CAMBRIDGE SURVEYS OF ECONOMIC LITERATURE

THE METHODOLOGY OF ECONOMICS

This book is an examination of the nature of economic explanation. The opening chapters introduce current thinking in the philosophy of science and review the literature on methodology. Professor Blaug then turns to the troublesome question of the logical status of welfare economics, giving the reader an understanding of the outstanding issues in the methodology of economics. This is followed by a series of case studies of leading economic controversies, whose purpose is not to settle substantive questions on which economists disagree, but rather to show how controversies in economics may be illuminated by paying attention to questions of methodology. A final chapter draws the strands together and gives the author's view of what is wrong with modern economics.

This is a revised and updated edition of a classic work on the methodology of economics, in which Professor Blaug develops his discussion of the latest developments in macroeconomics, general equilibrium theory, and international trade theory. A new section on the rationality postulate is also added.

CAMBRIDGE SURVEYS OF ECONOMIC LITERATURE

The literature of economics is expanding rapidly, and many subjects have changed out of recognition within the space of a few years. Perceiving the state of knowledge in fast-developing subjects is difficult for students and time-consuming for professional economists. This series is intended to help with this problem. Each book will be quite brief, giving a clear structure to and balanced overview of the topic, and written at a level intelligible to the senior undergraduate. The books will therefore be useful for teaching but will also provide a mature yet compact presentation of the subject for economists wishing to update their knowledge outside their own specializations.

The methodology of economics

OR HOW ECONOMISTS EXPLAIN

Second Edition

MARK BLAUG

Professor Emeritus
University of London

Consultant Professor
University of Buckingham

Visiting Professor
University of Exeter

CAMBRIDGE
UNIVERSITY PRESS

PUBLISHED BY THE PRESS SYNDICATE OF THE UNIVERSITY OF CAMBRIDGE
The Pitt Building, Trumpington Street, Cambridge CB2 1RP, United Kingdom

CAMBRIDGE UNIVERSITY PRESS
The Edinburgh Building, Cambridge CB2 2RU, United Kingdom
40 West 20th Street, New York, NY 10011-4211, USA
10 Stamford Road, Oakleigh, Melbourne 3166, Australia

First edition 1980
Reprinted 1981
Second edition 1992
Reprinted 1993, 1994, 1997

Printed in the United States of America

Typeset in Times

A catalogue record for this book is available from the British Library

Library of Congess Cataloguing-in-Publication Data is available

ISBN 0-521-43061-5 hardback
ISBN 0-521-43678-8 paperback

to my son, Tristan

In the choice of subject to-day [scope and method of economics], I fear that I have exposed myself to two serious charges: that of tedium and that of presumption. Speculations upon methodology are famous for platitude and prolixity. They offer the greatest opportunity for internecine strife; the claims of the contending factions are subject to no agreed check, and a victory, even if it could be established, is thought to yield no manifest benefit to the science itself. The barrenness of methodological conclusions is often a fitting complement to the weariness entailed by the process of reaching them.

Exposed as a bore, the methodologist cannot take refuge behind a cloak of modesty. On the contrary, he stands forward ready by his own claim to give advice to all and sundry, to criticise the works of others, which, whether valuable or not, at least attempts to be constructive; he sets himself up as the final interpreter of the past and dictator of future efforts.

– Roy F. Harrod, *Economic Journal*, 1938

CONTENTS

classical macroeconomics · Macroeconomics seen through Lakatosian spectacles

Part IV: What have we now learned about economics?

PREFACE

The first edition of this book was published in 1980. Since then we have seen seven major textbooks, three books of readings, an annotated bibliography, and of course hundreds of articles, all focused on economic methodology – not bad going for a mere decade of intellectual activity in a relatively minor branch of economics.[1]

[1] In chronological order and confining oneself strictly to books: H. Katouzian, *Ideology and Method in Economics* (1980); W. J. Samuels (ed.), *The Methodology of Economics. Critical Papers from the Journal of Economic Issues* (1980); J. Pitt (ed.), *Philosophy in Economics* (1981); B. J. Caldwell, *Beyond Positivism. Economic Methodology in the Twentieth Century* (1982); W. Stegmüller, W. Balzer, and W. Spohn (eds.), *Philosophy of Economics* (1982); L. A. Boland, *The Foundations of Economic Method* (1982); A. S. Eichner (ed.), *Why Economics Is Not Yet A Science* (1983); A. W. Coats (ed.), *Methodological Controversy in Economics: Historical Essays in Honor of T. W. Hutchison* (1983); W. L. Marr and B. Raj (eds.), *How Economists Explain. A Reader in Methodology* (1983); R. B. McKenzie, *The Limits of Economic Science* (1983); B. J. Caldwell (ed.), *Appraisal and Criticism in Economics: A Book of Readings* (1984); D. M. Hausman (ed.), *The Philosophy of Economics: An Anthology* (1984); P. Willes and G. Routh (eds.), *Economics in Disarray* (1984); J. J. Klant, *The Rules of the Game: The Logical Structure of Economic Theories* (1984); E. R. Weintraub, *General Equilibrium Analysis* (1985); A. Mingat, P. Salmon, and A. Wolfelsperger, *Méthodologie économique* (1985); D. McCloskey, *The Rhetoric of Economics* (1985); S. C. Dow, *Macroeconomic Thought. A Methodological Approach* (1985); T. Lawson and H. Pesaran (eds.), *Keynes' Economics: Methodological Issues* (1985); L. A. Boland, *Methodology for a New Microeconomics* (1986); P. J. O'Sullivan, *Economic Methodology and Freedom to Choose* (1987); J. Pheby, *Methodology and Economics: A Critical Introduction* (1988); N. de Marchi (ed.), *The Popperian Legacy in Economics* (1988); L. A. Boland, *The Methodology of Economic Model Building: Methodology After Samuelson* (1989); S. Roy, *Philosophy of Economics* (1989); D. A. Redman (ed.), *Economic Methodology. A Bibliography* (1989); J. C. Glass and W. Johnson, *Economics. Progression, Stagnation or Degeneration?* (1989); D. A. Redman, *Economics and the Philosophy of Science* (1991); S. Gordon, *The History and Philosophy of Social Science* (1991).

This explosion of the literature in the methodology of economics would alone have warranted a second edition, in order to take account of new developments in the field. Moreover, my central message has sometimes been misunderstood, no doubt because it was badly expressed, tempting me to restate my argument. In addition, some of the case studies in the second half of the book were too flimsy and others needed updating. Finally, new developments in macroeconomics, general equilibrium theory, and international trade theory encouraged me to prepare a new edition.

At first, I had ambitions to double the length of the original book by new chapters on post-Keynesian economics, experimental economics, game theory, and the crisis in econometrics, resolving the clash between Bayesian and classical theories of inference. But in the final analysis, intellectual laziness and a disinclination to rush in where even angels fear to tread have produced a second edition which is only marginally longer than and different from the first. I have amplified my discussion of general equilibrium theory, the Heckscher–Ohlin theory of international trade, monetarism, and the new classical macroeconomics, and have added a new section on the rationality postulate as the "hard core" of mainstream economics. In the main, however, the new edition is substantially the same book as the old. The ambitious additions I had hoped to insert I leave to another book.

Let me now try to restate the central message of the book by way of a comparison between my own account of the methodology of economics and that of Bruce Caldwell's *Beyond Positivism*.[2] Our two books are in striking agreement on many of the substantive issues in economic methodology: *methodology* is not just a fancy name for "methods of investigation" but a study of the relationship between theoretical concepts and warranted conclusions about the real world; in particular, methodology is that branch of economics where we examine the ways in which economists justify their theories and the reasons they offer for preferring one theory over another; methodology is both a descriptive discipline – "this *is* what most economists do" – and a prescriptive one – "this is what economists *should* do to advance economics"; finally, methodology does not provide a mechanical algorithm either for constructing or for validating theories and as such is more like an art than a science. We also agree that economic theories must sooner or later be confronted with empirical evidence as the final arbiter of truth but that empirical testing is so difficult and ambiguous that one cannot hope to find many examples of economic theories being decisively knocked down by repeated refutations (but there are nevertheless striking examples of precisely that phenomenon, as we shall see). It is vain to seek an empirical counterpart for

---

[2] The pages that follow borrow heavily from my "Comment" in Wiles and Routh (1984, pp. 30–6).

every theoretical concept employed, which is in any case an impossible objective, but we can achieve indirect testing by considering the network of fundamental concepts embedded in a particular theory and deducing their implications for some real-world phenomena. This is not to say, however, that predictions are everything and that it hardly matters whether assumptions are ''realistic'' or not. Economic theories are not simply instruments for making accurate predictions about economic events but genuine attempts to uncover causal forces at work in the economic system.

However, this is where the agreement between us stops. I argue in favor of *falsificationism*, defined as a methodological standpoint that regards theories and hypotheses as scientific if and only if their predictions are at least in principle falsifiable, that is, if they forbid certain acts/states/events from occurring. My reasons for holding this view are partly epistemological – the only way we can know that a theory is true or rather not false is to commit ourselves to a prediction about acts/states/events that follow from this theory – and partly historical – scientific knowledge has progressed by refutations of existing theories and by the construction of new theories that resist refutation. In addition, I claim that modern economists do in fact subscribe to the methodology of falsificationism: despite some differences of opinion, particularly about the direct testing of fundamental assumptions, mainstream economists refuse to take any economic theory seriously if it does not venture to make definite predictions about economic events, and they ultimately judge economic theories in terms of their success in making accurate predictions. I also argue, however, that economists fail consistently to practice what they preach: their working philosophy of science is aptly characterized as ''innocuous falsificationism.'' In other words, I am critical of what economists actually do as distinct from what they say they do.

Caldwell, on the other hand, doubts that falsificationism is a recommendable methodology: its structures are so demanding that little of economics would survive if it were rigorously applied. In addition, he can find few signs of economists practicing falsificationism even innocuously. Instead, he advocates ''methodological pluralism,'' or ''let a hundred flowers bloom,'' implying that various schools of thought in economics can be criticized from within, that is, in terms of the criteria they themselves avow. But if all methodological standards are equally legitimate it is difficult to see what sort of theorizing is ever excluded. From the ultrapermissive standpoint of ''methodological pluralism,'' it is not even obvious why we should require theories to be logically consistent, or to assert something definite about the real world, which after all carries the implication that they may be shown to be false.

Caldwell is clearly sympathetic to the methodology of falsificationism but he derives many of his negative conclusions about falsificationism from a subtle distinction between the methodology of *confirmationism* and that of falsificationism. He notes that most modern economists believe "that theories should be testable; that a useful means of testing is to compare the predictions of a theory with reality; that predictive adequacy is often the most important characteristic a theory can possess; and that the relative ordering of theories should be determined by the strength of confirmation, or corroboration, of those being compared" (Caldwell, 1982, p. 124). These four principles, he contends, define the methodology of confirmationism rather than falsificationism. Falsificationism is a tougher doctrine. In its simplest form, it can be stated in Caldwell's own words: "Scientists should not only empirically test their hypotheses, they should construct hypotheses which make bold predictions, and they should try to refute those hypotheses in their tests. Equally important, scientists should tentatively accept only confirmed hypotheses, and reject those which have been disconfirmed. Testing, then, should make a difference" (1982, p. 125).

Thus, the distinction between confirmationism and falsificationism rests partly on the degree to which theories are squeezed to yield risky implications liable to refutation and partly on whether refutations are taken seriously as possible reflections of fundamental error. Confirmationists make sure that their theories run few risks and, when faced with an empirical refutation, set about repairing the theory or amending its scope; they never abandon it as false. Falsificationists, on the other hand, deliberately run risks and regard repeated failures to predict accurately as a sign that alternative theories must be considered. Obviously, these distinctions are differences of degree, not of kind, and two methodologists may honestly disagree, as Caldwell and I do, as to whether modern economists are more appropriately characterized as "confirmationists" or "innocuous falsificationists."

There are good reasons why falsificationism is hard to practice in economics: any hypothesis is subject to other things being held constant and these other things are numerous and not always well specified; there are no well-attested, universal laws in economics and what general laws there are turn out to be statistical laws or tendencies lacking universal constants; to test a theory we must construct a model of the theory and, unfortunately, the same theory may be represented by a variety of models; and, finally, the data employed in any empirical test corresponds only crudely to the concepts in the theory being tested (Caldwell, 1982, pp. 238–42). However, exactly the same factors operate in physics, chemistry, and biology, albeit to a lesser degree. Indeed the so-called Duhem–Quine thesis states that it is logically impossible decisively to refute any theory, since any test of a theory involves the conjunction of initial conditions and the component elements of the theory, so that a refutation can always be blamed on inappropriate initial conditions. The way out of this dilemma is to lay down restrictions on what Popper calls "immunizing stratagems," adopted solely to protect theories against empirical refutations. These restrictions are important features of the methodology of falsificationism, which Caldwell along with so many other commentators on methodological issues simply ignores.

Let us agree that there are no tests in economics (or for that matter in any other science) that are unambiguously interpretable. But that is not to echo Caldwell that disconfirming tests are always ignored in economics or that they always lead to a repair job designed to make sure that there will be no further disconfirmations. The history of economics, and particularly modern economics, is replete with theories and hypotheses that were rejected because of repeated, if not decisive, empirical refutations. "It is not easy to think of a proposition in economics," Frank Hahn once said, "that all reasonable economists agree to have been decisively falsified by the evidence" (1987, p. 110). But actually it is perfectly easy. Of course, it all depends on whom we include as "reasonable economists" and what is meant by "decisively falsified." But here is an exemplary list: the wholesale rejection in the 1970s of the Phillips curve, interpreted as a stable trade-off between inflation and unemployment; the rejection in the 1980s of a stable velocity of money, scuttling the notion that inflation can be controlled merely by controlling the supply of money, even reducing it to zero in two to three years; the rejection again in the 1980s of the proposition that rational expectations make it impossible to alter real output or employment by monetary or fiscal policy; the rejection somewhere in the 1960s of Bowley's "law" proclaiming the constancy of the relative shares of national income going to capital and labor as well as everybody's "law" of the constancy of the capital–output ratio in the economy as a whole; the rejection in the 1950s of the Keynesian consumption function making current consumption a function solely of current income; the rejection in the 1930s of the Treasury view on the total crowding out of public expenditure in times of depression; the rejection again in the 1930s of the proposition that real wages fluctuate countercyclically – one could go on almost indefinitely expanding these examples. The notion that economic theories, like old soldiers, never die but only fade away is simply a myth perpetuated by constant repetition.

Thus, Caldwell has recently admitted that at least one of the many arguments he employed over the years as a persistent critic of falsificationism is "if not wrong . . . seriously incomplete."

My error was to claim that falsification is an inappropriate methodology for economics *because* most economic theories cannot be conclusively falsified. To buttress the claim I noted numerous obstacles to getting clean tests of theories in economics. . . . [But] *every* science encounters difficulties in coming up with clean refutations. . . . Thus it is not an effective argument against falsificationism to simply point out . . . that decisive refutations are rare. That problem always exists [1991, p. 7].

The remedy for the problem is quite simple: try harder! Of course, the recommendations to try harder must be capable of being implemented, that is, a prescriptive methodology like falsificationism must be descriptively adequate or at least not descriptively impractical. At this point in the argument, Caldwell again refers to his former conviction that falsificationism has never been practiced to any significant extent in economics: "neither Hutchison nor Blaug have been able to pinpoint paradigmatic episodes of falsificationist practice. Hutchison's examples (the refutations of Malthusian population theory and of certain unqualified versions of Keynesian and monetarist macroeconomics) involve instants in which usually, after fairly long periods of time, it became evident that a theory's predictions did not come to pass" (1991, p. 9). I hope that a reading of Chapter 12 below will convince any "reasonable economist" that the entire history of postwar macroeconomics furnishes a whole series of paradigmatic episodes of falsificationist practice, that is, instants in which it became evident rather quickly that "a theory's predictions did not come to pass."

Bruce Caldwell set the pattern for others' reactions to the first edition of this book. Daniel Hausman (1985; 1988; 1989) argued that falsificationism is never practiced because it is unpracticeable. Modern economists, he insisted, subscribe to what he calls "deductivism" or what I called "verificationism," whose patron saint is John Stuart Mill and not Karl Popper: "given how poorly supported are various auxiliary statements needed to derive economic theories, it is usually not sensible or responsible to follow Blaug's Popperian advice and to regard predictive failures as falsifying economic theories" (Hausman, 1989, p. 119).[3] After that, it is hardly surprising to be told that Hausman (1989, pp. 122–3) believes in descriptive, not prescriptive, methodology. Again and again, we shall find that falsificationism is an "aggressive methodology" which is critical of much of what passes as modern economics, whereas critics of falsificationism invariably adopt a "defensive methodology," arguing that the business of economic methodologists is to describe the actual practice of economists, which is, in brief, to make the best of a bad job. This is the old distinction between positive and normative economics in the realm of methodology: either we describe, explain, and endorse what economists actually do or we advocate best-practice economics on the supposition that many economists fall short of it.

Lawrence Boland does not go as far as Hausman: falsificationism is implementable but it is not actually implemented. "For Blaug, any practice of what he calls falsificationism amounts not only to devising models which are in principle refutable but also actively attempting to refute such models. With the exception of a brief moment in the LSE seminars, hardly any mainstream economists have advocated such a strict employment of the Popper–Samuel-

---

[3] Similarly Hargreaves-Heap (1989, chap. 2) uses the Duhem–Quine thesis to attack falsificationism, arguing that as empirical tests are always inconclusive, we have to settle for "understanding" in economics, according to which empirical evidence is relevant but not decisive for theory choice.

son methodological requirement of falsifiability'' (Boland, 1989, p. 10; also 1982, chaps. 10–11). Economists do worry about testability as a requirement of adequate economic models, Boland asserts, but they regard an empirical refutation as a challenge to improve the model so as to raise its ''degree'' of testability and not a reason to reject the theory underlying the model.

Klant (1984, pp. 184–6) and de Marchi (1988, pp. 12–13) likewise have deep misgivings about falsifiability in economics, regarding it as an ideal never attained in practice and at best only attainable to a degree; in short, they leave the door open to falsificationism as a normative methodology. Deborah Redman, on the other hand, has little use for such philosophers of science as Popper, Kuhn, and Lakatos, and regards the Popperian legacy in economics as almost wholly disastrous. Interpreting falsification as ''conclusive disproof,'' she has no difficulty in showing that it does not exist in science, from which it follows that ''defending a theory because it has not yet been 'falsified' . . . is in reality indefensible'' (Redman, 1991, p. viii). The logic of the argument is impeccable. Unfortunately, no one has ever defined falsification as equivalent to conclusive disproof and Popper spent pages and pages in *The Logic of Scientific Discovery* arguing against the thesis that one could ever conclusively disprove anything, pages which Redman (1991, pp. 32–5; also p. 124) actually quotes at length. Having established to her own satisfaction that economic theories cannot be falsified any more than physical theories in her sense of the term, she convicts me of self-contradiction: ''Blaug asserts that economists say their goal is falsification but they do not in fact practise falsification, and so economists are to be reprimanded for doing something that Blaug admits is impossible anyway'' (Redman, 1991, p. 119). Am I alone in thinking that this is a good example of winning an argument by inventing a straw man?

Finally, Bill Gerrard (1990, pp. 201–2), in a useful survey of recent books on economic methodology, winds up the argument by distinguishing between ''radical falsificationism'' and ''dogmatic falsificationism'':

Radical falsificationism recognises the fallibility of knowledge, stresses the role of empirical testing as a safety valve protecting subject fields from falling prey to dogmatism and acknowledges the difficulties involved in empirical testing as a result of the conglomerate nature of theories. Dogmatic falsificationism, on the other hand, treats empirical testing as an infallible and purely objective means of arriving at certain knowledge.

The first is the methodology of Popper, Gerrard declares; the second is Popperian methodology. He concludes: ''There seems a clear case for more of the methodology of Popper in economics and the elimination of the bastardized version that is Popperian method.''

Among the books Gerrard reviews is Donald McCloskey's *Rhetoric of Economics* (1985), a witty and provocative book expressly designed to purge economics of all prescriptive methodologies, such as falsificationism, verificationism, or what you will. Economists, argues McCloskey, pay obeisance to an outmoded philosophy of science, which he labels as "modernism," although it is usually labeled as "logical positivism." This matter of labels is not unimportant, for in no time at all he includes within modernism various propositions that have gained currency among economists but that have absolutely nothing to do with the philosophical movement known as logical positivism. Modernism, McCloskey tells us, is characterized by ten commandments, which include such notions as these: only the observable predictions of a theory matter to its truth; facts and values belong to different realms of discourse, so that positive propositions are always to be distinguished from normative ones; any scientific explanation of an event subsumes the event under a covering law; and introspection, metaphysical beliefs, aesthetic considerations, and the like may well figure in the discovery of any hypothesis but are irrelevant to its justification. Such notions, McCloskey points out, are now discarded by many professional philosophers – but economists have paid no attention to these reactions to "modernism" among philosophers and continue to believe that the only "fundamental" proof of an economic assertion is an objective, quantitative test. It is this naive belief in empirical testing as the hallmark of truth that is the real core of "modernism" and hence the Big Bad Wolf of McCloskey's book. "It is hard to disbelieve the dominance of modernism in economics," he remarks, "although an objective, quantitative test would of course make it, or any assertion, more believable and would be worth doing" (McCloskey, 1985, p. 11).

On the one hand, he deplores all hints of a prescriptive methodology; that is, no one is to lay down metatheoretical standards of what is to be considered a good or bad argument. On the other hand, "an objective, quantitative test would make it . . . more believable *and* would be worth doing" (my italics). Yes, it might make a proposition more believable if only because unphilosophical economists tend to take quantitative tests seriously. But why would it be worth doing if it has no bearing on the validity of the assertion? And if it has at least some bearing, why are we not told what bearing it has? McCloskey ridicules the reader who believes that there are some propositions in economics that are either true or false, in which case it is difficult to see why empirical testing should ever be worth doing.

If prescriptive methodology is out, what is left is descriptive methodology or what McCloskey prefers to call the study of "rhetoric" or "conversation." The word *rhetoric* has in recent years required a derogatory meaning, but at one time (roughly up to the nineteenth century) it meant simply the ways of producing an effect on one's audience by the careful use of language; it is the art of speaking or writing persuasively. McCloskey never gives a precise definition of the term *rhetoric* but the general idea of what he is after is, surely, plain enough. Moreover, he provides a number of worked examples of rhetorical analysis in the latter half of the book, based on the writings of Paul Samuelson, Robert Solow, John Muth, and Robert Fogel, which are instructive even if one does not share what McCloskey calls the "Anarchistic Theory of Knowledge in Economics."

The mystery is how McCloskey manages to examine the language used by economists without some criteria of "good" and "bad" language, some standards of what to look for in the linguistic devices employed by these economists to persuade their readers to believe them. The fact of the matter is, of course, that he does not manage it: these case studies of rhetorical analysis are filled with implicit metatheoretical judgments. As a case in point, Mc-Closkey's penultimate chapter attacks one of the worst characteristics of modern economics, the confusion between statistical significance tests and tests of substantive effects. This chapter veritably bursts with advice on "good" statistical practice, all of which I personally applaud. But where does such advice come from except from metatheoretical norms, otherwise known as methodology, that is, the logic of the methods employed by the practitioners of a subject. McCloskey is unalterably opposed to Methodology with a capital *M* but much in favor of methodology with a lowercase *m*. What this seems to mean is that you can prescribe many little things – don't shout; be open-minded; face up to the facts; don't fall for your own rhetoric; don't pronounce on large or small effects without giving standards of comparison; don't confuse statistical with substantive significance; replace Neyman–Pearson inference with Bayesian methods; and so on – but you may not prescribe big things, such as eschewing conclusions that are compatible with any and all factual evidence; always comparing one's conclusions with those of competing theories, if such exist; and avoiding changes to one's theories that have no other aim but to account for an empirical anomaly. Unfortunately, I fail to see a rational basis for the implied distinction between deplorable Methodology and salutary methodology, and McCloskey never provides such a basis.[4]

One can imagine a rhetorical analysis of the writings of Milton Friedman on monetarism. Friedman uses some explicit and implicit literary devices that seem to account for his enormous persuasive power and, hence, his influence on modern economics. Having studied these devices, I will probably ask myself at some time whether it is actually true that control of the supply of money is the key to the control of inflation in modern industrial economies. Silly boy, I can hear McCloskey saying, there is no such thing as truth in economics: "Economics, like geology or evolutionary biology or history itself is a historical rather than a predictive science" (McCloskey, 1985, p. 18). But geology, evolutionary biology, and history are retroactive sciences, that is, the validity of these propositions do depend *ex post facto* on empirical data

---

[4] For other critiques of McCloskey making more or less the same point, see Caldwell and Coats (1984), Rosenberg (1988), Gerrard (1990, pp. 208–12), and Backhouse (1992).

(consider the importance of fossil evidence to the debates on Darwinian theory). Is the same true of economics? Does the validity of monetarism depend, if not on the accuracy of its future productions, on the accuracy of its past retrodictions? Friedman did after all co-author a book on the *Monetary History of the United States, 1867–1960*. Did he verify monetarism by means of historical data on the money supply and the level of prices? Is this an important question to ask? Silly boy, you're doing Methodology again: off with your head!

The idea of studying how economists actually go about persuading one another is a good one, but it is false to assert that all reasons for believing an economic theory are equally valid and that economists in fact regard them as equally valid. However, this is precisely what McCloskey is saying.

Consider, for example, the sentence in economics, "The demand curve slopes down". The official rhetoric says that economists believe this because of statistical evidence – negative coefficients in demand curves for pig iron or negative diagonal items in matrices of complete systems of demand – accumulating steadily in journal articles. These are the tests 'consistent with the hypothesis'. Yet more beliefs in the hypothesis come from other sources: from introspection (what would I do?); from uncontrolled cases in point (such as the oil crisis); from authority (Alfred Marshall believed it); from symmetry (a law of demand if there is a law of supply); from definition (a higher price leaves less expenditure, including this one); and, above all, from analogy (if the demand curve slopes down for chewing gum, why not for housing and love too?). As may be seen in the classroom and seminar, the range of arguments in economics is wider than the official rhetoric allows [McCloskey, 1987, p. 174].

No doubt, there are many reasons for believing that demand curves are negatively inclined but there is little doubt that if the statistical evidence repeatedly ran the other way, none of these reasons would suffice to make economists believe in the "law of demand." Most "beliefs in the hypothesis" do *not* come from other sources, contrary to what McCloskey asserts, and, of course, they should not. Description and prescriptions agree perfectly with one another in this case as in so many others. And that is the gist of my argument.

I document in this book a striking continuity in the methodological precepts of modern economists, precepts that loosely correspond to Popper's falsificationist strictures. But at the same time, there is no denying that the practice of economists is at best an innocuous brand of falsificationism and at worst a Millian style of verificationism.[5]

---

[5] Canterberry and Burkhardt (1983), in an examination of 542 empirical articles in four major economics journals over the years 1973–8, found that only three articles attempted to falsify the hypotheses proposed; in all other cases the null hypothesis was accepted, demonstrating that economists confirm rather than falsify. But is this not

My fond belief that economists could be goaded into taking falsificationism more seriously has received some hard knocks over the last ten years. A number of general equilibrium and game theorists have in recent years expressed open hostility to falsificationism (see Chapter 8 below) and a conference on the application of Lakatos's philosophy of science to economics held in 1989 revealed a studious skepticism among the participants about the utility of Popperian and Lakatosian ideas in a subject like economics and, particularly, a disinclination to appraise economic theories in terms of their novel empirical content (de Marchi, 1991, pp. 504–6, 509). It was clear that many economists cannot abandon the notion that mere theoretical progress, a deeper understanding of some economic problems, is of value in itself even if it does not produce any substantive findings about the economy and even if it does not enhance our ability to predict the consequences of economic policies. In so doing, they reflect an increasing tendency in modern economics to pursue theorizing like an intellectual game, making no pretense to refer to this as any other possible world on the slim chance that something might be learned which will one day throw light on an actual economy.

In a letter to *Science,* Wassily Leontief (1982) surveyed articles published in the *American Economic Review* in the last decade and found that more than 50 percent consisted of mathematical models without any empirical data, while some 15 percent consisted of nonmathematical theoretical analysis, likewise without any empirical data, leaving 35 percent of the articles using empirical analysis.

Articles published in the AER

	1972–6 (%)	1977–81 (%)
1. Mathematical models without any data	50.1	54.0
2. Theoretical models without mathematical formulation and without data	21.2	11.6
3. Statistical methodology	0.6	0.5
4. Empirical analysis based on data developed by the author	0.8	1.4
5. Empirical analysis using statistical inference on published data	21.4	22.7
6. Other types of empirical analysis	5.4	7.9
7. Empirical analysis based on artificial simulation and experiment	0.5	1.9

Source: Leontief (1982)

what some of the critics of falsificationism, like Hausman, say? Yes, but they welcome it or else regard it as inevitable, while I deplore it and argue that it is corrigible.

Morgan (1988) has updated Leontief's findings, showing once again that half the articles published in the *American Economic Review* and the *Economic Journal* do not use data of any kind, a ratio that vastly exceeds that found in articles in physics and chemistry journals. Oswald (1991a) has confirmed Leontief's and Morgan's results in the area of microeconomics, concluding quite rightly that a large number of economists treat the subject as it if were "a kind of mathematical philosophy." Perhaps a better expression would be "social mathematics," that is, a brand of mathematics that appears to deal with social problems but does so only in a formal sense. What we have here is a species of formalism: the reveling in technique for technique's sake. Colander and Klamer (1987; 1988) have shown that students in American graduate schools perceive that analytical ability is the chief requirement for professional advancement and not knowledge of the economy or acquaintance with the economic literature. Students are usually shrewd observers of their own chosen profession and they have a sensitive nose for the "hidden agenda" in their curriculum. It is clear that American graduate students have correctly perceived that nothing succeeds in economics like mathematical pyrotechnics, supplemented on occasions by some fancy econometrics.

The fact that graduate education in economics emphasizes technical puzzle-solving abilities at the expense of imparting substantial knowledge of the economic system is simply a reflection of the empty formalism that has come increasingly to characterize the whole of modern economics. And why not? What after all is wrong with elegant economics practiced as an intellectual pastime? There are, I suppose, two answers to this question. One is that some of us suffer from "idle curiosity" about the economy. Much as we enjoy abstract, mathematically formulated economics, we cannot help wondering just how the economy actually works, and most of the lemmas of rigorous pure theory do not really satisfy the desire to understand how things hang together in the economic world. The second answer is that economics throughout its long history has been intimately connected with economic policy, with the desire to improve economic affairs, eradicate poverty, equalize the distribution of income and wealth, combat depressions, and so on, and never more so than in the recent postwar period. But if economists are going to take a stand on questions of economic policy, not to mention advising governments what to do, they must have knowledge of how the economic system functions: we *know* that privatization if accompanied by an increase in the numbers of producers improves the quantity and quality of the goods privatized; we *know* that a deficit on the balance of payments can be cured by devaluation and even how quickly it can be cured; we *know* that inflation can be reduced by a hard fiscal and monetary policy and even what it will take to cut inflation by a given percentage – or do we? All this is to say that economics must be first and foremost an empirical science or else it must abandon its age-old concern with "piecemeal social engineering."[6]

Granted that economists must ultimately judge their ideas by the test of empirical evidence – that analytical rigor may have to be traded off against practical relevance – it does not follow that they need to endorse the Methodology of falsificationism. The argument for an empirically minded economics might derive from methodological considerations with a lowercase m.[7] No doubt, but the fact remains that any metatheoretical recommendation is no better than the Methodology which underpins it. McCloskey notwithstanding, there is no logical or philosophical distinction between methodology and Methodology. And the Methodology which best supports the economist's striving for substantive knowledge of economic relationships is the philosophy of science associated with the names of Karl Popper and Imre Lakatos. To fully attain the ideal of falsifiability is, I still believe, the prime desideratum in economics.

---

[6] This argument has been most forcefully expressed by Hutchison (1988, pp. 172–3; 1992).

[7] Mayer (1992) argues this at some length in a new book whose title is its message: *Truth vs. Precision in Economics*.

PREFACE TO FIRST EDITION

A fatal ambiguity surrounds the expression "the methodology of . . ." The term *methodology* is sometimes taken to mean the technical procedures of a discipline, being simply a more impressive-sounding synonym for *methods.* More frequently, however, it denotes an investigation of the concepts, theories, and basic principles of reasoning of a subject, and it is with this wider sense of the term that we are concerned in this book. To avoid misunderstanding, I have added the subtitle, *How Economists Explain,* suggesting that "the methodology of economics" is to be understood simply as philosophy of science applied to economics.

To ask how economists explain the phenomena with which they are concerned is in fact to ask in what sense economics is a science. In the words of one prominent modern philosopher of science: "It is the desire for explanations that are at once systematic and controlled by factual evidence that generates science; and it is the organization and classification of knowledge on the basis of explanatory principles that is the distinctive goal of the sciences" (Nagel, 1961, p. 4). There can be no doubt that economics provides plenty of examples of "explanations that are at once systematic and controlled by factual evidence," and hence no time will be wasted defending the assertion that economics is a science. However, economics is also a peculiar science, set apart from, say, physics because it studies human actions and therefore invokes the reasons and motives of human agents as the "causes of things" and from, say, sociology and political science because it manages somehow to provide rigorous, deductive theories of human action that are almost wholly lacking in these other behavioral sciences. In short, the explanations of economists are a particular species of a larger genus of scientific explanations, and as such they present some problematic features.

What then is the nature of economic explanations? Insofar as these explanations consist of definite theories, what is the structure of these theories, and in particular, what is the relationship between the assumptions and the predictive implications of economic theories? If economists validate their theories by invoking factual evidence, is that evidence pertinent only to the predictive implications of these theories, or to their assumptions, or both? Besides, what is it that counts as factual evidence for economists? How is it that economic theories that purport to explain what *is* are also employed in almost identical form to demonstrate what *ought* to be? In other words, what exactly is the relationship between positive and normative economics or, in more old-fashioned language, the relationship between economics as a science and political economy as an art? These are the sort of questions that will preoccupy us in this book.

Economists have been worrying about these questions ever since the days of Nassau William Senior and John Stuart Mill, and much is to be learned by going back to these nineteenth-century writers to see what economists themselves have rightly or wrongly thought they were doing when they practiced economics. By 1891, John Neville Keynes managed to sum up the methodological thinking of a whole generation of economists in his deservedly famous *Scope and Method of Political Economy,* which may be regarded as a sort of of benchmark in the history of economic methodology. The twentieth century witnessed a similar summing-up in *The Nature and Significance of Economic Science* (1932) by Lionel Robbins, followed a few years later by a widely read book with a diametrically opposite thesis, *The Significance and Basic Postulates of Economic Theory* (1938) by Terence Hutchison. In more recent years, Milton Friedman, Paul Samuelson, Fritz Machlup, and Ludwig von Mises have all contributed important pronouncements on the methodology of economics. In short, economists have long been aware of the need to defend "correct" principles of reasoning in their subject, and although actual practice may bear little relationship to what is preached, the preaching is worth considering on its own ground. That is the task of Part II. Part I is a self-contained, brief introduction to current thinking in the philosophy of science, which develops several distinctions that will be used throughout the rest of the book (see Glossary at the back).

After surveying the literature on economic methodology in Part II, Chapters 3 and 4, we turn in Chapter 5 to the troublesome question of the logical status of welfare economics. At the end of that chapter, having gained a more or less complete view of the outstanding issues in the methodology of economics, we are ready to apply the conclusions we have reached to some leading economic controversies. Part III therefore provides a series of case studies, whose purpose is not to settle substantive questions on which economists now disagree among themselves but rather to show how every controversy in economics involves questions of economic methodology. The last chapter in Part IV draws the strands together in an attempt to reach some final conclusions; it is perhaps more personal than the rest of the book.

Too many writers on economic methodology have seen their role as simply rationalizing the traditional modes of argument of economists, and perhaps this is why the average modern economist has little use for methodological inquiries. To be perfectly frank, economic methodology has little place in the training of modern economists. Possibly, all this is now changing. After many years of complacency about the scientific status of their subject, more and more economists are beginning to ask themselves deeper questions about what they are doing. At any rate, there are growing numbers who suspect that all is not well in the house that economics has built. It is not my purpose to coach them to be better economists but, on the other hand, there is little point in merely describing what economists do without drawing some object lessons; at some stage, even the most impartial spectator must be willing to assume the role of umpire. Like many other modern economists, I too have a view of *What's Wrong With Economics?* to cite the title of a book by Benjamin Ward, but my quarrel is less with the actual content of modern economics than with the way economists go about validating their theories. I hold that there is nothing much wrong with standard economic methodology as laid down in the first chapter of almost every textbook in economic theory; what is wrong is that economists do not practice what they preach.

When Laertes tells Ophelia not to yield to Hamlet's advances, she replies: "Do not as some ungracious pastors do, / Show me the steep and thorny way to heaven, / Whiles like a puff'd and feckless libertine / Himself, the primrose path of dalliance treads." Twentieth-century economists, I believe, are much like those "ungracious pastors." I leave it to my readers to decide whether I have made my case in this book, but at any rate, the wish to make that case has been the principal motive for writing it.

The book is essentially addressed to undergraduate students of economics, that is, those who have learned some substantive economics but find it difficult, if not impossible, to choose between alternative economic theories. Such is the growing interest of professional economists in methodological problems that, I dare say, even some of my colleagues will find the book of interest. Other students of social science – sociologists, anthropologists, political scientists, and historians – are inclined either to envy economists for their apparent scientific rigor or else to despise them for being the lackeys of governments. It may be that they will find this book not so much an antidote to envy as a reminder of the benefits that economics derives and always has derived from its policy orientation.

This book has been too long in the making. The first chapter was drafted at the Villa Serbelloni in Bellagio, Italy, where I spent the month of November, 1976, thanks to the generosity of the Rockefeller Foundation. After I left the idyllic atmosphere of the Bellagio Study and Conference Centre, teaching and other research commitments kept me from getting back to the manuscript during the whole of the academic year 1976–7. Even then, it took me all of the calendar year 1978 to finish it. I received valuable comments, too numerous for comfort, on my first draft from Kurt Klappholz and Thanos Skouras. In addition, Ruth Towse read the entire manuscript, removing most, if not all, of my lapses from correct grammar. For this thankless task, I owe her a debt of gratitude that can only be paid in like coin.

PART I

What you always wanted to know about the philosophy of science but were afraid to ask

1

From the received view to the views of Popper

The received view

Anyone consulting some current textbooks in the philosophy of science will soon discover that the philosophy of science is a very strange subject: it is not, as might be expected, a study of the psychological and sociological factors that promote and encourage the discovery of scientific hypotheses; it is not an examination of the philosophical views of the world that are implicit in leading scientific theories; it is not even a reflection on the principles, methods, and results of the physical and social sciences, describing at the highest level of generality the pinnacles of scientific achievement. Instead, it appears to consist largely of a purely logical analysis of the formal structure of scientific theories, which seem to be more concerned with prescribing good scientific practice than with describing what it is that has actually passed as science; and when it mentions the history of science at all, it is written as if classical physics were the prototype science to which all other disciplines must sooner or later conform if they are to justify the title of "science."

This characterization of the philosophy of science is now somewhat out of date, reflecting as it does the heyday of logical positivism in the interwar years. Between the 1920s and 1950s, philosophers of science did more or less agree with what Frederick Suppe (1974) has called "The Received View on Theories." But the works of Popper, Polanyi, Hanson, Toulmin, Kuhn, Lakatos, and Feyerabend, to mention only the leading names, have largely destroyed this *received view* without, however, putting any generally accepted alternative conception in its place. In short, the philosophy of science has been in something of a turmoil ever since the 1960s, which complicates the task of providing a simple guide to the subject in the space of two chapters. On balance, there is much to be said for beginning with some principal features of the received view and only then moving on to the new heterodoxy,

3

using the work of Karl Popper as a watershed between the old and the new views of the philosophy of science.

The hypothetico-deductive model

The standard view of science in the middle of the nineteenth century was that scientific investigations begin in the free and unprejudiced observation of facts, proceed by inductive inference to the formulation of universal laws about these facts, and finally arrive by further induction at statements of still wider generality known as theories; both laws and theories are ultimately checked for their truth content by comparing their empirical consequences with all the observed facts, including those with which they began. This inductive view of science, perfectly summed up in John Stuart Mill's *System of Logic, Ratiocinative and Inductive* (1843) and remaining to this day the conception of science of the man-in-the-street, gradually began to break down in the last half of the nineteenth century under the influence of the writings of Ernst Mach, Henri Poincaré, and Pierre Duhem, and to be almost entirely reversed by *the hypothetico-deductive model of scientific explanation* that emerged after the turn of the century in the work of the Vienna Circle and the American pragmatists (see Alexander, 1964; Harré, 1967; and Losee, 1972, chaps. 10, 11).

Nevertheless, it was not until 1948 that the hypothetico-deductive model was written down in formal terms as the only valid type of explanation in science. This authorized version first appeared in a now famous paper by Carl Hempel and Peter Oppenheim (1965),[1] which argued that all truly scientific explanations have a common logical structure: they involve at least one universal law plus a statement of relevant initial or boundary conditions that together constitute the *explanans* or premises from which an *explanandum*, a statement about some event whose explanation we are seeking, is deduced with the aid of the rules of deductive logic. By a *universal law*, we mean some such proposition as "in all cases where events A occur, events B also occur," and such universal laws may be deterministic in form by referring to individual events B or statistical in form by referring to classes of events B; (thus, statistical laws take the form: "in all cases where events A occur, events B also occur with a probability of p, where $0 < p < 1$"). By the rules of deductive logic, we mean some sort of infallible syllogistic reasoning like "if A

---

[1] This was a more guarded version of the same thesis announced by Hempel (1942), which generated a great debate among historians about the meaning of historical explanations (see footnote 5). Earlier, less formally precise statements of the hypothetico-deductive model can be found in Popper's *The Logic of Scientific Discovery*, first published in German in 1934 and then in English in 1959 (1959, pp. 59, 68–9; also Popper, 1962, II, pp. 262–3, 362–4; Popper, 1976, p. 117), and indeed as early as 1843 in Mill (1973, 7, pp. 471–2).

is true, then *B* is true *A* is true; therefore *B* is true" (this is an example of what logicians call a *hypothetical syllogism*). It need hardly be added that deductive logic is an abstract calculus and that the logical validity of deductive reasoning in no way depends on the material truth of either the major premise "if *A* is true, then *B* is true," or the minor premise, "*A* is true."

It follows from the common logical structure of all truly scientific explanations, Hempel and Oppenheim went on to argue, that the operation called *explanation* involves the same rules of logical inference as the operation called *prediction,* the only difference being that explanations come after events and predictions before events. In the case of explanation, we start with an event to be explained and find at least one universal law plus a set of initial conditions that logically imply the statement of the event in question. In other words, to cite a particular cause as an explanation of an event is simply to subsume the event in question under some universal law or set of laws; for that reason one critic of the Hempel–Oppenheim thesis has called it "the covering law model of explanation" (Dray, 1957, chap. 1). In the case of prediction, on the other hand, we start with a universal law plus a set of initial conditions, and from them we deduce a statement about an unknown event; the prediction is typically used to see whether the universal law is in fact upheld. In short, explanation is simply "prediction written backwards."

This notion that there is a perfect, logical symmetry between the nature of explanation and the nature of prediction has been labeled the *symmetry thesis*. It constitutes the heart of the hypothetico-deductive or covering-law model of scientific explanation. The point of the model is that it employs no other rules of logical inference than that of deduction (the force of that remark will become clear in a moment). The universal laws that are involved in explanations are not derived by inductive generalization from individual instances; they are merely hypotheses, inspired conjectures if you like, that may be tested by using them to make predictions about particular events but which are not themselves reducible to observations about events.

The symmetry thesis

The covering-law model of scientific explanation has been attacked from a number of standpoints, and even Hempel himself, its most vigorous proponent, has retreated somewhat over the years in response to these attacks (Suppe, 1974, p. 28n). Most of the critics have seized on the symmetry thesis as the butt of all their objections. It has been argued that prediction need not imply explanation and even that explanation need not imply prediction. The former proposition, at any rate, is plain sailing: prediction only requires a correlation, whereas explanation cries out for something more. Thus, any linear extrapolation of an ordinary least squares regression is a prediction of sorts, and yet the regression itself may be based on no theory whatsoever of the relationship between the relevant variables, much less a notion of which are causes and which are effects. No economist needs to be told that accurate short-term economic forecasting, like accurate short-term weather forecasting, is perfectly possible with the aid of rules-of-thumb that yield satisfactory results, although we may have no idea why they do so. In short, it is only too obvious that it is perfectly possible to predict well without explaining anything.

This is not to say, however, that it is always easy to decide whether a particular scientific theory with an impressive predictive record achieves its results by fluke or by design. Some critics of the received view have argued that the covering-law model of scientific explanation is ultimately based on David Hume's analysis of causation. For Hume, what is called *causation* is nothing but the constant conjunction of two events that happen to be contiguous in time and space, the event that is prior in time being labeled the "cause" of the later event labeled "effect," although there is actually no necessary connection between them (see Losee, 1972, pp. 104–6). In other words, we can never be sure that causation is not simply correlation between event at time t and event at time $t + 1$. The critics have dismissed this Humean "billiard ball model of causation" and have instead insisted that genuine scientific explanation must involve an intervening mechanism connecting cause and effect, which guarantees that the relationship between the two events is indeed a "necessary" one (e.g., Harré, 1970, pp. 104–26, 1972, pp. 92–5, 114–32; and Harré and Secord, 1972, chap. 2).

The example of Newton's theory of gravitation, however, shows that the insistent demand for a truly causal mechanism in scientific explanation, if taken at face value, might well be harmful to scientific progress. Ignore everything about moving bodies, Newton said, except their positions, point masses, and velocities, and provide operational definitions for these terms; the resulting theory of gravity, incorporating the universal law that bodies attract each other with a force that varies directly with the product of their masses and inversely with the square of the distance between them, then enables us to predict the behavior of such diverse phenomena as the elliptical paths of planets, the phases of the moon, the occurrence of tides, the trajectory of missiles fired out of cannons, and even the rate at which apples fall from trees. Nevertheless, Newton provided no push-or-pull mechanism to account for the action of gravity – and none has ever been discovered – and he was unable to meet the objection of many of his contemporaries that the very notion of gravity acting instantaneously at a distance without any material medium to carry the force – ghostly fingers clutching through the void! – is utterly metaphysical.[2]

---

[2] We know that Newton was perfectly aware of this objection; as he wrote in a letter to a friend: "Gravity must be caused by an agent acting constantly according to certain laws, but whether this agent be material or immaterial I have left to the consideration of my readers" (quoted in Toulmin and Goodfield, 1963, pp. 281–2; see also Toulmin

Yet who could deny the extraordinary predictive power of Newtonian theory, particularly after the confirmation in 1758 of Edmond Halley's prediction of the return of "Halley's comet," topped in 1846 by Leverrier's use of the inverse-square law to predict the existence of a hitherto unknown planet, Neptune, from the observed aberrations in the orbit of Uranus; the fact that Newtonian theory sometimes scored misses as well as hits (witness Leverrier's fruitless search for another unknown "planet," Vulcan, to account for the irregularities in the motion of Mercury) was conveniently forgotten. In short, it can be argued that Newton's theory of gravity is merely a highly efficient instrument for generating predictions that are approximately correct for virtually all practical purposes within our solar system but which nevertheless fails really to "explain" the motion of bodies. Indeed, it was thoughts such as these that led Mach and Poincaré in the nineteenth century to assert that all scientific theories and hypotheses are merely condensed descriptions of natural events, neither true nor false in themselves but simply conventions for storing empirical information, whose value is to be determined exclusively by the principle of economy of thought – this is what is nowadays called the methodology of *conventionalism*.

Suffice it to say that prediction, even from a highly systematic and rigorously axiomatized theory, need not imply explanation. But what of the converse proposition: can we provide an explanation without making any prediction? The answer clearly depends on precisely what we mean by *explanation,* a question that we have so far carefully dodged. In the widest sense of the word, to explain is to answer a Why? question; it is to reduce the mysterious and unfamiliar to something known and familiar, thus producing the exclamation: "Aha, so that is how it is!" If this deliberately loose use of language is accepted, it would appear that there are scientific theories which generate a sense of Aha-ness and yet produce little or nothing in the way of prediction about the class of events with which they are concerned. A leading example, frequently cited by critics of the received view (e.g., Kaplan, 1964, pp. 346–51; Harré, 1972, pp. 56, 176–7), is Darwin's theory of evolution, which purports to explain how highly specialized biological forms develop from a succession of less specialized ones by a process of natural selection that acts to maximize reproductive capacity, without however being able to specify beforehand precisely what highly specialized forms will emerge under which particular environmental conditions.

Darwinian theory, say the critics, can tell us much about the evolutionary process once it has occurred, but very little about that process before it occurs.

and Goodfield, 1965, pp. 217–20; Hanson, 1965, pp. 90–1; Losee, 1972, pp. 90–3). Likewise, the history of the concept of hypnosis (through "animal magnetism" to "mesmerism" to "hypnosis") demonstrates that many well-attested natural phenomena, for example, the efficacious use of hypnosis as a medical anaesthetic, cannot be explained even now in terms of an intervening, causal mechanism.

It is not simply that Darwinian theory cannot spell out the initial conditions required for the operation of natural selection, but that it cannot provide definite universal laws about the survival rates of species under different environmental circumstances. Insofar as the theory predicts at all, it predicts the *possibility* of a certain outcome conditional on other events actually occurring and not the *likelihood* of that outcome if those events did occur. For example, it conjectures that a certain proportion of a species with the capacity to swim will survive the sudden inundation of its previously arid habitat, but it cannot predict what proportion will actually survive a real flooding and it cannot even predict whether this proportion will be larger than zero (Scriven, 1959).

It would be wrong to say that Darwinian theory commits the famous fallacy of *post hoc, ergo propter hoc,* that is, inferring causation from mere casual conjunction, because Darwin did provide a mechanism to account for the evolutionary process. The cause of the variation of species according to Darwin is natural selection, and natural selection expresses itself through a struggle for existence that operates via reproduction and chance variations on what he called "gemmules," much like domestic selection by animal breeders. Darwin's mechanism of inheritance was essentially a system whereby the traits coming from each parent were blended in the offspring, the traits being steadily diluted in successive generations. Unfortunately, the specified mechanism is faulty: no new species could so arise because any mutation, or "sport" as Darwin used to say, would fade away by blending within several generations to the point where it would cease to have any selective value. Darwin himself came to appreciate this objection, and in the last edition of *The Origin of Species* he made increasing concessions to the discredited Lamarckian concept of the direct inheritance of acquired characteristics in the effort to provide something like a tenable explanation of evolution.[3]

For Lamarck, the giraffe grows a longer neck because it wants to get at leaves higher up the tree and this acquired characteristic is handed down to its progeny, who in turn stretch their necks still further. According to Darwin, giraffes have offspring with necks of different lengths and the scarcity of leaves gives young giraffes with longer necks a better chance to survive, mate, and thus produce more giraffes with long necks like themselves; over generations this same effect eventually produces the long-necked giraffe we

---

[3] It is with some satisfaction that we note that Darwin was inspired by one economist, Thomas Malthus, and decisively criticized by another, Fleeming Jenkin, a professor of engineering at the University of Edinburgh (Jenkin, incidentally, was the first British economist to draw demand and supply curves). It was Jenkin who first demonstrated in an 1867 review of *The Origin of Species* (1859) that Darwin's theory was incorrect as Darwin stated it. It was this objection which *may* have caused Darwin to insert a new chapter in the sixth edition of *The Origin of Species,* resuscitating the ideas of Lamarck (see Jenkin, 1973, particularly pp. 344–5; Toulmin and Goodfield, 1967, chap. 9: Ghiselin, 1969, pp. 173–4; Lee, 1969; Mayr, 1982, pp. 512–14).

know. The two evolutionary mechanisms are radically different and for Darwin to have conceded even a jot to Lamarck was a serious compromise of his fundamental argument.

The irony is that by 1872, unknown to Darwin or to anyone else, Mendel had already discovered the idea of genes, that is, discrete units of heredity that are transmitted from generation to generation without blending or dilution. Mendelian genetics provided Darwinian theory with a convincing causal mechanism, but from our point of view, it left the status of the theory of evolution essentially where it was before: Darwinian theory seems to explain what it cannot predict and offers few supports for its arguments except indirect ones after the fact. Darwin was himself a self-declared advocate of the hypothetico-deductive model of scientific explanation (Ghiselin, 1969, pp. 27–31, 59–76; George, 1982, pp. 140–50), but the fact remains that for some he provides to this day "the paradigm of the explanatory but nonpredictive scientist" (Scriven, 1959, p. 477).

This is perhaps to overstate the case because Darwinism does rest on a number of specific contingent claims about reality – for example, that offspring vary in phenotypes, that such variations are systematically related to the phenotypes of the parents, and that different phenotypes leave different numbers of offspring in remote generations. And Darwinism does imply some definite predictions, for example, that species never reappear; thus, if the dodo came back, Darwinism would be refuted (Mayr, 1982, chap. 10; Rosenberg, 1985, chaps. 5–7). Similarly, to say that Darwinian evolution can explain the modern giraffe's neck but could never have predicted it beforehand is really to misunderstand Darwinian theory, which predicts, if it predicts at all, not for individuals (like giraffes) or for organs (like necks) but rather for traits or sets of traits. Darwin himself was keenly aware that certain facts, such as the existence of neuter insects and sterile hybrids, appeared to contradict his theory: a whole chapter of the *Origin of Species* was devoted to "miscellaneous objections to the theory of natural selection," that is, traits which could not have evolved by natural selection. In short, Darwinism is capable of being refuted by observations, quite apart from the fact that in recent times speciation à la Darwin has been directly observed (Ruse, 1982, pp. 97–108; Ruse, 1986, pp. 20–6). In that sense Darwinian evolution is not a logically different type of theory from, say, Newtonian mechanics or Einsteinian relativity (Williams, 1973; Flew, 1984, pp. 24–31; Caplan, 1985). Nevertheless, it may be granted that the covering-law model of scientific explanation with its corollary, the symmetry thesis, cannot easily accommodate the Darwinian theory of evolution.[4]

[4] Perhaps that is why Popper (1976, pp. 168, 171–80; also 1972a, pp. 69, 241–2, 267–8) once argued that the Darwinian theory of evolution is not a testable scientific theory

There are other examples of theories that appear to provide explanations without making definite predictions, such as Freudian depth psychology and Durkheim's theory of suicide, although any of them are susceptible to the retort that they are not truly scientific. But a still wider class of examples is furnished by all manner of historical explanations, which at best yield sufficient but not necessary conditions for a certain kind of event to occur or to have occurred; what historians explain is almost never strictly deducible from their *explanans* and hence does not result in anything like a strict prediction (or rather retrodiction). Historical explanations are indeed controlled by factual evidence like scientific explanations but the evidence is usually so sparse and so ambiguous as to be compatible with a large number of alternative and even conflicting explanations. It is difficult therefore to resist Hempel's (1942) argument that virtually all historical explanations are pseudo-explanations: they may be true or they may be false but we will rarely know which is the case and the historian is not typically prepared to help us to distinguish one from the other.

To sum up: we can make a case for the thesis of explanation-without-prediction but it is not a strong case and I myself remain persuaded that the covering-law model of scientific explanation survives all the criticisms it has received. This is clearly a controversial position but suffice it to say that we ought to be on our guard when offered an explanation that does not yield a prediction, that is, when instead of an explanation we are offered "understanding." "We understand the causes of earthquakes," Frank Hahn (1985, p. 10) tells us, "but we cannot at the moment predict them." On the contrary, however: geophysicists have made great progress in recent years in predicting earthquakes because they have come better to understand their precise causes. In any case, when understanding is not matched by predictability, we should ask, Is it because we cannot secure all the relevant information about the initial conditions, as with much of biological evolution, or is it because the explanation does not rest in any way on a universal law or at least a loose generalization of some kind, as with so many historical explanations? If the latter, I would argue that we are definitely being handed chaff for wheat because it is not possible to explain anything without reference to some larger set of things of which it is itself an element (see Elster, 1989).

Norms versus actual practice

We have seen that the covering-law model of scientific explanation excludes much of what at least some people have regarded as science. But

but rather "a metaphysical research programme – a possible framework for testable scientific theories."

this is precisely its aim: it seeks "to tell it like it should be" and not "to tell it as it is." It is this prescriptive, normative function of the covering-law model of explanation that its critics find so objectionable. They argue that, instead of stating the logical requirements of a scientific explanation, or the minimum conditions that scientific theories ideally should satisfy, our time would be better spent in classifying and characterizing the theories that are actually employed in scientific discourse.[5] When we do so, they contend, what we shall find is that their diversity is more striking than their similarity; scientific theories seem to lack properties common to them all.

In addition to deductive, lawlike, statistical, and historical explanations, which we have already mentioned, biology and social science in general furnish numerous examples of functional or teleological explanations, which take the form of indicating either the instrumental role that a particular unit of an organism performs in maintaining a given state of the organism, or that individual human action plays in bringing about some collective goal (see Nagel, 1961, pp. 20–6). These four or five types of explanations appear in a variety of scientific theories, and the theories themselves may in turn be further classified along various dimensions (e.g., Suppe, 1974, pp. 120–5; Kaplan, 1964, pp. 298–302). But even such detailed typologies of scientific theories raise difficulties because many theories combine different modes of explanation, so that it is not even true that all the scientific theories classed together under some common heading will reveal the same structural properties. In other words, as soon as we take a comprehensive view of scientific practice, there is simply too much material to permit a single "rational reconstruction" of theories from which we might derive methodological norms that all proper scientific theories are supposed to obey.

The tension between description and prescription in the philosophy of science, between the history of science and the methodology of science, has been a leading factor in the virtual overthrow of the received view in the 1960s (see Toulmin, 1977). That tension also makes itself felt in Karl Popper's treatment of the role of falsifiability in scientific progress, which has

---

[5] In the same way, historians have argued that the covering-law model of historical explanation misrepresents what historians actually do: history is an "idiographic" not a "nomothetic" subject, being concerned with the study of particular events and particular persons, not with general laws of development (see Dray, 1957; 1966). But the essence of Hempel's original argument was that even individual events cannot be explained except by invoking generalizations of some kind, however trivial, and that historians typically provide no more than an "explanation sketch" because they either fail to specify their generalizations, or else imply without warrant that they are well attested. The debate about the received view among philosophers of science is thus perfectly duplicated by the Hempel–Dray debate among philosophers of history (see McClelland, 1975, chap. 2, for a judicious and pointed summary).

proven to be one of the mainsprings of the opposition to the received view. A discussion of Popper's ideas will allow us to return to the symmetry thesis with new insights.

Popper's falsificationism

Popper begins with the distinction between science and nonscience, his so-called *demarcation criterion,* and ends with the attempt to devise standards for appraising competing scientific hypotheses in terms of their degrees of verisimilitude. In so doing, he moves steadily away from the received view in which the aim of the philosophy of science is rationally to reconstruct the untidy scientific theories of the past so as to make them conform with certain canons of scientific explanation. With Popper, the philosophy of science instead becomes a subject in which we seek methods of appraising scientific theories once they have been proposed.

Popper's starting point is a criticism of the philosophy of logical positivism as espoused by the Vienna Circle and embodied in what has come to be called *the verifiability principle of meaning.* This principle stipulates that all statements are either analytic or synthetic – either true by virtue of the definition of their own terms, or true, if true at all, by virtue of practical experience – and then pronounces all synthetic statements as meaningful if and only if they are capable, at least in principle, of being empirically verified (see Losee, 1972, pp. 184–90). Historically, the members of the Vienna Circle (Wittgenstein, Schlick, and Carnap) employed the verifiability principle of meaning primarily as a needle to puncture metaphysical pretensions in science and nonscience alike, implying that even some statements that passed as science and certainly all statements that did not profess to be scientific could be dismissed as meaningless.[6] In practice, the verifiability principle bred a deep suspicion of the use of nonobservable entities in scientific theories such as absolute space and absolute time in Newtonian mechanics, electrons in particle physics, valence bonds in chemistry, and natural selection in the theory of evolution. A typical product of this antimetaphysical bias of logical positivists was the methodology of *operationalism,* first advanced in 1927 and later widely disseminated in a series of influential books by Percy Bridgman. To discover the meaning of any scientific concept, Bridgman alleged, we need only specify the physical operation performed to assign numerical values

---

[6] By implication, statements like "God exists," "life is sacred," "war is evil," and "Rembrandts are beautiful" are all expressions of personal taste which have no logical or philosophical meaning. Clearly, they do have meaning of some sort and hence the very choice of language to express the verifiability principle of meaning was designed to inflame traditionalists of all kinds. The revolutionary flavor of logical positivism is perfectly captured by that all-time philosophical best-seller, Alfred Ayer's *Language, Truth, and Logic* (1936).

to it: length *is* the measurement of objects in a single dimension and intelligence *is* what is measured by intelligence tests (see Losee, 1972, pp. 181–4).

Popper rejects all such attempts to demarcate the meaningful from the meaningless and replaces them by a new demarcation criterion that divides all human knowledge into two mutually exclusive classes, labeled ''science'' and ''nonscience.'' Now, the traditional nineteenth-century answer to this demarcation problem was that science differs from nonscience by virtue of the use of the method of *induction:* science starts with experience and proceeds through observation and experiments to the framing of universal laws with the aid of the rules of induction. Unfortunately, there is a logical problem about the justification of induction, which has worried philosophers ever since the time of David Hume. To take a concrete example: men infer the universal law that the sun always rises in the morning from past experience of the sun rising in the morning; nevertheless, this cannot be a logically conclusive deduction, in the sense of true premises necessarily implying true conclusions, because there is absolutely no guarantee that what we have so far experienced will persist in the future. To argue that the universal law of the sun's rising is grounded in invariant experience is, as Hume put it, to beg the question because it shifts the problem of induction from the case at hand to some other case; the problem is precisely how logically to infer anything about future experience on the basis of nothing but past experience. At some stage in the argument, induction from particular instances to a universal law requires an illogical leap in thought, an extra element that may well lead from true premises to *false* conclusions. Hume did not deny that we constantly generalize from individual instances out of habit and the spontaneous association of ideas, but what he denied was that such inferences were logically justifiable. This is the famous *problem of induction*.

It follows from Hume's argument that there is a fundamental asymmetry between induction and deduction, between proving and disproving, between verification and falsification, between asserting truth and denying it. No universal statement can be logically derived from, or conclusively established by, singular statements however many, but any universal statement can be logically contradicted or refuted with the aid of deductive logic by only one singular statement. To illustrate with a favorite Popperian example (that actually originated with John Stuart Mill): no amount of observations of white swans can allow the inference that all swans are white, but the observation of a single black swan is enough to refute that conclusion. In short, you can never demonstrate that anything is materially true but you can demonstrate that some things are materially false, a statement which we may take to be the first commandment of scientific methodology. Popper exploits this fundamental asymmetry in formulating his demarcation criterion: science is that body of synthetic propositions about the real world that can, at least in principle, be falsified by empirical observations. Thus, science is characterized by its method of formulating and testing propositions, not by its subject matter or by its claim to certainty of knowledge; whatever certainty science provides is instead certainty of ignorance.

The line that is hereby drawn between science and nonscience is, however, not absolute: both falsifiability and testability are matters of degrees (Popper, 1959, p. 113; 1972b, p. 257; 1976, p. 42). In other words, we should think of the demarcation criterion as describing a more or less continuous spectrum of knowledge, at one end of which we find certain "hard" natural sciences such as physics and chemistry (next to which we get the "softer" sciences such as evolutionary biology, geology, and cosmology) and at the other end of which we find poetry, the arts, literary criticism, etcetera, with history and all the social sciences lying somewhere in between, hopefully nearer to the science than to the nonscience end of the continuum.

A logical fallacy

Let us hammer home the distinction between verifiability and falsifiability by a brief digression into the fascinating subject of logical fallacies. Given the hypothetical syllogism, "If A is true, then B is true; A is true; therefore B is true," the hypothetical statement in the major premise can be split up into the antecedent, "if A is true," and the consequent, "then B is true." In order to arrive at the conclusion, "B is true," we must be able to say that A is indeed true; in the technical language of logic, we must "affirm the antecedent" of the major premise in the hypothetical statement in order for the conclusion, "B is true," to follow with logical necessity. Remember the term *true* in this entire argument refers to logical truth, not factual truth.

Consider what happens, however, if we slightly alter the minor premise in our hypothetical syllogism to read: "if A is true, then B is true; B is true; therefore A is true." Instead of affirming the antecedent, we now "affirm the consequent" and try to argue from the truth of the consequent, "B is true," to the truth of the antecedent, "A is true." But this is fallacious reasoning because it is no longer the case that our conclusion must follow with logical necessity from our premises. A single example will illustrate the point: if Blaug is a trained philosopher, he knows how correctly to use the rules of logic; Blaug knows how correctly to use the rules of logic; therefore Blaug is a trained philosopher (alas, he is not).

It is logically correct to "affirm the antecedent" (sometimes called *modus ponens*), but it is a logical fallacy to "affirm the consequent." What we may do, however, is to "deny the consequent" (*modus tollens*), and that is always logically correct. If we express the hypothetical syllogism in its negative form, we get: "if A is true, then B is true; B is *not* true; therefore A is *not* true." To continue our earlier illustration: if Blaug fails to use correctly the rules of logic, we are indeed logically justified in concluding that he is not a trained philosopher.

To express the same point in more colloquial language: *modus ponens* in formal logic means that the truth of the premises is transmitted forward to the conclusions but falsity is not; *modus tollens,* on the other hand, means that the falsity of the conclusions is transmitted back to the premises but truth is not. The former tells us that when premises are demonstrated to be false, the truth or falsity of the conclusions is still an open question; the latter tells us that when the conclusions are false one or more of the premises must be false but that even if the premises were true, we still could not guarantee the truth of the conclusions.

Here is one reason why Popper lays stress on the idea that there is an asymmetry between verification and falsification. From a strictly logical point of view, we can never assert that a hypothesis is necessarily true because it agrees with the facts; in reasoning from the truth of the facts to the truth of the hypothesis, we implicitly commit the logical fallacy of "affirming the consequent." On the other hand, we can deny the truth of a hypothesis with reference to the facts because in reasoning from the absence of the facts to the falseness of the hypothesis, we invoke the logically correct process of reasoning called "denying the consequent" or *modus tollens*. To sum up the entire argument in a mnemonic formula, we might say: there is no logic of proof but there is a logic of disproof.

The problem of induction

If science is to be characterized by the endless attempt to falsify existing hypotheses and to replace them by ones that successfully resist falsification, it is natural to ask where these hypotheses come from. Popper (1959, pp. 31–2) follows the received view in rejecting any interest in the so-called "context of discovery" as distinct from the "context of justification" – the problem of the genesis of scientific knowledge is consigned to the psychology or sociology of knowledge – but he nevertheless insists that whatever is the origin of scientific generalizations, it is not induction from particular instances. Induction for him is simply a myth: not only are inductive inferences invalid, as Hume showed long ago, they are actually impossible (Popper, 1972a, pp. 23–9, 1972b, p. 53). We cannot make inductive generalizations from a series of observations because the moment we have selected certain observations among the infinite number of possible ones, we have already settled on a point of view and that point of view is itself a theory, however crude and unsophisticated. In other words, there are no "brute facts" and all facts are theory-laden – a fundamental idea to which we shall return. Popper, like Hume, does not deny that daily life is full of *prima facie* examples of induction but, unlike Hume, he goes so far as to deny that these are really bold generalizations strengthening what were previously mere hunches. In ordinary life as in science itself, Popper would say, we acquire knowledge and improve on it by a constant succession of conjectures and refutations, using the familiar method of trial and error. In that sense, we might say that Popper has not so much solved the problem of induction, one of his favorite claims, as dissolved it. In short, his claim to have "solved" the problem of induction is to some extent a play on words.[7]

To avoid misunderstanding, we need to spend a moment on the double sense of the term *induction* in common parlance. So far, we have spoken of induction in the strict logical sense as an argument that employs premises containing information about some members of a class in order to support a generalization about the whole class, thus including some unexamined members of the class. In Popper, as in Hume, induction in this sense is not a valid logical argument; only deductive logic affords what logicians call "demonstrative" or compelling arguments whereby true premises always entail true conclusions. But in science, and indeed in everyday thinking, we are continually confronted with arguments also labeled "inductive" that purport to show that particular hypotheses are supported by particular facts. Such arguments may be called "nondemonstrative" in the sense that the conclusions, although in some sense "supported" by the premises, are not logically "entailed" by them (Barker, 1957, pp. 3–4); even if the premises are true, a nondemonstrative inductive inference cannot logically exclude the possibility that the conclusion is false. Thus, "I have seen a large number of white swans; I have never seen a black one; therefore all swans are white" is a nondemonstrative, inductive inference that is not entailed by the major and minor premises: both of these may be perfectly true and yet the conclusion does not logically follow. In short, a nondemonstrative argument can at best persuade a reasonable person, whereas a demonstrative argument must convince even a stubborn person.

Popper's assertion that "induction is a myth" refers to induction as a demonstrative logical argument, not to induction as a nondemonstrative attempt to confirm some hypothesis, frequently involving an exercise in statistical inference.[8] On the contrary, as we shall see, Popper has much to say about

---

[7] The history of philosophy is simply littered with unsuccessful attempts to solve "the problem of induction." Even economists have not been able to resist the game of trying to refute Hume. For example, Roy Harrod (1956) wrote an entire book attempting to justify induction as a species of probability reasoning, probability being viewed as a logical relationship and not as an objective characteristic of events. The question at issue involves some deep conundrums in the very concept of probability that we cannot take up here (but see Ayer, 1970).

[8] The tendency to lose sight of the double meaning of the term "induction" is responsible for some of the attacks that have been leveled at Popper's strictures against

nondemonstrative induction, or what is sometimes called *the logic of confirmation*. All of which is to say that there is hardly anything more misleading than the common notion that deduction and induction are opposite mental operations, with deduction taking us from the general to the particular and induction from the particular to the general. The relevant contrast is never between deduction and induction but between demonstrative inferences that are certain and nondemonstrative inferences that are precarious (see Cohen, 1931, pp. 76–82; Cohen and Nagel, 1934, pp. 273–84).

Enormous confusion might be avoided if we could only enforce the linguistic usage of "adduction" for nondemonstrative styles of reasoning vulgarly labeled "induction" (Black, 1970, p. 137). For example, it is common to encounter statements like: all science is based on induction; deduction is merely a tool for clear thinking that cannot serve as an instrument for gaining new knowledge, being a kind of sausage machine that only produces at one end what must have gone in at the other; only by induction can we learn something new about the world and, after all, science is the accumulation of new knowledge about the world. This point of view, which is virtually a paraphrase from John Stuart Mill's *Logic,* is simply a frightful muddle of words. It supposes that induction is the opposite of deduction and that these two are the only methods of logical thinking. But there is no such thing as demonstrative induction, and adduction is by no means the opposite of deduction, but in fact is a totally different type of mental operation; adduction is the nonlogical operation of leaping from the chaos that is the real world to a hunch or tentative conjecture about the actual relationship that holds between the set of relevant variables. How this leap is made belongs to the context of discovery. Perhaps the study of this context ought not to be contemptuously dismissed, as is the wont of positivists and even Popperians, but the fact remains that the philosophy of science is and has been exclusively concerned with the next step in the process, namely, how initial conjectures are converted into scientific theories by stringing them together into a more or less tightly knit deductive structure and how these theories are then tested against observations. In short, let us not say that science is based on induction: it is based on adduction followed by deduction.

Immunizing stratagems

To return to Popper. There is frequent reference in Popper, particularly in his early writings, to the covering-law model of scientific explanation, but there is also an initial and growing distrust of the symmetry thesis. Predictions have an overriding importance for him in the testing of explanatory

inductivism (see, e.g., Grunbaum, 1976). Barker (1957) provides a good treatment of the issues, although his discussion of Popper leaves something to be desired; see also Braithwaite (1960, chap. 8).

theories, but this is not to say that he regards the *explanans* of a theory as nothing but a machine for generating predictions: "I consider the theorist's interest in *explanation* – that is, in discovering explanatory theories – as irreducible to the practical technological interest in the deduction of predictions" (1959, p. 61n; also 1972a, pp. 191–5; Popper and Eccles, 1977, pp. 554–5; and footnote 1 above). Scientists seek to explain and they derive the logical predictions that are inherent in their explanations in order to test their theories; all "true" theories are merely provisionally true, having so far defied falsification; alternatively expressed, all the material truth we possess is packed into those theories that have not yet been falsified.

Everything hangs, therefore, on whether we can in fact falsify theories, and even if we can, whether we can do so decisively. Long ago, Pierre Duhem argued that no individual scientific hypothesis is conclusively falsifiable, because we always test the entire *explanans,* the particular hypothesis in conjunction with auxiliary statements, and hence can never be sure that we have confirmed or refuted the hypothesis itself. Thus, any hypothesis can be maintained in the face of contrary evidence and, therefore, its acceptance or rejection is to some extent conventional. By way of an example: if we want to test Galileo's law of freely falling bodies, we will necessarily end up testing Galileo's law along with an auxiliary hypothesis about the effect of air resistance because Galileo's law applies to bodies falling in a perfect vacuum and perfect vacuums are, in practice, impossible to obtain; there is nothing to stop us then in setting aside a refutation of Galileo's law on the grounds that the measuring instruments failed to eliminate the effects of air resistance. In short, Duhem concluded, there are no such things as "crucial experiments" (see Harding, 1976). It was said of Herbert Spencer that his idea of tragedy was a beautiful theory killed by one discordant fact. Actually, he need not have worried: such tragedies never happen!

This conventionalist argument of Duhem is known nowadays as the Duhem–Quine thesis because it has been restated by Willard Quine, a modern American philosopher. Popper is not only aware of the Duhem–Quine thesis but indeed the whole of his methodology is conceived to deal with it. Since Popper is still regarded in some circles as a naive falsificationist, that is, as one who believes that a single refutation is sufficient to overthrow a scientific theory, it is worth citing his own endorsement of the Duhem–Quine thesis:

In point of fact, no conclusive disproof of a theory can ever be produced; for it is always possible to say that the experimental results are not reliable, or that the discrepancies which are asserted to exist between the experimental result and the theory are only apparent and that they will disappear with the advance of our understanding [Popper, 1965, p. 50; see also pp. 42, 82–3, 108].

It is because "no conclusive disproof of a theory can ever be produced" that we need methodological limits on the stratagems that may be adopted by scientists to safeguard their theories against refutation. These methodological limits are not superficial adjuncts to Popper's philosophy of science; they are absolutely essential to it. It is not always appreciated that it is not falsifiability as such that distinguishes science from nonscience in Popper; what does demarcate science from nonscience is falsifiability plus the methodological rules that forbid what he first called "*ad-hoc* auxiliary assumptions," later "conventionalist stratagems," and finally "immunizing stratagems" (Popper, 1972a, pp. 15–16, 30; 1976, pp. 42, 44).

If we read Popper's *The Logic of Scientific Discovery,* looking for phrases like "I propose the rule . . . ," "we shall adopt the methodological rule . . . ," etcetera, we shall find more than twenty such phrases. It is instructive to set out a sample of these:[9]

(1) . . . adopt such rules as will ensure the testability of scientific statements; which is to say, their falsifiability [1965, p. 49].

(2) . . . only such statements may be introduced in science as are inter-subjectively testable [1965, p. 56].

(3) . . . in the case of a threat to our system we will not save it by any kind of *conventionalist stratagem* [1965, p. 82].

(4) . . . only those [auxiliary hypotheses] are acceptable whose introduction does not diminish the degree of falsifiability or testability of the system in question, but on the contrary, increases it [1965, p. 83].

(5) Inter-subjectively tested experiments are either to be accepted, or to be rejected in the light of counter-experiments. The bare appeal to logical derivations to be discovered in the future can be disregarded [1965, p. 84].

(6) We shall take it [a theory] as falsified only if we discover a *reproducible effect* which refutes the theory. In other words, we only accept the falsification if a lower-level empirical hypothesis which describes such an effect is proposed and corroborated [1965, p. 86].

(7) . . . those theories should be given preference which can be most severely tested [1965, p. 121].

(8) . . . auxiliary hypotheses should be used as sparingly as possible [1965, p. 273].

(9) . . . any new system of hypotheses should yield, or explain, the old, corroborated, regularities [1965, p. 253].

It is these methodological rules, including that of falsifiability itself, that constitute the criterion of demarcation between science and nonscience in

---

[9] For a complete list of the rules, see Johannson (1975, chaps. 2, 4–11), a useful book by one who is, however, out of sympathy with all that passes nowadays as philosophy of science.

Popper. But why should anyone adopt such a demarcation criterion? "My only reason for proposing my criterion of demarcation," Popper declares, "is that it is fruitful: that a great many points can be clarified and explained with its help" (1965, p. 55). But fruitful for what? For science? The apparent circularity of the argument only disappears if we remind ourselves that the pursuit of science can be justified only in nonscientific terms. We want to gain knowledge of the world, even if it is only fallible knowledge, but why *we* should want such knowledge remains a profound but as yet unanswered metaphysical question about the nature of man (see Maxwell, 1972).

"Methodological rules," Popper (1959, p. 59) tells us, "are here regarded as conventions." Notice that he does not seek to justify his rules by appeal to the history of science, and indeed he specifically rejects the notion of methodology as a subject that investigates the behavior of scientists at work (1959, p. 52). It is true he makes frequent references to the history of science – Einstein being a special source of inspiration (1959, pp. 35–6) – but he does not assume that he has provided a rationale of what it is that scientists are doing, whether they are aware of it or not.[10] His aim appears to be to advise scientists how to proceed so as to encourage scientific progress and his methodological rules are frankly normative, like that famous rule of the medieval scholastics, Occam's Razor, which can be rationally discussed but which cannot be overthrown by historical counterexamples. In that sense, the title of Popper's magnum opus, *The Logic of Scientific Discovery,* is misleading on two scores.[11] The *logic* of scientific discovery is not a pure logic, that is, a series of analytic propositions; as he himself says, "the logic of scientific discovery should be identified with the theory of scientific method" (1959, p. 49), and that theory, as we have seen, consists of the falsifiability principle plus the negative methodological rules strewn throughout his writings.[12] Moreover, the theory of scientific method, even if we loosely describe it as a kind of logic, is not a logic of scientific *discovery* but rather a logic of justification, because the problem of how one discovers new fruitful scientific

---

[10]   Thus, Popper notes, Newton believed himself to have used the method of Baconian induction, which makes his achievements "even more admirable: they are achieved against the odds of false methodological beliefs" (Popper and Eccles, 1977, p. 190; also Popper, 1972b, pp. 106–7, 1983, pp. i–xxxi). Even Einstein, Popper (1976, pp. 96–7) grants, was for years a dogmatic positivist and operationalist. It is odd that Popper rarely invokes the name of Darwin, who, as a matter of fact, is unique among the great scientists of the past in being truly Popperian, going so far as to tell his readers about ways in which his theory might be disproved (see note 14 below).

[11]   This may be a question of bad translation: the German title, *Logik der Forschung,* is more accurately rendered as *The Logic of Inquiry.*

[12]   It is still common to find expositions of Popper that leave out the vital element of the methodological rules that prohibit "immunizing stratagems": see, e.g., Ayer (1976, pp. 157–9); Harré (1972, pp. 48–52); Williams (1975); and even Magee (1973).

hypotheses has been ruled out by Popper from the very beginning as a psychological puzzle.

Statistical inference

Many commentators have been deeply troubled by the notion of methodological principles that are not in some sense generalizations grounded in past scientific achievements. But economists are admirably equipped to appreciate the value of purely normative methodological rules, because they appeal to them every time they estimate a statistical relationship. As every elementary textbook of statistics tells us, statistical inference involves the use of sample observations to infer something about the unknown characteristics of an entire population, and in making that inference we can either be too stringent or too lax: we always run the risk of what is called Type I error, the decision to reject a hypothesis that is in fact true, but we also always run the risk of Type II error, the decision to accept a hypothesis that is in fact false, and there is in general no way of setting up a statistical test that does not in some degree involve both of these risks simultaneously. We are instructed to test a statistical hypothesis indirectly by forming a negative version of the hypothesis to be tested, the null hypothesis, H_O. The probability of Type I error or "size" of the test then consists of the probability of mistakenly rejecting H_O, and the probability of Type II error consists of the probability of mistakenly accepting it; the "power" of the test is the probability of correctly rejecting a false hypothesis which is equal to $(1 - \text{Prob. Type II error})$. We are further instructed to choose a small "size," say, 0.01 or 0.05, and then to maximize "power" consistent with that "size" or, alternatively expressed, to set the probability of Type I error at some arbitrary small figure and then to minimize the probability of Type II error for that given probability of Type I error. This finally produces a conclusion, such that a given hypothesis is established at the 5 percent level of significance, meaning that we are willing to take the risk of accepting that hypothesis as true when our test is so stringent that there is actually a one-in-twenty chance that we will reject a true hypothesis.

The object of this simple lesson in what has come to be known as the Neyman–Pearson theory of statistical inference is to demonstrate that any statistical test of a hypothesis always depends in an essential way on an *alternative hypothesis with which it is being compared,* even if the comparison is only with an artifact, H_O. But that is true not only of statistical tests of hypotheses but of all tests of "adductions." Is Smith guilty of murder? Well, it depends on whether the jury presumes him to be innocent until proven guilty, or guilty until he can prove himself to be innocent. The evidence itself, being typically "circumstantial" as they say, cannot be evaluated unless the jury first decides whether the risk of Type I error is smaller or greater than the risk

of Type II error. Do we want a legal system in which we never convict innocent people, which must come at the cost of occasionally allowing guilty
parties to go scot free, or do we ensure that guilty people are always punished,
in consequence of which we will of course occasionally convict innocent parties?

Now, scientists typically have a greater fear of accepting a falsehood than
of failing to acknowledge a truth; that is, they behave as if the cost of Type II
errors were greater than that of Type I errors. We may deplore this attitude as
stodgy conservatism, a typical manifestation of the unwillingness of those
with vested interests in received doctrines to welcome new ideas, or we may
hail it as a manifestation of healthy skepticism, the hallmark of all that is
salutory in the scientific attitude. But whatever our point of view, we must
perforce conclude that in this way what are considered methodological rules
enter into the very question of whether a statistical fact is accepted as a fact.
Whenever we say a relationship is statistically significant at a level of significance as low as 5 or even 1 percent, we commit ourselves to the decision
that the risk of accepting a false hypothesis is greater than the risk of rejecting
a true one, and this decision is not itself a matter of logic, nor can it be
justified simply by pointing to the history of past scientific accomplishments
(see Braithwaite, 1960, pp. 174, 251; Kaplan, 1964, chap. 6).

In view of the inherently statistical character of modern quantum physics
(Nagel, 1961, pp. 295, 312), these are not idle remarks pertinent only to a
social science like economics. Whenever the predictions of a theory are probabilistic in nature (and what predictions are not – any laboratory experiment
designed to confirm even so simple a relationship as Boyle's law will never
find the product of pressure and volume an exact constant), the notion of
assessing evidence without invoking normative methodological principles is
an absurdity. Popper's philosophy of science would have been much better
understood, much less attended with the misinterpretations that still abound
in the secondary literature, if he had made explicit reference from the outset
to the Neyman–Pearson theory of statistical inference.

It is true of course that this theory of hypothesis testing only emerged in
the writings of Jerzy Neyman and Egon Pearson between the years 1928 and
1935, becoming standard practice somewhere in the 1940s (Kendall, 1968),
and that Popper's *The Logic of Scientific Discovery* was first published in
German in 1934, too early perhaps to take advantage of these developments.
But Ronald Fisher, in a famous paper of 1930, had already developed the
concept of *fiducial inference*, which is virtually identical to the modern Neyman–
Pearson theory of hypothesis testing (Bartlett, 1968), and besides, Popper has
written a great deal on the philosophy of science since 1934. Popper's neglect
of the implications of the modern theory of statistical inference for the philosophy of science is the more surprising in that he begins his discussion of

probability in *The Logic of Scientific Discovery* with the insight that probability statements are inherently nonfalsifiable because they "do not rule out anything observable" (1965, pp. 189–90). "It is fairly clear," he goes on to say, "that 'practical falsification' can be obtained only through a methodological decision to *regard* highly improbable events as ruled out – as prohibited" (1965, p. 191). There is the gist of the Neyman–Pearson theory and, when put like that, it immediately becomes obvious that the principle of falsifiability requires methodological norms to give it bite. Popper's failure to exploit the Neyman–Pearson theory, and particularly his apparent reluctance to mention it, must thus be put down as one of those unsolved mysteries in the history of ideas.[13] I conjecture that it has something to do with his lifelong opposition to the use of probability theory to assess the verisimilitude of a hypothesis – a question too daunting to take up here – but that is only an inspired guess.

Degrees of corroboration

Although Popper denies the view that scientific explanations are simply "inference tickets" for making predictions, he nevertheless insists that scientific explanations cannot be appraised except in terms of the predictions which they imply. To verify the predictions of a theoretical explanation, to show that observable phenomena are compatible with the explanation, is all too easy: there are few theories, however absurd, that will not be found to be verified by some observations. A scientific theory is only really put to the test when a scientist specifies in advance the observable conditions that would falsify the theory.[14] The more exact the specification of those falsifying con-

---

[13] Lakatos (1978, I, p. 25n) notes that Popper's "falsificationism is the philosophical basis of some of the most interesting developments in modern statistics. The Neyman-Pearson approach rests completely on methodological falsificationism." But Lakatos does not comment on the fact that Popper fails ever to notice the Neyman-Pearson theory, which was developed independently of and largely prior to Popper's falsificationism. See also Ackermann (1976, pp. 84–5). Braithwaite (1960, p. 199n), after noting the intimate connection between the "problem of induction" and the early work of Fisher on significance tests, culminating in the inference theory of Neyman and Pearson, and, latterly, in the statistical decision theory of Abraham Wald, has a revealing footnote that reads: "Though several writers on logic refer to Fisher's 'maximum likelihood' method, I know of only two works on logic, C. W. Churchman, *Theory of Experimental Inference* (New York, 1948), and Rudolf Carnap, *Logical Foundations of Probability,* which refer to Wald's work – or indeed to Neyman and Pearson's work which is as old as 1933."

[14] It is interesting that Darwin (1859, pp. 228–9) offers precisely such a Popperian specification: "If it could be proved that any part of the structure of any one species had been formed for the exclusive good of another species, it would annihilate my theory, for such could not have been produced through natural selection"; he cites the rattlesnake's rattle as a case in point but immediately evades the issue of altruistic

ditions and the more probable their occurrence, the greater are the risks that the theory runs. If such a bold theory succeeds repeatedly in resisting falsification and if, in addition, it successfully predicts results that do not follow from competing theoretical explanations, it is judged to be highly confirmed or, as Popper prefers to say, "well corroborated" (1959, chap. 10). In short, a theory is corroborated, not if it agrees with many facts, but if we are unable to find any facts that refute it.

In traditional nineteenth-century philosophy of science, adequate scientific theories should satisfy a whole list of criteria, such as internal consistency, simplicity, completeness, generality of explanation (that is, the ability to imply or at least to throw light on a wide variety of phenomena – what William Whewell used to call "consilience of induction"), fecundity (that is, the power to stimulate further research), and perhaps even the practical relevance of the implications. It is worth noting that Popper struggles to reduce most of these traditional criteria to his overriding demand for falsifiable predictions. Obviously, logical consistency is "the most general requirement" for any theory because a self-contradictory explanation is compatible with any event and hence can never be refuted (Popper, 1959, p. 92). Likewise, it is obvious that the greater the generality of a theory, the wider the scope of its implications, the easier it is to falsify it; in that sense, the widespread preference for more and more comprehensive scientific theories may be interpreted as an implicit recognition of the fact that scientific progress is characterized by the accumulation of theories that have withstood severe testing. More controversially, Popper argues that theoretical simplicity may be equated to the degree of falsifiability of a theory, in the sense that the simpler the theory, the stricter its observable implications, and hence the greater its testability; it is because simpler theories have these properties that we aim for simplicity in science (Popper, 1965, chap. 7). It is doubtful that this is a convincing argument, since the very notion of simplicity of a theory is itself highly conditioned by the historical perspective of scientists. More than one historian of science has noted that the elegant simplicity of Newton's theory of gravitation, which so impressed nineteenth-century thinkers, did not particularly strike seventeenth-century contemporaries, and if modern quantum mechanics and relativity theory are true, it must be conceded that they are not very simple theories.[15]

> behavior by adding "I have not space here to enter on this and other such cases." The problem of how to account for altruism in animals remains an abiding concern of modern sociobiologists.
>
> [15] As Polanyi (1958, p. 16) has observed, "great theories are rarely simple in the ordinary sense of the term. Both quantum mechanics and relativity theory are very difficult to understand; it takes only a few minutes to memorize the facts accounted for by relativity, but years of study may not suffice to master the theory and to see these facts in its context."

Attempts to define precisely what is meant by a simpler theory have so far failed (Hempel, 1966, pp. 40–5), and Oscar Wilde may have been right when he quipped that the truth is rarely pure and never simple.

Be that as it may, Popper's reference to "degrees of corroboration" may suggest a metric of comparison between theories, but in fact he explicitly denies the possibility of giving a numerical expression to the degree of falsifiability of a theoretical system. First of all, no theory can ever be decisively falsified by any single experiment – the Duhem–Quine thesis. Second, although we may urge scientists not to evade falsification of their theories by "immunizing stratagems," we must recognize the functional value in certain circumstances of clinging tenaciously to a refuted theory in the hope that it can be repaired to cope with the newly discovered anomalies (Popper, 1972a, p. 30); in other words, the advice that Popperianism offers to scientists is by no means unambiguous. Third, most problems of theoretical appraisal involve not just a duel between a theory and a set of observations but a three-cornered fight between two or more rival theories and a body of evidence that is more or less satisfactorily explained by both theories (Popper, 1965, pp. 32–3, 53–4, 108). All three considerations doom the concept of degrees of corroboration of a theory to that of an *ex post* ordinal comparison that is inherently qualitative (Popper, 1972a, pp. 18, 59):

By the degree of corroboration of a theory I mean a concise report evaluating the state (at a certain time *t*) of the critical discussion of a theory, with respect to the way it solves its problems; its degree of testability; the severity of the tests it has undergone; and the way it had stood up to these tests. Corroboration (or degree of corroboration) is thus an evaluating *report of past performance*. Like preference, it is essentially comparative: in general, one can only say that the theory A has a higher (or lower) degree of corroboration than a competing theory B, in the light of the critical discussion, which includes testing, *up to some time t*. Being a report of past performance only, it has to do with a situation which may lead to preferring some theories to others. *But it says nothing whatever about future performances, or about the "reliability" of a theory. . .* I do not think that degrees of verisimilitude, or a measure of truth content, or falsity content (or, say, degree of corroboration, or even of logical probability) can ever be numerically determined, except in certain limiting cases (such as 0 and 1).

The problem of giving some precision to the concept of corroboration is further aggravated by the fact that rival theories may actually have slightly different domains, in which case they are not even, strictly speaking, commensurable. If, in addition, they each form part of a larger, interconnected system of theories, the task of comparing them in terms of their degrees of corroboration or verisimilitude becomes almost impossible. This central difficulty in Popperian methodology is well expressed by a somewhat mischievous "rational reconstruction" of his work, penned by one of his pupils, Imre Lakatos (1978, I, pp. 93–4).

Popper is the dogmatic falsificationist who never published a word: he was invented – and "criticized" – first by Ayer and then by many others . . . Popper₁ is the naive falsificationist, Popper₂ the sophisticated falsificationist. The *real* Popper developed from dogmatic to a naive version of *methodological* falsificationism in the twenties; he arrived at the *"acceptance rules"* of *sophisticated falsificationism* in the fifties. . . But the real Popper never abandoned his earlier (naive) *falsification rules*. He has demanded, until this day, that *"criteria of refutation"* have to be laid down before hand: it must be agreed which observable situations, if actually observed, mean that the theory is refuted. He still construes "falsification" as the result of a duel between theory and observation, without another, better theory *necessarily* being involved. . . Thus the real Popper consists of Popper₁ together with some elements of Popper₂.

Lakatos's characterization of Popper is perhaps unfair, but there is no doubt, as we shall see, that the attempt to differentiate his own product from that of Popper (Lakatos = Popper₃) is warranted: Popper concedes that scientists usually have a new theory up their sleeves before concluding that an old one is falsified, but he does not insist that they should have or must have such a new theory up their sleeves, which is Lakatos's main point (Lakatos, 1978, II, pp. 184–5, 193–200; also Ackerman, 1976, chap. 5).

A central conclusion

We have now reached one of our central conclusions: just as there is no logic of discovery, so there is no demonstrative *logic* of justification either; there is no formal algorithm, no mechanical procedure of verification, falsification, confirmation, corroboration, or call it what you will. To the philosophical question "How can we acquire apodictic knowledge of the world when all we can rely on is our own unique experience?" Popper replies that there is no certain empirical knowledge, whether grounded in our own personal experience or in that of mankind in general. And more than that: there is no sure method of guaranteeing that the fallible knowledge we do have of the real world is positively the best we can possess under the circumstances. A study of the philosophy of science can sharpen our appraisal of what constitutes acceptable empirical knowledge, but it remains a provisional appraisal nevertheless. We can invite the most severe criticism of this appraisal, but what we cannot do is to pretend that there is on deposit somewhere a perfectly objective method, that is, an intersubjectively demonstrative method, that will positively compel agreement on what are or are not acceptable scientific theories.

2

From Popper to the new heterodoxy

Kuhn's paradigms

We have seen that Popper's methodology is plainly normative, prescribing sound practice in science, possibly but not necessarily in the light of the best science of the past. To that extent, the Popperian methodology of falsificationism is in keeping with the received view on theories, although in many other respects it points away from the received view. In Kuhn's *The Structure of Scientific Revolutions* (1962), however, the break with the received view is almost total because his emphasis is not on normative prescription but rather on positive description. Moreover, the inclination to preserve theories and to render them immune to criticism, which Popper grudgingly accepts as a departure from best-practice science, becomes the central issue in Kuhn's explanation of scientific behavior. Kuhn regards *normal science,* that is, problem-solving activity in the context of an orthodox theoretical framework, as the rule and *revolutionary science,* or the overthrow of one framework by another in consequence of repeated refutations and mounting anomalies, as the exception in the history of science. It is tempting to say that for Popper science is always in a state of permanent revolution, the history of science being a history of continuous conjectures and refutations; for Kuhn, the history of science is marked by long periods during which the status quo is preserved, interrupted on occasions by discontinuous jumps from one ruling paradigm to another with no conceptual bridge for communicating between them.

To take our bearings, we must begin by defining terms. In the first edition of his book, Kuhn frequently employs the term *paradigm* in a dictionary sense to stand for certain exemplary instances of past scientific achievement that continue to serve as models for current practitioners. But he also employs the term in quite a different sense to denote both the choice of problems and the set of techniques for analyzing them, in places going so far as to give *para-*

27

digm a still wider meaning as a general metaphysical world outlook; the last sense of the term is, in fact, what most readers retain of the book. In the second edition of *The Structure of Scientific Revolutions* (1970), Kuhn admits to terminological imprecision in the earlier version[16] and suggests replacing the term *paradigm* by the term *disciplinary matrix:* " 'disciplinary' because it refers to the common possession of the practitioners of a particular discipline; 'matrix' because it is composed of ordered elements of various sorts, each requiring further specification" (Kuhn, 1970a, p. 182). But whatever language is employed, the focus of his argument remains that of "the entire constellation of beliefs, values, techniques and so on shared by the members of a given community," and he goes on to say that if he were to write his book again, he would start with a discussion of the professionalization of science before examining the shared "paradigms" or "disciplinary matrices" of scientists (1970a, p. 173).

These are not fatal concessions for the simple reason that the distinctive feature of Kuhn's ideas is not the concept of paradigms that everyone has seized on, but rather that of "scientific revolutions" as sharp breaks in the development of science, and particularly the notion of a pervasive failure of communications during periods of "revolutionary crisis." Let us remind ourselves of the building bricks of Kuhn's argument: the practitioners of normal science form an invisible college in the sense that they are in agreement both on the problems that require solution and on the general form that the solution should take; moreover, only the judgment of colleagues is regarded as relevant in defining problems and solutions, in consequence of which normal science is a self-sustaining, cumulative process of puzzle solving within the context of a common analytical framework; the breakdown of normal science, when it does break down, is heralded by a proliferation of theories and the appearance of methodological controversy; the new framework offers a decisive solution to hitherto neglected puzzles, and this solution turns out in retrospect to have long been recognized but previously ignored; the old and new generations talk past each other as unsolved puzzles in the old framework become corroborating examples in the new; since there is always loss of content as well as gain, conversion to the new approach takes on the nature of a religious experience, involving a *Gestalt* switch; and as the new framework conquers, it becomes in turn the normal science of the next generation.

The reader who is acquainted with the history of science thinks immediately of the Copernican revolution, the Newtonian revolution, the Darwinian revolution, or the Einstein-Planck revolution. The so-called Copernican revolution, however, took a hundred and fifty years to complete and was argued

---

[16] Masterman (1970, pp. 60–5) has in fact identified 21 different definitions of the term *paradigm* in the first edition of Kuhn's book.

out every step of the way;[17] even the Newtonian revolution took more than a generation to win acceptance throughout the scientific circles of Europe, during which time the Cartesians, Leibnizians, and Newtonians engaged in bitter disputes over every aspect of the new theory (Cohen, 1980, pp. 141ff, 1985, pp. 167–79).[18] Likewise, the Darwinian revolution fails to conform to Kuhn's description of scientific revolutions: there was no crisis in biology in the 1850s; the conversion to Darwin was swift but by no means instant; there was even something of a decline in Darwin's reputation at the turn of the century; and some two hundred years passed between the beginning of the Darwinian revolution in the 1740s and its modern version in the evolutionary synthesis of the 1940s (Mayr, 1972). Finally, the switch in the twentieth century from classical to relativistic and quantum physics involved neither mutual incomprehension nor quasi-religious conversions, that is, switches of *Gestalt,* at least if the scientists directly involved in the "crisis of modern physics" are to be believed (Toulmin, 1972, pp. 103–5).[19] It is hardly necessary, however, to argue these points, because in the second edition of his book Kuhn candidly admits that his earlier description of scientific revolutions suffered from rhetorical exaggeration: paradigm changes during scientific revolutions do not imply total discontinuities in scientific debate, that is, choices between competing but totally incommensurate theories; mutual incomprehension between scientists during periods of intellectual crisis is only a matter of degree; and the only point of calling paradigm changes "revolutions" is to underline the fact that the arguments that are advanced to support a new paradigm always contain nonrational elements that go beyond logical or mathematical proof (Kuhn, 1970a, pp. 199–200). As if this were not enough, he goes on to complain that this theory of scientific revolutions was misunderstood as referring solely to major revolutions, such as the Copernican, Newtonian, Darwinian, or Einsteinian; he now insists that the schema was just as much directed at minor changes in particular scientific fields, which might not

---

[17] The Copernican heliocentric theory is, by the way, the best example in the history of science of the abiding appeal of simplicity as a criterion of scientific progress: Copernicus' *De Revolutionibus Orbium Caelestium* failed to achieve the predictive accuracy of Ptolemy's *Almagest,* and it did not even get rid of all the epicycles and eccentrics that cluttered the geocentric Ptolemaic theory, but it was a more economical explanation of most, if not all, the known contemporary facts of planetary motion (Kuhn, 1957, pp. 168–71; also Bynum et al., 1981, pp. 80–1, 348–52).

[18] As Kuhn (1957, p. 259) himself pointed out in his earlier study of the Copernican revolution: "It was forty years before Newtonian physics firmly supplanted Cartesian physics, even in British universities."

[19] Of all the many critiques that Kuhn's book has received, none is more devastating than that of Toulmin (1972, pp. 98–117), who traces the history of Kuhn's ideas from its first announcement in 1961 to its final version in 1970. For a deeply sympathetic but in many ways equally critical reading of Kuhn, see Suppe (1974, pp. 135–51).

seem to be revolutionary at all to those outside "a single community, consisting perhaps of fewer than twenty-five people directly involved in it" (1970a, pp. 180–1).

In other words, in this later version of Kuhn any period of scientific development is marked by a large number of overlapping and interpenetrating paradigms; some of these may be incommensurable but certainly not all of them are; paradigms do not replace each other suddenly and, in any case, new paradigms do not spring up full-blown but instead emerge as victorious in a long process of intellectual competition.[20] It is evident that these concessions considerably dilute the apparently dramatic import of Kuhn's original message. What remains, however, is the emphasis on the role of normative judgments in scientific controversies, particularly in respect of the choice between competing approaches to science, together with a vaguely formulated but deeply held suspicion of cognitive factors like epistemological rationality, rather than sociological factors like authority, hierarchy, and reference groups, as determinants of scientific behavior. What Kuhn appears to have done is to fuse prescription and description, thus deducing his methodology of science from the history of science.

In one sense, Kuhn's *The Structure of Scientific Revolutions* is not a contribution to methodology but rather a contribution to the sociology of science. No wonder then that a confrontation between Kuhnians and Popperians produces something of an impasse. Thus, Kuhn (1970b, pp. 1–4, 19–21, 205–7, 238, 252–3) himself underlines the similarities between his approach and that of Popper, insisting that he is like Popper "a convinced believer in scientific progress," while nevertheless conceding the inherently sociological nature of his own work. Likewise, Popperians admit as a matter of fact that "there is *much more* Normal Science, measured in man-hours, than Extraordinary Science" (Watkins, 1970, p. 32; also Ackermann, 1976, pp. 50–3), but they regard such concessions to realism as irrelevant to the essentially normative focus of the philosophy of science; in Popper's own words, "to me the idea of turning for enlightenment concerning the aims of science, and its possible progress, to sociology or to psychology (or . . . to the history of science) is surprising and disappointing" (Popper, 1970, p. 57).

---

[20] In short, Kuhn eventually abandoned the four distinct theses that Watkins (1970, pp. 34–5) found embedded in his book, namely, (1) the paradigm-monopoly thesis – a paradigm brooks no rivals; (2) the incompatibility thesis – new paradigms are incompatible and incommensurable with old ones; (3) the no-interregnum thesis – scientists do not flounder between abandoning an old paradigm and embracing a new one; and (4) the *Gestalt*-switch or instant-paradigm thesis – when scientists switch over to the new paradigm, they do so instantly and totally.

Methodology versus history

Our discussion of Kuhn's book has brought us back full circle to the old puzzle about the relationship between normative methodology of science and positive history of science, a puzzle that has dogged the received view on scientific theories for over a generation. The puzzle is this: to believe that it is possible to write a history of science "as it actually happened" without in any way prejudging the distinction between "good" and "bad" science, without any prior notions of sound scientific practice, is to commit the inductive fallacy in the writing of intellectual history. If Popper is right about the myth of induction, those who want "to tell it as it is" will find themselves driven "to tell it as it should be": by telling the story of past developments one way rather than another, they will necessarily be revealing their implicit view of the nature of scientific explanation. In short, all statements in the history of science are methodology-laden.

On the other hand, it would seem that all statements about the methodology of science are likewise history-laden. To preach the virtues of *the* scientific method, while utterly ignoring the question of whether scientists now or in the past have actually practiced that method, is surely arbitrary; besides, in practice even Popper finds it impossible to resist reference to the history of science as a partial justification of his methodological views. We appear, therefore, to be caught in a vicious circle, implying the impossibility both of a methodology-free, totally descriptive historiography of science and an ahistorical, purely prescriptive methodology of science.[21] From this vicious circle, there is, I think, no real escape. To justify this assertion, we need to consider the work of Imre Lakatos, which is expressly designed to convert the vicious circle into a virtuous one. In a series of papers, largely published between 1968 and 1971, Lakatos developed and extended Popper's philosophy of science into a critical tool of historical research, taking as his maxim a paraphrase of one of Kant's dicta: "Philosophy of science without history of science is empty; history of science without philosophy of science is blind" (Lakatos, 1978, I, p. 102). This maxim perfectly expresses the puzzle or vicious circle in question.

---

[21] The vicious circle is perfectly expressed by one scientist who has frequently acknowledged his debt to Popper. Discussing the paradox of testing a scientific methodology by the practices of scientists, Peter Medawar (1967, p. 169) notes: "If we assume that the methodology is unsound, then so also will be our tests of its validity. If we assume it to be sound, then there is no point in submitting it to test, for the test could not invalidate it." For other evidence of the widespread recognition of the vicious circle by both philosophers and historians of science, see Lakatos and Musgrave (1970, pp. 46, 50, 198, 233, 236–8); Achinstein (1974); Hesse (1973); and Laudan (1977, chap. 5).

Scientific research programs

Popper's methodology of science is an *aggressive methodology* in the sense that by its standards some of what is called "science" can be dismissed as methodologically unsound. Kuhn's methodology, however, is a *defensive methodology* because it seeks to vindicate rather than criticize actual scientific practice.[22] The writings of Lakatos, on the other hand, may be understood as striking a compromise between the ahistorical, if not antihistorical, aggressive methodology of Popper and the relativistic, defensive methodology of Kuhn, a compromise that nevertheless stays firmly within the Popperian camp.[23] Lakatos is "softer" on science than Popper but a great deal "harder" than Kuhn, and he is always more inclined to criticize bad science with the aid of good methodology than to qualify methodological speculations by an appeal to scientific practice.

For Lakatos, as for Popper, methodology as such does not provide scientists with a book of rules for solving scientific problems; it is concerned with the logic of appraisal, a set of nonmechanical rules for appraising fully articulated theories. Where Lakatos differs from Popper, however, is that this logic of appraisal is employed by him at one and the same time as a historical theory that purports to retrodict the development of science. As a normative methodology of science, it is empirically irrefutable because it is derived from a particular view of epistemology. But as a historical theory, asserting that scientists in the past frequently did behave in accordance with the methodology of falsifiability, it is perfectly refutable. If the history of science fits the normative methodology, Lakatos seems to be saying, we have reasons additional to philosophical ones for subscribing to falsificationism; if it fails to do so, we are furnished with reasons for abandoning our normative principles. In other words, Lakatos insists that we cannot ultimately evade the task of examining the history of science with the aid of an explicit falsificationist methodology to see how large the area of conflict actually is.[24]

Lakatos begins by denying that individual theories are the appropriate units

[22] I owe the distinction between aggressive and defensive methodologies to Latsis (1974).

[23] Bloor (1971, p. 104) is wide of the mark, as we shall see, in characterizing Lakatos's work as "a massive act of revision, amounting to a betrayal of the essentials of the Popperian approach, and a wholesale absorption of some of the most characteristic Kuhnian positions." He is not alone, however, in seeing little difference between Kuhn and Lakatos (e.g., Green, 1977, pp. 6–7), thus missing the entire object of Lakatos's argument.

[24] This is, at any rate, how I read Lakatos. It must be said that he is not an easy author to pin down to a precise interpretation. His tendency to make vital points in footnotes, to proliferate labels for different intellectual positions, to coin new phrases and expressions, and to refer back and forth to his own writings – as if it were impossible to understand any part of them without understanding the whole – stands in the way of ready comprehension.

for making scientific appraisals; what ought to be appraised, and what inevitably is appraised, are clusters of more or less interconnected theories or *scientific research programs* (SRPs).[25] As a particular research strategy or SRP encounters falsifications, it undergoes changes in its auxiliary assumptions, which, as Popper had argued, may be content increasing or content decreasing, or as Lakatos prefers to say, represent either "progressive or degenerating problem shifts." An SRP is said to be *theoretically progressive* if a successive formulation of the program contains "excess empirical content" over its predecessor, that is, predicts "some novel, hitherto unexpected fact"; it is *empirically progressive* if "this excess empirical content is corroborated" (Lakatos, 1978, I, pp. 33–4). Conversely, if the SRP is characterized by the endless addition of ad hoc adjustments that merely accommodate whatever new facts become available, it is labeled "degenerating."

Yes, but what is a "novel fact"? A hitherto totally unsuspected implication of an SRP (such as the existence of the planet Neptune in the Newtonian SRP), or a fact which, while known, had previously lacked any theoretical explanation (such as Kepler's first law of planetary motion, the elliptical orbits of planets around the sun, which proved to be a simple deduction of the Newtonian formula for gravity). Clearly, the former is a much tougher criterion than the latter and the choice between them would therefore affect our Lakatosian judgment of the degree of progress of an SRP. Lakatos himself weakened his novel fact requirement and his followers soon settled on the loosest definition (Hands, 1991): a progressive SRP is one that succeeds more or less continually in making novel predictions, accounting systematically for new out-of-sample data; in short it does something more than to account, however ingeniously, for phenomena already known before the SRP was formulated, or worse, to account for only those that the SRP was expressly designed to explain.

In any case, the distinction between a progressive and a degenerating SRP is a relative, not absolute, distinction. Moreover, it is applicable, not at a given point in time, but over a period of time. The forward-looking character of a research strategy, as distinct from an isolated theory, defies instant appraisal. For Lakatos, therefore, an SRP is not "scientific" once and for all; it may cease to be scientific as time passes, slipping from the status of being "progressive" to that of being "degenerating" (astrology is an example), but the reverse may also happen (parapsychology?). We thus have a *demarcation criterion* between science and nonscience that is itself historical, involving the evolution of ideas over time as one of its necessary elements.

---

[25] If the concept of scientific research programs strikes some readers as vague, it must be remembered that the concept of theories is just as vague. It is in fact difficult to define the notion of *theory* even when the term is employed in a narrow, technical sense (Achinstein, 1968, chap. 4).

The argument is now extended by dividing the components of an SRP into rigid and flexible parts. "The history of science," Lakatos (1978, I, pp. 49–52) observes, "is the history of research programmes rather than of theories," and "all scientific research programmes may be characterized by their 'hard core', surrounded by a protective belt of auxiliary hypotheses which has to bear the brunt of tests." The hard core is treated as irrefutable by "the methodological decision of its protagonists" and it contains, besides purely metaphysical beliefs, a "positive heuristic," and a "negative heuristic," consisting in effect of a list of "do"'s and a list of "don't"'s. The protective belt contains the flexible parts of an SRP, and it is here that the hard core is combined with auxiliary assumptions to form the specific testable theories with which the SRP earns its scientific reputation.

Terms like *hard core* and *protective belt* are clearly chosen for their ironic overtones. To some extent the distinction is a logical one: if SRPs are continually evolving in the effort to deal with anomalies and to encompass new phenomena, it follows that some of their components must remain more or less the same or else we are in fact confronting entirely new SRPs; in short, there must be something like a "hard core" or relatively rigid part to an SRP. That is not to say that the hard core of an SRP is set in concrete at the birth of the program; on the contrary, it too evolves, but presumably much more slowly than the protective belt. The hard core, as we have said, consists of empirically irrefutable beliefs and hence amounts to what others have called "metaphysics."[26] In other words, there is no positivist obsession in Lakatos to get rid of metaphysics once and for all. Like Popper (1959, p. 38), Lakatos is convinced that scientific discoveries are impossible without metaphysical commitments; it is simply that the metaphysics of science is deliberately kept out of sight in the hard core, much like the playing cards in a game of poker are kept out of sight in the hands of the dealer, while the real game of science takes place in terms of the cards in the hands of the players, that is, the falsifiable theories in the protective belt.

Lakatos argues that Popper's falsifiability criterion requires not simply that a scientific theory be testable but that it be independently testable, that is,

---

[26] Lakatos's "hard core" expresses an idea virtually identical to that conveyed by Schumpeter's notion of "vision" in the history of economics – "the preanalytic cognitive act that supplies the raw material for the analytic effort" (Schumpeter, 1954, pp. 41–3) – or Gouldner's "world hypotheses," which figure heavily in his explanation of why sociologists adopt certain theories and reject others (Gouldner, 1971, chap. 2). Marx's theory of ideology may be read as a particular theory about the nature of Lakatos's "hard core"; Marx was quite right in believing that "ideology" plays a significant role in scientific theorizing but he was quite wrong in thinking that the class character of that ideology was decisive for the acceptance or rejection of scientific theories (see Seliger, 1977, particularly pp. 26–45, 87–94).

capable of predicting an outcome that is not also predicted by a rival theory. In that case, Popperian "corroboration" requires at least two theories and as much is true of SRPs. A particular SRP is judged superior to another if it accounts for all the facts predicted by a rival SRP and, in addition, makes extra predictions as well, some of which are empirically confirmed (Lakatos, 1978, I, pp. 69, 116–17). Lakatos illustrates the argument by analyzing Newton's gravitational theory – "probably the most successful research programme ever" – and then traces the tendency of physicists after 1905 to join the camp of relativity theory, which subsumes Newton's theory as a special case. He labels this move from the Newtonian to the Einsteinian SRP an "objective" one because most physicists acted as if they believed in the Lakatosian *methodology of scientific research programs* (MSRP).

It happens of course that this particular incident in the history of science involved virtually no Kuhnian loss of content in moving from a degenerating SRP to a progressive SRP: the Newtonian system may be taken to be a special case of Einstein's more comprehensive relativity theory. But not all history of science fits so neatly into the notion of steady, cumulative scientific progress in which older theories are constantly being superseded by newer, more general ones. Frequently, the gain of content in scientific progress comes at the expense of some loss of content, in which case we are back to the familiar Kuhnian problem of the incommensurability of successive research strategies. Nevertheless, Lakatos goes on to advance the somewhat startling claim that all history of science can be similarly described as the "rational" preference of scientists for progressive over degenerating SRPs, apparently because the content gain always exceeds the content loss, and he defines any attempt to do so as *internal* history of science (p. 102).

By way of contrast, *external* history is not just all the normal pressures of the social and political environment that we usually associate with the word *external,* but any failure of scientists to act according to MSRP; for example, preferring a degenerating SRP to a progressive SRP on the grounds that the former is simpler than the latter. Lakatos does not pretend for one moment that internal history can ever be the whole story: to do so would imply that scientists are always perfectly "rational," a proposition that he is too Kuhnian to entertain (pp. 130, 133). He grants that the claim that all history of science can be explained by a purely "internal" rational reconstruction may not be sustainable in the light of historical evidence, but he recommends that we give priority to internal history before resorting to external history. Alternatively, what we can do is "to relate the internal history *in the text,* and indicate in the footnotes how actual history 'misbehaved' in the light of its rational reconstruction" (p. 120), advice that he himself followed in his famous history of Euler's mathematical theorems on polyhedrons (Lakatos,

1976).[27] History of science written along these lines, Lakatos conjectured, would in fact need few footnotes referring to external history.

In reply to Lakatos's aspersions on his own sociopsychological theory, Kuhn (1970b, p. 256) minimizes the differences between them: "Though his terminology is different, his analytic apparatus is as close to mine as need be: hard core, work in the protective belt, and degenerating phase are close parallels for my paradigms, normal science, and crisis." He insists, however, that "what Lakatos conceives as history is not history at all but philosophy fabricating examples. Done in that way, history could not in principle have the slightest effect on the prior philosophical position which exclusively shaped it" (Kuhn, 1971, p. 143). Lakatos meets this argument by claiming that his own approach to the historiography of science is perfectly capable of postdicting novel historical facts, that is, facts that are unexpected in the light of the extant approaches of historians of science. In that sense, the "methodology of *historiographical* research programmes" may be vindicated by MSRP itself: it will prove "progressive" if and only if it promotes the discovery of novel historical facts (Lakatos, 1978, I, pp. 131–6). The proof of the pudding is therefore in the eating: it remains to be seen whether the history of science, natural or social, is more fruitfully conceived, not as a steady series of paradigmatic refinements punctured every few hundred years by a Kuhnian scientific revolution, but as a succession of progressive Lakatosian research programs constantly superseding one another with theories of ever-increasing empirical content.

Lakatos's concepts of SRP and MSRP have already inspired a whole series of reinterpretations of both familiar and unfamiliar episodes in the history of science (see Urbach, 1974; Howson, 1976), including some applications in economics that we will examine in some detail later in this book (see also de Marchi and Blaug, 1991). Whether these studies in fact demonstrate the heuristic power of Lakatos's metahistorical research program must be left to others to judge, but it is fair to say that Lakatos in the final analysis has the same difficulty that Popper experienced in steering a middle course between prescriptive arrogance and descriptive humility.

As we saw earlier, Popper would appear to advise scientists what to do – without however ruling out the possibility that scientific progress may be achieved by ignoring his advice. Similarly, Lakatos characterizes his MSRP

---

[27] It would be truer to say that his advice was a rationalization of his history of Euler's theorems, first published in 1964. This scintillating work is in the form of a Platonic dialogue, and all references to the history of mathematics are consigned to footnotes: it demonstrates that such age-old mathematical concepts as "rigor," "elegance," and "proof," which have long been considered to be matters of pure logic, have been subject to as much historical development as their scientific counterparts, "cogency," "simplicity," "deductive necessity," etcetera.

as an *ex post* appraisal of past scientific research programs that cannot be simply equated with heuristic advice to living scientists to desert a degenerating SRP and to join a progressive one. He preaches tolerance towards budding SRPs that have as yet failed to predict novel facts, and refuses to condemn scientists who cling to degenerating SRPs, provided that they honestly admit that their program is in fact degenerating. He adds, however, that editors of scientific journals are perfectly justified in refusing to publish the papers that result from degenerating SRPs and so are research foundations in refusing to finance them (Lakatos, 1978, I, p. 117). It is not difficult to see that these distinctions amount to a kind of intellectual schizophrenia, particularly as no time limits are specified for either scientists, learned journals, or research foundations. Feyerabend (1976, p. 324n) maliciously remarks that "one might comment on the futility of a point of view where a thief can steal as much as he wants, [and] is praised as an honest man by the police and by the common folk alike provided he tells everyone that he is a thief."

It is clear that Lakatos's effort to divorce appraisal from recommendation, to retain a critical methodology of science that is frankly normative, but which nevertheless is capable of serving as the basis of a research program in the history of science, must be judged either a severely qualified success or else a failure, albeit a magnificent failure.[28]

Feyerabend's anarchism

Many of the tendencies in Lakatos's writings to soften the "aggressive" features of Popperianism, to widen the limits of what is permissible, is carried further by some of the other recent critics of the received view on theories, such as Hanson, Polanyi, and Toulmin, and it is carried still further by Paul Feyerabend.[29]

All of these writers deny the positivist distinction between "the context of discovery" and "the context of justification" (see, in particular, Toulmin, 1972, pp. 478–84; Feyerabend, 1975, chaps. 5, 14). Of course, they agree that the logical and empirical justification of theories cannot be reduced to an exposé of their historical origins, but they nevertheless refuse totally to divorce *ex post* appraisals of validity from the study of the genesis of theories. In other words, all of them follow Kuhn and Lakatos in rejecting the Popperian program of a completely ahistorical philosophy of science, the more so as each of them repeatedly emphasizes the essentially public and cooperative

---

[28] The failure is confirmed by the valiant but unconvincing attempt of one of his pupils to reformulate Lakatos's MSRP: see Worrall (1976, pp. 161–76). For other cogent criticisms of Lakatos, see Berkson (1976) and Toulmin (1976).

[29] Gaston Bachelard, a French philosopher of science little known outside France, must be coupled with the English and American critics of the received view. For a commentary on Bachelard, see Bhaskar (1975).

character of scientific knowledge: it is interpersonal testability, captured by the notion of indefinitely replicable results, that is the hallmark of science and that alone distinguishes it from other human conceptual activities. Even in Michael Polanyi's book with its pointed title, *Personal Knowledge,* the basic argument about science contradicts the title: whatever scientific knowledge is, it is not purely personal knowledge that cannot be conveyed to others (e.g., Polanyi, 1958, pp. 21, 153, 164, 183, 292–4; see also Ziman, 1967, 1978). There may be disagreement as to what can be compellingly conveyed to others but there is no disagreement about the idea that scientific theories must be assessable in terms of observations that are at least in principle available to all observers. Once this is granted, however, it is immediately obvious that new observations will alter these assessments, in consequence of which an inevitable evolutionary element creeps into the appraisal of scientific theories. Thus, the Popperian assault on "the genetic fallacy," the muddling of historical origins with empirical validity, falls to the ground.

Another persistent note in the *new view on scientific theories* is the idea that all empirical observations are necessarily theory-laden and that even ordinary acts of perception, such as seeing, touching, and hearing, are profoundly conditioned by prior conceptualizations; as Hanson (1965, p.. 7), for whom this is virtually an *idée fixe,* expresses it: "there is more to seeing than meets the eyeball."[30] In this particular respect, the new view draws nearer to Popper, who long ago appreciated the paradox of demanding the vigorous testing of theories in terms of their observable predictions, while at the same time granting that all observations are really interpretations in the light of a theory. Far from evading an apparent contradiction, Popper wisely refused to define the term *observable:* "I think it should be introduced as an undefined term which becomes sufficiently precise in use" (Popper, 1959, pp. 103; also p. 107n). To some, this has always seemed a counsel of despair: we appear to be provided with garments that later prove to be transparent.[31] But those who have absorbed the import of the Duhem–Quine thesis, as well as the Lakatosian lesson that all testing involves a three-cornered fight between facts

---

[30] Economists should be well acquainted with Hanson's arguments: they are cited in the first chapter of Samuelson's *Economics* (1976, pp. 10–12). Some sociologists of science (Collins, 1985) carry the notion of theory-laden evidence one step further. Since experimentation is a skillful practice, it is never clear whether a second experiment has been carried out sufficiently well to count as a replica of a first experiment; further experiments are needed to test the quality of the second experiment – and so forth. In this way we can show that there really is no such thing as replication of laboratory experiments: every experiment is *sui generis* and thus the much-acclaimed replicability of scientific findings is, according to this point of view, just a myth.

[31] See the generally perceptive, but logic-chopping, nihilistic criticism of Popper along these lines by one Marxist writer: Hindess (1977, chap. 6).

and at least two rival theories, will take the theory-laden nature of empirical observations in their stride.

Yes, facts are to a greater or lesser extent theory-laden, but they need not be wholly constituted by the theories that they are adduced to support. Facts seem to come in three kinds. There are facts that are observed events, where the observations are so numerous or self-evident that the fact in question is universally accepted as conclusive. But there are also inferred facts, such as the existence of atoms and genes, that are not actually data of direct experience but that are, nevertheless, accorded the status of incontrovertible facts. Finally, there are still more hypothetical facts, where the evidence is either suspect or subject to competing interpretations (e.g., telepathy, poltergeists, and UFO sightings); the world is certainly full of mysterious "facts" that still await rational explanation (see Mitchell, 1974). In short, facts have at least some independence from theories if only because they may be true although the particular theory in question is false; they may be consistent at a lower level with a number of theories whose higher-level propositions are nevertheless in conflict; and the process of scrutinizing facts always involves a relative comparison between more or less fallible theories. Once we grant that completely certain knowledge is denied to us, there is nothing inherently uncomfortable about the profoundly theoretical nature of our very way of looking at facts about the real world.

However, if we couple the concept of theory-laden facts with the Kuhnian notion of content loss in successive theories, paradigms, or SRPs, so that competing theoretical systems become difficult to compare if not literally incommensurable, we reach a position in which there would appear to be no grounds whatsoever for a rational choice between conflicting scientific theories. It is this position of theoretical anarchism that Feyerabend argues with great wit and eloquence in his book, *Against Method,* going so far as to say that "flippant Dadaism" would be a better description of his stance than "serious anarchism" (Feyerabend, 1975, pp. 21, 189–96). Feyerabend's intellectual development as a philosopher of science has been aptly characterized as "a journey from an ultra-Popperian Popper to an ultra-Kuhnian Kuhn" (Bhaskar, 1975, p. 39).

Against Method argues, first of all, that there are no canons of scientific methodology, however plausible and firmly grounded in epistemology, that have not been violated with impunity at some point in the history of science; furthermore, some of the greatest scientists only succeeded by deliberately breaking every rule of sound procedure (Feyerabend, 1975, p. 23; also chap. 9). Second, the thesis that science grows by incorporating older theories as special cases of newer, more general theories is a myth: the actual overlap between rival and scientific theories is so small that even sophisticated falsificationism is deprived an anchorage in rational assessment (pp. 177–8). Third, scientific progress, however conceived or measured, only occurred in the past because scientists were never fettered by any philosophy of science: philosophy of science is one of those "bastard subjects . . . which have not a single discovery to their credit" and "the only principle that does not inhibit progress is: *anything goes*" (pp. 302, 23).

Science, Feyerabend insists, is "much more 'sloppy' and 'irrational' than its methodological image"; more than that, there is no demarcation criterion that could usefully distinguish it from nonscience, ideology, or even myth (pp. 179, 297). "Anything goes," he explains, "does not mean that there are no rational methodological principles but only that if we are to have *universal* methodological principles they will have to be as empty and indefinite as 'anything goes'; 'anything goes' does not express any conviction of mine, it is a jocular summary of the predicament of the rationalist" (1978, p. 188; also pp. 127–8, 142–3, 186–8). In short, he is not against method in science but rather against method in general, including his own advice to ignore methods ("to be a true Dadaist, one must also be an anti-Dadaist").

But it is not just methodology that Feyerabend wants to cut down to size; the real target of his skeptical barbs is the repressive influence of science itself and particularly the presumption of the scientific establishment that it alone has discovered correct methods for discovering truth: state and science must be separated, so that parents can exercise their right to have their children learn magic rather than science in publicly owned schools if that is what they wish (1975, p. 299). The only ultimate, higher-order value is freedom, not science. As one critic has put it: "for Feyerabend the only freedom that deserves the name is that of doing one's own thing in one's own way" (Bhaskar, 1975, p. 42). In the end, Feyerabend's book amounts to replacing the philosophy of science by the philosophy of flower power.[32]

Back to first principles

What are we to make of a skepticism, relativism, and voluntarism as extreme as that of Feyerabend, which succeeds in annihilating not only its

---

[32] Nothing critical said of Feyerabend's *Against Method*, however, can detract from its quality of outrageous "charm" in the best sense of that word: it is hilariously disrespectful of scientific academia, enamored of all underdogs, including Marxists, astrologers, and Jehovah's Witnesses and laughs at itself as well as others; indeed, it is difficult to know whether the author is not constantly pulling your leg. *Against Method* was widely reviewed and in a new book, Feyerabend (1978) reacts characteristically by answering his reviewers at twice the length of their original reviews, accusing them of misunderstanding, misinterpretation, downright distortion, evasion of issues, and worst of all lack of humour. He assures us that there are methods other than those favored by scientists that could supplement rational scientific procedures, but what they are, he does not say; his counterevidence largely consists of personal anecdotes of successful experience with unorthodox medicine. In a more recent book, he continues to defend astrology and even witchcraft as exemplifications of radical pluralism in all intellectual endeavors (Feyerabend, 1988).

own analysis and recommendations but also the very subject to which it is supposed to be contributing? Must we really conclude after centuries of systematic philosophizing about science that science equals myth and that anything goes in science as it does in dreams? If so, astrology is no worse or better than nuclear physics – after all, there is some confirming evidence for genethliacal astrology, predicting the occupational choices of individuals from the position of certain planets at their moment of birth;[33] witches can be just as real as electrons – the fact is that most educated people believed in witchcraft for over two centuries (Trevor-Roper, 1969); we have indeed been visited by supermen from outer space because von Däniken says so, using the age-old trick of verification without reference to well-attested alternative explanations; the planet Venus was ejected by Jupiter around 1500 B.C., nearly collided with Earth, and settled down to its present orbit only around 800 B.C., as Emmanuel Velikovsky would have us believe, thus vindicating the Bible as a more or less accurate account of contemporary catastrophes;[34] plants have emotions and can receive communications from human beings;[35] faith healing is on a par with modern medicine; and spiritualism is back in business as the answer to atheism.

If we resist such radical implications, let us be perfectly clear that the resistance cannot be grounded on the supposedly firm bedrock of epistemology. Nor can it rely on *praxis,* as Leninists like to say, that is, the practical experience of social groups acting on the basis of certain ideas; *praxis* will justify the anticommunism of McCarthy and the antisemitism of *The Protocols of Zion* as easily as the belief of a Trotskyite conspiracy in the Moscow Trials, being simply a fancy name for majority opinion.[36] The only answer that we

---

[33] See West and Toonder (1973, pp. 158, 162–74). Kuhn (1970b, pp. 7–10) for one has argued that "genethliacal" astrology (predicting the future of individuals) as distinct from "mundane" astrology (predicting the future of entire nations and races) must be admitted under Popper's demarcation criterion as a genuine science, albeit a refuted one. See also Eysenck (1979).

[34] Velikovsky's argument would be more plausible if it were set back a million years or so. His is a splendid example of a theory which fairly bristles with predictions, virtually all of which are ad hoc; in addition, he scores misses as frequently as successes (Goldsmith, 1977).

[35] This particular conjecture lacks a theory and rests solely on a few suggestive experimental results and, of course, its deep psychological appeal (see Tompkins and Bird, 1973).

[36] As Polanyi (1958, p. 183) has observed: "Almost every major systematic error which has deluded men for thousands of years relied on practical experience. Horoscopes, incantations, oracles, magic witchcraft, the cures of witch doctors and of medical practitioners before the advent of modern medicine, were all firmly established through the centuries in the eyes of the public by their supposed practical success. The scientific method was devised precisely for the purpose of elucidating the nature of things under more carefully controlled conditions and by more rigorous criteria than are present in the situations created by practical problems."

can give to the philosophy of anything goes is the discipline provided by the *ideals* of science. Science, for all its shortcomings, is the only self-questioning and self-correcting ideological system that man has yet devised; despite intellectual inertia, despite built-in conservatism, and despite the closing of ranks to keep heretics at bay, the scientific community remains loyal to the ideal of intellectual competition in which no weapons other than evidence and argument are permitted. Individual scientists sometimes fall short of those ideals but, nevertheless, the scientific community as a whole is the paradigm case of the open society.

The case for methodological monism

So far, in speaking of science, we have hardly mentioned *social* science, much less economics. To complete the groundwork for our later analysis of economic methodology, however, we must now raise a famous question in the philosophy of the social sciences: is there one scientific method applicable to all the sciences whatever their subject matter, or must social science employ a logic of inquiry that is uniquely its own? There are many social scientists who look to the philosophy of science to tell them how better to imitate physics, chemistry, and biology, but there are also some who are convinced that social science is in possession of an intuitive understanding of its subject matter that is somehow denied to the physical scientists. Even philosophers of science who are adamant in insisting that all the sciences must follow the same methodology sometimes lay down special requirements for valid explanation in social science. Thus, Popper in *The Poverty of Historicism* first announces the doctrine of *methodological monism* – ''all theoretical or generalizing sciences [should] make use of the same method, whether they are natural sciences or social sciences'' – and then prescribes a principle of *methodological individualism* for the social sciences: ''the task of social theory is to construct and analyse our sociological models carefully in descriptive or nominalist terms, that is to say, *in terms of individuals,* of their attitudes, expectations, relations, etc.'' (Popper, 1957, pp. 130, 136). All this is, to say the least, a little confusing to the beginner.

Let us begin by sorting out the argument for the *doctrine of the unity of sciences,* or what we call Methodological Monism. No one denies that the social sciences frequently employ different techniques of investigation from those common in the natural sciences, for example, participant-observer techniques in anthropology, social survey techniques in sociology, and multivariate statistical analysis in psychology, sociology, and economics in contrast to the technique of controlled laboratory experiments in many of the physical sciences. It is worth noting, however, that techniques of investigation perhaps differ no more between the social and natural sciences taken as a whole than between the individual natural sciences taken separately. But methodological monism has nothing to do with techniques of inquiry but rather with "the context of justification" of theories. The methodology of a science is its rationale for accepting or rejecting its theories or hypotheses. Thus, to hold that the social sciences should employ a methodology distinct from the natural sciences is to advocate the startling view that theories or hypotheses about social questions should be validated in ways that are radically different from those used to validate theories or hypotheses about natural phenomena. The categorical denial of such methodological dualism constitutes what we call methodological monism.

To this doctrine, there is an old and a new objection. The old objection is that of certain nineteenth-century German philosophers of the neo-Kantian school and revolves around the concept of *Verstehen* or "understanding." The new objection derives from some of Wittgenstein's later philosophical work having to do with the meaning of human actions, governed as they always are by social rules. Let us take these in turn.

The German term *Verstehen* denotes understanding from within by means of intuition and empathy, as opposed to knowledge from without by means of observation and calculation; in other words, first-person knowledge that is intelligible to us as fellow human beings, instead of third-person knowledge that may not correspond to anything that can be grasped in human terms. It is clear that natural scientists are denied this sort of participant, first-person knowledge because they cannot imagine what it would be like to be atoms or molecules.[37] But social scientists, concerned as they are with human actions, can enter sympathetically into the position of the human actors being analyzed, can draw on introspection as a source of knowledge about the behavior of these actors, and in this way can exercise an inherent advantage over the student of natural phenomena. Not only is *Verstehen* a necessary characteristic of adequate explanation in the social sciences, thus disqualifying such brands of psychology as Skinner's behaviorism, but it is also the source of unique strength as compared to the outsider's knowledge of physical scientists.

The methodological difficulty with *Verstehen* doctrine is the same as that with the use of introspection as a source of evidence about human behavior: how do we know that a particular use of *Verstehen* is reliable? If we challenge a specific act of empathy, how will the empathizer validate his method? If the validity of the empathic method can be independently established, it will usually turn out to be redundant. Besides, we may doubt whether social scientists are actually helped by the extra information gained by introspection and empathy because first-hand knowledge creates the nuisance problem of how to

---

[37] For an amusing defense of *Verstehen* doctrine under the heading "If Matter Could Talk," see Machlup (1978, pp. 315–32).

handle reports that are either deliberately or unwittingly misleading. Accordingly, it is easy to make a case for intuition and empathy as extra sources of knowledge available to social scientists that may aid the invention of suitable hypotheses about human behavior, but it is difficult to sustain the argument for *verstehende* social science in "the context of justification" (see Nagel, 1961, pp. 473–6, 480–5; Rudner, 1966, pp. 72–3; Lesnoff, 1974, pp. 99–104).

The new objection to methodological monism has been forcibly and even fatuously stated by Peter Winch in his much discussed *Idea of a Social Science* (1958) and it links up with some of Max Weber's methodological ideas, particularly the notion of *ideal types* that incorporate the meanings that human agents attach to their actions.[38] The central strand in this brand of thinking is that meaning is not a category open to causal analysis and that, so long as rule-guided human actions form the subject matter of social inquiry, explanation in social science must run not in terms of physical cause and effect but in terms of the motives and intentions of individuals. In other words, the kind of knowledge appropriate to social inquiry can only be gained by coming to "learn the rules," and coming to learn the rules in turn entails knowing the phenomena from the inside, that is, having the experience of behaving in conformity with those rules. Thus, the new objection to methodological monism ultimately blends into the old objection of *Verstehen* doctrine; both are subject to the same criticism that we are offered no interpersonally testable method of validating assertions about rule-governed behavior (Rudner, 1966, pp. 81–3; Lesnoff, 1974, pp. 83–95; Ryan, 1970, chaps. 1, 6).

The question of *Verstehen* and the meaningfulness of rule-guided action is intimately and indeed confusingly connected with the Popperian principle of *methodological individualism*. This principle asserts that explanations of social, political, or economic phenomena can only be regarded as adequate if they run in terms of the beliefs, attitudes, and decisions of individuals. This principle is opposed to the allegedly untenable principle of *methodological holism,* according to which social wholes are postulated to have purposes or functions that cannot be reduced to the beliefs, attitudes, and actions of the individuals that make them up. The force of Popper's insistence on methodological individualism is by no means clear from his own writings (Acker-

---

[38] Weber's ideal types are not any abstract conception but particular kinds of constructs specifically related to thinking, feeling human agents and the events resulting from the action of these agents (e.g., economic man, capitalism, bureaucracy, etc.). In short, Weber's definition of ideal types involves *Verstehen* as one of its essential elements. Weber's meaning was widely misunderstood, in part because it was obscurely expressed: ideal types are neither "ideal" nor "types." Both Burger (1976) and Machlup (1978, chaps. 8, 9) deal expertly with Weber's much-abused theory of ideal types.

mann, 1976, p. 166), and the 1950s saw a great debate on the question in which Popper himself did not participate.[39]

The debate succeeded in clearing away certain confusions that inevitably surround the imperative of methodological individualism. The expression "methodological individualism" was apparently invented by Schumpeter as early as 1908, and Schumpeter was also the first to distinguish methodological individualism from "political individualism," the former prescribing a mode of economic analysis that always begins with the behavior of individuals, while the latter expresses a political program in which the preservation of individual liberty is made the touchstone of government action (Machlup, 1978, p. 472). Popper does not make this distinction as clearly as Schumpeter did, and hence his defense of methodological individualism, or rather his criticism of methodological holism, is sometimes illegitimately hitched to the defense of political individualism (Popper, 1957, pp. 76–93); a similar tendency is detectable in Friedrich Hayek's (1973) earlier critique of "scientism," the slavish imitation of the methods of the physical sciences (Machlup, 1978, pp. 514–16), which appears to have inspired Popper to formulate the principle of methodological individualism.[40] Similarly, many of Popper's followers, if not Popper himself, derive methodological individualism from what has been called "ontological individualism," namely, the proposition that individuals create all social institutions and hence that collective phenomena are simply hypothetical abstractions derived from the decisions of real individuals. But although ontological individualism is trivially true, it has no necessary connection with the manner in which we should or should not investigate collective phenomena, that is, with *methodological* individualism.

One obvious interpretation of what is meant by methodological individualism is to equate it with the proposition that all the concepts of sociology are reducible and should be reduced to those of psychology. But Popper denounces this interpretation as psychologism. Popper's attack on psychologism, however, has been found unconvincing, and much of the debate has in fact turned on the distinction between irreducible "societal facts" or institutions and possibly reducible "societal laws," in the light of which Popper may be interpreted as insisting on the reduction of social laws to individuals and the relations between them. Unfortunately, Popper also argues that "the main task of the theoretical social sciences . . . is to trace the unintended social repercussions of intentional human action" (1972b, p. 342; also pp.

---

[39] Virtually the entire debate is reproduced in both Krimerman (1969, Pt. 7) and O'Neill (1973); but see also Nagel (1961, pp. 535–44); Lukes (1973); Ryan (1970, chap. 8); and Lesnoff (1974, chap. 4). In relation to economics, see Chapter 15 below.

[40] Hayek has backtracked on much of his earlier opposition to methodological monism and now takes up a stance that is Popper-with-a-difference: see Barry (1979, chap. 2), Hutchison (1992), Caldwell (1992).

124–5, 1962, II, p. 95; 1972a, p. 160n). But how is this possible if there is
no such thing as legitimate social laws, that is, propositions about wholes that
are more than the sum of propositions about their constituent parts? No doubt,
the theoretical individualism of economics and politics in the days of Hobbes
and Locke did culminate in the unintended-consequences doctrine of the eigh-
teenth-century Scottish philosophers – language, law, and even the market
mechanism are the unintended social consequences of individual actions undertaken for purely selfish reasons – but that is, surely?, no reason why the
study of the unintended by products of individual actions should now be made
a necessary or even a principal feature of the social sciences. But if it were,
what then becomes of the imperative of methodological individualism?

At this point, it is helpful to note what methodological individualism strictly
interpreted (or *Verstehen* doctrine for that matter) would imply for economics.
In effect, it would rule out all macroeconomic propositions that cannot be
reduced to microeconomic ones, and since few have yet been so reduced, this
amounts in turn to saying goodbye to almost the whole of received macroeconomics. There must be something wrong with a methodological principle that
has such devastating implications. The reference to economics is by no means
otiose because Popper himself has explained that methodological individualism must be interpreted as the application to social questions of the "rationality principle," or "zero method" applied to the "logic of the situation."
This method of situational analysis, he explains in his intellectual biography,

. . . was an attempt *to generalize the method of economic theory (marginal utility
theory) so as to become applicable to the other theoretical social sciences* . . . this
method consists of constructing a *model of the social situation,* including especially
the institutional situation, in which an agent is acting, in such a manner as to explain
the rationality (the zero-character) of his action. Such models, then, are the testable
hypotheses of the social sciences [Popper, 1976, pp. 117–18; also 1957, pp. 140–1;
1972a, pp. 178–9, 188].

Let us, by all means, commend methodological individualism as a heuristic
postulate: in principle, it is highly desirable to define all holistic concepts,
macroscopic factors, aggregate variables, or whatever they are called, in terms
of individual behavior if and when this is possible. But when it is not possible,
let us not lapse into silence on the grounds that we may not defy the principle
of methodological individualism. As one participant in the debate writes:

The most that we can ask of the social scientist . . . is that he keep the principle of
methodological individualism firmly in mind as a devoutly to be wished-for consum-
mation, an ideal to be approximated as closely as possible. This should at least help
assure that nevermore will he dally with suspect group-minds and impersonal 'forces',
economic or otherwise; nevermore will non-observable properties be attributed to equally

non-observable group entities. At the same time, he will not by methodological fiat be struck dumb about matters on which there is, no matter how imprecisely, a great deal to be said [Brodbeck, 1958, p. 293].

Now that we have reasserted methodological monism, even against Popper's apparent dilution of the doctrine, we do not mean to deny the relative immaturity of every social science, including economics compared to at least some of the physical sciences. Even if the difference between "hard" physical and "soft" social science is only one of degree, that degree is a large one. No social science can boast of the universal laws of modern chemistry, the numerical constants of particle physics, and the predictive accuracy of Newtonian mechanics. The comparison between social and natural science looks a little better in terms of biology, geology, physiology, and meteorology, but even here there is still a long gap between our knowledge of human behavior and our knowledge of natural phenomena.[41] There may be nothing to choose *in principle* between the methods of the physical and the social sciences, but *in practice* the divide between them is almost as great as that between the methods of social sciences and, say, the principles of literary criticism.

[41] See Machlup (1978, pp. 345–67) for a judicious attempt to deal with the grand question: are the social sciences really inferior? His answer is yes, but not as much as most people seem to think. Anyone who thinks that economics is unique in the weakness and indecisiveness of the evidence for its claims should look at "the Nemesis affair," the history of the hypothesis that the impact of a large meteorite 65 million years ago was the cause of the extinction of dinosaurs, that this was only one of many such extinctions over the last 250 million years, and that these extinctions are periodic and due to Nemesis, a companion star to our own sun that approaches the solar system every 30 million years (Raup, 1986).

PART II

The history of economic methodology

3

The verificationists, a largely nineteenth-century story

The prehistory of economic methodology

A subtle but significant difference separates the methodological writings of nineteenth-century economists from those of twentieth-century ones, or rather from those of modern economists in the last forty years or so. The great British nineteenth-century economic methodologists focused attention on the premises of economic theory and continually warned their readers that the verification of economic predictions was at best a hazardous enterprise. The premises were said to be derived from introspection or the casual observation of one's neighbors and in that sense constituted *a priori* truths, known, so to speak, in advance of experience; a purely deductive process led from premises to implications, but implications were true *a posteriori* only in the absence of disturbing causes. Hence, the purpose of verifying implications was to determine the applicability of economic reasoning and not really to assess its validity. The ingenuity of these nineteenth-century writers knew no bounds when it came to giving reasons for ignoring apparent refutations of an economic prediction, but no grounds, empirical or otherwise, were ever stated in terms of which one might reject a particular economic theory. In short, the great British nineteenth-century methodologists of economics were *verificationists,* not falsificationists, and they preached a *defensive methodology* designed to make the young science secure against any and all attacks.

If we count the publication of *The Wealth of Nations* in 1776 as marking the "birth" of economics as a separate discipline, the burgeoning science of political economy was just over fifty years old when Nassau William Senior published his *Introductory Lecture on Political Economy* (1827), the first self-conscious discussion of the problems of economic methodology, which he elaborated and extended a decade later in his *Outline of the Science of Political Economy* (1836). The year 1836 also saw the publication of John Stuart Mill's celebrated essay, *On the Definition of Political Economy; and on the*

51

Method of Investigation Proper to It (1836), which established his reputation as a leading commentator on economic questions, a reputation that he further enhanced by a major work on the philosophy of science, *A System of Logic* (1844), followed by the magisterial *Principles of Political Economy* (1848). The next important landmark is John Elliot Cairnes' *Character and Logical Method of Political Economy* (1875) and the entire era of classical methodology was summed up in unmistakably authoritative terms by John Neville Keynes in *The Scope and Method of Political Economy* (1890), a book that appeared in the same year as Alfred Marshall's *Principles of Economics,* with which it shares a common conciliatory methodological outlook.

This is not to say that Adam Smith, David Ricardo, and Thomas Malthus lacked methodological principles, but merely that they saw no need to state them explicitly, regarding them perhaps as too obvious to require defense. Adam Smith is a particularly striking case because he in fact employed radically different modes of reasoning in different parts of his works. Books I and II of *The Wealth of Nations* make liberal use of the method of comparative statics later associated with the work of Ricardo, whereas Books III, IV, and V of *The Wealth of Nations,* and most of *The Theory of Moral Sentiments,* exemplify the very different methods of the so-called Scottish historical school.

It is not easy to characterize these Scottish historical methods because neither Adam Smith, nor any other member of the School, ever wrote them down in so many words. In any case, they appear to consist, on the one hand, of a firm belief in the stages theory of history, resting on the interaction between definite "modes" or types of economic production and certain eternal principles of human nature, and on the other hand, of a profound commitment to simplicity and elegance as overriding criteria of adequate explanation in both the physical and the social sciences (see Skinner, 1965; Macfie, 1967, chap. 2; and Smith, 1776, pp. 15–43). Adam Smith did contribute an amazingly erudite essay in the philosophy of science, *The Principles which Lead and Direct Philosophical Enquiries; Illustrated by the History of Astronomy,* written around 1750, but only published posthumously in 1799.[1] Writing only sixty years after the appearance of Newton's *Principia,* Smith described the Newtonian method as one in which we lay down "certain principles, primary or proved, in the beginning, from whence we account for the several phenomena, connecting all together by the same chain." Given the pivotal role of sympathy for other human beings in *The Theory of Moral Sentiments* and that of self-interested behavior in *The Wealth of Nations,* both of these books must be regarded as deliberate attempts by Smith to apply this Newtonian method first to ethics and then to economics (Skinner, 1974, pp. 180–1), which is not

---

[1] Smith's essay on astronomy is now available as Vol. III in The Glasgow Edition of *The Works and Correspondence of Adam Smith* (1980).

to deny that he had a naive view of what constituted Newton's method. It is a striking fact that Smith credited the origin of science in the essay on astronomy, not to men's idle curiosity or the impulse to master nature, but to the simple desire to assuage "wonder, surprise, and admiration." Even his standard of judgment of scientific ideas was more often aesthetic than strictly cognitive, and he stressed the advantage of being able to explain different phenomena by a single familiar principle such as gravity almost as much, if not more, than the capacity to make accurate predictions. There is much *conventionalism* in Smith's account of both the Copernican and Newtonian revolutions, probably inspired by Hume's equally incipient conventionalism; that is to say, Smith refused to describe Newtonian mechanics as 'the truth', quite contrary to the general view at the time (Thompson, 1965, pp. 223–3; Lindgren, 1969, p. 901; Hollander, 1977, pp. 134–7, 151–2; and Skinner, 1974). However, there is little point in worrying about what Smith really meant to imply by his view of scientific theories as "imaginary machines" because his essay went entirely unnoticed by the English classical economists that came after him and indeed seems to have exerted no influence whatsoever on nineteenth-century philosophy of science.

In Ricardo, the historical, the institutional, and the factual, which had figured so prominently in the writings of Adam Smith, faded into the background, and even his social philosophy was discernible only in a number of innuendos (Hutchison, 1978, pp. 7–10, chap. 2). Although his methodological views can only be read between the lines, he was clearly a convinced advocate of what we nowadays call "the hypothetico-deductive model of explanation," vigorously denying that facts can ever speak for themselves. It is always difficult to know whether Ricardo regarded the predictions of his system – the rising cost of growing food, the pressure of population on the food supply, the rising share of income going to landlords, and the gradual disappearance of investment opportunities – as statements of purely conditional tendencies or as unconditional historical forecasts, because the hallmark of his style of writing is to minimize the distinction between abstract conclusions and concrete applications. Indeed, Schumpeter (1954, pp. 472–3) has labeled this propensity of Ricardo to apply highly abstract economic models directly to the complexity of the real world the "Ricardian Vice." On one hand, Ricardo told Malthus that his object was to elucidate principles and, therefore, he "imagined strong cases . . . that might show the operation of these principles"; on the other hand, he was forever telling Parliament that some of the conclusions of economics were "as certain as the principles of gravitation."[2] At any rate, there is no doubt that the message that his successors took from

---

[2] For a collection of Ricardo's throwaway remarks on methodology, see de Marchi (1970, pp. 258–9) and Sowell (1974, pp. 118–20).

his writings was that economics is a science, not because of its methods of investigation, but because of the certainty of its results.

Malthus had severe misgivings about Ricardo's methodology, particularly about Ricardo's habit of directing exclusive attention to the long-run equilibrium implications of economic forces, and he suspected, although he was never able clearly to express it, that there was in Smith an inductive method that was diametrically opposed to Ricardo's deductive approach. In practice, however, Malthus's style of reasoning was identical to that of Ricardo's and their wide disagreement on questions of value and the possibility of "general gluts" involved no substantive differences in methodology.

Mill's essay

Ricardo died in 1823, and the next decade saw a vigorous debate over the validity of the Ricardian system, accompanied by an attempt on the part of his chief disciples, James Mill and John Ramsay McCulloch, to identify Ricardianism with economics itself. Periods of intellectual controversy are likely to engender methodological clarifications, and so it was in this critical phase of English classical political economy. Both Senior and John Stuart Mill now saw the need to formulate the principles that governed the methods of investigation of political economists.

To Senior, we owe the first statement of the now familiar distinction between a pure and strictly positive *science* and an impure and inherently normative *art* of economics (a question that we will defer until Chapter 5), as well as the first explicit formulation of the idea that scientific economics rests essentially on "a very few general propositions, which are the result of observation, or consciousness, and which almost every man, as soon as he hears them, admits, as familiar to his thoughts," from which conclusions are then drawn that hold true only in the absence of "particular disturbing causes" (quoted by Bowley, 1949, p. 43). Senior went so far as to reduce these "very few general propositions" to four, namely, (1) that every person desires to maximize wealth with as little sacrifice as possible; (2) that population tends to increase faster than the means of subsistence; (3) that labor working with machines is capable of producing a positive net product; and (4) that agriculture is subject to diminishing returns (see Bowley, 1949, pp. 46–8). Here, as elsewhere in his writings, Senior was among the most original of the classical economists. Nevertheless, Mill's discussion of these same questions is at once more careful and penetrating than Senior's, and moreover, he paid much more attention than Senior did to the problem of verifying the conclusions of pure theory.

Mill's 1836 essay *On the Definition of Political Economy* begins with Senior's distinction between the science and the art of political economy, which is the distinction between a collection of material truths and a body of normative rules, and goes on to categorize the subject of economics, once again in the manner of Senior, as a "mental science," fundamentally concerned with human motives and modes of conduct in economic life (Mill, 1967, pp. 312, 317–18). This leads straightaway to a famous passage in which the much maligned concept of "economic man" is born. Long as it is, this passage deserves to be quoted almost in full, to be read and reread:

What is now commonly understood by the term "Political Economy" . . . makes entire abstraction of every other human passion or motive; except those which may be regarded as perpetually antagonizing principles to the desire of wealth, namely, aversion to labour, and desire of the present enjoyment of costly indulgences. These it takes, to a certain extent, into its calculations, because these do not merely, like other desires, occasionally conflict with the pursuit of wealth, but accompany it always as a drag, or impediment, and are therefore inseparably mixed up in the consideration of it. Political Economy considers mankind as occupied solely in acquiring and consuming wealth; and aims at showing what is the course of action into which mankind, living in a state of society, would be impelled, if that motive, except in the degree in which it is checked by the two perpetual counter-motives above adverted to, were absolute ruler of all their actions. . . . The science . . . proceeds . . . under the supposition that man is a being who is determined, by the necessity of his nature, to prefer a greater portion of wealth to a smaller in all cases, without any other exception than that constituted by the two counter-motives already specified. Not that any political economist was ever so absurd as to suppose that mankind are really thus constituted, but because this is the mode in which science must necessarily proceed. When an effect depends upon a concurrence of causes, those causes must be studied one at a time, and their laws separately investigated, if we wish, through the causes, to obtain the power of either predicting or controlling the effect ... . There is, perhaps, no action of a man's life in which he is neither under the immediate nor under the remote influence of any impulse but the mere desire of wealth. With respect to those parts of human conduct of which wealth is not even the principal object, to these Political Economy does not pretend that its conclusions are applicable. But there are also certain departments of human affairs, in which the acquisition of wealth is the main and acknowledged end. It is only of these that Political Economy takes notice. The manner in which it necessarily proceeds is that of treating the main and acknowledged end as if it were the sole end; which, of all hypotheses equally simple, is the nearest to the truth. The political economist inquires, what are the actions which would be produced by this desire, if, within the departments in question, it were unimpeded by any other. In this way a nearer approximation is obtained than would otherwise be practicable, to the real order of human affairs in those departments. This approximation is then to be corrected by making proper allowance for the effects of any impulses of a different description, which can be shown to interfere with the result in any particular case. Only in a few of the most striking cases (such as the important one of the principle of population) are these corrections interpolated into the expositions of Political Economy itself; the strictness of purely scientific arrangement being thereby somewhat departed from, for the sake of practical utility. So far as it is known, or may be presumed, that the conduct of mankind in the pursuit of wealth is under the collateral influence of any other of the properties of our nature than the desire of obtaining the greatest quantity of wealth with the least labour and self-denial, the conclusions of Political Economy will so far fail of being applicable to the explanation or prediction of real events, until they are modified by a correct allowance for the degree of influence exercised by the other cause [pp. 321–3].

Mill's definition of economic man has features that need underlining. Mill does not say that we should take the whole man as he is, staking our claim on correctly predicting how he will actually behave in economic affairs. This is a theory of ''real man'' that Senior held to throughout his life despite Mill's essay (see Bowley, 1949, pp. 47–8, 61–2) and that is also the standpoint that was later adopted by Alfred Marshall and, one dares say, all modern economists (see Whitaker, 1975, pp. 1043, 1045n; Machlup, 1978, chap. 11).[3] What Mill says is that we shall abstract certain economic motives, namely, those of maximizing wealth subject to the constraints of a subsistence income and the desire for leisure, while allowing for the presence of noneconomic motives (such as habit and custom) even in those spheres of life that fall within the ordinary purview of economics. In short, he operates with a theory of ''fictional man.'' Moreover, he emphasizes the fact that the economic sphere is only a part of the whole arena of human conduct. To that extent, political economy abstracts twice: once for conduct that is actually motivated by money income and a second time for conduct that involves ''impulses of a different description.''

Notice too that the Malthusian theory of population is admitted to be one of those ''impulses of a different description.'' It is frequently forgotten that the pressure of population on subsistence in Malthus rests essentially on what he called man's ''irrational passion'' to reproduce himself, which hardly tallies with the classical notion of man as a calculating economic agent. As is well known, Malthus admitted no checks to the pressures of population other than the positive ones of ''misery and vice'' and the preventive one of ''moral restraint,'' meaning the postponement of marriage accompanied by strict continence before marriage: Malthus never could bring himself to contemplate any voluntary limitation of family size after marriage. In later editions of his *Essay on Population,* Malthus conceded that moral restraint had indeed become an automatic check in the Britain of his day, being itself induced by

---

[3] It is just as well to remember that nothing like Mill's construct of economic man is found in the works of Adam Smith. In Smith, men certainly act on what they perceive to be their self-interest, but that self-interest is never conceived as being directed solely at pecuniary ends and as often as not is a matter of honor, ambition, social esteem, and love of domination rather than mere money (see Hollander, 1977, pp. 139–43; Winch, 1978, pp. 167–8).

population growth; in other words, he counterposed the "natural passion to procreation" to the equally natural Smithian tendency of each individual "to exert himself in bettering his condition" (see Blaug, 1978, pp. 74–5). Thus, the great Malthusian difficulty might be said to turn on the empirical question of whether married people in fact made rational calculations in respect of the number of children they brought into the world. It is clear, therefore, that the concept of economic man is intimately associated with the question of the validity of the Malthusian doctrine, that linchpin of the Ricardian version of classical economics.

It is also noteworthy that neither Mill nor Senior related the discussion of economic man to the role of nonpecuniary motives in workers' choices of occupations, which Adam Smith had shown in that remarkable chapter 10 of Book I of *The Wealth of Nations* to be a decisive element in the determination of wages (see Blaug, 1978, pp. 48–50). When we realize that these nonpecuniary motives involve much more than an "aversion to labour, and desire of the present enjoyment of costly indulgences," consisting in fact of the desire to maximize all kinds of psychic income even at the expense of money income, and to minimize the variance of uncertain income and not just to maximize its mean value, it is clear that the problem of specifying the compelling motives of economic man is a little more difficult than Mill made out. In modern language, it is not easy to decide even now what arguments should or should not enter into the utility functions that economic agents are said to maximize.

The pages on economic man in Mill's essay are followed immediately by the characterization of political economy as "essentially an *abstract* science" that employs "the method *a priori*" (1976, p. 325). The method *a priori* is contrasted with the method *a posteriori,* and Mill admits that the former term is somewhat unfortunate because it is sometimes used to designate a mode of philosophizing that is not founded on experience at all: "By the method *a posteriori* we mean that which requires, as the basis of its conclusions, not experience merely, but specific experience. By the method *a priori* we mean (what has commonly been meant) reasoning from an assumed hypothesis" (pp. 324–5). The hypothesis of economic man therefore is grounded on a kind of experience, namely, introspection and the observation of fellow men, but it is not derived from specific observations or concrete events. Since the hypothesis is an assumption, it might be totally "without foundation in fact," and in this sense it can be said that "The conclusions of Political Economy, consequently, like those of geometry, are only true, as the common phrase is, *in the abstract,* that is, they are only true under certain suppositions" (pp. 325–6).

Thus, by the *science* of political economy, Mill means a body of deductive analysis, resting on assumed psychological premises, and abstracting, even in respect of these premises, from all noneconomic aspects of human behavior:

When the principles of Political Economy are to be applied to a particular case, then it is necessary to take into account all the individual circumstances of that case; not only examining to which of . . . the circumstances of the case in question correspond, but likewise what other circumstances may exist in that case, which not being common to it with any large and strongly-marked class of cases, have not fallen under the cognizance of the science. These circumstances have been called *disturbing causes*.

   This constitutes the only uncertainty of Political Economy; and not of it alone, but of the moral sciences in general. When the disturbing causes are known, the allowance necessary to be made for them detracts in no way from scientific precision, nor constitutes any deviation from the *a priori* method. The disturbing causes are not handed over to be dealt with by mere conjecture. Like *friction* in mechanics, to which they have been often compared, they may at first have been considered merely as a nonassignable deduction to be made by guess from the result given by the general principles of science; but in time many of them are brought within the pale of the abstract science itself, and their effect is found to admit of as accurate an estimation as those more striking effects which they modify. The disturbing causes have their laws, as the causes which are thereby disturbed have theirs; and from the laws of the disturbing causes, the nature and amount of the disturbance may be predicted *a priori,* like the operation of the more general laws which they are said to modify or disturb, but with which they might more properly be said to be concurrent. The effect of the special causes is then to be added to, or subtracted from, the effect of the general ones [p. 330].

   It is because of the influence of disturbing causes that "the mere political economist, he who has studied no science but Political Economy, if he attempt to apply his science to practice, will fail" (p. 331).

   Because of the impossibility of conducting controlled experiments in human affairs, the mixed inductive-deductive method *a priori* is the only "legitimate mode of philosophical investigation in the moral sciences" (p. 327). But the specifically inductive method *a posteriori* comes into its own, "not as a means of discovering truth, but of verifying it":

We cannot, therefore, too carefully endeavour to verify our theory, by comparing, in the particular cases to which we have access, the results which it would have led us to predict, with the most trustworthy accounts we can obtain of those which have been actually realized. The discrepancy between our anticipations and the actual fact is often the only circumstance which would have drawn our attention to some important disturbing cause which we had overlooked. Nay, it often discloses to us errors in thought, still more serious than the omission of what can with any propriety be termed a disturbing cause. It often reveals to us that the basis itself of our whole argument is insufficient; that the data, from which we had reasoned, comprise only a part, and not always the most important part, of the circumstances by which the result is really determined [p. 332].

Although this is in many ways an impeccable statement of verificationism, it is noteworthy that Mill cannot bring himself to equate a failure to verify a prediction with a refutation of the underlying theory: a "discrepancy between our anticipation and the actual fact" shows, not that the original statement is wrong and therefore to be discarded, but only that it is "insufficient."

The passages on the need to verify our theories lead up to a superb statement of *tendency laws.*

Doubtless, a man often asserts of an entire class what is only true of a part of it; but his error generally consists not in making too wide an assertion, but in making the wrong *kind* of assertion; he predicated an actual result, when he should only have predicated a *tendency* to that result – a power acting with a certain intensity in that direction. With regard to *exceptions;* in any tolerably advanced science there is properly no such thing as an exception. What is thought to be an exception to a principle is always some other and distinct principle cutting into the former: some other force which impinges against the first force, and deflects it from its direction. There are not a *law* and an *exception* to that law – the law acting in ninety-nine cases, and the exception in one. There are two laws, each possibly acting in the whole hundred cases, and bringing about a common effect by their conjunct operation. If the force which, being the less conspicuous of the two, is called the disturbing force, prevails sufficiently over the other force in some one case, to constitute that case what is commonly called an exception, the same disturbing force probably acts as a modifying cause in many other cases which no one will call exceptions [p. 333].

Tendency laws

We have encountered tendency laws before, in Ricardo and in Malthus, and we would do well to digress for a moment to consider their justification in scientific work. The classical economists' reference to disturbing causes that were said to be capable of contradicting the conclusions of economic theories is echoed in the modern economists' appeal to *ceteris paribus* clauses that are invariably attached to general economic propositions or statements of economic "laws."[4] There is a widespread impression among laymen and students of science alike that *ceteris paribus* clauses abound in the social sciences but rarely occur in physics, chemistry, and biology. Nothing could be further from the truth, however. A scientific theory that could entirely dispense with *ceteris paribus* clauses would in effect achieve perfect closure: no variable that makes an important difference to the phenomena in

---

[4] For a history of the economists' use of the phrase *ceteris paribus,* see Rivett (1970, pp. 144–8).

question is omitted from the theory and the variables of the theory in effect interact only with each other and not with outside variables. Perhaps only celestial mechanics and nonatomic thermodynamics ever came near to achieving such perfect closure and completeness (Brodbeck, 1973, pp. 296–8). But even in physics, such highly closed and complete theories are exceptional, and outside of physics, there are few examples in natural science in which the relevant *cetera,* far from having to be held constant, are in fact terms within the theory.[5] Usually, *ceteris paribus* clauses appear in the natural sciences just as much as in the social sciences whenever a causal relationship is being tested: typically, they take the form of statements to the effect that other relevant initial conditions and relevant causal relations besides those being tested are assumed to be absent. In short, the natural sciences speak of auxiliary hypotheses that are present in every test of a scientific law – recall the Duhem–Quine thesis – whereas the social sciences speak of laws or hypotheses holding true if the *ceteris paribus* condition is satisfied. But the purpose in both cases is the same, namely, to exclude all variables other than those that are specified by the theory.

It might be said, therefore, that just about all theoretical propositions in both natural and social science are in fact tendency laws. But it is true that there is a world of difference between most tendency statements in physics and chemistry and virtually all such propositions in economics and sociology. For example, Galileo's quantitative law of falling bodies certainly carries with it an implied *ceteris paribus* clause, because all cases of free fall involve the resistance of air in which the body is falling. Galileo in fact employed the idealization of a "perfect vacuum" to get rid of the effect of what he called "accidents," but he gave estimates of the magnitude of the amount of distortion that results from factors such as friction, which the abstract law ignored. As we have just seen, Mill was perfectly aware of this characteristic of *ceteris paribus* clauses in classical mechanics: "Like *friction* in mechanics. . . . The disturbing causes have their laws, as the causes which are thereby disturbed have theirs" (Mill, 1976, p. 330). In the social sciences, however, and in economics in particular, it is quite common to encounter tendency statements with unspecified *ceteris paribus* clauses – a sort of catchall for everything that is unknown – or if specified, specified only in qualitative rather than quantitative terms. Thus, the Marxian "law" of the tendency of the rate of profit to decline is said to be subject to certain "counteracting causes" and, although these are spelled out, they are held to be set into motion by the very fall in the rate of profit which they counteract (Blaug, 1978, pp. 294–6). What we have, therefore, is one negative rate of change, enshrined in the basic law,

---

[5] "One can easily argue," observes Lakatos (1978, I, p. 18), "that ceteris paribus clauses are not exceptions, but the rule in science" (see also Nagel, 1961, pp. 560–1).

and several positive counteracting rates of change; the joint outcome of all these forces clearly could be either negative or positive.[6] In short, unless we somehow manage to restrict the meaning of a *ceteris paribus* clause, placing definite limits on the operation of "disturbing" or "counteracting causes," the entire argument fails to produce a refutable prediction even in terms of the direction of the total change, much less in terms of the magnitude of that change.

Mill had the benefit of a useful distinction made by Bishop Whately in 1831 between a tendency statement in the sense of (1) "the existence of a cause which, if *operating unimpeded,* would produce a result," and in the sense of (2) "the existence of such a state of things, that that result *may be expected to take place,*" despite the fact that it is actually impeded by disturbing causes (quoted by Sowell, 1974, pp. 132–3). As Mill himself put it: we often state a result when all we mean is "a *tendency* to that result – a power acting with a certain intensity in that direction. With regard to *exceptions;* in any tolerably advanced science there is properly no such thing as an exception" (Mill, 1976, p. 333). Whately's distinction may be said to state the minimum conditions that a justifiable tendency law must fulfill: it must be possible to say of any legitimate tendency statement whether it conforms to the first or the second of the two Whately definitions; otherwise, we will have failed to produce a consequence that can even in principle be falsified. It is evident that neither Marx's "law" of the declining rate of profit nor Malthus's "law" of population meet this requirement, and in both cases they made things even worse by suggesting that the "disturbing" or "counteracting" causes to the basic tendency are themselves induced by the tendency, so that the first of Whately's sense of the term, tendency statement, could never in fact be observed under any conceivable circumstances.

A *tendency statement* in economics may be regarded, therefore, as a promissory note that is only redeemed when the *ceteris paribus* clause has been spelled out and taken into account, preferably in quantitative terms.[7] After the clarity of Mill's exposition of these issues in his methodological essay,

---

[6] I have reexamined this Marxian debate in Blaug (1990, chap. 2) in the light of Marx's own ideas about economic methodology.

[7] I am paraphrasing Kaplan (1964, pp. 97–8); as he put it, "*A tendency law* is one put forward for a law in the strictest sense, to be achieved when the countervailing forces have been identified and taken into account. It follows that the scientific value of a tendency law depends on how effectively it serves to stimulate and guide the search for those other determinants or forces. In itself, it is only a promissory note, circulating freely in the world of science so long as public confidence can be maintained that it will eventually be redeemed for something like its face value. The clause 'other things being equal' is not the redemption but another phrasing of the promise." [For further discussion and illustrations of tendency laws in economics, see Fraser (1937, chap. 3); Hutchison (1938, pp. 40–6); and Kaufmann (1944, pp. 215–17).]

we can hardly refrain from asking whether he demonstrated the same clarity in his actual analysis of economic problems. Schumpeter (1954, p. 537n) once said: "The literal meaning of a methodological profession of faith is of little interest except for the philosopher . . . any objectionable piece of methodology is immaterial whenever it can be dropped without forcing us to drop any result of the analysis that is associated with it," and as much is true of any commendable piece of methodology. But before turning to Mill's economics to see if it exemplifies his methodological outlook, we must take a quick look at Mill's *Logic,* a work that first brought him to the wider attention of the public. We do so because in assessing his economics, it is important to remember that he was not only a considerable philosopher of science but also a trained logician (not to mention a psychologist, a political scientist, and a social philosopher).

Mill's *Logic*

Mill's *System of Logic* is not an easy book for modern readers to comprehend. It embodies, as we have said earlier, a deliberate disparagement of deductive logic (called *ratiocination*) as an intellectual sausage machine and a eulogy to the logic of induction as the only path to new knowledge. Underlying much of the argument is an attempt to demolish all beliefs in what Kant called synthetic *a priori* propositions, that is, intuitionism writ large, first in the area of moral beliefs and later in the area of logic and mathematics – Mill's view that mathematics is really a sort of quasi-experimental science is distinctly old-fashioned. Finally, after devoting almost the whole of the book to defending inductive methods in science and mathematics, Mill turns in the closing section to the methodology of what he called the "moral sciences" (meaning social sciences) where, surprisingly enough, he does allow that inductive methods are generally unavailing because of the frequency of composite causes from many forces. These three features of the book taken together make it both difficult to place the work in context and to relate it to his previous analysis of the methodology of economics.[8]

What Mill had to say about formal logic is largely spoiled by the indiscriminate manner in which he plays fast and loose with the double sense of the term *induction,* treating it sometimes as a logically demonstrative form of causal proof and sometimes as a nondemonstrative method of confirming and corroborating causal generalizations – *adduction* in our language – the latter procedure being in turn confused with the problem of discovering new causal laws.[9] But although Mill is forever entangling the origin of ideas with ques-

---

[8] There are numerous commentaries on Mill's *Logic.* I have found Nagel (1950), Anschutz (1953), McRae's introduction to Mill (1973), Ryan (1974, chap. 3), and Mawatari (1982–83) most useful.

[9] As Medawar (1967, p. 133) remarks: "Unfortunately, we in England have been brought

tions of their logical warrant, with him the theory of logic becomes essentially an analysis of scientific method relating to the evaluation of evidence, and his book is much better understood as a work on models and methods than a study of symbolic logic in the twentieth-century sense of the term. The two things for which Mill is best remembered by philosophers of science is his treatment of the canons of induction, interpreted as a set of nondemonstrative rules of confirmation – the *four methods* of agreement, difference, residues, and concomitant variations – and his analysis of causation, which attempted to solve Hume's "problem of induction" by introducing the principle of the uniformity of nature as a major premise in every causal explanation. Mill's four methods are still mentioned sometimes as a crude sketch of the logic of experimental research design, but his treatment of causation is now only discussed in order to show how difficult it is to fault Hume's proof of the impossibility of inductive certitude.[10]

Having advanced his four methods as both aids to the discovery of causal laws and ways of proving that they hold universally, he turns in the last section of the *Logic* to the social sciences, where he candidly admits that the four methods do not apply. They do not apply because of the plurality of causes at work, the intermixture of separate effects, and the impossibility of conducting

up to believe that scientific discovery turns upon the use of a method analogous to, and of the same logical stature as deduction, namely, the method of *Induction* – a logically mechanized process of thought which, starting from simple declarations of fact arising out of the evidence of the senses, can lead us with certainty to the truth of general laws. This would be an intellectually disabling belief if anyone actually believed it, and it is one for which John Stuart Mill's methodology of science must take most of the blame. The chief weakness of Millian induction was its failure to distinguish between the acts of mind involved in discovery and in proof.''

[10] The method of agreement states that "If two or more instances of the phenomenon under investigation have only one circumstance in common, the circumstance in which alone all the instances agree, is the cause (or effect) of the given phenomenon''; the method of difference states that "If an instance in which the phenomenon under investigation occurs, and an instance in which it does not occur, have every circumstance in common save one, that one occurring only in the former; the circumstance in which alone the two instances differ, is the effect or the cause, or an indispensable part of the cause, of the phenomenon.'' The method of residues states that "Subduct from every phenomenon such part as is known by previous inductions to be the effect of certain antecedents, and the residues of the phenomenon is the effect of the remaining antecedents.'' Finally, the method of concomitant variations states "Whatever phenomenon varies in any manner when another phenomenon varies in some particular manner, is either a cause or an effect of that phenomenon, or is connected with it through some fact of causation'' (Mill, 1973, VII, pp. 390, 391, 398, 401). Despite the plethora of commentaries on Mill's four "methods,'' it is difficult to improve on the older treatment of Cohen and Nagel (1934, pp. 249–72); see also Losee (1972, pp. 148–58). Mill's canons of induction are an excellent introduction to modern treatments of causal explanation, as for example Mackie's INUS model (see Blaug, 1990, p. 114, and Gordon, 1991, pp. 43–4, 396–8, 648).

controlled experiments. Hence, for the social sciences he advocates instead (1) the "geometrical or abstract method," (2) the "physical or concrete deductive method," and (3) the "historical or inverse deductive method." The first is said to be of limited use, being applicable only where a single cause produces all the effects. The third, after Auguste Comte, is concerned with establishing genuine laws of historical change resting on certain universal principles of human nature. It is the second "physical or concrete deductive method" which is supposed to be exemplified by political economy. It is also, we are told, the method used in astronomy whereby the laws of separate causes acting additively are first determined with the aid of the four methods, after which the deductions made from those laws are verified by reference to empirical observations (Mill, 1973, pp. 895–6). At this point, Mill inserted the passages on economic man from his 1836 essay, quoted earlier, and moved on to discuss "political ethology," the unborn but heralded deductive science of the formation of national character that would someday, he fondly believed, become the foundation of all social science.

There is more in this last section of Mill's *Logic:* a stout defense of methodological monism; a firm adherence to the principle of methodological individualism; and an insistence that positive and not normative analysis is the key to science even in the social field. But the sudden support for deductive methods after hundreds of pages extolling inductive ones, not to mention the fact that most of the discussion in this last section is about the then infant science of sociology and touches only incidentally on the already mature science of economics, is well calculated to leave the reader utterly confused about Mill's final views on the philosophy of the social sciences.

Five years after finishing the *System of Logic,* Mill published his authoritative *Principles of Political Economy,* which contains neither an explicit discussion of methodology nor any harking back to the *Logic* to show that the *Principles* exemplifies sound methodology. No wonder then that those who attacked Mill's views on logic made no attempt to see if he practiced in economics what he preached for science in general. Both William Whewell and Stanley Jevons championed the hypothetico-deductive model of scientific explanation in direct opposition to Mill: Whewell wrote a lengthy reply to Mill's *Logic* that attempted to approach a philosophy of scientific discovery through the history of science, drawing inspiration from Kant rather than Hume (Losee, 1972, pp. 120–8); and Jevons in his own major contribution to the philosophy of science, *The Principles of Science: A Treatise on Logic and Scientific Method* (1873), continually criticized "Mill's innovations in logical science, and especially his doctrine of reasoning from particulars to particular," adding that induction was not a species of logical inference but simply "the marriage of hypothesis and experiment" (see Harré, 1967, pp. 289–90; Medawar, 1967, pp. 149ff; Losee, 1972, p. 158; and MacLennan, 1972).

But neither of them related their arguments against Mill's *Logic* to Mill's *Principles,* despite the fact that Whewell was a pioneer in the mathematization of Ricardian economics, while Jevons was of course one of the three founders of marginalism and as firmly opposed to the influence of Mill in economics as to the influence of Mill in logic.

One explanation of this curious phenomenon of treating the two Mills as if they were two different writers is that neither the critics nor Mill himself saw any relationship between the *Logic* and the *Principles;* for all practical purposes, they might just as well have been written by two different authors. As Jacob Viner (1958, p. 329) once said: "The *Principles* has no single methodological character. As is the case with the *Wealth of Nations* of Adam Smith, some portions are predominantly abstract and *a priori;* in others, there is a substantial measure of factual data and of inference from history."

Mill's economics in practice

Let us now spend a moment to examine what Mill actually did by way of verifying the implications of his abstract, hypothetical Ricardian premises. The doctrine that Ricardo bequeathed to his followers (in 1815, 1817, and 1819) gave rise to a number of testable propositions – a rising price of corn, a rising rental share of national income, a constant level of real wages, and a falling rate of profit on capital – and it depended on others, especially the growth of population at a rate at least as fast as the growth of foodstuffs. Moreover, given the absence of freely imported corn in contemporary Britain, these were all positive predictions, not hypothetical ones, because Ricardo boldly denied that countervailing forces could annul them except "for a time" (see Blaug, 1973, pp. 31–3; Blaug, 1986, pp. xiii–xiv, 91–114). The Corn Laws were not repealed until 1846, and statistical evidence available in the 1830s and 1840s falsified every one of these Ricardian predictions. For example, diminishing returns in British agriculture were being offset by technical improvements as evidenced by steadily declining wheat prices from the high levels of 1818; rents probably did not rise in the 25 years between the death of Ricardo in 1823 and the appearance of Mill's *Principles* in 1848, either per acre or as a relative share of income; real wages certainly increased over the period; and population increased more slowly in Britain from 1815–48 than from 1793–1815. All these facts, with the possible exception of the one about rents, were acknowledged in Mill's *Principles,* and yet that book retained the Ricardian system without qualifications. Mill remained a faithful advocate of Ricardian economics not so much by ignoring the gap between his theory and the facts, but by adopting various "immunizing stratagems," of which the chief one was to empty the appropriate *ceteris paribus* clauses of whatever specific content they may once have had.

Much of the difficulty goes back to Ricardo's own ambiguous attitude to the time period required for the basic long-run forces of his system to assert their dominance over certain short-run, counteracting influences. Agriculture was said to be subject to historically diminishing returns, because technical progress could only be expected to postpone the effects of the rising cost of growing food without, however, being able permanently to overcome the scarcity of fertile soil; Ricardo even went so far as to argue that landlords would have no private incentive to introduce technical improvements in food production. Similarly, Ricardo recognized that workers might in time come to consume more manufactured goods rather than agricultural products, in which case the rising costs of growing food would not necessarily raise real wages and depress profits. Lastly, workers might also begin to practice "moral restraint," allowing capital to accumulate faster than the rate at which population grew, which would once again stave off the onset of the "stationary state." But all these were merely realistic concessions: Ricardo had no theory to explain either technical progress, or changes in the composition of the average worker's household budget, or the disposition of families to control their size. Nevertheless, it is probably fair to say that Ricardo's tendency statements were meant to be conditional predictions that might conceivably be falsified by the course of events.

On the other hand, Ricardo clearly thought that his theories were of material help to legislators because the various temporary checks would not in fact counteract the basic forces at work over the foreseeable future. Under pressure, he committed himself to a "short run" of about twenty-five years to exemplify the long-run effects of the causes he postulated (de Marchi, 1970, pp. 255–6, 263), which is not to say, however, that he would have advocated waiting for twenty-five years to see if his theories were true. The whole tenor of his approach was opposed to verification, at least if by verification we mean checking whether a theory is confirmed by the evidence rather than simply waiting to see whether some modifying circumstance has been left out of account (see O'Brien, 1975, pp. 69–70).

It has been truly said that "J. S. Mill's methodological position was no different from Ricardo's: Mill only formally enunciated the 'rules' which Ricardo implicitly adopted" (de Marchi, 1970, p. 266). As we have seen, Mill was a verificationist, not a predictionist: the test of a theory in social science is not *ex ante* predictive accuracy but *ex post* explanatory power – Mill was no believer in the symmetry thesis. If a theory fails to predict accurately, Mill would have said, a search should be made for sufficient supplementary causes to close the gap between the facts and the causal antecedents laid down in the theory because the theory is true in any case *as far as it goes* by the nature of its true assumptions. And sure enough, we can see this attitude at work in the pages of his *Principles*. When the book was published, twenty-five years had elapsed since Ricardo's death and the Corn Laws had been finally repealed two years earlier; over the next twenty-three years, Mill put the *Principles* through as many as six editions, and with each successive edition it became more and more difficult to deny the refutation of virtually every one of Ricardo's historical predictions, conditioned as they were on the absence of free trade (Blaug, 1973, pp. 179–82). The Malthusian theory of population, in particular, was now glaringly contradicted by the evidence, a fact that most economists of the period accepted (Blaug, 1973, pp. 111–20). But the Malthusian difficulty loomed large in Mill's social philosophy, and he managed somehow to retain it in the *Principles* as a comparative static proposition – if population were smaller, wages would be higher – while agreeing that the tendency of population to outstrip the means of subsistence had not in fact manifested itself (de Marchi, 1970, pp. 267–71). Similarly, he gave the same twist to the Ricardian doctrine that protection would raise corn prices and the rental share going to landlords (Blaug, 1973, pp. 181–2, 208), which made it virtually impossible to treat the repeal of the Corn Laws as a social experiment in the testing of the Ricardian system.

Even those who are most sympathetic to Mill's economics agree that he was at best a lukewarm verificationist.[11] The real issue is whether Mill, having conceded the increasing irrelevance of Ricardian theory as time passed, ought to have admitted that Ricardian theory was now not merely irrelevant but invalid. In successive editions of the *Principles* between 1848 and 1871, Mill steadily stretched the length of the period during which technical progress was permitted to postpone the effects of the law of diminishing returns in agriculture and hence the underlying tendency of the growth of population to exceed the growth of subsistence. Nevertheless, if we stick to the first edition of the *Principles* it can of course be argued that ''the period from Ricardo's death to Mill's *Principles* was too short to constitute a conclusive test for Ricardo's predictions,'' particularly as it is agreed that ''the predictive test was in any case not one on which either Ricardo or Mill was prepared to reject his analysis'' (de Marchi, 1970, p. 273). As for the later editions of the *Principles,* is it not asking too much of any thinker, some would say, that he should abandon a body of ideas to whose defense he had devoted a lifetime? Mill did recant the wages fund doctrine and that, after all, is more than was done by his immediate disciples such as Henry Fawcett or John Elliot Cairnes.

---

[11] As de Marchi (1970, pp. 272–3) expresses it in his defense of Mill: ''It cannot be said that Mill always attempted to test his theory against the facts. . . . Mill was sometimes willing to live with a gap between his deductive theory and the facts. . . . He was prepared to use factual information in confirmation of theory; but historical facts . . . were never allowed to rise above theory to take on a valid status of their own.'' For a radically different view of both Ricardo and Mill, which denies that either of them made even conditional predictions of the future, see Hollander (1985, 1, chap. 1, 2, particularly pp. 33, 126, 130).

The point, however, is not to condemn or to exonerate Mill, but rather to correctly depict both his methodological views and the way in which he applied them in practice.

Mill, together with all the writers in the classical tradition, appealed fundamentally to assumptions in judging validity, whereas modern economists, as we shall see, appeal basically to predictions. This does not mean that classical writers were disinterested in predictions; obviously, being involved with policy questions as they were, they could not have avoided making predictions. Rather, they believed that as true assumptions result in true conclusions, oversimplified assumptions, such as those of economic man, diminishing returns at a given state of technology, infinite elastic labor supply at a given wage rate, etcetera, lead necessarily to oversimplified predictions, which in any case are never borne out exactly by the course of events even if serious efforts are made to take account of the relevant disturbing causes. The disturbing causes that are omitted from the explanation of events are, after all, not just the relatively minor disturbing causes of an economic nature but also substantive noneconomic causes. Thus, in economics, as Mill had explained, we test the *applications* of theories to determine whether enough of the disturbing economic causes have been taken into account to explain what actually happens in the real world after allowing, in addition, for noneconomic causes. We never test the *validity* of theories, because the conclusions are true as one aspect of human behavior by virtue of the assumptions, which in turn are true by virtue of being based on self-evident facts of human experience. We are miles away, therefore, from the popular modern position that assumptions do not need to be tested directly, although it might be useful if they could be, that in the final analysis only predictions matter, and that the validity of an economic theory is established when the predictions to which it gives rise are repeatedly corroborated by the evidence.[12]

Cairnes's *Logical Method*

If there are any doubts left as to what really is classical methodology, they should be dispelled by an examination of John Elliot Cairnes's *Character and Logical Method of Political Economy,* published first in 1875 and then revised in 1888 when the marginal revolution was in full swing (to which it, nevertheless, makes only perfunctory reference). By this time of course we are fifty to sixty years away from the death of Ricardo and yet, as we shall

---

[12] See Hirsch (1980), who quite correctly raps a number of modern commentators, including myself, over the knuckles for glossing over the difference between classical verificationism and modern falsificationism. I now realize that my earlier characterization of classical methodology (Blaug, 1978, pp. 697–9) was misleading in this respect. Hirsch also holds that classical methodology is a defensible one, which is of course quite a different argument.

see, Cairnes is as firmly convinced of the fundamental validity of the basic Ricardian tendencies as was Mill. If there is any difference at all between Mill and Cairnes – and it is only a hair's breadth – it is that Cairnes is more strident and dogmatic in denying that economic theories can ever be refuted by a simple comparison between their implications and the facts. The explanation for this may lie in the personalities of the two men, but in addition, Cairnes had lived through the rise of the English historical school and was clearly irritated by the endless scorn that members of the school had poured on the unrealistic postulates of classical economics (see Coats, 1954; Koot, 1975, 1987).

Cairnes begins with the well-known proposition that political economy is a hypothetical, deductive science: its conclusions "will correspond with facts only in the absence of disturbing causes, which is, in other words, to say that they represent not positive but hypothetic truths" (Cairnes, 1888, p. 64). He quotes Senior as arguing that political economy should not be regarded as a hypothetical science but as one based on real premises. There is nothing hypothetical about the premises of political economy, avers Cairnes, because they are based on "indubitable facts of human nature and of the world"; "the desire to obtain wealth at the least possible sacrifice" and "the physical qualities of the natural agents, more especially land, on which human industry is exerted" are both facts, "the existence and character of which are easily ascertainable" (pp. 68, 73). In this respect, economics is actually at an advantage compared to the physical sciences: *The economist starts with a knowledge of ultimate causes. He is already at the outset of his enterprise, in the position which the physicist only obtains after ages of laborious research* (p. 87). It is true that the economist cannot generally conduct experiments, but he can conduct thought experiments in his mind and he can even carry out "direct physical experiment upon the soil" (pp. 88–93). Thus, his assumptions are not "conjectures" but are drawn from observations of which we have "direct and easy proof" (p. 95; also p. 100). What is meant, therefore, by asserting that political economy is a hypothetical science, Cairnes proceeds to explain, is that it is one which makes conditional predictions about events that are always subject to a *ceteris paribus* clause: "the doctrines of Political Economy are to be understood as asserting, not what *will* take place, but what *would* or what tends to take place, and in this sense only are they true" (p. 69; also p. 110).

There follow some excellent pages on the multiple meanings of the term *induction,* including our own two senses of the term (already mentioned), accompanied by the claim that the use of the hypothetico-deductive method as distinct from the inductive-classifying method is an unmistakable sign of the maturity of a discipline (pp. 74–6, 83–7). Because of the multiplicity of factors impinging upon economic life, the hypothetical truths of economics must always be supplemented by "such sorts of verification as economical inquiry admits of": "verification can never in economic inquiry be otherwise than very imperfectly performed; but this notwithstanding, if carefully conducted it is often capable of furnishing sufficient corroboration to the process of deductive reasoning to justify a high degree of confidence in the conclusions thus obtained," a remark whose impact is unfortunately diluted by citing Ricardo as "The writer who has employed this resource most freely and with the most effect" (pp. 92–3).

Economists are always willing to consider "the influence of subordinate principles in modifying the force of the more powerful causes," Cairnes claims, provided that they can be established beyond doubt. As examples, he offers Smith's analysis of wage differentials for identical labor in geographically contiguous labor markets and the theory of international prices in Ricardo and Mill as arising in both cases from the effects of the "subordinate principle" that labor is relatively immobile (p. 101). For an even better illustration, he goes to Tooke's demonstration in his *History of Prices* that the price level in Britain in the preceding decades had not varied in the same direction as the quantity of money. The explanation for this phenomenon, Cairnes argues, is the rise of deposit checks, which went so far as to reverse the causal relationship between the circulation of bank notes and the general level of prices (pp. 101–4). Hammering his point home, he adds:

It is not to be supposed that the discrepancy alluded to (between prices and the note circulation) goes the length of invalidating the elementary law that, *ceteris paribus*, the value of money is inversely related to its quantity. This still rests upon the same basis of mental and physical facts as every other doctrine of political economy, and must always constitute the fundamental principle in the theory of money. It merely showed that in the practical case the condition *ceteris paribus* was not fulfilled. The fact in question is no more inconsistent with the economic law, than the non-correspondence of a complex mechanical phenomenon with what a knowledge of the elementary law of mechanics might lead a tyro to expect is inconsistent with these elementary laws. A guinea dropped through the air from a height falls to the ground more quickly than a feather; yet no one would on this account deny the doctrine that the accelerating power of gravity is the same for all bodies [Cairnes, p. 103n].

A better illustration of the abuse of *ceteris paribus* clauses, when none of the *cetera* are even specified, much less quantified, would be hard to find.

Economic laws, Cairnes concludes, "can be refuted only by showing either that the principles and conditions assumed do not exist, or that the tendency which the law affirms does not follow as a necessary consequence from this assumption" (p. 110; also p. 118). In short, either prove that the assumptions are unrealistic or do not apply to the case in question, or else demonstrate a logical inconsistency, but never take a refuted prediction as a reason for abandoning an economic theory, particularly because only qualitative predictions are possible in economics (pp. 119ff).[13] To show that this is not a harsh interpretation of Cairnes's meaning, consider his stand on the Malthusian theory of population: the Malthusian theory is a tendency law and hence "is not inconsistent with the doctrine that subsistence should in fact be increased much faster than population"; indeed, he was perfectly willing to agree that "further investigation showed that subsistence in most countries, and in all improving countries, had in fact increased faster than population" (pp. 158, 164). Nevertheless, the Malthusian theory is true. Besides, he added, without it all the standard Ricardian theorems cannot be understood at all (pp. 176–7), a remark which of course provides the key to his defensive methodological attitude towards economic predictions. In other words, he espoused the Ricardian scientific research program and, therefore, clung to the Malthusian theory as an indispensable element in that program.

One more example will round off the argument. Ricardian rent theory, Cairnes admitted, does not appear correctly to predict the order of cultivation in new colonies. These sorts of "residual phenomena" may be fatal in physical science but not in economics.

It is always regarded as the strongest confirmation of the truth of a physical doctrine, when it is found to explain facts which start up unexpectedly in the course of inquiry. But the ultimate principles of Political Economy, not being established by evidence of this circumstantial kind, but by direct appeals to our consciousness or to our senses, cannot be affected by any phenomena which may present themselves in the course of our subsequent inquiries . . . nor, assuming the reasoning process to be correct, can the theory which may be founded on them. We have here no alternative but to assume the existence of a disturbing cause. In the case before us, e.g. under what circumstances rent may be found to exist, this can never shake our faith in the facts that the soil of the country is not equally fertile, and that the productive capacity of the best soil is limited, nor weaken our confidence in the conclusions drawn from these facts [pp. 202–3n].

Over and over again, in Senior, in Mill, in Cairnes, and even in Jevons, we have found the notion that "verification" is not a testing of economic theories to see whether they are true or false, but only a method of establishing the boundaries of application of theories deemed to be obviously true: one verifies in order to discover whether "disturbing causes" can account for the discrepancies between stubborn facts and theoretically valid reasons; if they

[13] Cairnes belied his assertion about the impossibility of exact quantitative predictions in economics with his own empirical work on the effects of the Australian gold discoveries; see Bordo (1975), an essay which, however, attempts almost desperately to assimilate Cairnes's methodology to a modern falsificationist position (Hirsch, 1978; Bordo, 1978).

do, the theory has been wrongly applied, but the theory itself is still true. The question of whether there is any way of showing a logically consistent theory to be false is never even contemplated.[14]

John Neville Keynes sums up

The 1880s have gone down in the history of economic thought as the decade of the famous *Methodenstreit* between Carl Menger and Gustav Schmoller, when the influence of the German historical school reached British shores and added to the charges of Cliffe Leslie and John Ingram, the most vociferous of the native historists. The object of John Neville Keynes's *The Scope and Method of Political Economy* (1891) was to reconcile the Senior-Mill-Cairnes tradition with the new claims of the historical school by taking his cue from Henry Sidgwick's tolerant methodological discussion in his *Principles of Political Economy* (1883) and by complementing Marshall's equally conciliatory attitude to this and other long-standing doctrinal disputes in his *Principles of Economics* (1891) (see Dean, 1983). But although Keynes commended Adam Smith as the ideal economist because of the way in which he combined abstract-deductive and historical-inductive reasoning, his book reveals a subtly disguised attempt to vindicate the abstract-deductive view of economics.[15] He struggled to make that view more palatable by continually emphasizing the fact that even the a priori method of classical political economy begins and ends with empirical observations, while reminding his readers that such stalwarts of the abstract-deductive method as Mill and Cairnes had both made important contributions to historical-inductive analysis by their studies of peasant proprietorship in the one case and slave labor in the other. Keynes might have pointed to a British heterodox tradition standing out against the Senior–Mill–Cairnes view of economics,[16] but instead he preferred to pit

---

[14] This remark applies just as much to Marx as to mainstream classical economics (see Blaug, 1990, chap. 21).

[15] This may explain Marshall's somewhat enigmatic comment in a letter to Foxwell, "as regards method, I regard myself midway between Keynes + Sidgwick + Cairnes and Schmoller + Ashley" (quoted by Coase, 1975, pp. 27–8). But then Marshall was a case of an able theorist who in all his methodological writings emphasized the collection and assembly of facts and consistently played down the role of abstract theory (see Coase, 1975).

[16] O'Brien (1975, pp. 66–8; also 1970, pp. 96–8) bundles Hume, Smith, Say, and McCulloch together into an inductivist group and contrasts them with the orthodox deductivists, namely, Ricardo, Senior, Torrens, Mill, and Cairnes. But it is doubtful whether this schema will stand examination. It is noteworthy also that Keynes makes only a passing reference to the isolated methodological protestations of Richard Jones in the 1830s. Perhaps here his instinct was better than that of the members of the English historical school who claimed Richard Jones as a forerunner: Jones's actual work on rents, as distinct from his programmatic announcements, reflected not so

Smith and Mill against Ricardo as models of how to properly apply the hypothetico-deductive method.

The book opens with a perfect summary of the Senior–Mill–Cairnes tradition which Keynes (1891, pp. 12–20) saw as made up of five distinct theses: (1) that it is possible to distinguish between a positive science and a normative art of political economy; (2) that economic events can be isolated at least to some extent from other social phenomena; (3) that the direct induction of concrete facts, or the method *a posteriori,* is inappropriate as a starting point in economics; (4) that the right procedure is the *a priori* method of starting from "a few and indispensable facts of human nature . . . taken in connexion with the physiological properties of the soil, and man's physiological constitution"; and (5) that economic man is an abstraction and hence that "political economy is a science of tendencies only, not of matters of facts." Finally, he adds – it might almost be called a sixth thesis –

Mill, Cairnes, and Bagehot, however, all insist that the appeal to observation and experience must come in, *before the hypothetic laws of the science can be applied* to the interpretation and explanation of concrete industrial facts. For it then has to be ascertained how far . . . allowance needs to be made for the operation of the disturbing causes. Comparison with observed facts provides a *test* for conclusions deductively obtained and *enables the limits* of their application to be determined [p. 17; my italics].

His summary of the historical school as holding an "ethical, realistic, and inductive" view of economics is equally succinct: the historical school denies each of the five Senior–Mill–Cairnes theses and, in addition, has a favorable rather than a negative attitude to government intervention in economic affairs (pp. 20–5).[17]

Keynes was fond of saying, as we have noted, that economics "must begin with observation and end with observation" (p. 227) and he had a keen sense of the double meaning of the term *induction,* whereby "the inductive determination of premisses" at the beginning of an argument involves a different logical operation from "the inductive verification of conclusions" at its end (pp. 203–4n, 227). Although he sometimes observed that the premises of economics "involve little more than the reflective contemplation of certain of the most familiar of every-day facts" (p. 229), his book serves to remind us

much a general inductive approach to economic questions as an explicit denial of Ricardo's assumption of perfect competition among landlords (see Miller, 1971).

[17] On the historical school in general, see Schumpeter (1954, pp. 107–24) and Hutchison (1953, pp. 145–52). On the *Methodenstreit* in particular, see Hutchison (1973), who concludes: "In fact the *Methodenstreit* was not basically a quarrel about methods so much as a clash of interests regarding what was the most important and interesting subject to study, pricing and allocation analysis, or the broad development and change of national economies and industries" (pp. 34–5).

once again that, as Viner (1958, p. 328) once said, "introspection . . . was universally regarded in the past, whatever may be the fashion today, as an 'empirical' technique of investigation, and sharply distinguished from intuition or 'innate ideas.' " Not only is introspection for Keynes an empirically grounded source of economic premises (pp. 173, 223) but "the law of diminishing returns can also be tested by experiment" (p. 181). It is true of course that Keynes never asked the question: how is it that introspection, which by definition is not an interpersonally testable source of knowledge, can ever constitute a truly empirical starting point for economic reasoning? Nor did he ever cite a single example of an actual experimental test of diminishing returns from the application of a variable input to a fixed quantity of land although such tests had in fact been carried out much earlier by Johann von Thünen and several other German agronomists. Nevertheless, Keynes is proof against the charge that the classical economists merely snatched their assumptions out of the air for purposes of analytical convenience and cared little if they were realistic or not (see Rotwein, 1973, p. 365).

Keynes also provides additional evidence that the concept of economic man in classical and neoclassical economics is an abstraction of "real man," not of "fictional man." Mill, as we have seen, was insistent on the notion that economic man was a hypothetical simplification that isolated a selected set of the motives that actually impel economic conduct. Senior was much closer to the modern view that it is merely a postulate of rationality, an assumption of maximizing behavior subject to constraints. Cairnes reinstated Mill's position, while emphasizing that the hypothesis of economic man is far from arbitrary. And ever since, economic man has been variously described as an axiom, an *a priori* truth, a self-evident proposition, a useful fiction, an ideal type, a heuristic construct, an indisputable fact of experience, and a typical behavior pattern of man under capitalism (Machlup, 1978, chap. 11). Now, Keynes argues strongly for the realism of the concept of economic man in the sense that self-interested economic behavior is said to actually dominate motives of altruism and benevolence under contemporary conditions (pp. 119–25). The premises of economics, he argues, are not chosen on an "as-if" basis: "while theory assumes the operation of forces under artificially simplified conditions, it still claims that the forces whose effects it investigates are *verae causae* in the sense that they do operate, and indeed operate in a predominating way, in the actual economic world" (pp. 223–4; also pp. 228–31, 240n).

However, no evidence except casual empiricism is offered in defense of this proposition. Thus, phenomena that apparently contradict the hypothesis of economic man are simply allowed to stand as exceptions to the rule. Thus, "the love of a certain country or a certain locality, inertia, habit, the desire for personal esteem, the love of independence or power, a preference for country life . . . are among the forces exerting an influence upon the distribution of wealth, which the economist may find it necessary to recognise" (pp. 129–31), and the Mill–Cairnes doctrine of noncompeting grades of labor, or as we would say nowadays, segmentation of labor markets, is commended as "a modification of the received theory of value . . . suggested by observation and having for its object to bring economic theories into closer relation with actual facts" (p. 227n).

To be sure, it is only when we come to verify the predictions of economic theory that we can judge the degree of realism of a particular set of assumptions, at which point Keynes quotes Mill's *Logic:* "the ground of confidence in any concrete deductive science is not the a priori reasoning itself, but the accordance between its results and those of observation a posteriori" (p. 231). But even then he hedges his bets: "we may have independent grounds for believing that our premises correspond with the facts . . . in spite of the fact that there is difficulty in obtaining explicit verification" (p. 233). Besides, since "in all cases where the deductive method is used, it [the qualification *ceteris paribus*] is present more or less," we must not "suppose theories overthrown, because instances of their operation are not patent to observation" (pp. 218, 233). To illustrate the pervasive influence of "disturbing causes," he discusses the failure of the repeal of the Corn Laws to bring about the immediate fall in wheat prices predicted by Ricardo, and he rounds off the argument by condemning Ricardo for displaying "undue confidence in the absolute and uniform validity of the conclusions reached" and for neglecting "the element of time" and "the periods of transition, during which the ultimate effects of economic causes are working themselves out" (pp. 235–6, 238).

Throughout these crucial pages on the "Functions of Observation in the Employment of the Deductive Method" in Keynes's book, we get the suggestion, undoubtedly derived from Marshall's influence, that economic theory as such cannot be expected to result in direct predictions, being instead an "engine of analysis" to be used in conjunction with a detailed investigation of the relevant "disturbing causes" in every case (see Hutchison, 1953, pp. 71–4; Hirsch and Hirsch, 1975; Coase, 1975; and Hammond, 1991). Keynes assures us that "the hypothesis of free competition . . . is approximately valid in relation to a large number of economic phenomena" (pp. 240–1), but he provides no guidance on how we might determine what is a valid approximation in any particular instance. His chapter on "Political Economy and Statistics" is somewhat simplistic and mentions no statistical technique other than diagrams. Of course, the modern phase of the history of statistics, associated with such names as Karl Pearson, George Yule, William Gossett, and Ronald Fisher, was just beginning in 1891 (Kendall, 1968). Keynes grants that statistics is essential in the testing and verification of economic theories, but he provides not so much as a single example of any economic controversy that was ever resolved by a statistical test, although such examples would not have been hard to find in the works of Jevons, Cairnes, and Marshall. In consequence, his readers are left with the overwhelming impression that since the assumptions of economic theory are generally true, its predictions are also generally true, and whenever they are not, diligent search of the facts will always reveal some ad hoc disturbing causes that must bear the blame for the discrepancy.

Robbins's *Essay*

Keynes's and Marshall's hope of a final reconciliation of all methodological differences was to be short-lived. The new century had hardly begun before the first rumblings of the American Institutionalists were heard, and by 1914 or thereabouts the writings of Veblen, Mitchell, and Commons had spawned a whole school of heterodox inductivists across the Atlantic; institutionalism rose to a crescendo some time in the 1920s, threatening at one moment to become the dominant stream in American economic thought. Nevertheless, by the early 1930s it was all but over, although more recently there has been something of a revival.

It was at this point that Lionel Robbins decided that it was time to restate the Senior–Mill–Cairnes position in modern language to show that what orthodox economists had done and were still doing made good sense. There were elements in Robbins's argument, however, such as the famous means-ends definition of economics and the claim of the unscientific character of all interpersonal comparisons of utility, which derived from the Austrian rather than the Anglo-American tradition of economics.[18] In a decade noted for great controversies in economics, Robbins's *An Essay on the Nature and Significance of Economic Science* (1932) stands out as a polemical masterpiece that generated a veritable furor. As the preface to the second edition in 1935 makes clear, the bulk of contemporary reactions to Robbins's *Essay* centered on Chapter Six with its insistence on the purely conventional nature of interpersonal comparisons of welfare. Also, in arguing that the science of economics is neutral with respect to the objectives of economic policy, Robbins was widely and erroneously interpreted as issuing a self-denying ordinance in regard to discussions of policy. On the other hand, his Austrian-type definition of economics – "Economics is a science which studies human behaviour as a relationship between [a given hierarchy of] ends and scarce means which have alternative uses" – seized on an aspect rather than a type of human

[18] Robbins was unusual among British economists of the day in that he quoted Austrian and German writers more frequently than English or American ones. However, he was deeply influenced by Philip Wicksteed's *Common Sense of Political Economy* (1910), an earlier attempt to import Austrian ideas into British economics.

behavior (Robbins, 1935, pp. 16–17; Fraser, 1937, chap. 2; Kirzner, 1960, chap. 6) that soon won the field and that is now echoed in the first chapter of every textbook on price theory.

"The main postulate of the theory of value," Robbins (1935, pp. 78–9) announced, "is the fact that individuals can arrange their preferences in an order, and in fact do so." This fundamental postulate is at once an *a priori* analytic truth, "an essential constituent of our conception of conduct with an economic aspect," and an "elementary fact of experience" (pp. 75, 76). Similarly, the principle of diminishing marginal productivity, another funda-mental proposition of value theory, follows both from the assumption that there is more than one scarce factor of production and from "simple and indisputable experience" (pp. 77, 78). Thus, neither of these are "postulates the existence of whose counterpart in reality admits of extensive dispute. . . . We do not need controlled experiments to establish their validity: they are so much the stuff of our everyday experience that they have only to be stated to be recognised as obvious" (p. 79; also pp. 68–9, 99–100, 104). Indeed, as Cairnes had said long ago, in this respect economics actually has the edge on physics: "In Economics, as we have seen, the ultimate constituents of our fundamental generalisations are known to us by immediate acquaintance. In the natural sciences they are known only inferentially. There is much less reason to doubt the counterpart in reality of the assumption of individual pref-erences than that of the assumption of the electron" (p. 105). This is of course nothing but the familiar *Verstehen* doctrine, which was ever a favorite ingre-dient of Austrian economics. The *Verstehen* doctrine always goes hand-in-hand with a suspicion of methodological monism and this note too is found in Robbins: "less harm is likely to be done by emphasizing the differences between the social and the natural sciences than by emphasizing their similar-ities" (pp. 111–12).

Again, in the wake of Cairnes, Robbins denies that economic effects can ever be predicted in quantitative terms; even estimates of the elasticity of demand, which might appear to suggest the opposite, are in fact highly un-stable (pp. 106–12). What the economist possesses is merely a qualitative calculus, which of course may or may not apply in a particular case (pp. 79–80). He emphatically rejects the allegation of the historical school that all economic truths are relative to time and place, pours scorn on the American institutionalists – "not one single 'law' deserving of the name, not one quan-titative generalisation of permanent validity has emerged from their efforts" – and roundly endorses "the so-called 'orthodox' conception of the science since the time of Senior and Cairnes" (pp. 114, 82).

Next, he poses a contrast between "realistic studies" that "test the range of applicability of the answer when it is forthcoming" and a theory, "which is alone capable of supplying the solution" (p. 120), and sums up: "the *va-*

lidity of a particular theory is a matter of its logical derivation from the general assumptions which it makes. But its *applicability* to a given situation depends upon the extent to which its concepts actually reflect the forces operating in that situation,'' a statement which is then illustrated in terms of the quantity theory of money and the theory of business cycles (pp. 116–19). There follows, as we might expect, a number of pages on the dangers that are inherent in all tests of economic predictions (pp. 123–7).

In the famous and controversial sixth chapter, Robbins denies the possibility of making objective interpersonal comparisons of utility because they ''can never be verified by observation or introspection'' (pp. 136, 139–41). In a devastating critique of the use of introspection as an empirical source of economic knowledge, published a few years later in 1938, Hutchison (1938, pp. 138–9) points out the logical contradiction between adopting *intra*personal comparisons of utility as a warranted basis of consumer theory, while denying *inter*personal comparisons of utility as a basis of welfare economics. And certainly, it is peculiar to base so much in the theory of value on the assumption that other people have much the same psychology as oneself, while denying the same sort of reasoning in framing assumptions about other people's welfare. Alternatively expressed, if there are no objective methods for inferring anything about the *welfare* of different economic agents, there are also no objective methods for inferring anything about the *preferences* of different economic agents. Thus, the assumption that ''individuals can arrange their preferences in an order, and in fact do so,'' while no doubt ''the stuff of everyday experience,'' is contradicted by some consumer behavior that is also ''the stuff of everyday experience'': consumption patterns rigidly maintained out of habit, despite changing circumstances; shopping sprees and impulse buying that may be wildly inconsistent with previous preference orderings; consumption motivated solely by the desire to learn about one's own preferences from experience, not to mention consumption motivated, not by one's own preferences, but by one's perception of other people's preferences, as in so-called bandwagon and snob effects (Koopmans, 1957, pp. 136–7). In short, the proposition that all economic agents have well-defined preference orderings – that they are rational maximizers – is clearly false (see Chapter 15 below). Apriorism, the belief that economic theories are grounded in intuitively obvious axioms, is actually no less dangerous in the theory of demand than it is in the theory of welfare economics.

It is fortunate that in the case of Robbins we have for once a methodologist's afterthoughts on his earlier methodological pronouncements. Almost forty years after the *Essay,* Robbins published his autobiography in which he glanced back at the reception of his own *Essay on the Nature and Significance of Economic Science*. He remained unpersuaded by most of the criticisms that the book received, but in retrospect he agreed that he had paid too little attention to the problem of testing both the assumptions and the implications of economic theory: "the chapter on the nature of economic generalizations smacked too much of what nowadays is called essentialism . . . it was written before the star of Karl Popper had risen above our horizon. If I had known then of his pathbreaking exhibition of scientific method . . . this part of the book would have been phrased very differently" (Robbins, 1971, pp. 149–50; also 1979).

To show that Robbins's earlier hostility to quantitative investigations were by no means unique to him but were widely shared by many leading economists in the 1930s, consider the observations of John Maynard Keynes (1973, pp. 296–7) in a letter to Roy Harrod, written in 1938 (the references to Schultz are to Henry Schultz, whose *Theory and Measurement of Demand* [1938] constitute a milestone in the early history of econometrics):

It seems to me that economics is a branch of logic, a way of thinking; and that you do not repel sufficiently firmly attempts *à la* Schultz to turn it into a pseudo-natural science. One can make some quite worthwhile progress merely by using your axioms and maxims. But one cannot get very far except by devising new and improved models. This requires, as you say, 'a vigilant observation of the actual working of our system'. Progress in economics consists almost entirely in a progressive improvement in the choice of models. . . .

But it is of the essence of a model that one does not fill in real values for the variable functions. To do so would make it useless as a model. For as soon as this is done, the model loses its generality and its value as a mode of thought. That is why Clapham with his empty boxes was barking up the wrong tree and why Schultz's results, if he ever gets any, are not very interesting (for we know beforehand that they will not be applicable to future cases). The object of statistical study is not so much to fill in missing variables with a view to prediction, as to test the relevance and validity of the model.

Economics is a science of thinking in terms of models joined to the art of choosing models which are relevant to the contemporary world. It is compelled to be this, because, unlike the typical natural science, the material to which it is applied is, in too many respects, not homogeneous through time. The object of a model is to segregate the semi-permanent or relatively constant factors from those which are transitory of fluctuating so as to develop a logical way of thinking about the latter, and of understanding the time sequence to which they give rise in particular cases.

Good economists are scarce because the gift for using 'vigilant observation' to choose good models, although it does not require a highly specialised intellectual technique, appears to be a very rare one.

In the second place, as against Robbins, economics is essentially a moral science and not a natural science. That is to say, it employs introspection and judgements of value.[19]

---

[19] For discussion of Keynes's highly ambivalent attitude to econometrics, see Stone (1980) and Patinkin (1982, chap. 7).

Modern Austrians

The case for believing that economic truths – based as they are on such innocent and plausible postulates as a maximizing consumer with a consistent preference ordering, a maximizing entrepreneur facing a well-behaved production function, and active competition in both product and factor markets – require verification only to check that they do apply in any particular case was never stated with more verve and eloquence than in Robbins's *Essay*. Nevertheless, this was also the last time in the history of economic thought that the verificationist thesis was defended in these terms. Within a few years, the new wind of falsificationism and even *operationalism* was to blow through economics, encouraged by the growth of econometrics and the rise of Keynesian economics (despite Keynes's own lack of sympathy for quantitative research). Of course, old-fashioned methodological principles, like old soldiers, never die – they only fade away. While the rest of the economics profession since World War II has rejected the complacent stance of the verificationists, a small group of latter-day Austrian economists have returned to a more extreme version of the Senior–Mill–Cairnes tradition.

This school of so-called modern Austrian economics takes as its patron saints, not Carl Menger or Eugen von Böhm-Bawerk, but Ludwig von Mises and Friedrich Hayek. They were inspired by Hayek's attack on "scientism" or methodological monism and his emphasis of the principle of methodological individualism. But a more direct inspiration was Mises's *Human Action: A Treatise on Economics* (1949) with its statement of *praxeology,* the general theory of rational action, according to which the assumption of purposeful individual action is an absolute prerequisite for explaining all behavior, including economic behavior, constituting indeed a synthetic *a priori* principle that speaks for itself.[20] Mises's statements of radical apriorism are so uncompromising that they have to be read to be believed: "What assigns economics its peculiar and unique position in the orbit of pure knowledge and of the practical utilization of knowledge is the fact that its particular theorems are not open to any verification or falsification on the ground of experience . . . the ultimate yardstick of an economic theorem's correctness or incorrectness is solely reason unaided by experience" (Mises, 1949, p. 858, also pp. 32–41, 237–8; 1978). Together with radical apriorism goes an insistence on what Mises terms *methodological dualism,* the essential disparity in approach be-

---

[20] The same view appeared earlier in his *Grundprobleme der Nationaloekonomie* (1933). The appeal to Kantian synthetic *a priori* principles, that is, propositions that refer to the real world but are nevertheless prior to and independent of experience (such as our concept of time as being irreversible, so that an effect can never precede a cause, etcetera) was deliberate and reflected Mises's profound antipathy to logical positivism.

tween social and natural science grounded in *Verstehen* doctrine and the radical rejection of any kind of quantification of either the premises or the implications of economic theories (Mises, 1949, pp. 55–6, 347–9, 863–4). Although all this is said to be a continuation of Senior, Mill, and Cairnes, the notion that even the verification of assumptions is unnecessary in economics is, as we have seen, a travesty and not a restatement of classical methodology.

In short, the essential ingredients of the methodology of this new brand of Austrian economics, numbering among its adherents such names as Murray Rothbard, Israel Kirzner, and Ludwig Lachmann, appear to be (1) an absolute insistence on methodological individualism as an *a priori* heuristic postulate; (2) a deep suspicion of all macroeconomic aggregates, such as national income or an index of prices in general; (3) a firm disavowal of quantitative testing of economic predictions and, in particular, the categorical rejection of anything that smacks of mathematical economics and econometrics; and lastly (4) the belief that more is to be learned by studying how market processes converge on equilibrium than by endlessly analyzing, as most modern economists do, the properties of final equilibrium states.[21] There is much to be said for the fourth and last of these methodological tenets, which derives from the Hayekian influence on modern Austrian economics, but the first three ing from Mises smack of an antiempirical undertone in the history of continental economics that is wholly alien to the very spirit of science. In the 1920s, Mises made important contributions to monetary economics, business cycle theory and of course socialist economics, but his later writings on the foundations of economic science are so idiosyncratic and dogmatically stated that we can only wonder that they have been taken seriously by anyone. As Paul Samuelson (1972, p. 761) once said:

In connection with slavery, Thomas Jefferson has said that, when he considered that there is a just God in Heaven, he trembled for his country. Well, in connection with

---

[21] For recent restatements and defenses of Mises's praxeology, see Kirzner (1976), Rizzo (1978), and Rothbart (1957, 1976). For a devastating critique of Misesian apriorism by a modern Austrian, see Lavoie (1986), while Caldwell (1982, pp. 128–33) provides a criticism of Austrian methodology "from within its own framework." Finally, Rizzo (1982) provides a fascinating but unconvincing attempt to reconstruct Austrian methodology in Lakatosian terms.

The three dominant strands of Austrian economics – subjectivism, apriorism, and the teleological mode of explanation in terms of the purposive choices of individual agents – are not all integral to the Austrian position. O'Sullivan (1987) argues that a subjectivist and teleological interpretation of human action does not entail a commitment to apriorism and does not obviate the need to verify both the assumptions and the implications of economic theories. He thus advocates an Austrian methodology without the Austrian prejudice against empirical testing.

the exaggerated claims that used to be made in economics for the power of deduction and a priori reasoning – by classical writers, by Carl Menger, by the 1932 Lionel Robbins . . . , by disciples of Frank Knight, by Ludwig von Mises – I tremble for the reputation of my subject. Fortunately, we have left that behind us.

Yes, I do believe that we have.

4

The falsificationists, a wholly twentieth-century story

Ultraempiricism?

The year 1938 saw the publication of *The Significance and Basic Postulates of Economic Theory* by Terence Hutchison, and with it the explicit introduction of Popper's methodological criterion of falsifiability into economic debates. That Hutchison should have recognized the significance of Popper's demarcation criterion as early as 1938 is itself remarkable: Popper's *Logik der Forschung* (1934) was then almost completely unknown, and even so famous a popularization of the philosophical ideas of the Vienna circle as Ayer's *Language, Truth, and Logic* (1936) completely missed the significance of Popper's critique of the verifiability principle of meaning. To some extent, even Hutchison failed to realize the novelty of Popper's thinking: although he cited Popper frequently, he laid down the fundamental criterion that economic propositions that aspire to the status of "science" must be capable, at least conceivably, of being put to an interpersonal empirical test without any acknowledgment to Popper (Hutchison, 1938, pp. 10, 19, 26–7, 48, 49, 126, 156).[22] Hutchison's principal target of attack was apriorism in all its varieties, but in assailing the postulates of orthodox economics that were said by Mises and Robbins to be intuitively obvious, he overstated his case and so spoiled what might have been a decisive effort to reorient the methodology of interwar economics.

At the center of Hutchison's argument is the notion that all economic prop-

---

[22] When asked a few years later by Frank Knight to state his philosophical starting point, it is significant that Hutchison (1941, p. 735) mentioned the British empiricists as well as Mach, Schlick, and Carnap in Vienna without, however, referring to Popper. For a later treatment of methodological issues in economics by a philosopher of the social sciences that is simply Hutchison in different language, see Kaufmann (1944, chap. 16); he too makes no mention of Popper.

ositions can be exhaustively classified into either tautological propositions or empirical ones, the former being those that do not forbid any conceivable state of the world and the latter those that do forbid at least some conceivable states (1938, p. 13). Whatever we may think of such a dichotomous classification of scientific propositions – some modern philosophers have questioned this positivist dogma that all statements can be neatly divided into logically nec-essary, "analytic" propositions and logically indeterminate, "synthetic" ones (Nagel, 1961, p. 371) – the fact remains that Hutchison tended to characterize most economic propositions as tautologies. In so doing, he blurred the vital distinction in economics between assertions that are simply disguised defini-tions and assertions that, while testable in principle, are so stated as to delib-erately defy practical testing.

For example, metaphysical, "hard core" propositions in economics, such as the belief that the price system invariably acts to harmonize the interests of all economic agents or that all economic agents always act rationally in their own interests, are indeed assertions about the real world but are nevertheless irrefutable even in principle because they do not appear to forbid any events from occurring. Similarly, Hutchison dismissed economic propositions with unspecified *ceteris paribus* clauses as tautologies (1938, p. 42), whereas in fact they are simply untestable empirical assertions about the real world. Con-sider the two statements: the imposition of a tax on cigarettes will, *ceteris paribus,* raise their price, and the imposition of a tax on cigarettes will, *ceteris paribus,* lower their price; they cannot both be tautologies because they are actually incompatible with each other. As they stand, both are "synthetic" propositions about reality and yet neither is testable even in principle because the *cetera* are not enumerated. Thus, if a statement is in principle falsifiable, it does forbid some conceivable event or set of events. But the obverse does not hold: a statement may forbid some conceivable set of events and yet be irrefutable even in principle, as indeed are all tendency statements with un-specified *ceteris paribus* clauses.

This criticism of Hutchison originates with Klappholz and Agassi (1967). Instead of Hutchison's two-way classification into analytic-tautological prop-ositions and synthetic-empirical ones, consigning most economic concepts to the former category, Klappholz and Agassi propose a three-way classification into (1) analytic-tautological propositions, (2) synthetic-empirical proposi-tions that are nevertheless untestable even in principle, and (3) synthetic-empirical propositions that are testable at least in principle, with the con-sequence of reducing the number of economic concepts that fall into the first category and increasing the number that fall into the second. Hutchison, they contend, frequently criticizes economists for expressing tautologies when in fact they are pronouncing untestable empirical assertions: "From his surveys of economic theory one gets the impression that most economic theorists of his day uttered almost nothing but tautologies, although his book appeared two years after Keynes's *General Theory*. Yet Keynes was undoubtedly concerned with empirical issues'' (Klappholz and Agassi, 1967, p. 28).[23]

Hutchison's principal methodological prescription is that scientific economic inquiries should be confined to empirically testable statements. Unfortunately, he is rather vague about the question of whether the requirement of testability refers to the assumptions or to the predictions of economic theory. On balance, he seems to emphasize the testing of postulates, or what we now call assumptions, as suggested in the very title of his book, and this impression is strengthened by his response to Fritz Machlup's subsequent accusation of *ultraempiricism:* Machlup (1978, pp. 143–4) cites Hutchison as a prime example of an ultraempiricist, meaning one who would ''insist on independent verification of all assumptions by objective data obtained through sense observation,'' thus proposing ''a program that begins with facts rather than assumptions.'' Hutchison (1956) denies the charge of ultraempiricism and has no difficulty in showing that many of the statements in his book about the importance of testability referred, not to the assumptions, but to ''the finished propositions'' of economics.

Nevertheless, the burden of the book suggests otherwise and even the rejoinder to Machlup, written almost twenty years after the book, contains hints of Hutchison's long-standing conviction that empirical work in economics is just as usefully applied to the assumptions as to the predictions of theory. Thus, Machlup argues that the direct testing of such fundamental assumptions as utility maximization on the part of households and profit maximization on the part of business firms by, say, the interrogation of large numbers of consumers and entrepreneurs is ''gratuitous, if not misleading''; to this remark Hutchison (1956, p. 48) replies: ''it does not matter in principle whether the specification of the conditions of a test of this fundamental assumption [of rationality] is obtained 'directly' and 'independently', or by working back 'indirectly' from the specified tests of the conclusions to the assumptions from which the conclusions are deduced.'' Actually, it matters a great deal and it matters ''in principle'': it is precisely on this issue that Hutchison parts company with Machlup and, as we shall see, with Friedman's influential 1953

---

[23] Hutchison was quite right in arguing that economists did (and do) protect substantive empirical propositions by presenting them as if they were tautologies and definitions; contrariwise, they sometimes manage miraculously to extract substantive economic insights from what are in fact tautological identities (see Leontief, 1950; Klappholz and Mishan, 1962; also Hutchison, 1960; Klappholz and Agassi, 1960; Hutchison, 1966; Latsis, 1972, pp. 239–41; Rosenberg, 1976, pp. 152–5).

"Essay on the Methodology of Positive Economics." Machlup is not far wrong in labeling the Hutchison of 1956 and even more the Hutchison of 1938 as a "reluctant ultra-empiricist" (Machlup, 1978, pp. 493–503).

Apriorism once again

If we are to do historical justice to Hutchison's book, however, we need to remind ourselves once again of the strength of apriorism in the 1930s, namely, the methodological view that economics is essentially a system of pure deductions from a series of postulates derived from inner experience, which are not themselves open to external verification. Thus, the publication of Hutchison's book was greeted by a wild and confusing essay-length review by Frank Knight, expressing profound irritation with what he took to be Hutchison's "positivism," denying that truth in economics is anything like truth in the natural sciences, affirming the *Verstehen* doctrine in economics,[24] and concluding: "It is not possible to 'verify' any proposition about 'economics' behaviour by any 'empirical' procedure, if the key words of this statement are defined as they must be defined to be used with relevance and precision" (Knight, 1956, p. 163; also pp. 164, 168). When Hutchison (1941) restated his position, Knight came back with the categorical denial that propositions about economic behavior can be empirically tested because economic behavior is goal-directed and, therefore, depends for its meaning on our intuitive knowledge of its purposive character:

My point was and is that the categorical contrast drawn by Mr. Hutchison, and so many others [?], between propositions which can be tested and the "value conceptions of common sense", and the insistence that only propositions of the former character are admissible in economic theory, is a false pretense and must simply be abandoned. The testable facts are not really economics . . . This inability to test may or may not be regarded as "too bad"; anyhow, it is the truth [Knight, 1941, p. 753; see also Latsis, 1972, pp. 235–6].

It is curious that Knight, who in the early 1930s had become one of the principal opponents of the Austrian theory of capital, should have continued

---

[24] Similarly, Machlup (1978, pp. 152–3), in attacking Hutchison's ultraempiricism, declares: "This, indeed, is the essential difference between the natural and the social sciences: that in the latter the facts, the data of 'observation,' are themselves results of interpretations of human actions by human actors. And this imposes on the social sciences a requirement which does not exist in the natural sciences: that all types of action that are used in the abstract models constructed for purposes of analysis be 'understandable' to most of us in the sense that we could conceive of sensible men acting (sometimes at least) in the way postulated by the ideal type in question."

throughout his life to take his methodological views straight from Mises and company (see Gonce, 1972; Hirsch and Hirsch, 1976, pp. 61–5).

It remains only to say that Hutchison in recent years has continued to insist on the relevance of Popper's methodological prescriptions for economics, while conceding that the advocacy of methodological monism is apt to be almost as dangerous as the methodological dualism favored by advocates of *Verstehen* doctrine.

Regarding the views expressed in that earlier essay [*The Significance and Basic Postulates of Economic Theory*], I would still support for economics the criterion of testability and falsifiability. However, though this earlier essay could be claimed to have been, in many ways, a sceptical work by the standards of 1938, its optimistic "naturalism" seems now indefensible: that is, its suggestions that the "social sciences" could and would develop in the same manner as physics and the natural sciences . . . It seems highly misleading to insist on certain general similarities between the natural and social sciences (although such general similarities certainly exist), and to assert that the differences are only ones "of degree," *without* making it clear how important in practice these differences are [Hutchison, 1977, p. 151; see also pp. 57, 59–60; and Hutchison, 1938, pp. vii–x].[25]

Operationalism

In the same year that Ayer popularized logical positivism in *Language, Truth, and Logic,* Percy Bridgman reaffirmed the methodology of operationalism in *The Nature of Physical Theory* (1936). A year later, Paul Samuelson began writing his Ph.D. thesis on the *Foundations of Economic Analysis,* which carried the subtitle *The Operational Significance of Economic Theory.* The thesis was finally published in 1948 and was immediately recognized as a major landmark in economic theory, not so much because of its methodology, but because of its demonstration that the standard assumptions of constrained maximization are not sufficient to derive most economic predictions: the method of comparative statics is empty unless a corresponding dynamic system is specified and shown to be stable – this is the so-called *correspondence principle* (Samuelson, 1948, pp. 262, 284).

One of the central purposes of his book, Samuelson declares, is to derive "operationally meaningful theorems" in economics: "By a *meaningful* theorem I mean simply a hypothesis about empirical data which could conceivably be refuted if only under ideal conditions" (p. 4; also pp. 84, 91–2, 172, 220–1, 257). Ironically enough, however, this is not operationalism as that term is usually understood. The methodology of operationalism, as laid down by Bridgman, is fundamentally concerned with the construction of certain cor-

---

[25] For a review of Hutchison's entire career as a methodologist, see Coats (1983).

respondence rules that are supposed to connect the abstract concepts of a scientific theory to the experimental operations of physical measurement. What Samuelson's definition of operationally meaningful theorems amounts to, however, is Popperian falsificationism expressed in the language of the Vienna circle.

Samuelson goes on to draw a fundamental distinction in comparative static reasoning between what has since come to be called the *quantitative calculus* and the *qualitative calculus*. It is rarely possible in economics to specify the magnitude of the change in the endogenous variables that results from a change in one or more exogenous variables, but we must insist as a minimum requirement, Samuelson argues, that we can determine the algebraic sign of the change: "The usefulness of our theory emerges from the fact that by our analysis we are often able to determine the nature of the changes in our unknown variables resulting from a designated change in one or more parameters. In fact, our theory is meaningless in the operational sense unless it does imply some restrictions upon observable quantities, by which it could conceivably be refuted" (p. 7; also pp. 19, 21, 24ff, 257, 350–1). By applying the criterion of the qualitative calculus to some of the main pillars of received theory, Samuelson concludes that there is little empirical content in the modern theory of consumer behavior (pp. 90, 92, 97–8, 117, 172), and he is equally skeptical about the principal tenets of the "new welfare economics" which purport to make meaningful statements about welfare without resorting to comparisons between individuals (pp. 244, 249).

The notion of an operationalist research program in economics has been consistently ridiculed by Machlup. Reading Bridgman uncharitably (and probably unfairly), Machlup interprets operationalism as ruling out all mental constructs in theory formation, after which it is easy to show that this is tantamount to eliminating all mathematical formulations of a theory. If, on the other hand, we admit such mental operations as mathematical functions, Machlup argues, the methodological force of operationalism is fatally compromised: theories made up only of operational concepts measurable in physical terms would amount to nothing more than lower-level generalizations about empirical regularities (Machlup, 1978, chap. 6, especially pp. 179–83). This is so obvious that it would hardly be worth saying were it not for the emotive impact of the adjective in the expression "operational theory," which, in Samuelson at any rate, is employed as a synonym for "empirical." Machlup (1963, pp. 56–7) even goes so far as to deny that the concept of equilibrium is deserving of the description "operational" – "Equilibrium as a tool for theoretical analysis is not an operational concept; and attempts to develop operational counterparts to the construct have not been successful" – which seems to miss the significance of the qualitative calculus. The idea of equilibrium is, surely, nothing more than the prediction that the real-world observable counterparts of the endogenous variables of economic models will remain constant so long as the real-world counterparts of the exogenous variables remain constant (Finger, 1971). In short, an operational theory is simply a falsifiable one. Without mentioning the name of Samuelson, Machlup himself seems to imply as much when he says:

It is not easy to know what the economists who have used the phrase "operational theory" really meant by this designation. They have not furnished any illustrations or examples for their designation . . . What the economists could have meant when they called for "operational theory" is . . . that a theory ought to have sufficient links with the practical domain, with data of observation. Links are "sufficient" if they allow us . . . to subject the theoretical system to occasional verification against empirical evidence [1963, p. 66].

Precisely!

Donald Gordon (1955) makes a more promising effort to pin down the meaning of operationalism in economics. He begins very much in the manner of Bridgman by defining an *operational proposition* as one that states or implies an operation that could in principle be performed, the results of which would constitute a test of the proposition. But he allows the "operation" of introspection in addition to the physical operations of recording, compiling, and computing (1968, pp. 48–9) – just as Bridgman allowed pencil-and-paper thought experiments – as a result of which his definition of operationalism is almost indistinguishable from Popper's definition of falsifiability. He then applies the correspondence principle to reinterpret Samuelson's definition of operationally meaningful theorems: if a functional relationship among observable variables is to have *operational significance,* the function must be shown to be dynamically stable, that is, any departure from the equilibrium solution of the endogenous variables motivates behavior that impels a return to the original equilibrium solution; the test of the stability of a function is the applicability of the qualitative calculus, implying in turn that the associated *ceteris paribus* clause is subject to definite restrictions.

Thus, in the usual interpretation of ordinary demand curves, where we hold constant the tastes of buyers as well as their incomes and the prices of closely related commodities, the given incomes and prices are the *cetera* that restrict the demand curve to certain empirically observable situations, whereas the assumption of given tastes is an empirical hypothesis that the demand does not shift, or shifts little, over the period of observation. It follows that, in principle, there is no valid distinction between the *quantitative* and the *qualitative* calculus. If we can make qualitative predictions about the demand for a product, it must be because its demand curve stays put over the period of observation, in which case we may perhaps be able to predict its quantitative slope and elasticity. On the other hand, if we cannot make quantitative predictions about demand because the demand curve has shifted, we also cannot derive qualitative predictions about the variations in demand. In practice, however, the distinction between the quantitative calculus and qualitative calculus is vital to the requirement of operational significance, or, as I would prefer to say, to the requirement of falsifiability (Gordon, 1955, pp. 50–1).

The important principle that seems to be established by this argument is that we can infer the existence of something like a well-defined, negatively inclined demand function for butter (1) if we can correctly predict the algebraic sign of the change in the quantity of butter demanded consequent upon a change in its price, and (2) if we can safely assume with the aid of the correspondence principle that the butter market is dynamically stable. In the *Foundations,* Samuelson frequently relies on casual empiricism to satisfy condition (2), thus letting condition (1) do all the work in obtaining operationally meaningful theorems. To illustrate the point, consider the well-known argument by which some teachers of first-year economics "prove" the proposition that the marginal propensity to consume in a Keynesian macroeconomic model must be less than unity: if it were equal to or greater than unity, it follows by the definition of terms that the Keynesian multiplier would be infinite, in which case the model would display the dynamic characteristic of explosive instability; but the real world displays no such explosive instability; therefore, the marginal propensity to consume must have a value of less than unity. Q.E.D. Replying to Gordon in reference to all such arguments, Samuelson (1966, pp. 1769–70) draws back from some of his earlier optimism in the *Foundations.* The correspondence principle, he explains, is at best a heuristic device and "In *Foundations* . . . , I stepped forward as a man of the world and casual empiricist and stated my opinion that the hypothesis of dynamical stability was a 'realistic' one to make. I am no longer so sure of this . . . your theoretical model or system will always be an idealized representation of the real world with many variables ignored; it may be precisely the ignored variables that keep the real world stable."

The qualitative calculus and the correspondence principle have been further developed and put to subsequent use in the testing of economic theories (e.g., Archibald, 1961; 1965; Lancaster, 1962, 1966a), but to say more of this now is to run ahead of our story. At this point, we must turn to the centerpiece of postwar economic methodology, the one essay on methodological questions that virtually every modern economist has read at some stage in his or her career: Milton Friedman's "Essay on the Methodology of Positive Economics" (1953). Its central thesis that economists should not bother to make their assumptions "realistic" aroused a storm of controversy that took almost a decade to die down,[26] and so subtle is Friedman's argument that even now it

---

[26] So famous is Friedman's thesis that it has even become the subject of widely dissem-

is difficult to find two economists who will agree on precisely what it was that Friedman said. In part, this is because the essay pursues two quite different theses, which are presented as if one were the corollary of the other, though they actually have very little to do with each other.

The irrelevance-of-assumptions thesis

Friedman opens his essay by setting out the old Senior–Cairnes–Keynes distinction between normative and positive economics, after which he asserts the essential methodological unity of all the physical and social sciences, including economics in its positive part. There follows a statement of the nature of that unified methodology (despite the Popperian ring of the passage, it makes no explicit reference to Popper, or, for that matter, to any other philosopher of science):

Viewed as a body of substantive hypotheses, theory is to be judged by its predictive power for the class of phenomena which it is intended to "explain." Only factual evidence can show whether it is "right" or "wrong" or, better, tentatively "accepted" as valid or "rejected." As I shall argue at greater length below, the only relevant test of the *validity* of a hypothesis [notice that "only"] is comparison of its predictions with experience. The hypothesis is rejected if its predictions are contradicted ("frequently" or more often than predictions from an alternative hypothesis); it is accepted if its predictions are not contradicted; great confidence is attached to it if it has survived many opportunities for contradictions. Factual evidence can never "prove" a hypothesis; it can only fail to disprove it, which is what we generally mean when we say, somewhat inexactly, that the hypothesis has been "confirmed" by experience [Friedman, 1953, pp. 8–9].

From here, Friedman moves swiftly to his main target, namely, the notion that conformity of the assumptions of a theory with reality provides a test of validity different from, or additional to, the test of its predictions. This widely held view, he writes, "is fundamentally wrong and productive of much mischief" (p. 14). Not only is it unnecessary for assumptions to be realistic, it is a positive advantage if they are not: "to be important . . . a hypothesis must be descriptively false in its assumptions" (p. 14). This flamboyant exaggeration is what Samuelson later christened "the extreme version of the *F*-twist."

It is far from clear, as many commentators have noted (Rotwein, 1959, pp.

inated jokes. O'Brien (1974, p. 3) says that students at Belfast University told him the following story (I heard the same story told at a party of economists in Bangkok four years earlier): "An economist, an engineer and a chemist were stranded together on a desert island with a large tin of ham but no tin-opener. After various unsuccessful exercises in applied science by the engineer and the chemist aimed at opening the tin, they turned in irritation to the economist who all the while had been wearing a superior smile. 'What would you do?', they asked. 'Let us assume we have a tin-opener', came the unruffled reply."

564–5; Melitz, 1965, pp. 40–1; Nagel, 1961, pp. 42–4, 1968), what is meant by "realism" of assumptions. The assumptions of economic theory are some-times said to be "unrealistic" in the sense of being abstract. As we have just seen, this is certainly one of Friedman's meanings: "realistic" assumptions are descriptively accurate in the sense that they take account of all the relevant background variables and refuse to leave any of them out. Friedman has of course no difficulty in showing that absolutely any theory that is not an exact replica of reality idealizes the behavior of economic actors and oversimplifies the assumed initial conditions and hence is descriptively inaccurate. Like-wise, he also has no difficulty in showing that if simplicity is a desirable criterion of good theory, all good theories idealize and oversimplify outra-geously.

But there is another sense in which the assumptions of theories in a social science like economics may be said to be "realistic," namely, whether they ascribe motives to economic actors that we, fellow human beings, find com-prehensible. *Verstehen* doctrine tells us that this is a desideratum of adequate theorizing in the social sciences. Friedman in later portions of his essay leans heavily on this interpretation of the phrase "realism of assumptions," and he rejects it as categorically as he does the interpretation of descriptive accuracy: whether businessmen testify that they strive to maximize returns, or even whether they recognize the meaningfulness of the question being put to them, is no test of the "realism" of what he calls "the maximization-of-returns hypothesis" because a Darwinian process of competitive rivalry guarantees that only those who actually maximize will survive. Under a wide range of circumstances, he writes, "individuals behave as-if they were seeking ration-ally to maximize their expected returns . . . and had full knowledge of the data needed to succeed in this attempt" (p. 21). We may now rephrase Fried-man to read: "to be important . . . a hypothesis must be descriptively false in its assumptions" in the sense of imputing as-if motives to economic actors that they could not possibly hold consciously (like assuming that billiard play-ers calculate the angle and momentum of billiard balls every time they drive a ball into a pocket); all that matters is whether the theory grounded on as-if motives has predictive value. This is about as radical a rejection of *Verstehen* doctrine as we could ask for and is tantamount to the methodology of *instru-mentalism:* theories are *only* instruments for making predictions or, better still, inference tickets that warrant the predictions that we make (Coddington 1972, pp. 12–13). Thus, the as-if formulation of economic hypotheses not only refuses to offer any causal mechanism linking business behavior to the maximization of returns; it positively rules out the possibility of such an ex-planation.

But there is still a third sense in which the assumptions of theories may be said to be "unrealistic," and it is perhaps this interpretation that most of

Friedman's critics have had in mind. It is the case where the assumptions are believed to be either false or highly improbable in the light of directly perceived evidence about economic behavior (for example, when business firms are observed to commit themselves to a fixed rule-of-thumb for pricing their products irrespective of economic circumstances). However, while continuing to deny the need to test assumptions directly, Friedman does allow for "The Use of 'Assumptions' as an Indirect Test of a Theory," to cite the heading of an important but frequently overlooked section of his essay (pp. 26–30). That is to say, the assumptions of one theory regarded as false on grounds of casual empiricism may figure as the implications of a wider theory whose consequences can be or have been tested, in which case these assumptions may be shown to be false in a particular domain but not in another.

This raises an important methodological point about the role of assumptions in theorizing: it is, among other things, to specify the range of the intended applications of a theory. As Friedman aptly observes: "the entirely valid use of 'assumptions' in *specifying* the circumstances for which a theory holds is frequently, and erroneously, interpreted to mean that the assumptions can be used to *determine* the circumstances for which a theory holds" (p. 19). In other words, we should not inspect the assumptions of the theory of perfect competition to see whether it can be applied to the cigarette industry, because if the theory is properly formulated, the circumstances under which it applies are specified as among its essential components; we know before we begin that the theory of perfect competition cannot apply to the highly concentrated cigarette industry. Once we eliminate any reference to a theory's domain of application, we render it untestable because every refutation can be countered by the argument that it has been incorrectly applied. But, having introduced this important methodological clarification, Friedman immediately spoils the point by allowing the theory of perfect competition to apply to any firm whatsoever, depending on circumstances: "there is no inconsistency in regarding the same firm as if it were a perfect competitor for one problem and a monopolist for another" (p. 36; also p. 42). In other words, he reverts once again to an extreme instrumentalist interpretation of economic theories.[27]

---

[27] We must, surely, agree with Archibald (1963, pp. 69–70) when he conjectures, suppose "we can successfully predict some of the behaviour of an economic unity from theory A and some from theory B; where A is right B would be wrong, and vice versa. One way of interpreting the situation is: 'different theories for different problems'. Another is: 'A and B are both refuted'. How do we now proceed? My view is that the correct predictions of both A and B constitute part of our stock of useful knowledge, available for what I call engineering purposes, but that both A and B are, as scientific hypotheses, refuted. We might now endeavour to construct a more general theory, incorporating A and B. Part of such a theory would be the specification of the circumstances in which each subtheory would hold. Such a theory would be susceptible of refutation, since the specification might be wrong. In the case of the

Having distinguished the three senses in which assumptions may be said to be realistic or unrealistic, it must be added that Friedman considerably aggravates the problem of gauging his meaning by writing throughout his essay about "assumptions" in quotation marks without the slightest regard for the different logical status of various kinds of assumptions. He does not even explicitly distinguish between initial conditions, auxiliary hypotheses, and boundary conditions. As Archibald (1959a, pp. 64–5) has pointed out, *assumptions* in economics may refer to (1) statements of motivation such as utility and profit maximization; (2) statements of overt behavior of economic agents; (3) statements of the existence and stability of certain functional relationships; (4) restrictions on the range of variables to be taken into account; and (5) boundary conditions under which the theory is held to apply. The issue of realism of assumptions is clearly very different for each of these five assumptions.

Likewise, Melitz (1965, p. 42) distinguishes between "auxiliary" assumptions, which are used in conjunction with a theoretical hypothesis in order to deduce its logical consequences, and "generative" assumptions, which serve to derive the hypothesis itself. Despite the fact that every assumption may serve in either capacity, depending on the particular prediction in question, some frequently employed assumptions in economics usually function in one role rather than the other: *ceteris paribus* is typically an auxiliary assumption, whereas profit maximization is typically a generative assumption. Although the "realism" of both kinds of assumptions may be relevant, a discrepancy between the auxiliary assumptions and reality is more serious for the test of a theory than the lack of "realism" of the generative assumptions since the latter are usually capable of a number of alternative interpretations. Suffice it to say that the entire thesis of the irrelevance of assumptions has been bedeviled from the outset by the indiscriminate use of the term *assumptions*.

Machlup, coming to Friedman's rescue, distinguishes a whole class of assumptions, postulates, or fundamental hypotheses: " 'heuristic principles' (because they serve as useful guides in the analysis), 'basic postulates' (because they are not challenged for the time being), 'useful fictions' (because they need not conform to the 'facts' but only be useful in 'as-if' reasoning), 'procedural rules' (because they are resolutions about the analytical procedures to be followed), 'definitions assumptions' because they are treated like purely analytical conventions)" (Machlup, 1978, p. 145; see also Musgrave, 1981). In any theory, these types of fundamental assumptions have to be supplemented by what he calls "assumed conditions," that is, initial conditions specified as to type of case, type of setting, and type of economy to

monopoly-competition mixture my complaint is precisely that it is an *ad hoc* mixture and *not* a general theory which includes the appropriate specification, and it is therefore *not* susceptible of refutation."

which the theory is to be applied and from which a deduced outcome is to be inferred for purposes of testing (pp. 148–50). He agrees that to verify a theory (he always speaks of verification rather than falsification), the "assumed conditions" must correspond to observable situations, but he exempts all the fundamental assumptions from such scrutiny. That consumers are able to rank their preferences in a consistent order and that entrepreneurs prefer more profit to less if each is equally risky are fundamental assumptions "which, though empirically meaningful, require no independent empirical tests" (p. 147). Not only are such direct, independent tests "gratuitous," Machlup adds, they are even "misleading" because "the fundamental assumption [of maximization] may be understood as an idealization with constructs so far removed from operational concepts that contradiction by testimony is ruled out" (p. 147). That does not mean that it is inviolate, he grants, because it may be rejected together with the theoretical system of which it is a part, if and when a more satisfactory system is available.

In short, Machlup takes the view that a theory is never wholly discredited, even in contexts where its fundamental assumptions are known to be false, unless a better theory can be and perhaps has been offered. He concedes that the assumption of consistent utility-maximizing and profit-maximizing behavior are contrary to fact for some consumers and entrepreneurs (p. 498). The problem as he sees it is that we cannot know how significant deviations from, say, profit-maximizing conduct are except in the context of specific predictions. Therefore, we ought "to accept maximizing conduct as a heuristic postulate and to bear in mind that the deduced consequences may sometimes be considerably out of line with observed data. We can, to repeat, test empirically whether the outcome of people's actions is most of the time reasonably close to what one would expect if people always acted as they are unrealistically assumed to act" (p. 498).[28] This divides the methodological arena, according to Machlup, between extreme apriorists such as Mises, Knight, and Robbins at one end and ultraempiricists such as Hutchison at the other end, with the middle ground between these two extremes occupied by Zeuthen, Samuelson, Lange, Friedman, and presumably himself: "none of them holds that no conceivable kind of experience could ever cause him to give up his

---

[28] Similarly, Bear and Orr (1967, p. 195), without endorsing the irrelevance-of-assumptions thesis, argue that assumptions are difficult to test in economics and hence it is legitimate, as a second-best approach, to treat assumptions that do not flatly contradict anything observable as correct and to proceed directly to a test of predictions. "It is wrong categorically," they say, "to disregard predictions from a perfectly competitive model on the ground that any of the four or five inadequately rationalized intermediate textbook conditions of perfect competition do not hold. Such a rejection is erroneous because of the difficulty in establishing how widely or how significantly the actual situation varies from the perfect competition ideal, or, indeed of establishing what an appropriate ideal of perfect competition may be."

theory, and none of them wants his fundamental assumptions empirically tested independently of the propositions with which they are combined when the theory is applied'' (p. 495).

The big bad wolf, therefore, is he who insists on the direct verification of fundamental assumptions as the critical test of the validity of a theory in advance of, or independently from, a test of its predictions. But was there ever such a bad wolf? What the critics of Friedman have argued is (1) that accurate predictions are not the *only* relevant test of the validity of a theory and that if they were, it would be impossible to distinguish between genuine and spurious correlations; (2) that direct evidence about assumptions is not necessarily more difficult to obtain than data about market behavior used to test predictions or, rather, that the results of examining assumptions are not any more ambiguous than the results of testing predictions; (3) that the attempt to test assumptions may yield important insights that help us to interpret the results of predictive tests; and (4) that if predictive testing of theories with patently counterfactual assumptions is indeed all that we can hope for, we ought to demand that our theories be put to extremely severe tests.[29]

To underline points (2) and (3), let us spend a moment on what is meant by a "test" of assumptions. Now, it may be agreed that any attempt to interrogate businessmen as to whether they seek to maximize profits, or to equate marginal revenue and marginal costs, or to discount the returns from a capital project at the cost of capital to the firm, is bound to produce ambiguous answers whose interpretation will usually beg the very same question that is being investigated. But other inquiries are possible: not "what are the objectives of the firm?" but "what are the bits of information that are collected before making strategic decisions?" or "how are such decisions actually made and how are conflicts within the firm about strategic output and investment decisions actually resolved?" The traditional theory of the firm treats the firm as if it were a "black box" without explicating its internal decision-making machinery. An inquiry that seeks to throw light on the nature of the "black box" must, surely, illuminate the attempt to test the predictions of the black-box theory of business behavior and, in any case, without such an inquiry the predictions of the theory are almost as difficult to test as are the assumptions.

Amazingly enough, Friedman actually concedes this argument: asking businessmen what they do and why they do it, he notes at one point in his

---

[29] See Koopmans, 1957, p. 140; Archibald, 1959a, pp. 61–9; Rotwein, 1959, p. 556, 1973, pp. 373–4; Winter, 1962, p. 233; Cyert and Grunberg, 1963, pp. 302–8; Melitz, 1965, p. 39; De Alessi, 1965; Klappholz and Agassi, 1967, pp. 29–33; Rivett, 1970, p. 137; McClelland, 1975, pp. 136–9; Coddington, 1976a; Rosenberg, 1976, pp. 155–70; Naughton, 1978; in defense, see Machlup, 1978, p. 153n; Pope and Pope, 1972 a, 1972b. For a survey of some of Friedman's critics, see Boland (1979), which however gives the critics too little credit.

essay, is "almost entirely useless as a means of *testing* the validity of economic hypotheses," although it may be useful in "suggesting leads to follow in accounting for divergences between predicted and observed results" (Friedman, 1953, p. 31n). So, apparently, the testing of motivational assumptions has some limited role to play in validating theories, point (1), and, furthermore, it may prove productive in interpreting the results of predictive tests, point (3), from which we may therefore infer point (2). Indeed, rereading Friedman's essay we are struck by the fact that he is careful never to say that the realism of assumptions is *irrelevant* without preceding it by the adverb *largely*. In other words, he avoids the extreme versions of the *irrelevance-of-assumptions thesis,* or what Samuelson has dubbed the *F*-twist.

The *F*-twist

The debate surrounding Friedman's essay was considerably confused by Samuelson's attempt to reduce Friedman's argument to the "basic version of the *F*-twist," in the course of which he dropped his earlier advocacy of "operationalism" and instead opted for the methodology of "descriptivism," which left most of the combatants with the feeling that Friedman's methodology might be objectionable but Samuelson's new methodology was worse.

According to Samuelson, the *F*-twist comes in two versions: a basic version, which asserts that the lack of realism of a theory's assumptions is relevant to its validity, and an extreme version, which ascribes positive merit to unrealistic assumptions on the grounds that a significant theory will always account for complex reality by something simpler than itself. Ignoring the extreme version, he concentrates his attack on the basic *F*-twist:

. . . is fundamentally wrong in thinking that unrealism in the sense of factual inaccuracy even to a tolerable degree of approximation is anything but a demerit for a theory or hypothesis [1966, p. 1774].

. . . the doughnut of empirical correctness in a theory constitutes its worth, while its hole of untruth constitutes its weakness. I regard it as a monstrous perversion of science to claim that a theory is *all the better for its shortcomings;* and I notice that in the luckier exact sciences, no one dreams of making such a claim [1972, p. 761].

But admitting that we ought to worry about factually inaccurate assumptions, the real question is whether we should discard a theory merely because its assumptions are known to be unrealistic. However, on that question Samuelson is silent. When we recall that even Friedman only asserted that unrealistic assumptions are "largely" irrelevant for assessing the validity of a theory, and adding the fact that many of the motivational assumptions of economic theories involve directly unobservable variables, we are not actually any the wiser as a result of Samuelson's vehement condemnation of the *F*-twist.

Samuelson goes so far as to supply a logical proof of the error of the *F*-twist (1966, pp. 1775–6), but that proof presupposes a perfectly axiomatized "Euclidean" theory whose wholly deductive structure ensures that assumptions, theoretical propositions, and the consequences of those propositions all mutually imply one another. In fact, most economic theories are not completely axiomatized and do not possess a simple logical structure, which is precisely why there is some point in distinguishing the assumptions of theories from their implications (see De Alessi, 1971, pp. 868–9; Machlup, 1978, p. 481; Pope and Pope, 1972b, p. 236; Wong, 1973, p. 321). Moreover, even a completely axiomatized theory that is in principle decomposable into its assumptions cannot be empirically tested unless it is supplemented by initial conditions and more or less "realistic" auxiliary assumptions that provide measurable proxies for the analytical variables that appear in the theory. Thus, the Samuelson proof of the fallacy of the *F*-twist seems to have reference only to the formal role of theory as an analytical filing system for organizing our ideas about reality and not to the substantive role of theory as an "explanation" of reality (see McClelland, 1975, pp. 139–41; Rosenberg, 1976, pp. 170–2).

We would have thought that the weakest link in Friedman's argument is his commitment to the methodology of *instrumentalism*. Once theories are seen as nothing but instruments for generating predictions, the thesis of the irrelevance of assumptions is irresistible. "The only relevant test of the *validity* of a hypothesis," Friedman tells us, "is comparison of its predictions with experience." But such a comparison may show that a particular theory predicts extremely accurately although the theory as such provides no explanation, in the sense of a casual mechanism, to account for the prediction. Science, it might be argued, ought to do better than merely predict accurately. But instead of questioning Friedman's implicit recourse to the symmetry thesis, Samuelson himself invokes the symmetry thesis by opting for the methodology of *descriptivism:*

A Gallup poll count of the mail would seem to show there is a widespread will to disbelieve in my rather hardboiled insistence upon "theory" as (strategically simplified) description of observable and refutable empirical regularities . . . a description (equational or otherwise) that works to describe well a wide range of observable reality is all the "explanation" we can ever get (or need desire) here on earth . . . *An explanation, as used legitimately in science, is a better kind of description and not something that ultimately goes beyond description* [Samuelson, 1972, pp. 765–6; also 1966, p. 1778].

Apart from the fact that the methodology of descriptivism is a little old-fashioned (Nagel, 1961, pp. 118–29), we wonder what is the purpose of this strenuous insistence that the answer to the question "why?" is always an answer to the question "how?" In the final analysis, Samuelson is almost as defensive about economics as is Friedman.

Instrumentalism is an excessively modest methodology, and so is descriptivism, which is simply a poor man's version of instrumentalism (Boland, 1970; Wong, 1973; Caldwell, 1980; but see Hammond, 1990). But apart from excessive modesty, what is wrong with instrumentalism? Its weakness is that of all black-box theorizing that makes predictions without being able to explain why the predictions work: the moment the predictions fail, the theory has to be discarded in toto because it lacks an underlying structure of assumptions, an *explanans* that can be adjusted and improved to make better predictions in the future. It is for this reason that scientists usually do worry when the assumptions of their theories are blatantly unrealistic.

Both writers have been charged with saying the same thing in different words. They have also been charged with failing to practice what they preach. Machlup (1978, pp. 482–3) refers to Samuelson's international factor-price-equalization theorem (see Chapter 11 below) to show that Samuelson is as much an *F*-twister as Friedman, in the sense that he too infers apparently significant real-world consequences from theoretical assumptions admitted to be patently counterfactual. And Archibald (1961, 1963) has argued convincingly that Stigler and Friedman attack Chamberlin's theory of monopolistic competition, not on the grounds of its poor predictive record, but on grounds of consistency, simplicity, relevance, etcetera, that is, on the basis of the theory's assumptions rather than its predictions. But waiving such debating points, what is striking is that Friedman, Machlup, and Samuelson, each in their own way, adopt what we have earlier called a defensive methodology whose principal purpose seems to be to protect economics against the carping criticism of unrealistic assumptions, on the one hand, and the strident demand of severely tested predictions, on the other (Koopmans, 1957, pp. 141–2; Latsis, 1976, p. 10; Diesing, 1985). We have dealt with the first half of this defense, but we have as yet said nothing about the second half.

The Darwinian survival mechanism

Fritz Machlup, while urging the importance of empirical research in economics, is nevertheless keen to underline the inconclusiveness of all tests of economic hypotheses. We have already noted that he prefers the language of verification to that of falsification, but he is perfectly aware of the Popperian argument that verified theories are simply those that have so far resisted falsification: "testing an empirical hypothesis results either in its disconfirmation or its non-disconfirmation, never in its definitive confirmation" (Machlup, 1978, p. 140). With the aid of this terminological clarification, we can now consider his skepticism about empirical testing in a field like economics:

Where the economist's prediction is *conditional,* that is, based upon specified conditions, but where it is not possible to check the fulfillment of all the conditions stipulated, the underlying theory cannot be disconfirmed whatever the outcome observed. Nor is it possible to disconfirm a theory where the prediction is made with a stated *probability* value of less than 100 per cent; for if an event is predicted with, say, 70 per cent probability, any kind of outcome is consistent with the prediction. Only if the same "case" were to occur hundreds of times could we verify the stated probability by the frequency of "hits" and "misses." This does not mean complete frustration of all attempts to verify our economic theory. But it does mean that the tests of most of our theories will be more nearly of the character of illustrations than of verifications of the kind possible in relation with repeatable controlled experiments or with recurring fully-identified situations. And this implies that our tests cannot be convincing enough to compel acceptance, even when a majority of reasonable men in the field should be prepared to accept them as conclusive, and to approve the theory so tested as "not disconfirmed," that is, as "O.K." [p. 155].

This passage may be read as a perfectly valid criticism of "naive falsificationism," restating the Duhem–Quine thesis, but it may also be read as a plea for still more "sophisticated falsificationism": it is precisely because tests of economic theories are "more nearly of the character of illustrations than of verifications" that we need as many illustrations as possible. But that implies that economists should concentrate their intellectual resources on the task of producing well-specified falsifiable predictions, that is, assigning less priority to such standard criteria of appraisal as simplicity, elegance, and generality, and more priority to such criteria as predictability and empirical fruitfulness. It is fairly clear from the drift of Machlup's argument here and elsewhere, however, that he would order his priorities precisely the other way round (see Melitz, 1965, pp. 52–60; Rotwein, 1973, pp. 368–72). Throughout his long career, in which he has returned repeatedly to the methodological problems of economics, Machlup has been singularly ingenious in discounting all tests of economic theories that critics have devised, but he has never stated what evidence, if it materialized, he would be willing to regard as a refutation of, say, the neoclassical theory of business behavior or the marginal productivity theory of the demand for factors (e.g., Machlup, 1963, pp. 190, 207). There is little point in commending empirical work, as he certainly does, if it never really makes a difference to the beliefs one holds.[30]

[30] Machlup (1978, p. 46) has recently described himself as "a conventionalist – in the sense of one who accepts as meaningful and useful basic propositions that make no assertions but are conventions (resolutions, postulates) with regard to analytic procedure."

Friedman's attitude to empirical testing is somewhat different from that of Machlup: although he agrees that "There is never certainty in science, and the evidence for or against a hypothesis can never be assessed completely 'objectively' " (Friedman, 1953, p. 30), he is convinced that the neoclassical research program has been frequently tested and, moreover, that it has passed most of these tests with flying colors. First of all, he argues, as we have seen, that competition represents a Darwinian process that produces exactly the same results that would ensue if all consumers maximized their utility and all business firms maximized their profits, as a result of which the neoclassical model predicts correctly even though its assumptions may be counterfactual. (The classic statement of this argument is by Armen Alchian, and we will therefore label it the Alchian thesis.) Furthermore,

An even more important body of evidence for the maximization-of-returns hypothesis is experience from countless applications of the hypothesis to specific problems and the repeated failure of its implications to be contradicted. This evidence is extremely hard to document: it is scattered in numerous memorandums, articles and monographs concerned primarily with specific concrete problems rather than with submitting the hypothesis to test. Yet the continued use and acceptance of the hypothesis over a long period, and the failure of any coherent, self-consistent alternative to be developed and widely accepted, is strong indirect testimony to its worth [pp. 22–3].

This is without doubt the most frustrating passage in Friedman's entire essay because it is unaccompanied by even a single instance of these "countless applications." No doubt, when the price of strawberries rises during a dry summer, when an oil crisis is accompanied by a sharp rise in the price of oil, when stock market prices tumble after the threat of a switch to a hard money policy, we may take comfort in the fact that the implications of the maximization-of-returns hypothesis have once again failed to be refuted. However, given the multiplicity of hypotheses that could account for the same phenomena, we can never be sure that the repeated failure to produce such refutations is not a sign of the reluctance of economists to develop and test unorthodox hypotheses. It would be far more convincing to be told what economic events are excluded by the maximization-of-returns hypothesis, or better still, what events, if they occurred, would impel us to abandon the hypothesis. As Archibald (1959a, p. 62) has justly remarked, the true purport of the passage about "countless applications" is "to encourage complacency and to discourage that sceptical re-examination of the allegedly obvious that is the prerequisite of progress." It suggests that Friedman, despite what he says elsewhere, is not really interested in testing the maximization-of-returns hypothesis and is instead seeking to confirm it. As we know, there is no hypothesis so strange but that it is confirmed by evidence all around us. Besides, the age of a maintained hypothesis and the absence of a widely accepted rival do not provide "*strong* indirect testimony to its worth," to quote Friedman's own words; every fallacious doctrine that was ever held has been defended on such grounds.

There remains what I have labeled the Alchian thesis, that is, the notion that all motivational assumptions in microeconomics may be construed as as-if statements. This may be viewed as a knockdown version of the irrelevance-of-assumptions thesis – it is pointless to debate the realism of as-if assumptions because such assumptions are by definition neither true nor false – or else as a radical reinterpretation of the maximization-of-returns hypothesis that in effect shifts the locus of rational action from the individual to the social plane. By leaning heavily on the Alchian thesis, Friedman is in fact repudiating the methodological individualism that is commonly held to be embedded in the neoclassical approach to economic questions: instead of deriving testable predictions in-the-large from the rational action of individual agents in-the-small, the predictions of microeconomics are instead derived from a new kind of causal mechanism, namely, a dynamic selection process that rewards those businessmen who for whatever reasons act as if they were rational maximizers, while penalizing those who act in some other way by bankruptcy. This is not a behaviorist reinterpretation of traditional theory but rather a new theory. It is what I earlier referred to as Friedman's second methodological thesis whose theoretical implications are so far-reaching that it is amazing how widely it has been accepted and how little its special features have been noticed (but see Koopmans, 1957, pp. 140–1; Archibald, 1959a, pp. 61–3; Winter, 1962; Diesing, 1971, pp. 59–60, 299–303; Nelson and Winter, 1982, pp. 139–44.)[31]

The reference to a *dynamic* selection process shows immediately what is wrong with the appeal to the Alchian thesis: traditional microeconomics is largely, if not entirely, an analysis of timeless, comparative statics, and as such it is strong on equilibrium outcomes but weak on the process whereby equilibrium is attained. "Let the apparent immediate determinant of business behavior be anything at all – habitual reaction, random choice, or whatnot," Friedman (1953, p. 22) tells us; "Whenever this determinant happens to lead to behavior consistent with rational and informed maximization of returns,

---

[31] Thus, Harry Johnson (1968, p. 5), endorsing the irrelevance-of-assumptions thesis, states without qualification: "it has been shown . . . that whether firms consciously seek to maximize profits and minimize costs or not, competition will eliminate the inefficient firms; and that whether consumer behaviour is rational or purely random, the demand curves for a product will tend to slope downwards as in the Marshallian analysis. In consequence, it is possible for economists to treat the economy as an interdependent system responding to change according to certain general principles of a rational kind, with considerably more confidence than appeared justifiable thirty years ago." For other echoes of the Darwinian thesis, see Winter (1962, p. 1n).

the business will prosper and acquire resources with which to expand; and whenever it does not, the business will tend to lose resources." But the process whereby some firms prosper when their actual behavior approaches maximizing behavior takes time, and no reason has been given for believing that those firms, having prospered in one period, will act consistently in the next period; in other words, "habitual reaction" may, but "random chance" certainly will not, result in any cumulative tendency for profitable firms to grow relative to those that are not profitable. As Sidney Winter (1962, p. 240) expresses it in his systematic critique of the Alchian thesis:

There is then a basic difficulty in the existing statements of the selection argument, a difficulty which is rooted in the fact that the relative deviations from profit maximization of different firms may change through time. Since there has been no careful treatment of the dynamic process by which some patterns of behavior are shown to be viable and others nonviable, it has escaped notice that firms cannot in general be unambiguously ranked in terms of their closeness to maximising behavior. Such a ranking must, in general, presume a particular state of the environment, but the environment is changed by the dynamic process itself.

To vindicate the Alchian thesis, we need to be able to predict behavior in disequilibrium situations, that is, we need to supplement the standard theory of the firm by a so far missing theory of entry and exit relating to the appearance and disappearance of firms in the economic environment. Suppose there are increasing returns to scale in production, or any other technologically based cost advantages; if a nonmaximizing firm gains an initial advantage over a maximizer, say, by entering the industry earlier in time, the scale advantage may allow that nonmaximizer to grow faster than the maximizer and to do so irreversibly; in consequence, the only firms that we observe are firms that fail to maximize profits and that indeed carry "slack" (Winter, 1962, p. 243). Even the mere presence of differentiated products and associated advertising in an industry may produce a similar result. Now, of course, we can define a set of assumptions – constant returns to scale, identical products, perfect capital markets, reinvestment of all profits, etcetera – that will support the Alchian thesis, but that procedure will only bring us back full circle to the question of the "realism" of assumptions (pp. 242–5). In a nutshell, the problem with the Alchian thesis is the same as the problem of reading progress into "the survival of the fittest" in Darwinian theory: to survive, it is only necessary to be better adapted to the environment than one's rivals, and we can no more establish from natural selection that surviving species are perfect than we can establish from economic selection that surviving firms are profit maximizers. What is true of firms is true of techniques: once a technique gets a head start, an entire industry may be locked into a technique that is actually suboptimal. A beautiful example of this is the survival of the generally acknowledged nonoptimal typewriter keyboard with which we are all familiar (David, 1985).

We sum up our long analysis of Friedman's essay by reiterating its three central arguments, all of which combine to provide a sweeping warrant for economists of all persuasions to build abstract models without excessive anxiety on the grounds of implausible assumptions: (1) assumptions are "largely" irrelevant to the validation of theories, which ought to be judged "almost" solely in terms of their instrumental value in generating accurate predictions; (2) standard theory has an excellent predictive record as judged by "countless applications . . . to specific problems"; and (3) the dynamics of competition over time accounts for this splendid track record, whatever are the facts of either overt behavior or the motivation for behavior on the part of individuals. No wonder that Friedman's persuasively argued essay has been found extremely comforting to a whole generation of economists!

Looking back at the entire debate surrounding Friedman's essay, we cannot help being struck by the lack of methodological sophistication that it displayed. The notion that theories can be neatly divided into their essential components and that the empirical searchlight is to be directed solely at the implications and never at any other parts of a theory can only be understood as a reaction to a century of critical bombardment of orthodox theory, first by the German historical school and subsequently by the American institutionalists. The style of this criticism, which was invariably accompanied by the crudest of objections to the assumptions of standard theory, paying absolutely no attention to its predictive content, inevitably produced the reaction among defenders of received doctrine that "assumptions are largely irrelevant." It is as though generations of physicists had ridiculed Newton's theory of gravity on the grounds that he committed himself to the patently unrealistic assumption that the masses of moving bodies are concentrated at their center, which might well have induced Newton to reply that predictions are everything and assumptions nothing. Faced with the accusation that no theory with counterfactual assumptions can be taken seriously, the thesis of the irrelevance of assumptions is *almost* excusable.

Friedman has done major work in his long career in monetary economics, macroeconomics, microeconomics, and welfare economics. In addition, he has written as much popular economics as ten financial journalists added together. Much of that work does exemplify his methodological principles but some of it contradicts it, say, by leaning heavily on plausibility of assumptions as a reason for believing certain economic theories. That may be because while sounding superficially as if he were indebted to Popper, in fact he owes more to John Dewey than to Karl Popper: he is a pragmatist rather than a falsificationist. This point of view is argued persuasively in a fascinating recent book by Hirsch and de Marchi (1990), a book which threatens to start off a new round in the debate on "what Friedman really meant" in his essay on the methodology of positive economics.

Naive versus sophisticated falsificationism

We are almost at the end of our story of explicit methodological controversy in modern economics and the rest of it can be quickly told. The late 1950s saw the publication of two books on economic methodology, both of which denied that economics is a science. Sidney Schoeffler's study of *The Failures of Economics* (1955) is reminiscent of a prewar book by Barbara Wootton, *Lament for Economics* (1938), although it goes much further in denying the scientific claims of economics. Schoeffler's central argument is simplicity itself: the entire hypothetico-deductive tradition of economic theorizing is a blind alley and economists must investigate the whole of the social fabric, abandoning the pretension that there is such a thing as an autonomous discipline of economics; scientific predictions are only possible when there are universal laws unrestricted as to circumstances, and since the economic system is always open to noneconomic forces and the play of chance, there can be no economic laws and hence no economic predictions as such (Schoeffler, 1955, pp. 46, 162). All this is in fifty-four pages, after which the rest of the book consists of a series of case studies of the failures of particular economic models.

This wholly negative indictment is capped by a positive proposal for a new kind of economics, which surprisingly enough turns out to be a general theory of rational action based on inductive studies of decision making (pp. 189–221). There is little point in separating the sense from the nonsense in Schoeffler's argument (but see Klappholz and Agassi, 1967, pp. 35–8), because any methodological prescription that amounts to wiping clean the entire slate of received economics and to starting all over again from scratch may be dismissed out of hand as self-defeating: economists have always ignored and will always continue to ignore the advice of those who claim that because one cannot run, it is pointless to try to walk.

Andreas Papandreou's *Economics as a Science* (1958) employs a somewhat different but equally extreme argument that turns on a distinction between *models* and *theories:* for Papandreou, models, unlike theories, cannot be refuted because their relevant "social space" is not adequately characterized; but even "basic theories" in economics have to be supplemented by auxiliary assumptions, or "correspondence rules" that relate the theoretical variables of the theory to the actual world to become the "augmented theories" that are genuinely refutable. His indictment of current practice in economics is simply that economists rarely formulate "augmented theories" and instead are satisfied either with "models" or with "basic theories," which are virtually irrefutable *ex post* explanatory schema (Papandreou, 1958, pp. 9–11, 136, 139, 144–5; also 1963).

In essence, Papandreou is making a case by generalizing the Duhem–Quine thesis, which he somehow interprets as a peculiar difficulty of *economic* theories (see pp. 134–5). Although he emphasizes the importance of "empirical meaningfulness," he seems to confine "basic theories" to quantitative comparative statics and to deny that economics can boast at least some confirmed qualitative predictions. But it is never easy to decide just what he does mean because the entire argument is buried beneath formal mountains of a new set-theoretical language for economics (see Klappholz and Agassi, 1967, pp. 33–5; Rosenberg, 1976, pp. 172–7). Papandreou's strident positivism appears to have spawned a disciple who applied the essentials of the argument to the theory of consumer behavior (Clarkson, 1963), but of that more anon (see Chapter 6 below).

The next item in our chronology is Joan Robinson's *Economic Philosophy* (1962), a puzzling little book that depicts economics as partly a scientific study of society and partly a vehicle for propagating ideology, that is, special pleading of a politically apologetic kind, but whose cumulative impact is to suggest that received economics is much more the latter than the former. Popper is mentioned as demarcating a metaphysical proposition from a scientific one, and the inherent difficulties in social science of producing clinching evidence for theories are given as the reason that ideology so frequently creeps into the argument: "economics limps along with one foot in untested hypotheses and the other in untestable slogans" (Robinson, 1962, p. 25; also pp. 3, 22–3). The book ends with a plea for not abandoning "the hope that economics can make an advance towards science" (p. 146), but no guidance is offered as to how this is to be achieved.

This brings us to the first edition of Richard Lipsey's popular textbook, *An Introduction to Positive Economics* (1963), whose opening chapter on scientific method amounted to a frank espousal of Popperian falsificationism in its "naive" version, namely, the belief that scientific theories can be faulted by a single decisive test. "Naive falsificationism" in the first edition gave way to "sophisticated falsificationism" in the second edition: "I have abandoned the Popperian notion of refutation and have gone over to a statistical view of testing that accepts that neither refutation nor confirmation can ever be final, and that all we can hope to do is to discover on the basis of finite amounts of imperfect knowledge what is the balance of probabilities between competing hypotheses" (Lipsey, 1966, p. xx; see also p. 52n).[32] The viewpoint that this

---

[32] The source of this *volte-face* was events at the London School of Economics, where Lipsey taught at the time, in the years from 1957 to 1963, a story well told by de Marchi (1988).

passage exemplifies appears in all the subsequent editions of the book, and to this day Lipsey's textbook remains the outstanding Popper-inspired introduction to elementary economics, which continually emphasizes throughout all its pages the need to assess empirical evidence in favor of a particular theory relative to the evidence supporting rival theories.

Back to essentialism

At this point, we may be tempted to echo Hutchison's recently expressed opinion that by now "Perhaps a majority of economists – but not all – would agree that improved predictions of economic behaviour or events is the main or primary task of the economist" (Hutchison, 1977, p. 8). It is never easy to assess the balance of opinion on a matter such as this but suffice it to say that there are plenty of indications that the majority, if it is a majority, represents no more than 51 percent of modern economists. Radical economists, Marxists and neo-Marxists, post-Keynesian and neo-Keynesians, institutionalists, and heterodox economists of all kinds, who together constitute a sizeable portion of the younger generation, would certainly not agree that economic theories must ultimately stand or fall on the basis of their predictions, or that empirical testing of hypotheses constitutes, as it were, the Mecca of the modern economist (see Blaug, 1990, pp. 60–2). Even Benjamin Ward's aggressive catalog of *What's Wrong With Economics?* (1972), one of the best efforts to date to reassess economics through Kuhnian spectacles, denies that the failure to emphasize the empirically falsifiable consequences of theories is one of the major flaws of modern economics (Ward, 1972, p. 173).

To show how far an anti-Popperian methodology actually prevails in some quarters of the profession, we need only examine a radical methodological contribution by Martin Hollis and Edward Nell, *Rational Economic Man*, subtitled *A Philosophical Critique of Neo-Classical Economics* (1975).

This book examines the unholy alliance between neoclassical economics and logical positivism, without however mentioning either Popper, Lakatos, or any other positivist later than the young Ayer (some of Popper's works are cited in the bibliography but no explicit or implicit reference to his ideas appears in the text). Positivism, they argue, is a false philosophy and neoclassical economics must fall with it: the positivist thesis of the separability of facts and values, on the one hand, and facts and theories, on the other, is untenable because all facts are theory-laden and all theories are value-laden. A more satisfactory epistemology can be built on *rationalism* by which they mean the demonstration that there are Kantian "synthetic" *a priori* truths: "Our strategy depends on being able to pick out what is essential and then to insist that what is essential is therefore to be found in practice" (Hollis and Nell, 1975, p. 254; also p. 178). Economic systems must reproduce themselves and this fact of reproduction is therefore *the* "essence" of economic systems that alone can furnish a sound basis for economic theory. The trouble with neoclassical economics, they say, is that there is nothing in the framework that guarantees that firms and households will reconstitute themselves on a period-to-period basis.

After this, we might have expected to learn that "sound" economic theory is modern growth theory, which is of course fundamentally concerned with the infinitely reproducible, steady-state properties of economic growth paths. But no, the only alternative to neoclassical economics that incorporates the essential aspect of "reproduction" is classical-Marxian economics, meaning actually neo-Ricardian economics leaning heavily on the work of Sraffa rather than Marx (Hollis and Nell, 1975, pp. 188, 195). The concluding chapter of the book, giving a brief sketch of "Classical-Marxian Economics on Rationalist Foundations," seems to retract much of what has gone before: suddenly recalling that capitalism is subject to periodic business cycles and perhaps even to final collapse, the authors concede that "systems in fact often fail to reproduce themselves," in which case it is difficult to see why so much was made of "reproduction" as the essence of economic problems.

Hollis and Nell try to saddle "positive economists" with the problem of induction; by demolishing induction they believe that they have scotched any notion of a fruitful neoclassical research program. They inveigh against the typical assumptions of neoclassical economics, particularly the perfect information assumptions, in apparent ignorance of Hutchison who, as early as 1938, made many of their points, and they stress various genuine difficulties in the attempt to test economic theories as if no one before them had ever suspected such problems. In some mysterious sense, classical-Marxian economics is supposed to escape all these difficulties, but of course it does so only by evading the empirical yardstick for validating theories. Indeed, it is clear that their rationalistic, essentialist approach to economic knowledge leaves no role whatever for quantitative-empirical research. Their book simply wipes out all the advances in methodological thinking in postwar economics that Popperianism ushered in. We might almost say that if they had read Popper's many devastating comments on the philosophy of essentialism (Popper, 1957, pp. 26–34; also Popper, 1976, pp. 18–21, 197–8; Popper and Eccles, 1977, pp. 172–94), their book would have been deprived of its *raison d'être*.

This is perhaps as good a place as any to say a few more words about the philosophy of *essentialism,* which will raise its ugly head once or twice more in the course of our discussion. Essentialism goes back to Plato and Aristotle for whom knowledge or "science" begins with observations of individual events and proceeds by simple inductive enumeration until grasping by intuition that which is universal in the events – their "essence" – which is then enshrined in a definition of the phenomenon in question. The doctrine that it is the aim of science to discover the true nature or essence of things and to describe them by means of definitions had an enormous influence on Western thought right up to the nineteenth century. Popper contrasts this brand of *methodological essentialism* with the *methodological nominalism* that came into scientific debates with Newton, according to which the aim of science is to describe *how* things behave in various circumstances with the aid of universal laws, and not to determine *what* they really are.

Popper has long argued that essentialism has damaging effects on social theories because it encourages an antiempirical tendency to solve problems by the use of definitions. Hollis and Nell never in fact tell us how to go about selecting *the* "essence" of economic systems; they imply that it amounts to abstracting "correctly" but they provide no criterion for assessing "correct" abstraction other than crude realism.[33] Adherents of essentialism are inclined to settle substantive questions by reaching for a dictionary of their own making, and Hollis and Nell exemplify this tendency to perfection: reproduction is *the* "essence" of economic systems because *we* tell you so!

Institutionalism and pattern modeling

Have I covered the entire menu of possible economic methodologies? Some would say not. They discern in the writings of the American institutionalists a mode of explanation that is neither apriorism, conventionalism, operationalism, instrumentalism, descriptivism, nor falsificationism: it is what has been called *pattern modeling* because it seeks to explain events or actions by identifying their place in a pattern of relationships that is said to characterize the economic system as a whole (Wilber and Harrison, 1978). Pattern modelers, we are told, reject all forms of "atomism" and refuse to abstract from any part of the whole system; their working hypotheses are relatively concrete and close to the system being described, and if they generalize at all, they do so by developing typologies; their explanations emphasize "understanding" rather than "predictions," and they view an explanation as contributing to understanding if new data fall into place according to the stated patterns.

I have no doubt that this is a more or less accurate description of the methods of some institutionalists such as Thorstein Veblen, Clarence Ayers, and perhaps Gunnar Myrdal. But it is difficult to find anything like pattern modeling in the writings of John R. Commons, Wesley Clair Mitchell, and John Kenneth Galbraith, whom some would regard as leading institutionalists. It is clear that all of these writers are united in some respects: none of them will have any truck with concepts of equilibrium, rational behavior, instantaneous

---

[33] Thus, Nell (1972a, p. 94) writes elsewhere, "we must examine the definitions and assumptions of our models for their realism, and for the extent to which they incorporate the essentials. If they are realistic, the working of the model should mirror that of the economic system in a relatively simple and abstract form."

adjustments, and perfect knowledge, and they all favor the idea of group behavior under the influence of custom and habit, preferring to view the economic system more as a biological organism than as a machine. But that is a far cry from saying that they share a common methodology, that is, a common method of validating their explanations (see Blaug, 1978, pp. 710–13, 726–7). There may be such a thing as a school of institutionalism, but it clearly has no unique methodology denied to orthodox economists.

A much better description of the working methodology of institutionalists is what Ward (1972, chap. 12) labels *storytelling,* which he argues also describes much orthodox economics, particularly of the applied kind. Storytelling makes use of the method of what historians call *colligation,* the binding together of facts, low-level generalizations, high-level theories, and value judgments in a coherent narrative, held together by a glue of an implicit set of beliefs and attitudes that the author shares with his readers. In able hands, it can be extremely persuasive, and yet it is never easy to explain afterwards why it has persuaded.

How does one validate a particular piece of storytelling? One asks, of course, if the facts are correctly stated; if other facts are omitted; if the lower-level generalizations are subject to counterexamples; and if we can find competing stories that will fit the facts. In short, we go through a process that is identical to the one that we regularly employ to validate the hypothetico-deductive explanations of orthodox economics. However, because storytelling lacks rigor, lacks a definite logical structure, it is all too easy to verify and virtually impossible to falsify. It is or can be persuasive precisely because it never runs the risk of being wrong.

Perhaps economic problems are so intractable that storytelling is the best that we can do. But if such is the case, it is odd that we should actually recommend the safe methodology of storytelling and deplore the risky methodology of falsificationism. Surely, the more falsificationism, the better?

The current mainstream

Nothing like an overwhelming consensus has emerged from our survey of postwar economic methodology. But despite some blurring around the edges, it is possible to discern something like a mainstream view. Despite the embarrassment of the *F*-twist, Friedman and Machlup do seem to have persuaded most of their colleagues that direct verification of the postulates or assumptions of economic theory is both unnecessary and misleading; economic theories should be judged in the final analysis by their implications for the phenomena that they are designed to explain. At the same time, economics is held to be only a "box of tools," and empirical testing can show, not so much whether particular models are true or false, but whether or not they are applicable in a given situation. The prevailing methodological mood is not only highly protective of received economic theory, it is also ultrapermissive within the limits of the "rules of the game": almost any model will do provided it is rigorously formulated, elegantly constructed, and promising of potential relevance of real-world situations. Some famous economists, like the late John Hicks for example, even manage at one and the same time to pooh-pooh empirical testing and to emphasize the policy implications of economic theories, a patently schizophrenic position (see Blaug, 1990, chap. 5). Modern economists frequently preach falsificationism, as we have seen, but they rarely practice it: their working philosophy of science is aptly described as "innocuous falsificationism."[34]

To substantiate this charge, we will examine the empirical status of a selected sample of ruling economic theories. Before we do so, however, we need to digress to consider the troublesome question of welfare economics. One of the features that distinguishes economics from physics, chemistry, and biology is that propositions in economics frequently serve at one and the same time as explanations of behavior and as stipulated norms for behavior. There is little or nothing in the modern philosophy of science that helps us to judge theories that deduce the nature of a social optimum from certain fundamental value judgments. Is this perhaps why so many modern economists fail to take falsificationism seriously?

[34] I owe this happy phrase to Coddington (1975, p. 542).

5

The distinction between positive and normative economics

Hume's guillotine

The distinction between positive and normative economics, between "scientific" economics and practical advice on economic policy questions, is now 150 years old, going back to the writings of Nassau Senior and John Stuart Mill. Somewhere in the latter half of the nineteenth century, this familiar distinction in economics became entangled, and almost identified with, a distinction among philosophical positivists between "is" and "ought," between facts and values, between supposedly objective, declarative statements about the world and prescriptive evaluations of states of the world. Positive economics was now said to be about facts and normative economics about values.

Then in the 1930s, the *new welfare economics* came along to provide a normative economics that was allegedly free of value judgments, after which it appeared that the distinction between positive and normative economics was one between noncontroversial facts and values, on the one hand, and controversial values, on the other. The result was to enlarge traditional, positive economics to include the whole of pure welfare economics, leaving normative economics to deal with specific policy issues, where nothing much can be said about values or ends apart from what politicians tell us. What is involved here are some horrible, logical confusions that laid economists open to wholesale attack on the very idea of value-free, positive economics. There is clearly much sorting out to be done here, after which we hope to reinstate the positive-normative distinction as yet another Popperian methodological norm peculiarly relevant to a policy science like economics.

It was David Hume in his *Treatise of Human Nature* who long ago laid down the proposition that "one cannot deduce ought from is," that purely factual, descriptive statements by themselves can only entail or imply other factual, descriptive statements and never norms, ethical pronouncements, or

112

prescriptions to do something. This proposition has been aptly labeled "Hume's guillotine" (Black, 1970, p. 24), implying as it does a watertight logical distinction between the realm of facts and the realm of values.

Hume's guillotine:
equivalent antonyms

positive	normative
is	ought
facts	values
objective	subjective
descriptive	prescriptive
science	art
true/false	good/bad

But how do we tell whether a given utterance is an is-statement or an ought-statement? It is clearly not to be decided by whether the sentence containing the statement is or is not grammatically formulated in the indicative mood, because there are sentences in the indicative mood, like "murder is a sin," which are thinly disguised ought-statements dressed up as is-statements. Nor is it decided by the fact that people agree more readily to is-statements than to ought-statements, since it is easy to see that there is far less agreement, say, about the factual proposition that the universe originated without super-natural intervention in a big bang eons ago than about the normative proposition that, say, we should not eat babies. An is-statement is simply one that is either materially true or false: it asserts something about the state of the world – that it is such and such, and not otherwise – and we can employ interpersonally testable methods to discover whether it is true or false. An ought-statement expresses an evaluation of the state of the world – it approves or disapproves, it praises or condemns, it extols or deplores – and we can only employ arguments to persuade others to accept it.

Surely, it will be objected, the normative proposition that we should not eat babies can likewise be tested by interpersonally testable methods, say, by a political referendum? But all that a political referendum can establish is that all of us agree that eating babies is wrong; it cannot establish that it *is* wrong. But it will again be objected, this is just as true of every interpersonally test-able verification or falsification of an is-statement. Ultimately, a factual, de-scriptive is-statement is held to be true because we have agreed among our-selves to abide by certain "scientific" rules that instruct us to regard that statement as true, although it may in fact be false. To say that there are "brute facts" that we must accept whether we like it or not is to commit the inductive fallacy, and besides, the Neyman–Pearson theory of statistical inference should have taught us by now that the acceptance of every fact in science necessarily implies a risky decision made under uncertainty, involving a definite, but unknown, chance of being wrong. Thus, we accept or reject is-statements on grounds that are themselves conventions and in this sense even "The Scientist *qua* Scientist Makes Value Judgements," to cite the title of a well-known methodological paper (Rudner, 1953). Moral judgments are usually defined as prescriptions enjoining a certain kind of behavior, which everyone is supposed to comply with in the same circumstances. But are assertions about facts not exactly the same kind of judgments, enjoining certain kinds of attitude rather than certain kinds of behavior?

There have been persistent doubts among moral philosophers in recent years about the is-ought dichotomy, largely along the lines that moral judgements are not simply expressions of feelings, or imperatives commanding someone to act, but actually special kinds of descriptive statements about the world (Hudson, 1969; Black, 1970, chap. 3). The argument we have been developing against the implications of Hume's guillotine, however, is rather different. I am not asserting for one moment that ought-statements are logically equivalent to is-statements but rather that the acceptance or rejection of is-statements is not a very different cognitive process from the acceptance or rejection of ought-statements; my contention is that there are no empirical, descriptive is-statements regarded as true that do not rely on a definite social consensus that we "ought" to accept that is-statement.

Methodological judgments versus value judgments

Nagel (1961, pp. 492–5) seeks to protect Hume's guillotine against precisely this sort of objection by drawing a distinction in social science between two types of value judgments – characterizing value judgments and appraising value judgments. *Characterizing value judgments* involve the choice of subject matter to be investigated, the mode of investigation to be followed and the criteria for judging the validity of the findings, such as adherence to the canons of formal logic, the selection of data in terms of reliability, explicit prior decisions about levels of statistical significance, etcetera; in short, everything that we have earlier called methodological judgments. *Appraising value judgments,* on the other hand, refer to evaluative assertions about states of the world, including the desirability of certain kinds of human behavior and the social outcomes that are produced by that behavior; thus, all statements of the "good society" are appraising value judgments. Science as a social enterprise cannot function without methodological judgments, but it can free itself, at least in principle, Nagel contends, of any commitment to appraising or normative value judgments.

At a deep philosophical level, this distinction is perhaps misleading. Ultimately, we cannot escape the fact that all nontautological propositions rest for their acceptance on the willingness to abide by certain rules of the game, that is, on judgments that we players have collectively adopted. An argument about facts may appear to be resolvable by a compelling appeal to so-called objective evidence, whereas an argument about moral values can only be resolved by a hortatory appeal to the emotions, but at bottom both arguments rest on certain definite techniques of persuasion, which in turn depend for their effectiveness on shared values of one kind or another. But at the working level of a scientific inquiry, Nagel's distinction between methodological and normative judgments is nevertheless real and significant.

Every economist recognizes that there is a world of difference between the assertion that there is a Phillips curve, a definite functional relationship between the level of unemployment and the rate of change in wages or prices, and the assertion that unemployment is so deplorable that we ought to be willing to suffer any degree of inflation to get rid of it. When an economist says that every individual should be allowed to spend his income as he or she likes, or that no able person is entitled to the support of others, or that governments must offer relief to the victims of inexorable economic forces, it is not difficult to see that he or she is making normative value judgments. There are long-established, well-tried methods for reconciling different methodological judgments. There are no such methods for reconciling different normative value judgments – other than political elections and shooting it out at the barricades. It is this contrast in the methods of arbitrating disagreements that gives relevance to Nagel's distinction.

We have overstated the case in suggesting that normative judgments are the sort of judgments that are never amenable to rational discussion designed to reconcile whatever differences there are between people. Even if Hume is right in denying that ''ought'' can be logically deduced from ''is,'' and of course ''is'' from ''ought,'' there is no denying that ''oughts'' are powerfully influenced by ''ises'' and that the values we hold almost always depend on a whole series of factual beliefs. This indicates how a rational debate on a disputed value judgment can proceed: we pose alternative factual circumstances and ask, should these circumstances prevail, would you be willing to abandon your judgment? A famous and obvious example is the widespread value judgment that economic growth, as measured by real national income, is always desirable; but is it, we might ask, even if it made the bottom quartile, decile, quintile of the size distribution of personal incomes absolutely worse off? Another example is the frequently expressed value judgment that capital punishment is always wrong. But if there were incontrovertible evidence that capital punishment deterred potential murderers, we might ask, would you still adhere to your original opinion? And so on.

In thinking along these lines, we are led to a distinction between ''basic'' and ''nonbasic'' value judgments, or what I would prefer to call pure and impure value judgments: "A value judgment can be called 'basic' to a person if the judgment is supposed to apply under all conceivable circumstances, and it is 'nonbasic' otherwise" (Sen, 1970, p. 59). So long as a value judgment is nonbasic or impure, a debate on value judgments can take the form of an appeal to facts, and that is all to the good because our standard methods for settling disputes about facts are less divisive than those for settling disputes about values. It is only when we finally distill a pure value judgment – think of a strict pacifist opposition to any and all wars, or the assertion that "I value this for its own end" – that we have exhausted all the possibilities of rational analysis and discussion.[35] There is hardly any doubt that most value judgments that are expressed on social questions are highly impure and hence perfectly amenable to the attempt to influence values by persuading the parties holding them that the facts are other than what they believe them to be.

Value-free social science?

Once we have cleansed the impurities in impure value judgment by a rational debate, we are left with factual statements and pure value judgment between which there is indeed an irreconcilable gulf on anyone's interpretation of the concept of "facts" and the concept of "values." Even if we leave value judgments to be as impure as they usually are, we have so far only demonstrated that the difference between the methods of reaching agreement on methodological judgments and value judgments is one of degree, not of kind. Nothing that we have said should imply that this difference in degree is not worth bothering about.

To argue that the difference is so small as to be negligible takes us straight into the camp of certain radical critics who assert that absolutely all propositions about social phenomena are value-impregnated and hence lack "objectivity." As Nagel (1961, p. 500) points out, this assertion proves too much: it is either itself uniquely exempt from the charge, in which case there is at least one objective statement that can be made about social questions, or it is itself value-loaded, in which case we are locked into an infinite regress and are driven towards extreme subjectivism in which simply all opinions count equally. Moreover, the case against the very possibility of any value-free, "objective" social science is usually dressed up with all sorts of irrelevancies, boiling down to the denial of any meaningful distinction between methodological and normative judgments.

The doctrine of value-free social science asserts, first of all, that the logical

---

[35] Roy (1989, pp. 30–1, 106–8) in a heavy-handed assault on moral skepticism – the thesis that it is impossible to resolve all disagreements about normative economics by reasoning or argument – seems to deny the claim that there are any pure value judgments, which, surely?, goes too far. However, his insistence that economists should not shy away from moral discourse as they usually do is well taken.

status of factual, descriptive is-statements is different in kind from that of normative, prescriptive ought-statements, and second, that the methodological judgments that are involved in reaching agreement on is-statements differ in important ways from those used to reach a consensus on normative value judgments. The claim that social science can be value-free in this sense does not deny that ideological bias creeps into the very selection of the questions that social scientists investigate, that the inferences that are drawn from factual evidence are sometimes influenced by values of a particular kind, nor even that the practical advice that social scientists offer is frequently loaded with concealed value judgments, the better to persuade rather than merely to advise. The argument does not rest in any way on the supposed impersonal detachment of individual social scientists but rather on the social aspects of scientific activity, on the critical tradition of a scientific community that constantly weeds out the competing biases of individual scientists. Max Weber made all this perfectly clear over fifty years ago when he laid down the doctrine of *Wertfreiheit* (freedom from value) and there is really no excuse for misunderstanding of his meaning at this late stage.[36]

Obviously, Weber did not deny that social science as it is actually practiced is shot through with political bias; it is precisely for that reason that he preached the *possibility* of value-free social science. Moreover, *Wertfreiheit* did not for him imply that the valuations of human beings cannot be rationally analyzed. On the contrary, he insisted that *Wertungsdiskussionen* (discussions on values) were not only possible but of the greatest utility. They could take the form of (1) examining the internal consistency of the value premises from which divergent normative judgments are derived; (2) deducing the implications of those value premises in the light of the practical circumstances to which they are applied; and (3) tracing the factual consequences of alternative ways of realizing normative judgments (Weber, 1949, pp. 20–1; and Runciman, 1968, pp. 564–5). It is clear, therefore, that Sen's distinction between basic and nonbasic, or pure and impure value judgments, inviting a rational discourse on the value judgments that people actually hold, is completely Weberian in spirit.[37]

Few of those who attack the doctrine of *Wertfreiheit* have the courage of their own convictions. After marshaling all the standard arguments against the *Wertfreiheit* camp, they usually end up by saying that we are all in favor of objective truth and "impartial science," although how there can be such things if "ises" are inextricably tied up with "oughts" is not made clear. If there are not at least some descriptive, factual assertions about social uniform-

[36] See Runciman (1972); Cahnman (1964); Hutchison (1964, pp. 55–6, 58–9); and Machlup (1978, pp. 349–53, 386–8).

[37] At this point, it is instructive to read Ward (1972, chaps. 13–15) on the legal system as a value-consensus-producing mechanism.

ities that are value-free (apart from the characterizing value judgments implied in methodological judgments), it seems difficult to escape the conclusion that we have the license to assert whatever we please.

The denial of objectivity in social science is more common in sociology than in economics. Indeed, economists are traditionally complacent about the is-ought dichotomy, believing apparently that it needs only to be stated clearly to be self-evident (see Klappholz, 1964). It has not been easy, therefore, to find examples of economists tripping over themselves by first denying that economics can be value free and then affirming that some economic opinions are nevertheless more valid than others. But perhaps a single, instructive example will suffice.

A sample of the attack on *Wertfreiheit*

Robert Heilbroner (1973) begins his attack by denying the doctrine of methodological monism: the difference between the social and the physical sciences is that human actions are subject to both latent willfulness and conscious purposiveness and without assumptions as to the meaning of those actions no conclusions can be drawn from social facts. "It is at this juncture," he declares, "that value judgement enters the picture." Enters how? One example that he gives is "an obvious political bias observable in the choice of research tasks arrogated to itself by the profession" (p. 137). In Nagel's sense, however, this is a methodological and not a value judgment.

Conceding that these points have been made many times before, Heilbroner goes on to say that he prefers to examine "a less well-explored aspect of the problem lodged in the interstices of economic analysis itself, rather than in the underlying premises of economic thought" (p. 138). Economists are not scientifically detached in assessing economic theories, he declares, giving a somewhat less than wholly convincing illustration: "the unwillingness of economists to admit the phenomenon of imperialism as a proper subject for economic investigation, or their dogged adherence to a benign theory of international trade in the face of disquieting evidence that trade has failed to benefit the poorer lands" (pp. 138–9). Economists, like all social investigators, he adds, cannot help being emotionally involved with the society of which they are members: "every social scientist approaches his task with a wish, consciously or unconsciously, to demonstrate the workability or unworkability of the social order he is investigating" (p. 139). In the face of "this extreme vulnerability to value judgments," economists cannot be impartial or disinterested: "thus, value judgments, partly of a sociological kind, partly with respect to behavior, have infused economics from its earliest statements to its latest and most sophisticated representations" (p. 141).

At this point, we must digress briefly to comment on Heilbroner's loose use of the term *value judgments* to include any and all untestable metaphysical propositions that color the vision of an economist, making up what Lakatos called the "hard core" of his theories. If I assert that capitalism has done and will do more for the workers than any other alternative economic system, I am not expressing a value judgment but rather revealing my hard-core vision. Fortunately, I will not be judged on my vision but instead on the theories that the vision generates in "the protective belt." Unless some such distinction is drawn, the thesis that social science is value-impregnated becomes trivial: value impregnation is now a universal feature of all theoretical propositions and hence not a special problem of the social sciences. To show that Heilbroner is not alone in simply bundling all propositions other than purely factual assertions together under the indiscriminate label of "value judgments," consider the widespread belief since Robbins that interpersonal comparisons of utility are value judgments that have no place in "scientific" welfare economics. But statements about interpersonal comparisons of utility are not value judgments but merely untestable statements of fact: they are either true or false, but to this day we know of no method of finding out which is the case (Klappholz, 1964, p. 105; Barrett and Hausman, 1991). Value judgments may be untestable but not all untestable statements are value judgments (Ng, 1972).

Similarly, there is a tendency to define value judgments as any persuasive statement expressed in emotive language, utterly ignoring the fact that purely descriptive assertions, or indeed definitions of terms, can be just as persuasive as value judgments proper (Klappholz, 1964, pp. 102–3). Adding to the confusion, there is the equally pronounced tendency to identify value judgments with ideological statements (see, e.g., Samuels, 1977). *Ideology* is one of those words that everyone defines for himself to express whatever ideas he does not like. According to the Marxist doctrine of ideology, which we can only vaguely discern in the unsystematic and sometimes contradictory assertions of Marx and Engels (Seliger, 1977), men do not possess truths but merely creeds that mask some set of material interests, and this is true of all men except for the members of the privileged proletariat class and their self-conscious spokesmen (such as Marx and Engels). But if ideology is "false consciousness," the distortion of truth, we cannot recognize ideology for what it is without some nonideological criterion for distinguishing truth from falsehood, in which case it might be more helpful to be told what that criterion is (Ryan, 1970, pp. 224–41; Barnes, 1974, chap. 5). Be that as it may, ideological statements may be usefully defined as value judgments parading as statements of facts (Bergmann, 1968), a definition which purges the Marxist theory of ideology of its tendentious overtones and rescues what is valuable in it. On this definition, value judgments themselves are not ideological statements, although all ideological statements are disguised value judgments.

With these clarifications, we return to Heilbroner's assault on the doctrine of value-free economics. "I do not believe that economists should aim at value-free analysis," he declares. Nevertheless, he adds: "I must state with all the force at my command that I do not believe that the economist has the right, in the name of value-advocacy, to tamper with data, to promote or promulgate policy recommendations without supporting evidence, or to pass off his value-laden conclusions as possessing 'scientific' validity" (pp. 133, 142). He candidly admits that this sounds "like a contradiction in terms" (p. 138), but he believes that the circle can be squared by following the methods of the natural sciences. These methods consist, he believes, in "the openness of the procedures by which science goes about its task, exposing itself to . . . painful self-scrutiny with regards to its premises, experiments, reasoning, conclusions." And "since economists perform few experiments that can be rerun in a laboratory, their results cannot be so easily falsified as those of the natural scientists, but they can be equally subject to scrutiny and criticism in the forum of expert opinion" (pp. 142–3).

These are sentiments we can only applaud. But why spend pages and pages persuading us that the whole of economics is absolutely contaminated with value judgments, the latter being indiscriminately defined to include untestable statements, emotively phrased propositions, and ideological assertions, only to conclude at the end that it is possible to salvage a body of positive economic findings that is apparently objective? And are we likely to accumulate such a body of objective findings sooner rather than later if we go around declaiming against the very possibility of value-free economics?

Solutions to the impossibility of *Wertfreiheit*

Heilbroner's attack on value-free economics pales into insignificance next to that of Gunnar Myrdal, who has made the concept of value-impregnated social science one of the major themes of his lifetime's work. But his solution for the difficulties that value impregnation creates is quite different from Heilbroner's, or indeed from that of any other critic of *Wertfreiheit*.[38]

Myrdal's solution is not to suppress value judgments in the interests of science, nor to make it clear at which point they necessarily enter the argument, thus dividing positive from normative economics, but rather to declare them boldly at the outset of the analysis. In this way, he supposes, our results are mysteriously imbued with true objectivity: "The only way in which we can strive for 'objectivity' in theoretical analysis is to expose the valuations into full light, make them conscious, specific and explicit, and permit them to determine the theoretical research . . . there is nothing wrong, *per se,* with

---

[38] See the sophisticated criticism of *Wertfreiheit* by Scott Gordon (1977), who, like Heilbroner, concludes that social science is hopelessly value-impregnated but, nevertheless, argues for objectivity as a criterion of performance in scientific work, at least as an unattainable ideal.

value-loaded concepts if they are clearly defined in terms of explicitly stated value premises" (Myrdal, 1970, pp. 55–6; see also Hutchison, 1964, pp. 44–5, 48–9, 69n, 109, 115n). Like most critics of *Wertfreiheit,* Myrdal too defines virtually everything that is not a statistic as a "value judgment" (pp. 73–6) but we must assume that he goes further in making the radical denial that there are any ethically neutral, factual assertions whatever in economics. Because if I can assert that the import elasticity of demand for automobiles in Britain in, say, 1979 is 1.3 and this number is either true or false regardless of my wishes or yours, I have produced at least one proposition in positive economics whose objectivity does not depend on declaring my values.

According to Myrdal, it is impossible to distinguish positive from normative economics and to pretend to do so can only involve self-deception. But is it really vain to try to separate the empirical testing of economic hypotheses without overt recourse to our hopes and wishes, if only as an ideal at which to aim, from the expression of approval or disapproval of certain states of the world? It may be granted that there is no absolutely watertight distinction between positive and normative economics, as there is no absolutely watertight distinction between means and ends; but to declare the ubiquity and inevitability of value judgments, without examining precisely how and at what point they enter a piece of economic reasoning, is well calculated to usher in a style of relativism in which all economic opinions are simply a matter of personal choice.[39] The hour of the therapeutic influence of the positive-normative distinction, forcing economists to explicate their value judgments, is not yet past. "The normative-positive distinction," as Hutchison (1964, p. 191) has rightly observed, "*should* be clearly maintained as far as it *can* be – even at the cost, sometimes, of effective persuasion." Here is yet another Popperian methodological norm to add to our previous list (see Chapter 1 above).

A brief historical sketch

We have now cleared most of the ground for approaching the heart of the matter: how is it that certain economic propositions, like the famous marginal equivalences of Pareto optimality, appear in subtly different guises in both positive and normative economics?

A brief historical sketch of the positive-normative distinction will help to set the stage for an analysis of this question. The distinction first makes its appearance in the writings of Senior and the younger Mill in the form of a distinction between the "science" and the "art" of political economy. In passing from the science to the art, they realized that extrascientific, ethical premises necessarily make their appearance, and they also appreciated that

[39] See Lesnoff (1974, pp. 156–8). Hutchison (1964, chap. 2) on "The Sources and Roles of Value Judgments and Bias in Economics" says almost all that can be said on the subject.

noneconomic elements borrowed from other social sciences were required in addition to value judgments to give meaningful advice on practical problems (Hutchison, 1964, pp. 29–31). In short, they held the now surprising view that the economist cannot advise *qua* economist, not even if the science of economics is supplemented by appropriate value judgments, and Senior even went so far at one point in his life as to deny that economists should ever give advice (Bowley, 1949, pp. 49–55; Hutchison, 1964, p. 32; O'Brien, 1975, pp. 55–6).

Cairnes followed in Senior's and Mill's footsteps, expressing himself, as was his wont, more forcibly than ever they did: "Economic science has no more connection with our present industrial system than the science of mechanics has with our present system of railways" (Cairnes, 1965, p. 38). John Neville Keynes distinguished usefully, not just between a positive science and a normative art, as his forebears had done, but between (1) a "positive science," (2) a "normative or regulative science," and (3) an "art," that is, a system of rules for the attainment of given ends: "The object of a positive science is the establishment of *uniformities,* of a normative science the determination of *ideals,* and of an art the formulation of *precepts*" (Keynes, 1955, p. 35). The notion of a "normative science" as a bridge between the "positive science" and the "art" of political economy comes very close, as we shall see, to the aspiration of modern welfare economics.

But Neville Keynes's trichotomous classification did not win acceptance, and other English economists of the period simply echoed the old positive-normative distinction without adding anything new to it (Hutchison, 1964, pp. 32–41; Smyth, 1962). On the continent, however, both Walras and Pareto drew the dividing line, not between positive and normative economics, but between pure and applied economics (Hutchison, 1964, pp. 41–3); and for Pareto, if not for Walras, pure economics included only positive economics and excluded both what Neville Keynes called the "normative or regulative science" and the "art" of economics.[40] Pareto asserted, in his now famous statement of the conditions for optimality, that perfect competition would automatically maximize *collective ophelimity* (he despised the term *utility* for its overtones of cardinality) in the sense that no reallocation of resources could make anyone better off without at least making one person worse off. As far as he was concerned, this was a proposition of pure economics, which was completely independent of any ethical value judgments. Indeed, what we now call *Pareto optimality* was for him simply a definition of maximum collective ophelimity; but collective ophelimity was only a subset of a more general

---

[40] Tarascio (1966, pp. 46–50, 127–36) contends that Pareto, like Weber, argued, not for a rigid divorce between pure and applied studies, but only for the subjective minimization of normative judgments in the social sciences. But this is not how I read Pareto.

social ophelimity that belonged to the province of sociology, and Pareto was always insistent that pure economics by itself can solve no practical problems (Tarascio, 1966, p. 8).

For situations other than competitive equilibrium, Pareto offered no guidance on changes that might increase or reduce collective ophelimity. In the 1930s, John Hicks and then Nicholas Kaldor provided *compensation tests* by defining an improvement in economic welfare as any change that *might* make someone better off in his own terms without making anyone else worse off. To recommend that such a potential Pareto improvement (PPI) should actually be paid to compensate a victim of an economic change was of course to make a value judgment, but no value judgment whatsoever was involved if the economist merely described a change as a PPI. On this slender foundation, resting indeed on the subtle distinction between a possible improvement and a desirable one, was reared the ''new'' value-free welfare economics, powerfully assisted by the Robbinsian thesis that the arch villain of value judgments was that of making cardinal comparisons between the utility of different parties.[41]

Pareto optimality, like the set of equilibrium prices generated by a regime of perfect competition, is only defined with reference to a given initial distribution of resources among the members of society, and what is true of Pareto optimality is also true of PPI. This restriction is sometimes expressed by saying that the Pareto rule provides only a partial ordering of states of the economy, lacking as it does a criterion for choosing among the infinite potential distributions of resource endowments. The new value-free welfare economics likewise took the prevailing distribution of factor services as given, thus invoking no value judgment so long as compensation payments are not actually recommended. It was Bergson's 1938 paper on the *social welfare function,* given wider prominence by Samuelson in his *Foundations,* which first planted the idea that society, expressing itself through its political representatives, does in fact compare the utilities of different individuals; these comparisons are, so to speak, recorded in a social welfare function that aggregates the preferences of individuals in a social ranking of states of the economy. Once in possession of such a function, the economist might assess a given change in policy as a PPI, after which the social welfare function may be consulted to determine whether compensation payments should actually be made. By now it was difficult to resist the conclusion that welfare economics is avowedly and unashamedly normative, a point of view which may be said to be the dominant orthodox view (see Hennipman, 1976, pp. 40–1).

However, there have always been those who have gone back to Pareto

---

[41] For a brief survey of the new welfare economics, see Blaug (1980, pp. 585–608, 611–13) and the references cited there.

himself in regarding Paretian welfare economics as a branch of positive economic theory, as neutral and objective as any other part. It is worth examining this argument with some care.

Positive Paretian welfare economics

The heretical view that Paretian welfare economics does not depend upon a foundation of value judgments was defended with great vigor by Archibald (1959b). His argument is basically a simple one: Paretian welfare economics investigates the efficiency of alternative arrangements for satisfying *given* wants in the light of the choices that individuals themselves make in their own interests; thus, no evaluation of these wants is required for the Paretian theorems (pp. 320–1). An individual's preference map is identical with his welfare map, and to say that his welfare is higher in state *B* than in state *A* is simply to say that he would choose *B* rather than *A* were he free and able to do so. Paretian welfare economics simply asks: under what arrangements will this individual's choice be expanded from *A* to *B* without a contraction in someone else's choices, or alternatively expressed, under what arrangements will a PPI materialize? Value judgments only come into the picture when the crucial step to prescription is taken (p. 327).[42] Provided we do not prescribe, our arguments do not rest at any point on approval or disapproval and are hence subject to empirical refutation like all other propositions in positive economics. Even "the familiar Paretian proposition, such that: if a perfect market is in equilibrium, there is no change which permits an expansion of choice of any consumer(s) without contracting the choice of at least one other consumer" is empirically falsifiable, at least if stated in terms of a falsifiable demand theory (p. 325).

Archibald sums up thus: "The theorems of welfare economics are theorems in positive economics; they are concerned with the relationship between *given* ends and available means . . . We have a single dichotomy in economics, between positive enquiries into how something may be done, and normative recommendations that it should be done" (pp. 320–1).

Hennipman (1976) is another writer who espouses the technical, objective interpretation of Pareto optimality: "Propositions like those that, under certain assumptions, perfect competition is a sufficient condition of Pareto optimality, and that monopoly, tariffs and externalities cause a welfare loss are positive statements, which are true or false, independently of ethical or ideo-

---

[42] Archibald, therefore, avoids the mistake that Harrod (1950, pp. 389–90) made when he expressed a similar line of argument: "If an individual prefers a commodity or service X to Y, it is economically better that he should have it. . . . The economic good is thus the preferred. . . . In appraising institutions and practices and making recommendations, the economist has this criterion in mind; it constitutes his standard of good and bad."

logical beliefs'' (p. 47). Pareto optimality rests on three fundamental postulates: (1) consumer sovereignty – only self-chosen preferences count as individual preferences or yardsticks of individual welfare (in popular parlance: an individual is the best judge of his welfare); (2) nonpaternalism – social welfare comprises the welfare of every individual member of society (except children and lunatics) and nothing else but the individual members of society; and (3) unanimity – only unanimous reallocations of resources count as improvements in social welfare. On the basis of these three postulates, it is possible to demonstrate what Samuelson has colorfully labeled the *invisible hand theorem,* namely, the equivalence between an equilibrium in a perfectly competitive economy and the conditions for a Pareto optimum.

Hennipman agrees that the three postulates of Paretian theory are usually interpreted as value judgments, from which it follows that Pareto optimality is a normative concept (p. 51). But like Archibald, he argues that the first postulate may be interpreted in a positive sense as saying that individual preferences are taken as given, without implying that everyone is actually the best judge of what is good for him or her. Similarly, the second postulate may be read as denying the existence of independent community interests (such as the interest of the "State") and that is a matter of fact and not a matter of liking or disliking: "it is an arithmetic truism that 'every individual counts' when the economic welfare of the members of society is the subject of inquiry" (p. 53). Finally, the third postulate, which Hennipman does not discuss, is simply a redefinition of Pareto optimality in terms of the meaning that Pareto himself gave to the concept; hence, it raises no issues that are not included in the first two.

For Hennipman, as for Archibald, the quintessential purpose of normative economics is to make policy recommendations, and the contribution of Pareto optimality in that context is at best a modest one: it provides only a partial ranking of alternative social states; it is static and ignores the welfare of future generations except insofar as they are taken into account by individuals in the present generation; and it disregards all collective goals that are not somehow the sum of individual goals. Nevertheless, Paretian theory, Hennipman insists, also has a role to play in positive economics in spelling out the implications of economic behavior. Thus, the statement that monopoly, tariffs, and externalities bring about welfare losses is not to be construed, he argues, as a recommendation to take action to eliminate them; in short, to demonstrate the existence of a PPI is one thing and to call for action to do something about it is another (pp. 54–5).

All that is needed to reverse the objective interpretation of Pareto optimality is to introduce the value judgment that it would be desirable to eliminate the "inefficiency" implied by the existence of a PPI. "In this minute variation," Hennipman remarks, "lies the core of the controversy" (p. 58), a sentence that ought to be underlined. To sum up his argument: if we stick to the purely neutral interpretation of Pareto optimality, the Pareto criterion lays down no policy prescriptions; it merely asserts that, when a particular economic configuration creates the opportunities to reap a PPI, there are goods and services available for distribution that can make someone better off without making anyone else worse off – there is in this case no such thing as a free lunch; but it denies that such a distribution of extras is desirable and in cases where someone is made worse off as a result of it, it cannot recommend compensation payments to the losers.

The invisible hand theorem

What are we to make of this somewhat strained argument that the concept of Pareto optimality, so patently shot through with value judgments, may nevertheless be given a perfectly objective, value-free interpretation? On purely logical grounds, the Archibald–Hennipman argument is impeccable: taking individual preferences for granted and treating social choice as being made up entirely of individual choices are both methodological judgments, not value judgments. Even so, to force children to attend school whether they like it or not, to outlaw the sale of drugs but to permit the sale of alcohol, and to prohibit the sale of human organs is to compromise consumer sovereignty by a whole series of value judgments. Similarly, the insistence that the rain forests of Brazil must be preserved against the declared interests of timber producers and consumers is yet to commit oneself to another value judgment, qualifying the nonpaternalism implied by the Pareto criterion. Even waiving these points and accepting the Archibald–Hennipman thesis so far as it goes, it requires simply superhuman detachment not to slip in the "simple" assumption that the elimination of a PPI is desirable, particularly if we go beyond Pareto himself by dropping the third unanimity postulate, thereby allowing for potential compensation payments to the victims of an economic change. Welfare economics is, after all, that branch of economics concerned with the ethical criteria by which we decide that one economic state of the world is more desirable than another, and to speak of *positive* welfare economics is literally to revel in paradoxical language. No argument should be knocked down merely because it abuses linguistic conventions, but the case for operating with two interpretations of Pareto optimality, one of which is value-free and wholly within positive economics and the other of which is value-laden and therefore part of normative economics, does seem to be splitting hairs.

The bedrock of the argument is the meaning of the invisible hand theorem. It is true that the market mechanism allows individuals to be the best judge of their own interests, positively encourages them to act independently of others ("no *tu*-ism" as Wicksteed used to say), produces a collective result in which only individual preferences count as arguments in the social welfare function, and grinds out a functional and personal distribution of income that is not necessarily in conformity with ethical notions of distributive justice. We need only add an appropriate underlying technology (excluding increasing returns to scale) and some conditions about information and transaction costs (eliminating such externalities as may arise as well as "public goods") to arrive at an equilibrium under perfect competition that is Pareto-optimal. This is the invisible hand theorem, and to state it or to prove it appears to involve only the purely objective outcome of market processes. Thus, the invisible hand theorem seems to be a theorem of positive economics, in which case Archibald and Hennipman win the argument hands down.

If the invisible hand theorem is a theorem of positive economics, it is empirically falsifiable because positive economics is that branch of economics that contains all the falsifiable hypotheses of economics. But the invisible hand theorem is not falsifiable. Archibald, as we have seen, claims that it is, although he ingenuously adds that it is so only in terms of "a refutable theory of demand," meaning one which can rule out the existence of positively sloped demand curves. But as we shall show (see Chapter 6 below), the received theory of demand predicts positively inclined demand curves as happily as negatively inclined ones. Thus, we cannot preclude the possibility that a perfectly competitive equilibrium would leave at least one consumer facing a positively inclined demand curve for at least one *Giffen good* in consequence of which there exists a PPI: a reduction in the price of the Giffen good expands his choices, and since he now buys less rather than more of the Giffen good, it releases resources to expand rather than to contract the choices available to other consumers of normal goods. Thus, there does exist a reallocation of resources that would make at least one consumer better off without making anyone else worse off, which contradicts the invisible hand theorem. Since the invisible hand theorem is not falsifiable, it does not belong to positive economics but to normative economics.

The concept of Pareto optimality and the associated concept of PPIs *should* not be confused with theorems of positive economics. If this implies that economists must give up the notion that there are purely technical, value-free efficiency arguments for certain economic changes, and indeed that the very terms "efficient" and "inefficient" are terms of normative and not positive economics, so much the better: immense confusion has been sown by the pretense that we can pronounce "scientifically" on matters of "efficiency" without committing ourselves to any value judgments.

The dictatorship of Paretian welfare economics

Having placed Paretian welfare economics firmly within the camp of normative economics, I cannot resist a few comments on the more curious features of modern welfare economics, although the subject is strictly speaking a digression from our main theme. The three postulates of Paretian welfare economics (consumer sovereignty, nonpaternalism, and unanimity) are frequently described as innocuous because they command either universal or almost universal assent. The belief that almost everyone accepts the Paretian postulates is sometimes interpreted to mean that Paretian welfare economics is value-free. This is still another nonsense definition of value judgments: value judgments are those ethical prescriptions that are controversial.

We will lose no time criticizing this definition but it is worth remarking that the Paretian postulates by no means command universal assent. It certainly cannot be argued that absolutely everybody would regard a PPI as unequivocally desirable. It is not only those on the left of the political spectrum who would reject postulate (1) on individual welfare and particularly postulate (2) on social welfare. Even classical liberals have recently rebelled against what they call "the dictatorship of Paretian welfare economics," which sanctions a wide range of state interventions to achieve Pareto optimality, thus repairing the defects of the invisible hand by the extremely visible hand of government. Liberals, argue Rowley and Peacock (1975), accept a trade-off between freedom and individualism; they are willing to brook infringement of individual liberty, but only if the action secures greater freedom for others; liberalism is essentially concerned with the maintenance and extension of negative freedom, in the sense of denying coercion of some individuals by others, and this may conflict with consumer sovereignty, Paretian postulate (1). At any rate, the value premises that underlie the philosophy of classical liberalism cannot be reduced to the three postulates of Paretian welfare economics. Without further exploring Rowley and Peacock's argument, it serves to vindicate the view that there is much less acceptance of the Paretian value judgments than economists like to think. Actually, economists are rather poor at assessing other people's values: inasmuch as they have deliberately eschewed *Wertungsdiskussionen*, they have largely denied themselves the analysis of value judgments as a fruitful area of research. And the absurd thesis that uncontroversial value judgments are not value judgments at all has not helped matters.

The economist as a technocrat

Even those who reject the notion of Paretian welfare economics as positive economics may nevertheless believe that there is much that the economist *qua* economist can usefully say on questions of public policy without invoking value judgments. The case is usually made in terms of the distinction between means and ends, between instruments and objectives, which immediately reminds us of Robbins's famous definition of economics as the science that studies the allocation of scarce means among given but competing ends. Let governments decide their "objective function" defined in terms of the multiple ends or goals of economic activity; it is the task of economists to delineate the "possibility function," the costs and benefits of alternative allocations of scarce means; provided the means-ends distinction is rigidly maintained, economic advice to governments is, or rather can be, value-free.[43] Thus runs the textbook message on the role of the economist as a technocratic policy adviser.

In one sense, this is nothing but the is–ought, facts–values, positive–normative dichotomy all over again, and as such it is subject to the same difficulties that these distinctions give rise to. Just as we earlier advocated the divorce between positive and normative economics as a clarifying and therapeutic methodological convention, so we might similarly commend the textbook picture of the economic consultant to governments, keeping his value judgments scrupulously out of sight, as an ideal at which to aim rather than a description of what actually takes place. This was indeed Robbins's intent when he warned the profession that economists *qua* economists cannot legitimately recommend a particular course of public action.

There are problems about this party line, however, that reach beyond the difficulties of the positive-normative distinction. The notion is that the economist displays the menu of alternative possibilities, and then *the* decision maker chooses from that menu in the light of his preference function. Unfortunately, economic advice is typically sought, not just to elucidate the possibility function, but also the preference function. The decision maker seeks advice on both ends and means. How indeed is that economist supposed to discover the decision maker's preference function among objectives without imposing his own? Asking him will usually produce a blank stare: if the decision maker is a politician, he is committed first of all to maximizing electoral support and that is best secured by blurring objectives, not by revealing them. Nor can the economist deduce the politician's preference function by studying his past behavior: he may be inconsistent between one decision and another; he may have altered his preference function over time as a result of learning-by-doing; besides, circumstances themselves are changing and this itself makes inference difficult. Furthermore, the concept of a single decision maker is, in any case, a convenient fiction; typically, decision making in respect of public policy is carried out by teams, whose members may well disagree about ends; in consequence, successive policies may express conflicting ends, depending on which member of the team has the upper hand at

---

[43] A single reference will suffice to document this traditional argument. Lange (1967, p. 8), after pointing out that it is necessary to reach an interpersonal agreement on the objectives of economic policy, continues with "once the objectives are stated and certain assumptions are made about empirical conditions, the rules of 'ideal' use of resources are derived by the rules of logic and verified by the rules of verification. This procedure is interpersonally objective."

any moment of time. But if the economist cannot discover the preference function that underlies policy decisions, neither can be evaluate past decisions nor improve future ones.

Further reflections along these lines begin to suggest that there is indeed something wrong with the purist view à la Robbins that draws a rigid distinction between the means and ends of public policy: it supposes that decision makers first choose their goals and then hunt about for policies to achieve them. In point of fact, any decision maker starts with on-going activities and gradually begins to define his objective in the light of his experience with policies. In other words, decision makers do not try to get what they want; rather they learn to want by appraising what they get. Means and ends are indissolubly related, and evaluation of past decisions, or technical advice about future decisions, searches in vain for a social preference function that is not there.

This view of decision making, so different from the classic textbook view, has been forcefully argued in recent years by a number of economists and political scientists. A single reference is Braybrooke and Lindblom, *A Strategy of Decision,* with the revealing subtitle, *Policy Evaluation as a Social Process.*[44] Braybrooke and Lindblom (1963) reject all comprehensive approaches to decision making, purporting to lay down global rules for arriving at optimal decisions, and instead advocate what they call *disjointed incrementalism:* it is disjointed because decision making, far from being swallowed whole, is repeatedly attacked in bits and pieces; it is incremental because it considers only a limited range of policies that differ only incrementally from existing ones; disjointed incrementalism does not merely adjust means to ends but explores the ends while applying the means, in effect choosing means and ends simultaneously.

It is perfectly clear that Braybrooke and Lindblom have achieved a much more realistic view of the role of economic advice to decision makers. Obviously, decision making, particularly public decision making, never achieves more than a third-best solution, if only because the time required to collect adequate information to secure an improvement in ''fine tuning'' is the ultimate scarce resource. But can we not retain the textbook picture of value-free, technical economic advice to governments as an ideal type, while admitting and even emphasizing that economic advice in the real world will never closely correspond to the ideal? But here is an ideal type, which, if Braybrooke and Lindblom are right, can never be approximated in reality, and hence this very model of the advisory function contributes to systematic

---

[44] See also Wildavsky (1964, particularly chap. 5); Churchman (1968, pp. 11–12), and Dror (1968, 1971), the last of which contains a not altogether convincing critique of Braybrooke and Lindblom. Lindblom (1965, 1968) has since continued the argument further.

self-deception among economists. We have seen this brand of self-deception at work in encouraging the view that there is a promising field of *positive* Paretian welfare economics, which is either entirely free of value judgments or else rests on innocuous value judgments that allegedly command universal assent.

Economic advice must ultimately rest on the falsifiable hypotheses of positive economics, on the demonstration that the empirical relationships between economic variables are this and not that.[45] The moment economists go beyond such demonstrations, they have entered the wholly different realm of normative economics, where their skills, such as they are, are largely underdeveloped because of a long-standing tradition in modern economics to deny both the value aspects of economic beliefs and the realities of policy making. The scope of positive economics is smaller and that of normative economics larger than is frequently made out by economists.

Biases in assessing empirical evidence

All scientific hypotheses have philosophical, social and even political undertones, which may prejudice scientists in evaluating the evidence for and against a particular hypothesis (one need only think of the scientific reactions to Darwin's theory of natural selection and Einstein's relativity theory). Ideological biases and special pleading of all kinds are a universal feature of scientific work for which the only remedy is the public criticism of other scientists relying on the shared professional standards of the subject. So far, therefore, there is nothing to choose between economics and any other scientific discipline.

However, there are special biases to which economists are prone that have no parallel in the physical sciences. A potent source of these special biases lies in the intimate association between certain propositions in positive economics and something very like those same propositions in normative economics. "At least from the time of the physiocrats and Adam Smith," Samuelson (1948, p. 203) once observed, "there has never been absent from the main body of economic literature the feeling that in some sense perfect competition represented an optimal situation." The modern invisible hand theo-

---

[45] Thus, Lowe (1977) argues at great length that positive economics has now lost whatever powers of prediction it once had because the modern industrial system is too unstable to permit its behavior to be accurately predicted; he therefore proposes a method of "instrumental inference" as the basis of a new science of political economics in which certain macroeconomic goals are first laid down by politicians and then economists devote their efforts to studying the private incentives that are required to keep the economic system on the path that will attain these goals. But he never explains how an economic advisor, deprived of positive economics, is supposed to throw light on the relationship between private incentives and individual action. For a whole volume devoted to criticizing Lowe's proposal, see Heilbroner (1969).

rem provides rigorous support for that feeling: given certain conditions, every long-run, perfectly competitive equilibrium yields a Pareto-optimal allocation of resources, and every Pareto-optimal allocation of resources is attainable via a long-run, perfectly competitive equilibrium. Of course, this leaves out the justice of the underlying distribution of endowments in competitive equilibrium – and much besides. Nevertheless, every economist feels in his bones that the invisible hand theorem is not just an abstract proof of hypothetical significance in the stratosphere of ideas. Somehow, it seems just as relevant to socialism as to capitalism, coming close indeed to providing a universal justification for the price mechanism as a rationing device in literally any economy. If this is not what economics is ultimately about, why bother with it?

It is hardly surprising, therefore, that economists fight tooth and nail when faced with an empirical refutation of a proposition in positive economics involving the assumption of perfect competition. For what is threatened is not just that particular proposition but the entire conception of economic "efficiency" that gives *raison d'être* to the subject of economics. No wonder then that intellectual tenacity in the face of empirical refutations, the tendency to protect falsified theories by ad hoc immunizing stratagems (see Chapter 1), has loomed and continues to loom so large in the history of economics.

Heilbroner, as we have seen, accused economists of lacking detachment in the assessment of empirical evidence. But what scientist is ever so detached? It is simply untrue that the study of the universe evokes no emotions, whereas the study of society necessarily does. Religion is the oldest and deepest source of ideological preconceptions, and science advances by rolling back the answers of religion. Besides, when natural scientists express views on such policy issues as biological warfare, global warming, nuclear energy, sterilization, vivisection, etcetera, they are just as likely as anyone else to mix facts and values and to misrepresent the actual state of the evidence. It is not in these terms that we can distinguish between physics and economics.

The limitations of economics as an empirical science derive from other sources. They stem principally from the fact that the theorems of welfare economics are forever spilling over from normative economics into the appraisal of evidence in positive economics. Economists tend to polarize into "planners" or "free marketeers," and they are inclined to read the empirical evidence for and against particular economic hypotheses in the light of these polarized attitudes (Hutchison, 1964, pp. 63, 73–82).[46] The true state of af-

---

[46] As Krupp (1966, p. 51) has aptly observed: "The degree of confirmation of an entire theory is highly intertwined with value judgements which reflect, among other things, the selection of its constituent hypotheses. It is not coincidental, therefore, that the advocates of the theories of competitive price will simultaneously defend diminishing returns to scale, a low measure of economic concentration, the demand-pull explanation of inflation, a high consumption function, the effectiveness of monetary policies

fairs is almost the opposite of what Friedman (1953, p. 6) makes it out to be when he ventures the opinion that "different predictions about the importance of so-called 'economies of scale' account very largely for divergent views about the desirability or necessity of detailed government regulation of industry and even of socialism rather than private enterprises."

Was there ever an economist who came to believe in either socialism or capitalism because of the compelling empirical evidence about economies of scale? For that matter, it is probably not economic arguments at all that turn economists into planners or free marketeers. We can look high and low in the body of received economic doctrine without so much as encountering a well-formulated attack on, or justification for, private ownership of the means of production. There are economic arguments for private ownership having to do with the built-in tendency towards technical dynamism in a regime of atomistic competition but these must be set against a similarly built-in tendency towards recurrent slumps, not to mention inequalities in the size distribution of personal income. The fundamental link between economic freedom and political freedom, however, is rarely discussed, possibly because mainstream economists are embarrassed to admit that what really lies behind their preference for private over public ownership of industry is a definite piece of reasoning in political theory.[47] Joan Robinson (1962, pp. 138–9) hits the nail on the head in a marvelously succinct passage:

It is possible to defend our economic system on the ground that, patched up with Keynesian correctives, it is, as he put it, the "best in sight". Or at any rate that it is not too bad, and that change is painful. In short, that our system is the best system that we have got. Or it is possible to take the tough-minded line that Schumpeter derived from Marx. The system is cruel, unjust, turbulent, but it does deliver the goods, and, damn it all, it's the goods that you want. Or, conceding its defects, to defend it on political grounds – that democracy as we know it could not have grown up under any other system and cannot survive without it. What is not possible, at this time of day, is to defend it, in the neoclassical style, as a delicate self-regulating mechanism, that has only to be left to itself to produce the greatest satisfaction for all.

I fancy that, wording apart, the four defenses Robinson offers do cover the standard view and that the third of them outweighs all the others for those who "defend our economic system."

Even among the majority of economists who believe in capitalism, "free

on full employment, the insignificance of externalities, and the general pervasiveness of substitution rather than complementarity as a basic relation of the economic system."

[47] But not everyone is embarrassed, for example, Hayek (1960), Friedman (1962), and Machlup (1978, p. 126). Also, Lipsey (1989, p. 390) frankly discusses the political appeal of the invisible hand theorem.

marketeers'' of various kinds, there are profound differences of opinion on the degree to which income inequalities in our society are remediable by ordinary economic policies. For example, in a survey of the views of academic, business, and government economists in the United Kingdom, compared to politicians and journalists, Samuel Brittan (1973) showed that economists as a community tend to have distinctive views on public policy that set them apart from others in any public discussion: they have an appreciation of the functions of the price mechanism as a method of allocating resources in accordance with relative scarcities and the revealed preferences of consumers that is lacking among noneconomists. Nevertheless, whether a particular economist is willing to subscribe to the ''liberal economic orthodoxy'' frequently depended on whether ''he was prepared to treat questions of the allocation of resources on their own merits, in the belief that any major undesired effect on the distribution of income could be offset, or more than offset, by the tax and social security system'' (p. 23; see also Kearl, and others, 1979; Frey, and others, 1984; and Ricketts and Shoesmith, 1990). There is little ground, therefore, for Friedman's (1953, p. 5) optimistic view that all of us are more divided about the predicted effects of policy actions by governments than about questions of fundamental values.

Earlier, we argued that few people hold pure value judgments and that, despite Hume's guillotine, the realm of ''ises'' continually invades the realm of ''oughts.'' but now we have argued that is-statements are constantly being assessed in the light of ought-statements. This is no paradox. The mutual interplay of facts and values is precisely the fuel that fires scientific work, no less in the social than in the physical sciences. Scientific progress comes only when we strive to maximize the role of facts and minimize the role of values. If economics is to progress, economists must give absolute priority to the task of producing and testing falsifiable economic theories. In the final analysis, it is only the mechanism of hypothesis testing that can be relied on to weed out political and social prejudices at a rate faster than the one at which they are being continually recreated by new circumstances. The Mecca of economics is not, as Marshall thought, biology, or any other branch of science. The Mecca of economics is the method of science itself.

PART III

A methodological appraisal of the neoclassical research program

6

The theory of consumer behavior

Introduction

We are now ready to put our knowledge of methodology to practical use in the appraisal of economic theories. In so doing, we must always begin by stating what Popper calls the "problem-situation" to which the theory is supposed to be a solution. This obvious point is all too frequently neglected. Next, we must decide what it is that the theory actually predicts. This too is an obvious point and yet, as we shall see, it may be a very difficult question to answer. But since we have come so far, we must attempt to assess the evidence bearing upon the theory's predictions without, however, neglecting the nature of the "explanation" that underlies these predictions. Does the theory provide a causal mechanism that takes us systematically from the actions of economic agents and the operations of economic institutions to the outcomes predicted by the theory?

None of these questions can be fruitfully discussed if all that is available to us is a single theory. Scientific theories can only be meaningfully assessed in terms of competing hypotheses for the simple reason that methodology provides no absolute standards to which all theories must conform: what it does provide are criteria in terms of which theories may be ranked as more or less promising. Thus, the appraisal of economic theories is essentially a matter of asking: which of all the competing theories is the one best fitted to survive?

What follows constitutes a series of case studies, each of which illustrates one or more methodological lessons. Sometimes the lesson is that the empirical content of a theory has been exaggerated or completely misunderstood; sometimes it is to show why there are good reasons for retaining a theory despite the fact that it has been frequently refuted; and sometimes it is simply to demonstrate that leading economists with well-defined methodological views are nevertheless loath to follow their own precepts. These case studies are not selected at random: each constitutes a satellite research program within a larger

137

core program that is frequently called *neoclassical economics,* although "mainstream, orthodox economics" would be a better label. This is not to say that we deal exhaustively with every aspect of the neoclassical research program – it would take a whole series of books to do justice to that subject. All that we can manage to do here is to suggest the flavor of such a comprehensive appraisal of neoclassical economics, to trace some of the interconnections between different but complementary subprograms, and to show how every part of the larger core program draws strength from the other parts on the frequently unchecked assumption that the other parts are highly corroborated.

Throughout the following chapters that make up Part III of the book, we will keep asking ourselves: what indeed is the ultimate "hard core" of the neoclassical research program; that is, what is it that makes an analysis of, say, crime or the supply of money a piece of neoclassical economics rather than Marxist, radical, institutional, or what-have-you economics? Furthermore, in what circumstances should we contemplate an alternative research program with a different "hard core" and a different set of positive and negative "heuristics," particularly when that alternative research program is addressed to a different range of questions and is associated with different methodological standards? The answers to these momentous questions will emerge gradually in the course of Part III. We will turn to them explicitly in the final chapter of Part IV.

Is the law of demand a law?

The history of economics abounds in economics laws proclaimed with capital letters: Gresham's Law, Say's Law, Engel's Law, the Law of Demand and Supply, the Law of Diminishing Returns, the Law of Diminishing Marginal Utility, etcetera. The term *law,* however, has gradually acquired a somewhat old-fashioned ring and economists now prefer to present their most cherished general statements as "theorems" rather than "laws." At any rate, if by laws we mean well-corroborated, universal relations between events or classes of events deduced from independently tested initial conditions, few modern economists would claim that economics has so far produced more than one or two laws.[1] But such commendable methodological modesty may

---

[1] Samuelson (1966, p. 1539) remarks that years of experience have taught him "how treacherous are economic 'laws' in economic life: e.g. Bowley's Law of constant relative wage share; Long's Law of constant population participation in the labor force: Pareto's Law of unchangeable inequality of incomes; Denison's Law of constant private saving ratio; Colin Clark's Law of a 25 per cent ceiling on government expenditure and taxation; Modigliani's Law of constant wealth–income ratio; Marx's Law of the falling rate of real wage and/or the falling rate of profit; Everybody's Law of a constant capital–output ratio. If these be Laws Mother Nature is a criminal by nature" (see also Hutchison, 1964, pp. 94–5).

be carried too far. After all, there is little agreement among philosophers of science about the necessary and sufficient conditions that a scientific statement must satisfy to qualify it as a law of science, and for that matter, there are various kinds of laws that play different roles in different types of scientific theories (see Chapter 1 above; also Rosenberg, 1976, chaps. 4–6). Thus, whatever are the linguistic habits of economists, it is difficult to deny the famous law of demand the status of a scientific law.

It is not easy to decide, however, whether the law of demand is a "deterministic law," a "statistical law," or a "causal law." If the law of demand refers to individuals, asserting that the quantity demanded of any commodity by a consumer will always vary inversely with its money price, the claim that it expresses an invariable concomitance of events can be dismissed out of hand: the law will be contradicted if so much as one consumer judges the quality of the commodity in question by its price. But if it refers to the market conduct of a group of consumers of a homogeneous commodity, it is probably true to say that it was, at least until the time of Marshall, regarded as a deterministic law, that is, an empirical regularity that simply admitted of no exceptions. Since Marshall, however, it has in fact been regarded as a statistical law of market behavior, having a probability of occurrence that is close to, but by no means equal to, unity. Every first-year student of economics learns that, subject to conditions regarding tastes, expectations, incomes, and other prices, a rise in the price of a good is followed by a fall in the quantity demanded unless, however, the good in question is either a Giffen or a snob good; in short, market demand curves may be negatively or positively inclined. Nevertheless, there is overwhelming empirical evidence, as we shall see, that most market demand curves are negatively inclined: the "law of downward-sloping demand," as Samuelson (1976, p. 61) calls it, is in fact one of the best-corroborated statistical "laws" of economics.

On the other hand, the law of demand may also be construed as a "causal law," that is, one which explains human actions in terms of the reasons, desires, and beliefs of "rational" human agents, which form the causal mechanism that leads from a decline in price to an increase in quantity demanded (Rosenberg, 1976, pp. 53–5, 73–7, 108–21). Be that as it may, economists do not assert that human agents are "rational" by definition and to that extent the law of demand remains a lawlike empirically refutable statement about economic responses to changing prices.

Moreover, the law of demand is no simple inductive generalization from a set of atheoretical observations. On the contrary, it is alleged to be a logical deduction from what must be the nearest thing in economics to a completely axiomatized theory, the modern static theory of consumer behavior. The theory has a long and complex history that has been frequently told (see Blaug, 1980, pp. 328–55, 368–70), proceeding from the introspective cardinalism of Jevons, Menger, Walras, and Marshall to the introspective ordinalism of Slutsky, Allen, and Hicks, to the behaviorist ordinalism of Samuelson's revealed preference theory, to the behaviorist cardinalism of the Neumann–Morgenstern theory of expected utility, to Lancaster's theory of commodity characteristics, not to mention more recent stochastic theories of consumers' behavior. All along, its purpose was to somehow justify the notion of a negatively inclined demand curve from fundamental and compelling axioms of individual behavior. After all, neither individual nor market demand curves are directly observable entities; all that is observed at any time is a single point on the market demand curve for a commodity. We are thus driven to estimate demand curves statistically, and that is only possible in situations where we can make strong assumptions about the conditions of supply in the relevant market. This identification problem was first stated explicitly in the 1920s, but even nineteenth-century economists recognized the problem implicitly. Thus, the early pioneers of demand theory really had only two choices: to follow Augustin Cournot and Gustav Cassel in asserting downward-sloping demand curves as a crude empirical generalization, or to deduce the law of demand from a set of primitive assumptions about economic behavior. Given the importance of negatively inclined demand curves as an essential element in competitive price theory, it is hardly surprising that they chose the latter course.

It was Marshall who first drew attention to the fact that the so-called universal law of demand is unfortunately subject to a possible exception, namely, *Giffen's paradox,* the case where, to express it in modern language, the negative-income effect of a price change is so large in absolute terms as to cancel out the negative substitution effect of that change. The fact that Sir Robert Giffen never actually stated Giffen's paradox (Stigler, 1965, p. 379; also Mason, 1989, chaps. 6, 7) is of considerable significance: Marshall was looking, as it were, for Giffen's paradox and, therefore, was determined to find it. He realized that for practical purposes, we must define individual demand curves as subject to a *ceteris paribus* clause that includes tastes, expectations about future prices, the money incomes of consumers, and all prices other than the one under consideration. So defined, however, it was not possible to argue that there is in fact one "universal" law of demand.

Marshall also flirted, as Friedman has shown (see Blaug, 1980, pp. 351–3, 369), with a constant-*real*-income interpretation of demand curves in which the prices of all closely related goods are varied inversely to the price of the good in question (in practical terms, we divide money income by a Laspeyres price index) so as to "compensate" the consumer for any change in real income caused by the price change. Such a constant-real-income or compensated demand curve must indeed be negatively inclined under the very conditions implied in its construction, and hence, Friedman argued, we ought to choose this interpretation as the more preferable one because it alone has an unambiguously testable implication. Alas, a compensated demand curve is never observed, whereas we do at least observe one point on the constant-*money*-income demand curve. The constant-real-income formulation of demand curves is thus an evasion of issues: the income effect of a price change is as integral a part of real-world consumer behavior as is the substitution effect and to leave it out is to adjust the world to fit our theories rather than the other way around.[2] So long as we are interested in the total change in quantity demanded resulting from a given change in price, we want to measure both the income and the substitution effect.

From indifference to revealed preference

The Slutsky–Allen–Hicks decomposition of price responses into income and substitution effects, and the invariably negative sign of the substitution effect, are the only substantive achievements of the immense intellectual efforts of literally hundreds of economists applied for over a century or more to the pure theory of consumer behavior. This theory, as Lancaster (1966b, p. 132) said, "now stands as an example of how to extract the minimum of results from the minimum of assumptions." It is silent on the decision of consumers to purchase durable goods, to save, and to hold wealth in one form rather than another. It is addressed to the decision to buy perishable goods, and in particular to the decision to allocate available income between perishable goods, and yet it cannot even predict what particular goods will in fact be consumed. Far from generating testable economic hypotheses about demand behavior, inspiring and guiding empirical research, the theory has almost consistently lagged behind, rather than led, statistical studies of demand. Although family budget studies of the effect of income on consumers' expenditures were well established by the 1870s, the role of income as a key variable in demand was not theoretically recognized until the 1890s and it was not systematically analyzed until the 1930s (Stigler, 1965, p. 211). Similarly, the first modern statistical demand studies began in earnest just before World War I (Stigler, 1965, p. 219 ff), and yet the development of Allen–Hicks indifference theory in the 1930s owed absolutely nothing to the real advances that had by then been made in the empirical understanding of demand.

Indifference theory, coming after a generation of hostile but ineffective

---

[2] If only we could conveniently ignore the income effect of a price change, demand theory would be so much simpler. Thus Becker (1976, pp. 159–60) demonstrates that for a wide variety of household decision rules, including decisions determined by the throw of a dice, market demand curves would still be negatively inclined (essentially because price rises restrict, while price falls enlarge, the opportunity set). This demonstration assumes a constant-real-income and not a Marshallian constant-money-income demand curve.

criticism of marginal utility theory by the leaders of American institutional-ism,[3] reaffirmed the concept of economic man as possessed of what John Maurice Clark called an "irrationally rational passion for dispassionate cal-culation," while taking inordinate pride in deriving all the classical results from an ordinal rather than a cardinal utility calculus. The concept of "indif-ference," involving as it does pairwise comparisons between commodity bun-dles that are infinitesimally close to each other, is just as introspective and unobservable as the concept of cardinal comparisons between marginal utili-ties.[4] This is of no consequence if the formulation makes it easier to generate empirically significant predictions about consumer behavior. But as a matter of fact, the apparatus of indifference curves is of no help in telling us before-hand which demand curves have negative rather than positive slopes: since we can never directly observe either the substitution or the income effect (the income effect being defined with reference to an original level of total utility), we cannot measure the size of one to add it to the other for purposes of predicting the total change in the quantity demanded resulting from a change in price. As before, the theory of consumer behavior remains an *ex post facto* rationalization of all final demand outcomes, whatever they are. We can con-firm the law of demand, but we can never disconfirm it.

The classic exposition of indifference theory was presented in the first three chapters of Hicks's *Value and Capital* (1939), by which time Samuelson had already won the race to prove the same old results from a still smaller number of assumptions. Samuelson's *revealed preference theory* (RPT) proposed to purge the theory of consumer behavior of the last vestiges of utility by restrict-ing it to operational comparisons between value (quantity times price) sums. If consumers prefer more goods to less, choose only one definite bundle of goods in every budget situation, and behave consistently in successive choices, they will buy less of a good when its price rises if they would have bought more of that good when their incomes rose. This generalized law of demand, or, "fundamental theorem of consumption theory" as Samuelson called it, includes all of the observable implications of indifference theory and, in ad-dition, has the advantage of inferring consumers' preferences from their re-vealed behavior, not the other way round. Moreover, the income effect in RPT is measurable in principle, being the change in income opposite in sign

---

[3] For a review of this great interwar debate on the psychological foundation of econom-ics, see Coats (1976). A little book by Sargant Florence (1927) wonderfully recreates the atmosphere of this old-fashioned controversy.

[4] The derivation of indifference curves from simulated choice experiments has a long if sparse history, going back to a pioneering attempt in 1931 by the psychologist Louis Thurstone and repeated only twice since then. A recent, more sophisticated attempt by MacCrimmon and Toda (1969) produced positive but mixed evidence for the three familiar properties of indifference curves: (1) nonintersection, (2) negative slope, and (3) curvature convex to the origin.

to the change in price that is required to restore the original bundle of goods that was purchased.

Nevertheless, RPT is just as difficult to refute as indifference curve analysis: unless we have prior information about the income elasticity of demand for a commodity, we cannot predict in advance from the fundamental theorem of consumption theory that the quantity demanded of it will vary inversely with price. Of course, we can infer that this outcome will be the more likely, the smaller is the proportion of total expenditure accounted for by this commodity, but this inference is just as easily, if not more easily, drawn from the older Marshallian theory of consumer behavior.

Subsequent developments succeeded in axiomatizing RPT to the point where its assumptions and conclusions were so firmly connected that the established truth of one was sufficient to establish the truth of the other and vice versa (Houthakker, 1961, pp. 705–8). As such, it provides a perfect example of our earlier contention (see Chapter 4) that the logical distinction between "assumptions" and "implications" disappears in a perfectly axiomatized theory. RPT can be used to derive all the standard properties of demand curves that were earlier derived via cardinal and ordinal utility theory. What is called "rational" choice in utility theory translates into "preferring more to less," "consistency," and "transitivity" in RPT. In short , RPT and the theory of utility are logically equivalent, and Samuelson's original claims on behalf of RPT as a new approach to the problem of consumer behavior must, therefore, be rejected as unwarranted.[5] To that extent, the demand by some "aggressive" methodologists for the independent testing of the assumptions of RPT (Clarkson, 1963, pp. 55–6, 62–3, 79, 83) misses the point. We do not have to argue, à la Friedman, that Freud and Marx have taught us that people do not know why they behave the way they do and that, in any case, the business of social science is to trace the unintended social outcomes of individual actions, not to examine the degree of conscious awareness that individuals dis-

[5] As Wong (1978) has shown, Samuelson has in fact changed his mind twice over in respect of the aim of RPT: in the original 1938 article (Samuelson, 1966, chap. 1), the point of the theory was to derive the main results of Hicksian ordinal utility theory without resorting to the notion of indifference or indeed any other nonobservable terms; in a 1948 paper (Samuelson, 1966, chap. 9), in which he actually christened the new approach, RPT becomes the basis for an operational method of constructing an individual 's indifference map from observations of his market behavior, thus solving a problem that the earlier article had shown to be spurious; finally, in a 1950 paper (Samuelson, 1966, chap. 10), RPT receives yet another interpretation, namely, to explore and establish the observational equivalent of ordinal utility theory, which again seems to conflict with the objectives of the first as well as with the objectives of the second paper. To add to the confusion, Samuelson has also changed his mind at least once about his basic methodology: in 1938, he was an "operationalist," whereas by 1963 he had retreated to the more modest methodology of "descriptivism" (see Chapter 4 above).

play. RPT is a case where a test of the "realism" of implications is logically equivalent to a test of the "realism" of assumptions.

The predictive power of RPT in respect to demand relationships is of course no better than the older theories of consumer behavior: it too is empirically irrefutable unless reinterpreted as a statistical law because it relies on unrestricted universal statements. Although RPT is praised for promoting an emphasis on the observable implications of consumption theory (Houthakker, 1961, p. 713), it is difficult to find much evidence that it has inspired new empirical research on demand. It asserts, for example, that the order of a consumer's preferences is revealed by the chronological sequences of his choices when prices are changing, which immediately implies that it has little to contribute to an explanation of the demand for durable goods – since the services of durable goods are not necessarily consumed in any fixed relation to their date of purchase, choices among durable goods may not disclose a consumer's preferences (Morgenstern, 1972, p. 1168).

But apart from this limitation, there is the much more serious difficulty that it is a theory of the choices of a single consumer, whereas the measurement and testing of demand hypotheses is fundamentally concerned with market behavior. The conventional theory of individual consumer behavior, whether of the older or the newer variety, is in fact miles removed from the sort of market demand data that economists typically work with. For empirical demand analysis, the question of whether we may assume the very existence of utility functions – a stable set of preference orderings among consumers – looms much larger than the endlessly debated theoretical questions of cardinality versus ordinality or indifference versus revealed preference.

Empirical work on demand

In their authoritative survey of empirical research on demand relationships since World War II, Brown and Deaton (1972) noted that much empirical work on demand had been purely "pragmatic" and carried out with very little reference to any theory of consumer behavior (pp. 1150–2). Even where there was an attempt to draw on the conventional theory, many research workers had simply ignored the problem of aggregating individual demand into aggregate demand behavior, in effect treating average *per capita* demand data as if they were generated by a single consumer with an average *per capita* income. In general, they observed, the theory of consumer behavior "does not provide what might have been expected, the ideal way of setting up experiments in demand analysis" (p. 1154). The theory was of course never meant to apply to a particular individual but rather to a statistical, average individual. "It is therefore reasonable to regard the theory as no more than a fable (or in modern jargon, a paradigm) which suggests restrictions enabling the solution of an otherwise intractable problem of estimation and interpretation'' (p. 1168). Indeed, if all consumers were to behave exactly according to the pure theory of consumer behavior, the Engel curves of consumers would be parallel straight lines and estimation of demand relationships would become virtually impossible. Unfortunately, however, ''we are not aware of any thoroughgoing attempts to build truly aggregate systems of demand relations'' (p. 1170).

''Most applied work,'' Brown and Deaton went on to say, ''has in fact emphasised estimation rather than testing. . . . More rigorous testing had to wait until it became possible to estimate complete systems of demand functions'' (pp. 118–19). The assumption that demand functions are homogeneous of degree zero in prices and money incomes, which is one of their standard properties assumed in price theory, has in fact been rejected in some tests of complete systems of demand equations (pp. 1189–95; see also Gilbert, 1991). More generally, they concluded that there has been an ''overemphasis on the substitution effects of price changes''; ''for many practical purposes the effects of changes in income are of greater importance than those of changes in prices'' (pp. 1157, 1154). Finally, they observed that ''the problem of how changes in the distribution of income affect average *per capita* consumption behaviour . . . is perhaps . . . the most important missing link in the construction of an adequate empirically applicable theory of consumer demand'' (p. 1158).

In the circumstances, there is a good deal to be said for Mishan's proposal to wipe the slate clean of the theory of consumer behavior: ''after all the display of technical virtuosity associated with such theorems, there is nothing the practising economist can take away with him to help him come to grips with the complexity of the real world. Indeed, he would be no worse off if he remained ignorant of all theories of consumer's behaviour accepting the obviously indispensable 'Law of Demand' on trust'' (Mishan, 1967, pp. 82–3). But on trust of what? Presumably, on trust of the evidence. And, indeed, there is hardly any doubt that most economists, even those who would violently repudiate Mishan's iconoclasm, affirm the law of demand because of the weight of empirical evidence and not because of the theoretical dictates of the pure theory of consumer behavior. Besides, as we have argued, the pure theory of consumer behavior is not empirically refutable: the statistical law of demand is only derivable from that theory by the addition of an extra auxiliary assumption, asserting the likelihood that any negative income effect will be too small to offset the negative substitution effect of a price change.

This is the decisive answer to such apriorists as Mises and Robbins, and for that matter Keynes, who claim that economics must confine itself to qualitative predictions but rule out all quantitative predictions as pointless (see

Chapter 3 above and Lipsey, 1989, p. 160). Actually, without empirical measurement of income elasticities, even so basic a concept as the negative slope of demand curves cannot be established as generally valid.

The importance of Giffen goods

A cursory glance at some leading textbooks in economics suffices to establish the point that the law of demand is asserted as a law because of the assessment of the evidence relating to income elasticities. Samuelson (1985, p. 417n) simply ignores the evidence: the text assumes that all demand curves are negatively inclined, while a footnote admits that some demand curves may be positively sloped. Alchian and Allen (1964, pp. 54, 62–4) likewise ignore the statistical evidence but mention some casual evidence for the law of demand (e.g., lower prices of fruits and vegetables when they are in season), declaring that it is "a law simply because it describes a universal, verified truth about people's consumption and market behavior." Lipsey (1989, p. 164) contains a thorough and characteristically frank discussion of the problem:

. . . the modern theory of demand makes an unequivocal prediction only when we have extraneous information about income elasticities of demand . . . if we have no knowledge about the income effect we can still hazard a probabilistic statement. The great weight of existing evidence suggests that if we had to guess with no prior knowledge whether the demand curve for some commodity X was downward or upward sloping, the former choice would be the odds-on favourite.

Stigler (1966, pp. 24, 71–2) is even more emphatic: "all known demand curves have negative slopes."

How can we convince a sceptic that this "law of demand" is really true of all consumers, all times, all commodities? Not by a few (4 or 4,000) selected examples, surely. Not by a rigorous theoretical proof, for none exists – it is an empirical rule. Not by stating what is true, that economists believe it, for we could be wrong. Perhaps as persuasive a proof as is readily summarized is this: if an economist were to *demonstrate* its failure in a particular market, at a particular time, he would be assured of immortality, professionally speaking, and rapid promotion. Since most economists would not dislike either reward, we may assume that the total absence of exceptions is not from lack of trying to find them.

Hicks (1956, pp. 66–8, 93–4) is perhaps the only modern economist to attempt to rationalize the lack of evidence for upward-sloping demand curves by a theoretical argument: Giffen goods, he contends, are rarely observed because positive stretches in demand curves tend to produce unstable equilibria, implying apparently that most equilibria in the real world are patently stable.

Enough has now been said to establish the contention that the general view of Giffen goods as theoretical curiosities is based on nothing more than a broad assessment of the empirical evidence about market demand. In view of that fact, however, it is striking how many textbooks devote pages and pages to expounding the intricacies of the theory of consumer behavior, while hardly mentioning – much less teaching students to appreciate – the vast literature on the empirical measurement of demand. To be sure, there are some notable exceptions (e.g., Baumol, 1965, chap. 10; Green, 1976, chap. 9; Lipsey, 1989, chap. 9), but in general, the pedagogical inclination of modern economists is to assign overwhelming importance to the postulates or axioms of consumer theory, while consigning its implications for demand behavior to the higher reaches of the subject to be studied, if at all, at a later date. To follow Mishan and to dismiss the axioms altogether smacks too much of replacing a theory by the empirical evidence for that theory. Nevertheless, the intellectual effort that is traditionally devoted to the assumptions as distinct from the consequences of the pure theory of consumer behavior is almost in inverse proportion to their relative significance.

Lancaster's theory of characteristics

The empirical evidence about market demand behavior is, as we have seen, ambiguous and difficult to evaluate. For that reason alone, inspection of the assumptions of the theory is never redundant. Besides, even at this late stage, such a reexamination of assumptions may reveal unsuspected limitations; a reworking of the assumptions may well produce surprisingly new variations on old themes. A case in point is Kelvin Lancaster's new approach to consumer behavior, which takes as its starting point the old idea that consumers do not value goods for their own sake; rather they value them for the services that they render. The new element that Lancaster (1966b, 1971) adds is that these services or "characteristics" are usefully conceived as objectively measurable components, the same for all consumers, which are combined in fixed proportions to make up an individual good, these goods being in turn combined into a bundle of consumption "activities." The personal element in consumer choice arises from the choice between these fixed vectors of characteristics embodied in different bundles of goods. Thus, consumers are depicted as maximizing, not a utility function, but a transformation function, which depicts the utility derived by transforming a particular collection of characteristics into a particular collection of goods.

Lancaster (1966b, pp. 135, 152–3) is only too aware that the new theory may be thought "to run the danger of adding to the economist's extensive collection of non-operational concepts": there are severe practical problems in assigning empirical coefficients to the consumption technology. But in principle, he insists, the task is a manageable one and the result is "a model very many times richer in heuristic explanatory and predictive power than the conventional model of consumer behaviour" (pp. 154–5). A major implication of Lancaster's analysis is that consumers generally occupy corner equilibria in most dimensions of choice switching from corner to corner in response to price changes, so that continuous adjustments along something like an indifference curve are in fact never observed. In addition, the new theory is said to throw light on the "intrinsic" substitutability and complementarity between goods, on occupational choices, on asset holdings and on the role of advertising in promoting the introduction of new goods (pp. 144–51).

However, the examples that Lancaster provides of the empirical predictions of the new theory that are said to be denied by orthodox doctrine are less than wholly persuasive: (1) that wood will not be a close substitute for bread but that red cars of a given make will be a close substitute for gray cars of the same make; (2) that goods may be entirely displaced from the market by new goods or by a change in price; (3) that the labor-leisure choices of workers will have a marked occupational pattern; (4) that a monetary asset may entirely disappear from the economy (Gresham's law); (5) that individual choices may be completely unaffected by price changes; and (6) that certain breaks in the spectrum of cross-elasticities between goods, defining a commodity group, may be intrinsic and impervious to price changes. What is in doubt is not that these are genuine predictions of the new theory that cannot be derived from traditional consumer theory, but whether these are well-confirmed predictions and, furthermore, whether the two theories actually differ in their predictions when they address the same range of phenomena.

The "problem-situation" or critical empirical issue in the theory of consumer behavior is, as we have seen, the sign of the slope of the market demand curve for goods, and we may ask, therefore, whether Lancaster's theory casts further light on the famous question of the likelihood of Giffen goods. Lancaster (1966b, p. 145) himself conjectured that his theory creates new presumptions for the improbability of Giffen goods, that is, the greater likelihood of negatively inclined market demand curves. But some of his followers suggest the very opposite (Green, 1976, p. 161; Lipsey and Rosenbluth, 1971), adding that a new look at the existing evidence will bear them out.

The argument is that the demand for certain characteristics of goods may be satiated in an affluent society; if goods have different characteristics, it follows that any good may be a Giffen good at any level of income if it has a comparative advantage in a satiated characteristic. Thus, Giffen-like effects and hence positively sloped market demand curves may be more common than has previously been thought. Curiously enough, something like this was once asserted by Marshall in private correspondence when he used the example of consumer choice between two competing modes of transport within a given travel budget in circumstances where railways had a comparative advantage in time costs over canal boats but not in comfort, convenience, etcetera; an increase in the price of canal travel might then increase rather than decrease the demand for canal boats (Pigou, 1956, p. 441). Be that as it may, the Lipsey–Rosenbluth thesis has been contested on the grounds that it depends critically on the linear relationship between goods and characteristics postulated in the Lancaster model (Mason, 1989, pp. 122–6). We cannot hope to adjudicate this issue here but such disagreements do begin to suggest that it is too early to tell just what are the implications of the new theory of consumer characteristics.

It would be a methodological error of the now familiar sort to insist that the theory is not worth considering until it has been shown that the "characteristics" of goods are measurable in an operational sense – the assumptions of theories must be "realistic," or else – and in any case the particularly troublesome assumption of fixed proportions in the production of characteristics is a convenient simplification that is not strictly necessary to its results. The vital question remains: what are the refutable predictions about market behavior that are generated by the new theory and are these in fact predictions of "novel facts" that are capable of discriminating between the old and the new theory? There is little doubt that the Lancaster theory is richer in content than the old, which is hardly surprising since it includes the old as a special case, but it is far from clear that this increase in generality is accompanied by new substantive results of a testable kind. The fact that the new theory has received little development since its original formulation, particularly in application to empirical problems, creates further grounds for skepticism of its fecundity. We can detect the impact of Lancaster's theory in the common tendency to calculate "hedonic indices" of price movements to allow for changes in the quality of goods, but that is at best an indirect rather than a direct influence. On balance, it remains true to say that the new theory has so far failed to take off, and it is anybody's guess whether it ever will.

There is nothing in economic methodology that will help us to improve on that guess: methodology can sharpen the appraisal of new ideas but, in the final analysis, budding research programs such as the Lancaster theory of characteristics must prove their worth by their actual impact on the work of economists.

7

The theory of the firm

The classic defense

If the function of the orthodox theory of consumer behavior is to justify the notion of negatively inclined demand curves, the function of the orthodox theory of the firm is to justify the notion of positively inclined supply curves. The orthodox or neoclassical theory of the single-product firm, using only output or price as a strategic variable in a static but highly competitive environment, has been with us for 140 years (ever since Cournot more or less invented it in 1838), during which time it has been repeatedly criticized, particularly in respect of its central assumption that businessmen strive to maximize money profits subject to the constraints of technology and the prevailing pattern of demand.

It has been argued that business firms actually maximize a multivariate utility function that includes profits, leisure, prestige, liquidity, control, etcetera; that they maximize total sales subject to a minimum level of profits rather than profits themselves; that they do not maximize at all but "satisfice" by adjusting their profit targets in the light of experience so as to reach aspiration levels; that they cannot maximize because of prevailing uncertainty and, therefore, adopt rules-of-thumb like full-cost pricing; and that they do not want to maximize but instead to survive and hence operate in terms of administrative rules that serve to keep them one step ahead of their rivals. Such criticisms and their associated proposals for reconstructions of the theory of business behavior have greatly multiplied in the last thirty years, virtually amounting to what some commentators have described as the breakup of the traditional theory of the firm (Nordquist, 1967).

The classic defense of the traditional textbook theory, vigorously stated by Machlup in the famous Lester–Machlup debate of 1946, is that marginal analysis in general and the neoclassical theory of the firm in particular does not aim to provide a complete explanation of business conduct in all its aspects but rather to predict the effects of specific changes in market forces. The battered and bruised neoclassical theory of the firm deserves to survive because of its ability to produce verifiable predictions of the qualitative kind such as: "an increase in demand leads to a rise in both output and product prices"; "a rise in money wages causes a fall in employment"; "a lump sum tax on business profits will have no effect on output"; and so forth. Most of the alternative theories are not even capable of making such weak predictions, and generally speaking, they tell a better story at the expense of indeterminate results.

Admittedly, the textbook business firm is an "ideal type" that is patently unrealistic: for example, instead of conceiving of entrepreneurs as maximizing an index of preferences that includes pecuniary and nonpecuniary returns, on analogy with the consumer in the theory of demand, the utility function of businessmen is reduced to directly observable monetary returns; moreover, the elements of time, uncertainty, and the costs of obtaining information are put aside as unnecessary complications. Nevertheless, the theory is simple, elegant, internally consistent and it produces definite, qualitative predictions that are well corroborated. Such is Machlup's (1978, chaps, 16, 26) argument and, for that matter, the argument of Friedman in defense of what he calls "the maximization-of-returns hypothesis" (see Chapter 4 above).

Such defenses might carry conviction if only they were accompanied by a detailed examination of the predictive successes of traditional theory. We need not embrace the methodology of "instrumentalism" to agree that any simple theory that accurately predicts the direction of change of fundamental economic variables should not be declared out of court simply because it involves "unrealistic" assumptions; let us simply agree to work towards more realistic assumptions in the future. But the difficulty is precisely that of assessing the predictive record of the standard theory of the firm, and in making that assessment we typically receive little help from the staunch partisans of the theory. After all, the theory is as frequently contradicted as confirmed by casual evidence. For example, the theory predicts unequivocally that a profit maximizing firm in a perfectly competitive market will not advertise: it has no incentive to do so because it faces a perfectly elastic demand curve and can sell all it can produce. But many firms do advertise their differentiated product from which we may conclude either that demand curves facing firms are always downward sloping, in which case most of the standard predictions of the theory do not follow, or that the prevailing market structure is one of monopolistic rather than perfect competition; the theory of monopolistic competition, however, does not provide unambiguous predictions of the effect of a change in costs or demand on the price of the product, the size of the plant, or the number of firms in the industry (see Blaug, 1985, pp. 391–6, 423–4).[6] We are thus left with the weak conclusion that the neoclassical theory of the firm simply does not apply to most manufacturing firms producing final consumer goods and not even to all firms producing intermediate goods.

Similarly, the prediction of traditional theory that a rise in money wages *ceteris paribus* will lead to a fall in the volume of employment offered by firms is not borne out by evidence on short-run employment functions, which seem to exhibit remarkable stability in the face of wage inflation; on the other hand, if employment always varied negatively with money wages in the long run, we should observe well-behaved Phillips curves relating the rate of unemployment to the rate of change of money wages, which in general we do not observe. No doubt, we can relax the traditional theory by various ad hoc adjustments of its assumptions so as to account for the stability of short-run and the instability of long-run employment functions, but in so doing we lose both the simplicity and sharpness of its standard predictions. Keynes asserted in *The General Theory* that real wages varied countercyclically (rising as employment fell and vice versa), exactly as predicted by the orthodox theory of the firm. Dunlop and Tarshis then showed that U.S. and U.K. real wages fluctuated procyclically, a finding which Keynes was only too happy to accept; but further work has demonstrated that even Dunlop and Tarshis analyzed a special case and that, in general, procyclical product wages are just as common as countercyclical ones (Michie, 1991; Fisher, 1991, p. 17).

To take a final example, the traditional theory of the firm predicts that a proportionate tax on business income, such as the corporate income tax, is not shifted by the firm to its customers in the short-run, because the tax reduces the level of profits but not the volume of output at which profits are

---

[6] Samuelson (1967, pp. 108–9n), alarmed that criticism of Chamberlin's monopolistic competition theory might give comfort to the Friedman–Stigler view that there is no real alternative to the theory of perfect competition, felt impelled to say: "although I personally emphasized in my *Foundations of Economic Analysis* . . . the importance of the empirically testable implications of second-order maximization inequalities, I must dissociate myself from Archibald's criticism of the Chicago criticism, which consists of Archibald's demonstration that the Chamberlin theory has few unambiguously signed implications of my *Foundations* type. If the real world displays the variety of behavior that the Chamberlin–Robinson models permit – and I believe the Chicago writers are simply wrong in denying that these important empirical deviations exist – then reality will falsify *many* of the important qualitative and quantitative *predictions* of the competitive model. Hence, by the pragmatic test of predictive adequacy, the perfect-competition model fails to be an adequate approximation. . . . The fact that the Chamberlin–Robinson model is 'empty' in the sense of ruling out few empirical configurations and providing only formalistic descriptions, is not the slightest reason for abandoning it in favor of a 'full' model of the competitive type *if reality is similarly* 'empty' and 'non-full.' "

maximized. There is considerable evidence, however, that the corporate income tax is in fact shifted (Ward, 1972, p. 18), and this is relevant, although not necessarily clinching, evidence against the neoclassical theory of the firm (and, by the way, in favor of the sales-maximization hypothesis). Thus, there is little doubt that the traditional theory of business behavior does not pass the test of casual empiricism with flying colors. Of course, no theory ever does, but perhaps we have now said enough to suggest that an evaluation of the evidence for and against the standard theory of the firm cannot be settled simply by a shrug of the shoulder and a finger pointed at the real world.

Despite the scores of assaults on the traditional theory of business behavior over a period of more than thirty years, it has somehow managed to survive in textbooks and in countless applications to applied problems in microeconomics. How is this remarkable longevity to be explained? To attribute its survival entirely to the stubborn influence of tradition is too easy. To attribute that survival instead to its ability to produce empirically verified predictions is to leave unexplained the curious lack of interest that most economists display in the actual predictive record of conventional theory. We cannot even claim that the traditional theory predicts as well as or better than any of the alternative theories of business behavior produced thus far, because Baumol's constrained sales maximization theory and Williamson's managerial theory, to cite only two of a number of alternative theories, imply quite different comparative static predictions from standard theory – and yet few attempts have been made to compare the respective track records of these competing theories (but see Cyert and Hendrick, 1972). The basic problem is that we simply cannot evaluate the traditional theory of the firm without evaluating the whole of neoclassical price theory: the theory of the firm is only a single strand in what is in fact a more comprehensive scientific research program in microeconomics. In praising or condemning the conventional theory of the firm, we necessarily pass judgment on the power of the larger research program of which it forms an integral part.

By placing the theory of the firm in its appropriate theoretical context, we do no more than borrow a leaf from Lakatos's methodology of scientific research programs (MSRP). Indeed, we can gain a much better appreciation of the fecundity of MSRP by considering what it has to teach us about the evaluation of the traditional theory of business behavior. It is convenient to do so by way of a critical examination of Spiro Latsis's indictment of the traditional theory of the firm, the first attempt in the literature to provide a case study of MSRP in economics.

Situational determinism

Latsis begins with the proposition that all theories of perfect, imperfect, and monopolistic competition may be considered together as forming part of the same neoclassical research program in business behavior with one identifiable "hard core," one "protective belt," and one "positive heuristic" (see Chapter 1 above). The "hard core," he argues, is made up of "(1) profit-maximisation, (2) perfect knowledge, (3) independence of decisions, and (4) perfect markets" (Latsis, 1972, p. 209; 1976, p. 23). Without quarreling about the choice of language, we must underline the fact that the "hard core" of an SRP is made up of metaphysical propositions, that is, empirically irre-futable ones; hence, if items (1) to (4) are called the "assumptions" of the theory of the firm, as in the common parlance of economists, any question of their "realism" or lack of realism betrays a misunderstanding of their meth-odological status. In order to convert this "hard core" into a theory of the firm in the "protective belt" of the research program, the core propositions must be supplemented by auxiliary assumptions, such as "(1) product homo-geneity, (2) large numbers, and (3) free entry and exit" (1972, p. 212; 1976, p. 23), whose presence or absence in any particular case is subject to inde-pendent verification; in short, we may legitimately ask whether the auxiliary assumptions are "realistic," in the sense of being descriptively accurate, be-cause they supply the criteria of applicability of the theory. The "positive heuristic" of the neoclassical SRP consists of a set of directives that reduce to the single rule: derive the comparative static properties of theories. More specifically, (1) divide markets into buyers and sellers; (2) specify the market structure; (3) create "ideal type" definitions of the behavioral assumptions; (4) set out the relevant *ceteris paribus* conditions; (5) translate the situation into a mathematical extremum problem and examine first- and second-order conditions; and so forth (1972, pp. 212–13; 1976, p. 22).

Latsis's label for the neoclassical research program in business behavior is "situational determinism" because "under the conditions characterising per-fect competition the decision maker's discretion in choosing among alterna-tive courses of action is reduced simply to whether or not to remain in busi-ness" (1972, p. 209; 1976, p. 25).[7] This seems to ignore the fact that, apart from remaining in business, the competitive firm also has to decide what output to produce. But the nub of the argument is that competitive firms either produce the profit-maximizing level of output or no output at all: "I shall call situations where the obvious course of action (for a wide range of conceptions of rational behavior) is determined uniquely by objective conditions (cost, demand, technology, numbers, etc.), 'single exit' or 'straightjacket' situa-tions" (1972, p. 211; 1976, p. 19).

In other words, once an independent decision maker with a well-behaved profit function in a perfect competitive market is given perfect information

---

[7] The phrase "situational determinism" is derived from Popper's *Open Society* where *the* method of economic theory is described as "analysis of the situation, the situa-tional logic."

about the situation he faces, there is nothing left for him to do, according to neoclassical theory, but to produce a unique level of output, or else to go out of business. There is no internal decision-making machinery, no information search, no rules for dealing with ignorance and uncertainty, and no entrepreneurship of any kind whatsoever: the problem of choice among alternative lines of action is so far reduced to its simplest elements that the assumption of profit maximization automatically singles out the best course of action. The motivational assumptions of orthodox theory, Latsis concludes, could be weakened from profit maximization to bankruptcy avoidance without affecting its predictions (1972, p. 233; 1976, p. 24).

But what are these predictions? The purpose of the theory is to answer such questions as "(1) Why do commodities exchange at given prices? (2) What are the effects of changes in parameters (say, demand) on the variables of our model once adjustment has taken place?" (1972, pp. 212–13). Latsis spends little time considering such qualitative predictions of the theory under given circumstances. Here and there, he does refer to evidence indicating that highly competitive industries sometimes fail to behave in the way predicted by the theory (1972, pp. 219–20; 1976, p. 28) but for the most part he takes it for granted that traditional theory has a poor predictive record without even bothering to argue the case.

He has little difficulty in showing that the habitual appeal to conditions of perfect competition as an approximation to reality fails to specify the limits of applicability of the traditional theory of profit maximization, so that even the behavior of oligopolists has come to be analyzed with the same tools. But such criticism tells us nothing about "the degree of corroboration" of a theory. For that, we need a report on the past performance of the theory in terms of the severity of the tests it has faced and the extent to which it has passed or failed these tests (see Chapter 1 above). Latsis provides no such report. In part, this is because of his central argument that all the program's successive versions have failed to generate significant empirical results. But the fact of the matter is that they were thought to do so. For example, the Chamberlin tangency solution was supposed to predict excess capacity in the case of many sellers with differentiated products. Similarly, theories of joint profit maximization under conditions of oligopoly were supposed to predict price rigidity. We cannot avoid asking, therefore, whether these predictions are borne out by the evidence.

Thus, it is difficult to escape the conclusion that Latsis's characterization of the neoclassical theory of the firm as "degenerating" (1972, p. 234; 1976, p. 30) is actually based on an examination of the theory's assumptions rather than its testable implications. This conclusion is strengthened by considering his discussion of the Carnegie school of business behavior as a research program that rivals the neoclassical theory of the firm. He draws a useful distinction in the writings of Simon, Cyert and March, Williamson, and Baumol between behavioralism proper and organizationalism, the former emphasizing learning and slack in a constantly changing and only partially known environment, the latter emphasizing the survival needs of organizations. *Behavioralism* is applicable to a single decision maker but *organizationalism* denies that there are such animals and insists that the objectives of decision makers should not be postulated *a priori* but ascertained *a posteriori* by observation of decision making in the real world. Traditional theory turns the decision maker into a cipher, whereas both behavioral and organizational theories focus attention on the nature and characteristics of the decision-making agent or agents; they do so by repudiating all "hard core" concepts of optimization, rejecting even the notion of a general analytical solution applicable to all business firms facing the same market situation.

It would be premature, Latsis argues, to attempt an appraisal of the Carnegie school as a budding research program. The approach may have potential for problems to which the traditional theory is unsuited but "neoclassical theory gives some simple answers to questions which we cannot even start asking in terms of behaviouralism (namely, in the domain of market structure and behaviour)" (1972, p. 233). Likewise, the Carnegie school has not "successfully predicted any unexpected novel fact" and "as a research programme, it is much less rich and much less coherent than its neoclassical opponent" (1972, p. 234). But lest this imply the superiority of traditional theory, Latsis hastens to add that these are incommensurable research programs: "the two approaches are, in my view, importantly different and mutually exclusive over an extensive area" (1972, p. 233).[8]

In other words, the neoclassical research program is condemned as "degenerating" although it has no rival in its own domain, and furthermore, the condemnation is based on the logic of "situational determinism" and not on the track record of its empirical predictions. In the final analysis, therefore, Latsis denies the essence of Lakatos's MSRP: neoclassical theory is primarily rejected because it is theoretically sterile and only secondarily because it fails to be empirically corroborated. There is nothing wrong with such a criticism,

---

[8] Loasby (1976, chaps. 7, 11) reaches the same conclusions, while relying on Kuhn rather than Lakatos to provide a methodological framework, but he is even more severe than Latsis in condemning the traditional theory of the firm for ignoring the internal decision processes of business enterprises (see also Leibenstein, 1979, pp. 481–4). In reply to Latsis, Machlup (1978, p. 525) has seized eagerly on the admission of incommensurability between behavioralism and marginalism, claiming that "a research programme designed to result in theories that explain and predict the actions of particular firms can never compete with the simplicity and generality of the marginalist theory, which, being based on the constructs of a fictitious profit-maximiser, cannot have the ambition to explain the behaviour of actual firms in the real world."

but it is less than might have been expected from an application of MSRP to economics.

Competitive results despite oligopoly

Modern industrial economies are characterized by a manufacturing sector that is almost entirely made up of a few, large producers, where the typical market structure is one of oligopoly rather than of perfect or monopolistic competition. Competition among the few is not like competition among the many, principally because fewness of numbers introduces the phenomenon of interdependence of decision making, in consequence of which the behavior of every firm depends critically on what it believes to be the behavior of other firms, and so on ad infinitum. Here too the story starts with Cournot, whose model of oligopolistic competition effectively banished all the interesting complications of mutual interdependence. Since then, numerous special theories of oligopoly have sought to produce determinate results despite the phenomenon of mutual interdependence, but all with little success. Few economists would disagree with Martin Shubik's (1970, p. 415) cryptic summary of the status of oligopoly theory: "There is no oligopoly theory. There are bits and pieces of models: some reasonably well analyzed, some scarcely investigated. Our so-called theories are based upon a mixture of common sense, uncommon sense, a few observations, a great amount of casual empiricism, and a certain amount of mathematics and logic."

The neoclassical theory of the firm is inapplicable to situations of oligopoly, not because its assumptions are ''unrealistic'' but because its antecedent or boundary conditions are not satisfied. In principle, therefore, it is pointless to attempt to test its predictions by examining the behavior of Unilever or U.S. Steel, because whatever the outcome of such an investigation, it could have no bearing on the empirical status of the neoclassical theory of the firm. Nevertheless, the principal qualitative predictions of that theory are widely employed in applied economics to provide rough-and-ready answers to questions that cut across the entire spectrum of business firms, including firms that are clearly oligopolists. The notion is that, despite the existence of monopoly and oligopoly, the dynamic process of rivalry between giant corporations produces results that approximate the outcome of a perfectly competitive process, so that, lo and behold!, the neoclassical theory of the firm is a useful parable and provides robust conclusions even in situations that violate virtually all the auxiliary assumptions of the theory. It has been argued (Lipsey, 1989, pp. 281–2; also Nelson and Winter, 1982, pp. 356–65) that this belief is so vague as to be of little use in making predictions and reaching policy decisions. Vague it certainly is, but that is not to say that such a point of view does not imply definite predictions about economic behavior. In truth, the theoretical contention that the behavior of all firms approaches that of competitive firms in the long run is a different theory of business behavior from the static neoclassical one: it is a dynamic theory of the *process* of competition as distinct from a static theory of the equilibrium *end-state* of competition – this is a distinction we have met before when we discussed the Alchian thesis (see Chapter 4 above).

In appraising that dynamic theory, we face the difficulty that it is rarely stated in such a way as to be testable even in principle. On the one hand, the process of competition implies that an industry is open to potential newcomers – it is "contestable" in the language of Baumol, Panzar, and Willig (1986). On the other hand, it is generally believed that large size and some barriers to entry are required to provide the necessary risk insurance that induces innovational investment – growth requires big business, as Schumpeter liked to say; that a reduction of entry barriers to an oligopolistic industry nevertheless reduces costs and prices; and that the larger the number of firms in an industry, the greater is the degree of price flexibility and sometimes even the rate of technical dynamism. But such notions are almost never tied together into any coherent exposition of the theory of workable competition under conditions of big business, although elements of that theory appear in Adam Smith, in John Stuart Mill, and particularly in Alfred Marshall (see Loasby, 1990; Williams, 1978, chap. 4; and Backhouse, 1990).

What we have, on the one hand, is a rigorous theory of business behavior under conditions of perfect competition, which no longer commands universal assent among modern economists and which in any case is not testable under conditions of oligopoly and, on the other hand, a loosely constructed theory of workable competition, which commands nearly universal assent but which is insufficiently specified to be potentially falsifiable. We are left with an almost perfect defense of the concept of competitive equilibrium: it does not apply, strictly speaking, to most industrial situations in which we are interested, and yet even there it mysteriously gives us many of the same results (see Yamey, 1972). As McClelland (1975, p. 125) puts it: "A cornerstone of microeconomics, both theoretical and applied, is the belief that the marginal equivalences of the neoclassical model are achieved to a tolerable degree, in whatever economic situation is being analyzed. To date, that belief – for all its importance – is largely an untested hypothesis."

To some this is a foregone conclusion because they have long doubted that economic behavior is explicable in terms of a timeless equilibrium system. Books such as Janos Kornai's *Anti-Equilibrium* (1971), George Shackle's *Epistemics and Economics* (1973), Brian Loasby's *Choice, Complexity and Ignorance* (1976), Alfred Eichner's *The Megacorp and Oligopoly* (1976), Richard Nelson and Sidney Winter's *An Evolutionary Theory of Economic Change* (1982), and the writings of the new "Austrian economics" (see Chapter 4 above) insist on the fact that economic decisions are made under conditions of pervasive uncertainty and incomplete knowledge; the passage of time involves learning and hence economic decisions are in principle irreversible; thus, equilibrium economics with its concept of rational action cannot be applied to an explanation of economic behavior over time. It follows that any precise, predictive economic science is impossible: the purpose of theory is not to predict what will happen but only to classify various possible outcomes (Shackle, 1973, pp. 72–3) or to simulate probable outcomes using preselected parameter values and randomly generated data (Nelson and Winter, 1982, chaps. 7, 8, 12–14).

Needless to say, we repudiate such radical anti-Popperian conclusions, and we reassert the need to carry out Samuelson's program of the "qualitative calculus," not to mention the "quantitative calculus." If prediction of human behavior were truly impossible, if none of us could predict anything about the behavior of other people, economic life itself, not to mention theories about economic life, would be unimaginable. Not only would the total incapacity to predict economic events wipe out traditional economic theory: it would wipe out every other type of economics, as well as all pretenses of offering advice to governments and business enterprises.

No doubt, the postulate that economic agents act rationally in their own interests with perfect knowledge and correct expectations only makes sense when we are in equilibrium, while complicating the story of how we get there from a situation of disequilibrium: in equilibrium, market prices carry all the knowledge we need but out of equilibrium they systematically mislead us. On the other hand, how are we to take account of incorrect expectations and incomplete knowledge? There is one set of correct expectations based on complete knowledge for each and every economic situation but there is an endless variety of incorrect ones. To simply classify all types of incorrect expectations and all possible states of ignorance is virtually to foresake generalization of any kind (Hutchison, 1977, pp. 70–80). Even Herbert Simon, with his concept of "bounded rationality" as a constructive replacement for the notion of "maximisation under certainty," does not pretend to be capable as yet of making general pronouncements on the decision-making process in business organizations (see Simon, 1979). In short, the call to abandon the maximization-under-certainty postulate has not so far been attended by any really convincing proposal to put something else in its place.

In respect of the traditional theory of the firm, however, the vital question remains that of testing its predictions in a world that rarely satisfies the conditions required to apply it. It may be that the theory has little predictive power outside agriculture and the stock market, in which case we ought perhaps to clear our minds to consider nonequilibrium theories of the firm, provided, however, that these imply definite predictions about economic outcomes. What we cannot do is to continue to operate with equilibrium concepts while denying that their consequences are ever observed in the real world. As Hutchison (1965, pp. 105–6) said long ago: "To justify special preoccupation with the position of equilibrium it is necessary to assert as an empirically testable truth that there is a tendency towards this position in our economic system, or that readjustments in general come quicker than new disturbances occur."

8

General equilibrium theory

Testing GE theory

It was Léon Walras in 1874 who first suggested that the maximizing behavior of consumers and producers can and, under certain conditions, will result in an equilibrium between amounts demanded and supplied in every product and factor market of the economy. This proposition of the possibility and even the likelihood of general equilibrium (GE) was not rigorously proved until the 1930s, but long before that date the sort of crude proof that Walras himself had supplied carried conviction with an increasing number of economists. Insofar as Walrasian GE is a logical consequence of the maximizing behavior of economic agents, rigorous existence proofs of GE seemed to provide an independent check on the validity of various partial equilibrium theories. However, modern industrialized economies frequently display disequilibrium and perhaps even chronic disequilibrium in labor markets. Can we then infer that the manifest failure of an economy to exhibit an equilibrium in all markets also falsifies such microeconomic theories as the utility-maximizing theory of consumer behavior and the profit-maximizing theory of the firm? No, because the widespread occurrence of economies of scale in certain industries, not to mention the phenomenon of externalities, suggests straightaway that some of the initial conditions of GE theory are not satisfied; GE theory, therefore, is inapplicable rather than false.

It could be argued, however, that GE theory is simply inadequately formulated for purposes of testing its central implication that there exists at least one equilibrium configuration of prices in all markets of the economy. For example, it has proved difficult to incorporate money into the GE schema without introducing an assumption of pervasive uncertainty. But the theory of consumer behavior, the theory of the firm, and the marginal productivity theory of the demand for factors are all based on the assumption of certainty of knowledge of future outcomes. In other words, any attempt to test GE theory

161

as a whole involves something more than the traditional armory of micro-economic propositions of the partial equilibrium variety.

However, to talk of testing GE theory at all seems to strike a false note. Even if we observed conditions of full employment, we could hardly verify the existence of GE in all markets simply by looking. In one sense, GE theory makes no predictions: it attempts to establish the logical possibility of GE without showing how it will come about and even without claiming that it will actually come about as a result of spontaneous forces. To be sure, Walras himself believed that he had provided an explanation of how real-world com-petitive markets would reach equilibrium via the process of *tâtonnement* or "groping." But there are serious deficiencies in the Walrasian notion of *tâ-tonnement* (see Blaug, 1980, pp. 578–80; and Walker, 1987), and to this day it is not possible to show that a final equilibrium in the economy as a whole is independent of the path taken towards equilibrium or that, of all the pos-sible paths chosen, the one that is actually adopted will and must converge on equilibrium. All modern work on GE theory of the Arrow–Debreu variety has been confined to "existence theorems" – theorems that state the conditions under which a GE system has an unique solution – and to questions of the stability of equilibrium once equilibrium is attained. In other words, we are almost as far away as Walras was from discovering the real-world counterpart of the equilibrating forces invoked by GE theory.

A theory or a framework?

Arrow–Debreu proofs of the existence of GE depend critically on two assumptions: that consumption and production sets are convex and that every economic agent owns some resources valued by other agents. The global stability of such an equilibrium depends in turn on the presence of some dy-namic process that guarantees that every economic agent has knowledge of the level of aggregate demand and that no final transactions are actually car-ried out except at equilibrium prices. Some of these assumptions may be relaxed a little to accommodate increasing returns to scale in a minority of industries and even a measure of monopolistic competition in all industries. But the existence of oligopoly, not to mention the presence of externalities in consumption and production, destroys all GE solutions as it does all other notions of competitive equilibrium.

Since GE theory has no empirical content, it is difficult to justify the very term *theory,* and its most prominent defenders have indeed been careful to label it a *framework* or *paradigm* (see Hahn, 1984, pp. 44–5). The operative question is not why we should need such a framework but why we should go on investing scarce intellectual resources in continually refining and elaborat-ing it. What if anything do we learn from the GE framework about the way actual economic systems function? The traditional defense of the framework was that precise statements of the necessary and sufficient conditions required to produce GE would somehow throw light on the way in which equilibrium is actually attained in the real world. But, more recently, the GE framework has been defended entirely in negative terms: what we are now told is that it facilitates the decisive refutation of commonly held but invalid arguments (Arrow and Hahn, 1971, pp. vi–vii).

There is by now a long and fairly imposing line of economists from Adam Smith to the present who have sought to show that a decentralized economy motivated by self-interest and guided by price signals would be compatible with a coherent disposition of economic resources that could be regarded, in a well-defined sense, as superior to a large class of possible alternative dispositions. Moreover, the price signals would operate in a way to establish this degree of coherence. It is important to understand how surprising this claim must be to anyone not exposed to this tradition . . . It is not sufficient to assert that, while it is possible to invent a world in which the claims made on behalf of the ''invisible hand'' are true, these claims fail in the actual world. It must be shown just how the features of the world regarded as essential in any description of it also make it possible to substantiate these claims. In attempting to answer the question ''Could it be true?'', we learn a good deal about why it might not be true.

The claim that GE ''theory'' is merely making precise an economic tradition that is as old as Adam Smith, thus enabling us to show just why Pareto-optimal, competitive equilibrium may never actually materialize, is a historical travesty. To be sure, there are elements of the invisible hand theorem in Adam Smith as well as in Alfred Marshall. Nevertheless, the Smith–Marshall analysis of workable or free competition is essentially in a different tradition from that of Walras and Pareto. If indeed ''GE is strong on equilibrium and very weak on how it comes about'' (Hahn, 1984, p. 140), the Smith–Marshall analysis is, by way of contrast, weak on equilibrium and very strong on how it comes about: it is more a study of the competitive process than of the end-state of competitive equilibrium (Loasby, 1976, p. 47; Backhouse, 1990). Adam Smith's approval of ''the invisible hand'' of competition was based on the notion that it promoted ''the division of labor,'' his name for technical progress, and the expansion of wants; in short, it raised living standards even of the poorest members of society. Similarly, Marshall's guarded assertions in favor of capitalism were based on the dynamic consequences of a competitive economy and not on the efficient allocation of resources achieved by the action of a static model of perfect competition. But historical pedigrees apart, the connection between GE ''theory'' and the invisible hand theorem is a tenuous one. The invisible hand theorem is either a descriptive or an evaluative claim about the nature of perfect competition (see Chapter 5 above), whereas the GE framework does not claim to describe the real world in any sense whatsoever and certainly not to evaluate it.

The GE construction, as Frank Hahn (1984, pp. 47–8) frankly admits:

> . . . makes no formal or explicit causal claims at all: for instance it contains no presumption that a sequence of actual economic states will terminate in an equilibrium state. However, it is motivated by a very weak causal proposition. This is that no plausible sequence of economic states will terminate, if it does at all, in a state which is not an equilibrium. . . . It will be seen that this is not a strong proposition in that no description of any particular process is involved. It is also clear that weak as this claim is, it may be false.

We can examine the internal consistency of the GE framework, conceived as a purely logical exercise, but how would we demonstrate the falsity of the ''very weak causal proposition'' that if a sequence of economic states is plausible, it will terminate in an equilibrium state? The word ''plausible'' surely suggests a reference to real-world conditions, and yet the GE framework would seem to lack any bridge by which to cross over from the world of theory to the world of facts.

It is important to recognize that the interpretation of the meaning of GE theory has gone through a 180-degree revolution since Walras's own times. Walras himself seems to have conceived of his model as an admittedly abstract but not misleading representation of the manner in which competition drives prices to their equilibrium values in a capitalist society (Walker, 1984). Similarly, when GE theory was revived in the 1930s by Hicks and Samuelson, having almost disappeared from view in the previous fifty years, it was common to regard it as a reasonable description of an actual capitalist economy. Thus, in the Great Socialist Calculation Debate of the 1930s, Oskar Lange argued that the planning bureau under socialism could employ a procedure for equilibrating prices that was similar to that ostensibly employed under capitalism, namely the method of trial-and-error enshrined in Walras's *tâtonnement* (Lavoie, 1985, pp. 120–1). Lange's *Economic Theory of Socialism* (1936) was a work in which many prewar economists first learned of the Walrasian system but, more importantly, they learned of it as having immense significance for coming to grips with substantive economic issues, whereas nowadays it is defended as a purely formal statement of the concept of GE, telling us what we meant by a logically consistent equilibrium model. Not even the most enthusiastic modern advocates of GE theory pretended for one moment that it provides any kind of description of, or prescription for, a capitalist economy.

Practical relevance

Nevertheless, Hahn (1984, pp. 44–15; 1985, pp. 19–20) assures us the GE framework is of ''great practical significance'' because it can be used to refute all sorts of ill-considered policy views about exhaustible resources, floating exchange rates, and foreign aid. But after claiming practical relevance for Arrow–Debreu GE "theory," Hahn (1984, p. 69) concedes that "the paradigm is of course of ambitious generality and for very many important purposes a much more modest Marshallian apparatus will do very well." And again but more damagingly:

We thus find it reasonable to require of our equilibrium notion that it should reflect the sequential character of actual economies. . . . This in turn requires that information processes and costs, transactions and transaction costs and also expectations and uncertainty be explicitly and essentially included in the equilibrium notion. This is what the Arrow–Debreu construction does not do. I do not believe that therefore it is quite useless. But certainly it is the case that it must relinquish the claim of providing necessary descriptions of terminal states of economic processes [Hahn, 1984, p. 53].

Much more could be said about Hahn's densely argued defense of GE "theory," which at times seems to conflate equilibrium analysis in general and GE analysis as a particular version thereof.[9] "The student of GE believes," Hahn (1984, p. 137) observes, "that he has a starting point from which it is possible to advance towards a descriptive theory." Nevertheless, the continuous refinements in GE "theory" in recent decades, steadily weakening its axioms and generalizing its boundary conditions (see Weintraub, 1977), have failed to bring us any closer to such a descriptive theory. In sum, it is difficult to resist Loasby's (1976, p. 50) conclusion that the GE research program has generally combined "fierce rigour in the theory and unheeding slackness in its application."

The empirical content of GE theory is nil because no theoretical system couched in such completely general terms could possibly predict any economic event or, to use Popperian language, forbid any economic event that might conceivably occur. It is true that the Walrasian system can be simplified by aggregation, as for example the famous Hicks–Hansen IS-LM version of Keynesian economics reduced to four equations; it is also true that the qualitative or comparative static properties of such simplified GE systems can be checked against empirical observations (does investment increase when the interest rate declines? , and so forth). Likewise, Herbert Scarf's (1987) computational algorithm for solving GE systems has encouraged a number of economists in recent years to employ large-scale GE models to provide numerical estimates of the impact of policy changes, such as amendments of the tax system. But few of these models have been tested to check whether they actually give more accurate answers than much simpler partial equilibrium

[9] For other commentaries on Hahn's arguments, see Coddington (1975); Loasby (1976, pp. 44–50, 1990, chap. 8) ; and Hutchison (1977, pp. 81–7).

models. The superiority of such applied GE models is fundamentally an empirical question because their construction is costly. Taking account of all interdependencies is of course better than ignoring them but it is also much harder work and the payoff in predictability may not warrant the extra effort.

It is clear that we must distinguish between radically different theoretical conceptions traveling under the same label. We can speak of GE theory in at least two senses. The first is Walras's original notion of multimarket equilibrium: Does it exist? Is it unique? Is it stable? Is it path-independent? Let us agree from now on to call this the Walras–Arrow–Debreu GE theory or Walrasian GE theory for short. The second is the wider notion of an economic model expressed as a set of simultaneous equations defined in terms of a large number of endogenous variables. Let us agree to call this the GE *model* as distinct from the Walrasian GE *theory*.

There can be no question that the GE model as distinct from the GE theory has definite empirical content. Indeed, its only *raison d'être* is to demonstrate the difference it makes to assume that everything else remains constant in a partial equilibrium treatment of an economic problem. At the same time we need constantly to remind ourselves that there is nothing obvious or commonplace about a GE view of a problem: all-round multimarket equilibrium is a feature of certain models of the economy and not necessarily a reflection of how that economy is constituted. Thus we assume too readily after studying GE theory that prices are actually determined simultaneously in the real world when in fact a sequential process of price determination – first the price of coal, then the price of steel, and then the price of automobiles – is a more plausible representation of how prices come to be set in the course of competitive rivalry.

In any case, the question is not one of approving or condemning the Walrasian apparatus in toto but of deciding whether GE *theory* deserves the precedence over GE *models* in the pecking order of professional economics which it currently enjoys; in particular, whether it does not constitute something like a blind alley, an intellectual game, from the standpoint of generating substantive hypotheses about economic behavior. As Franklin Fischer has said:

the very power and elegance of [general] equilibrium analysis often obscures the fact that it rests on a very uncertain foundation. We have no similarly elegant theory of what happens out of equilibrium, of how agents behave when their plans are frustrated. As a result we have no rigorous basis for believing that equilibrium can be achieved or maintained if disturbed [Fischer, 1987, p. 26; see also De Vroey, 1990].

This lacuna in GE theory produces the curious anomaly that perfect competition is possible only when a market is in equilibrium. It is impossible when a market is out of equilibrium. It is impossible when a market is out of equilibrium for the simple reason that perfectly competitive producers are price-takers, not price-makers. But if no one can make the price, how do prices ever change to produce convergence on equilibrium? This problem is perhaps a minor blemish in an apparatus which has no role for money, for stock markets, for bankruptcies, or for true entrepreneurship (Geanakoplos, 1987).

Nevertheless, despite the acknowledgments of such limitations of GE theory, its leading protagonists continue to insist on its usefulness. Thus, both Arrow (Feiwel, 1987, pp. 197–8, 281–2, 331–2) and Hahn (1985, pp. 19–22) defend GE theory as a benchmark of rigorous foundation from which to judge such un-Walrasian phenomena as increasing returns to scale, externalities, imperfect competition, and Keynesian underemployment equilibrium. But all of these phenomena were discovered and investigated independently of the Walrasian tradition, and apart from the realization that they are not capable of being incorporated in something as rigorous as GE theory, it is difficult to see what GE reasoning has contributed to their analysis.

One problem in such arguments is the apparently irresistible appeal to the notion of analytical rigor. Alas, there is a trade-off in economics (and not only in economics) between rigor and relevance. Theories that are truly rigorous are rarely practically relevant and theories that are eminently relevant are rarely analytically rigorous. If we argue in favor of a market economy compared to a command economy because of the dynamic characteristics of a competitive regime in fostering technical dynamism and cost-cutting innovations, and perhaps even political freedom to match economic freedom, our argument is anything but rigorous; it is, however, extremely relevant. On the other hand, if we prove that multimarket equilibrium is possible no matter how large the number of markets, our demonstration is rigorous but has no relevance whatsoever.

When GE theory is questioned along these lines, its advocates invariably fall back on GE *models* as accounting for the value of GE reasoning (see Arrow in Feiwel, 1987, pp. 201–2, 205–6; also Hausman, 1981, 1981a). But the undoubted value of GE models in no way justifies GE theory. On the contrary, excessive concern about the latter threatens to demote economics to a peculiarly degraded type of social mathematics. Economists are sometimes accused of physics envy – "scientism" as Hayek called it – but it would be nearer the mark to say that economists suffer from mathematics envy. The point has been strikingly asserted in an exhilarating essay by Donald Mc-Closkey:

From everywhere outside of economics except the Department of Mathematics the proofs of existence of competitive equilibrium, just to take them as concrete examples, will seem strange. They do not claim to show that an actual existing economy is in equilibrium, or that the equilibrium of an existing economy is desirable. The blackboard problem thus solved derives more or less vaguely from Adam Smith's assertion that capitalism is self-regulating and good. But proofs of existence do not prove or disprove Smith's assertion. They show that certain equations describing a certain blackboard economy have a solution but they do not give the solution to the blackboard problem, much less to an extant economy. Indeed the problem is framed in such general terms that no specific solution even to the toy economy on the blackboard could reasonably be expected [McCloskey, 1991, p. 8; see also Morishima, 1991].

Precisely, Roy Weintraub (1985) has argued at book length: GE theory must be appraised as any research line in mathematics and not as a theory that could conceivably be falsified. Indeed, GE theory must be construed as the Lakatosian "hard core" of the neoclassical SRP and as such it is of course empirically empty. He then proceeds to tell the story of the development of GE existence proofs over the years 1930 to 1954, presented as a case study in the "hardening" of that hard core. He never questions the significance of existence proofs or the fact that some of the best minds of modern economics devoted a quarter of a century to an achievement which is, to say the least, of somewhat dubious value. Besides, the notion that GE theory is the hard core of the neoclassical SRP is questionable on both conceptual and historical grounds. There was neoclassical economics long before the revival of GE theory in the 1930s. Surely ?, Marshallian economics is neoclassical economics and yet Marshall relegated GE to a brief appendix in his *Principles*. Similarly, modern economics is full of partial equilibrium theories that draw little even on GE models and certainly not at all on GE theory. In short, there is something wrong with Weintraub's story. What seems to have happened historically is that GE theory invaded neoclassical economics and in the process transformed it into an increasingly technical, highly formal apparatus for talking about an economy as if that talk corresponds to a real economy.

Once an economist has committed himself to the meaningfulness of GE theory, it is a striking fact that in no time at all he or she will be found damning the methodology of falsificationism as outmoded positivism. Thus, Weintraub (1985, pp. 169–71; 1989) insists that all economics facts are theory-laden and hence that all notions of theories being created to rationalize facts, and facts being used to corroborate theories, are just methodological confusions. Likewise, Hahn (1984, pp. 4–5; 1985, pp. 10–11) pours cold water on falsifiability and insists that there is "understanding" without predictability. Arrow (1987, p. 242) is less categorical in reflecting falsificationism but even he draws back from the relentless demand for empirical validation. Asked in an interview "What criteria would you use to evaluate the soundness of an alternative theory?," he replied:

Persuasiveness. Does it correspond to our understanding of the economic world? I think it is foolish to say that we rely on hard empirical evidence completely. A very important part of it is just our perception of the economic world. If you find a new concept, the question is does it illuminate your perception? Do you feel you understand what is going on in everyday life? Of course, whether it fits empirical and other tests is also important [see also Aumann in Feiwel, 1987, pp. 313–15].

But so what? Not all economists are engaged in GE theory, so why decry the work of Arrow, Debreu, McKenzie, Hurwicz, Sonnenschein, etcetera? It is only one kind of economics after all. On the contrary, however: it is the most prestigious economics of all and has set standards that all economists aspire to reach. Enormous intellectual resources have been invested in its endless refinements, none of which has even provided a fruitful starting point from which to approach a substantive explanation of the workings of an economic system. Its leading characteristic has been the endless formalization of purely logical problems without the slightest regard for the production of falsifiable theorems about actual economic behavior, which, we insist, remains the fundamental task of economics. The widespread belief that every economic theory must be fitted into the GE mold if it is to qualify as rigorous science has perhaps been more responsible than any other intellectual force for the purely abstract and nonempirical character of so much of modern economic reasoning.

9

Marginal productivity theory

Production functions

The orthodox theory of the firm makes the strong assumption that it is always possible to specify a function, the so-called production function, which expresses the *maximum* volume of physical output that can be obtained from all technically feasible combinations of physical inputs, given the prevailing level of freely available technical knowledge about the relationship between inputs and output. It is customary to classify the inputs into more or less homogeneous classes, which ought to carry the labels "man-hours," "machine-hours," and "acres-per-year," and not "labor," "capital," and "land," because the inputs in question are supposed to be flow and not stock variables. On the further convenient assumption that the microproduction function so defined is smoothly differentiable and the strictly necessary assumption that the firm is profit maximizing (no value being placed on the psychic income of entrepreneurs), the theory then proceeds to derive the input demand functions as inverse forms of the marginal productivity equations. If factor and product markets are competitive, firms will hire workers, machines, and space until wage rates, machine rentals, and land rentals are equal to their respective marginal value or marginal revenue products.

If the supplies of these factor services are exogenously determined, this theory may be said to "determine" wage and rental rates. For the firm, it would be truer to say that factor prices "determine" marginal products than that marginal products "determine" factor prices. Even for factor markets as a whole, this is only a so-called marginal productivity theory of factor prices on the assumption that factor supplies are given. As Denis Robertson used to say, factor prices "measure" the marginal products, and what "determines" factor prices is not so much the first derivatives of the production function as the maximizing behavior of producers. The equality of factor prices and marginal products is an equilibrium solution of a set of simultaneous equations,

170

and it seems pointless to select "marginal productivity" as a sort of prime mover. For this and other reasons, it would be a great advantage if the phrase "marginal productivity theory of distribution" were banished from the literature.

Most of the great neoclassical economists of the nineteenth century refused to aggregate the microproduction functions of firms into an aggregate production function for the economy as a whole and instead used marginal productivity theory to tackle special problems in the spirit of partial equilibrium economics, or else, like Walras, they operated with the notion of the entire disaggregated array of *n* production functions. Furthermore, they went out of their way to deny the belief that marginal productivity theory provided ready-made answers to the great questions of property ownership and distributive justice; all of them had learned the lesson taught by John Stuart Mill: the laws of distribution, unlike the laws of production, are capable of being decisively affected by collective action.

The notion that the functional distribution of income may be explained simply by invoking the principles of marginal productivity, as enshrined in an aggregate production function of the simple Cobb–Douglas variety, was broached virtually for the first time in Hicks's *Theory of Wages* (1932), in particular Chapter 6 of that book. After some years largely devoted to exploring Hicks's invention of *the elasticity of substitution,* the Keynesian revolution caused the range of issues Hicks had opened up to fall into disfavor. It was only after World War II that what Samuelson had called the neo-neoclassical theory of production and distribution caught the imagination of economists. After Solow's seminal article of 1957, estimation of aggregate production functions for purposes of measuring the sources of growth and drawing inferences about the nature of technical change became a widespread practice in economic research, ignoring the profound difficulties that surround the entire concept of an *aggregate* production function (see Blaug, 1980, pp. 469–71).

Much of this empirical work was little more than "measurement without theory."[10] What emerged in the process was the *simpliste* marginal productivity theory that characterized a large number of journal articles in the 1960s: one or two outputs, two inputs, twice differentiable, aggregate production functions obeying constant returns to scale, malleable homogeneous capital,

---

[10] In an authoritative review of the literature on production functions, Walters (1963, p. 11) concluded: "After surveying the problems of aggregation, one may easily doubt whether there is much point in employing such a concept as an aggregate production function. The variety of competitive and technological conditions we find in modern economies suggests that we cannot approximate the basic requirements of sensible aggregation except, perhaps, over firms in the same industry or for narrow sections of the economy."

a monotonic relationship between the capital–labor ratio and the rate of return on capital, disembodied technical progress classified as neutral or factor saving, perfect competition, instantaneous adjustments, and costless information. Even "the new quantitative economic history" of that decade became thoroughly infected by this style of theorizing in which dramatic conclusions about the past were derived from the global measurement of a few well-selected microeconomic variables (see McClelland, 1975, pp. 194– 201, 230–7).

What practical inferences can be drawn from a *simpliste* marginal productivity theory of distribution? Radical critics of orthodox economics are persuaded that questions of unions, the corporate power structure, the state of aggregate demand, and government policies toward incomes and prices, all of which seem to be relevant to problems of income distribution, are somehow relegated to "sociology" by neo-neoclassical theory, which explains wages and profits simply by technology, consumers' preferences, and given factor supplies. This criticism should not be lightly shrugged off but it does involve a certain confusion of language. By a *theory of distribution,* the critics mean a theory of distributive shares, whereas in orthodox economics, the theory of income distribution is a theory of factor pricing: until Hicks there was in fact no theory of the share of wages and profits in national income that commanded universal assent. Since Hicks we have such a theory, but its precise significance is frequently misunderstood. For better or for worse, it does not prohibit the belief that the "class struggle" has a lot to do with the determination of distributive shares and even with the rate of wages and profit.

The Hicksian theory of relative shares

The Hicksian theory grafted a three-way classification of innovation in terms of relative shares on a standard marginal productivity theory of factor pricing, deliberately gearing the argument to the economy as a whole. According to Hicks, "neutral" technical change leads to an unchanged capital–labor ratio at constant relative factor prices; but according to Harrod, it leads instead to a constant capital–output ratio at a given rate of interest; both agree that it would leave the relative shares of wages and profits unaffected (see Blaug, 1980, pp. 472–8). In subsequent years, a great deal of energy was spent in the effort to show that these two definitions only come to the same thing if the aggregate production function is of the type that involves an elasticity of substitution of unity such as, for example, the Cobb–Douglas production function. Measurement with aggregate data usually confirmed the Cobb–Douglas hypothesis but at the industry level it soon proved necessary to fit production functions with nonunitary elasticities of substitution, such as the so-called CES (constant elasticity of substitution) production function. In all such cases, the evidence lends itself only too readily to Hicksian interpretations for the simple reason that the Hicksian theory is entirely taxonomic, capable of accounting for anything and everything.

In a comprehensive survey of the literature on technical progress, Kennedy and Thirlwall (1972, p. 49) conclude: "Neither the finely competitive model nor the minor monopoly-oligopoly departures prepare us for predicting the distributive influences of technical change; at best we have definitions of 'Harrod-neutral' and 'Hicks-neutral' technical progress . They permit us to be wise in explanation, ex post, but ex ante all seems obscure." Similarly, reviewing the theory of income distribution, Johnson (1973, p. 42) minces no words in making the same point, that "the elasticity of substitution, as employed in distributive theory, is a tautology, in the same way as the Marshallian concept of elasticity of demand is a tautology . . . in both cases, the economic problem is measurement, not statements about the implications of hypothetical measurement." He goes on to observe that "no theoretical apparatus will explain functional shares . . . in fundamental causal terms, but what can be done is to measure changes in observable inputs and then, in the light of theoretical concepts, interpret the outcome" (1973, p. 191). Unfortunately, when the theoretical concepts themselves, such as the aggregate production function, are only tenuously related to microeconomic behavior, interpretation of the outcome may not carry us any further. Even the theory of induced innovations, which for a while seemed to offer the exciting prospect of explaining technical change endogenously as a process whereby firms "learn" to extrapolate past trends in the factor-saving bias of technology, has gradually petered out for lack of coherent microeconomic foundation (Bronfenbrenner, 1971, pp. 160–2; Blaug, 1980, pp. 481–4; Nordhaus, 1973). No wonder a leading book on income distribution by a "cautious supporter" of neoclassical economics eventually arrives at the conclusion that "In the present state of the science, prediction of income shares is beyond our capabilities" (Pen, 1971, p. 214).[11]

In some ways, it is difficult to understand why anyone should want to predict relative shares. Such predictions have virtually no practical relevance for collective bargaining because, depending on how the shares are measured, we can make the figures come out almost as we like (Blaug, 1980, p. 511). Nor are relative shares a particularly interesting theoretical problem. It is of course true by definition that labor's share of total income is equal to the average rate of wages and salaries divided by the average product of labor in the entire economy; likewise, the profit share is by definition equal to the

---

[11] Lipsey (1989, pp. 339–40), almost alone among textbook writers, agrees with Pen and doubts that a testable theory of macrodistribution, if and when it comes along, will be a marginal productivity theory. Hicks (1965, p. 172), however, remained persuaded that there is some life left in the old apparatus.

average rate of profit on capital invested divided by the average product of capital (or multiplied by the capital-output ratio). But the average products of labor and capital are not behavioral variables in standard theory; economic agents do not maximize or minimize them; no producers or consumers, no workers or capitalists, respond to them; they are just *ex post* magnitudes that can be and have been measured, but which nevertheless lack a definite theoretical status. It is perfectly possible, therefore, to have a theory of wages or a theory of the rate of profit, without having a theory of the share of wages and profits, and vice versa. The fact of the matter is that the distributive shares are the outcome of a wide variety of forces and any theory that attempts to tackle them directly finds itself making so many heroic, simplifying assumptions that the results are simply analytical curiosities. Apart from obeisance to past traditions, and particularly some of the questions posed by Ricardo, I personally can find no persuasive reasons to justify the obsessive preoccupation with distributive shares in the writings of both critics and defenders of marginal productivity theory.

So long as we stick to the orthodox theory of functional income distribution cast in general equilibrium terms, we are unlikely to come up with answers that will shake the world. In that theory, I repeat, the functional distribution of income may be said to be "determined" by the initial distribution of resources among households, their preferences, the production functions of firms, and the behavioral motives of both households and firms. But the theory does not "explain" why equilibrium obtains, if indeed it does obtain, or why it should continue to obtain, and in that sense it fails to provide a *causal* explanation of the functional distribution of incomes. In short, the neoclassical, as well as the neo-neoclassical theory of functional income distribution, is a much more modest theory than many of its enemies would have us believe. As Hahn (1972, p. 2) rightly says:

I call a theory of distribution neoclassical if it employs a model of perfect competition in permanent equilibrium . . . This theory has nothing simple to offer in answer to the question why is the share of wages, or of profits, what it is. The question is prompted by our interest in the distribution of income between social classes, and social class is not an explanatory variable of neo-classical theory . . . On the one hand, neo-classical practitioners have not been able to resist the temptation to make the theory yield simple answers to sociologically motivated questions. On the other hand, economists impressed by the inadequacy of the model for such questions . . . have criticized it on logical grounds where, as it happens, it is particularly robust.

Testing marginal productivity theory

The marginal productivity theory of factor pricing is a modest theory. It is also a highly abstract theory: it is formulated in terms so general as to make it virtually useless for answering specific questions about, say, the structure of wages in labor markets. This is nicely illustrated by a series of questions posed by Lester Thurow (1975, pp. 211–30) in his "Do-It-Yourself Guide to Marginal Productivity."

Are workers paid their marginal product at each instant of time, or are they only paid their marginal product over the course of an entire working life? If Gary Becker's distinction between "general training" and "specific training" is to be believed (see Blaug, 1972, pp. 192–9), the earnings of workers receiving general training is necessarily less than their current marginal product, the opposite being true of workers receiving specific training. *General training* is defined as training that raises the trainee's productivity irrespective of which firm he works for, whereas *specific training* is defined as training that only enhances the future productivity of trainees in the firm providing it. Firms operating under competitive conditions have no incentive to pay the costs of general training because they cannot guarantee that they will be able to retain trained workers. As a result, the costs of general training programs are passed on to trainees in the form of reduced earnings during the training period. On the other hand, workers receiving specific training must earn as much as they could earn elsewhere if they are to have an incentive to stay with the firm in question; firms recoup these specific training expenses by paying trained workers less than their marginal product. Thus, if we examine the wages of young workers, it is only those receiving specific training who can be expected to earn their current marginal product; if we look at old workers, however, it is only those who earlier received general training who can be expected to earn their current marginal product; in general, few workers in a perfectly competitive labor market earn their current marginal product. Clearly, in these circumstances it is not going to be easy to test the marginal productivity theory of wages.

Next, we may ask whether it is individual workers who are paid their marginal product, or whether instead it is groups of workers with identical skills who are all paid alike, say, because of the difficulty of identifying better and worse workers with a common skill, in consequence of which some workers in that skill category will be paid more and some will be paid less than their individual marginal products would warrant. Similar arguments apply to other ways of grouping workers such as workers of a given sex, age, and educational qualification in a particular industry, where again firms may pay these groups the same wage at least initially because of the problem of accurately measuring the marginal product of individuals. If, as is frequently asserted, much industrial work is carried out by teams of workers coordinating their efforts, members of the team may be paid their average marginal product not only initially but throughout their working lives simply because their individual contribution to output cannot be identified; here too no individual worker will earn precisely his own particular marginal product. Once again, we see how formidable are the problems of testing the comparative static predictions of marginal productivity theory.

All these difficulties would exist even under conditions of perfect competition in both product and factor markets. In the real world, many of the wages we will observe will be earned in industries that are not competitive, producing under conditions of increasing returns to scale, in which case some inputs must be paid less than their marginal products and these may well be labor inputs. Furthermore, the observed wages may be disequilibrium wages and in any case they will be influenced by labor supply conditions in different local labor markets, not to mention the unequal distribution of preferences for psychic income among workers.

Next, there are the nonmarket clearing theories of Keynesian macroeconomics that purport to explain the persistence of involuntary unemployment even in cyclical booms (see Lindbeck and Snower, 1985). One of these is the so-called "efficiency wage theory," according to which employers are willing to pay workers a premium over and above the competitive wage, that is, more than their marginal value or marginal revenue product and more than the wage for which workers as a whole are prepared to work. They do so because they find it difficult to distinguish high-quality from low-quality workers and know that a wage equal to the average marginal product of all workers will give high-quality workers an incentive to quit in order to locate better offers elsewhere. Furthermore, workers must be monitored to prevent shirking and malingering and the higher the wage, the larger the penalty of being fired after being caught shirking. In either case, wages are set above competitive levels as a method of retaining superior labor and providing workers with an incentive to work diligently. In short, we should not expect to observe wages equal to the marginal productivity of labor under normal circumstances (Fisher, 1991, pp. 27–8; Nickell, 1991, pp. 153–7).

Perhaps we have now said enough to suggest that the famous or infamous marginal productivity theory of wages has never been spelled out in sufficient detail to be of much use in accounting for the observed pattern of relative wages. No wonder, therefore, that it has rarely been tested, and even where efforts have been made to put it to the test, the results have been inconclusive. If any one-sentence summary of the evidence is possible, the most we can say is that marginal productivity theory is fairly successful in correctly predicting extremely long-run changes in interindustry and interoccupational wage differentials; on the other hand, it is singularly unsuccessful in correctly predicting short-run movements in wage differentials (see Burton and others, 1971, particularly pp. 275–80; Perlman, 1969, chaps. 4, 5).[12] The empirical status

---

[12] Perlman's textbook in labor economics stands out among many of its rivals for its thoroughly Popperian flavor.

of the marginal productivity theory of factor pricing, therefore, remains uncertain. Of course, this is just as true of many other economic theories. Nevertheless, marginal productivity theory has suffered more than most theories from the failure to specify its range of application to concrete problems. It has largely remained, throughout its long history, a perfectly general thesis without specific content.

10

Switching, reswitching, and all that

Measurement of capital

The marginal productivity theory of wages has never lacked critics at any stage in its history but, at least until recently, the marginal productivity theory of interest was allowed to pass more or less unscathed. In the 1950s, however, Joan Robinson, soon followed by a number of other Cambridge economists (Cambridge, United Kingdom, that is), launched an entirely new attack on the so-called marginal productivity theory of distribution, directed in particular at the Hicksian two-inputs-one-output simplification of the neo-classical theory of factor pricing. The stock of capital in an economy, it was argued, being a collection of heterogeneous machines rather than a homogeneous fund of purchasing power, cannot be valued in its own technical units, although apparently "labor" and "land" can be so measured; the valuation of capital necessarily presupposes a particular rate of interest, and this means that the rate of interest cannot be determined by the marginal product of capital without reasoning in a circle; hence, marginal productivity theory cannot explain how the rate of interest is determined.

Much of this criticism falls to the ground if we replace the *simpliste* formulation of marginal productivity theory by the disaggregated Walrasian version, which neither invokes nor implies the concept of aggregate production function, nor indeed the notion of the aggregate capital stock as an economic variable. Moreover, the idea that the aggregation of capital goods poses unique difficulties not encountered in the aggregation of labor inputs, not to mention the aggregation of physical outputs, is simply a popular misunderstanding (Blaug, 1980, p. 408). Even if it is necessary to measure capital in its own technical units in order to make gross comparisons between economies in different stationary equilibrium states, the issue of finding a natural unit in which to measure capital does not arise if we are only concerned, as we always are for purposes of the qualitative calculus, with marginal variations

178

around an equilibrium position. For such variations, different capital goods are indeed aggregated into a fund of purchasing power; the uniform equilibrium rate of interest on money capital invested in competing activities only emerges because investors care nothing about the actual physical variety of capital goods.

The existence of a demand function for capital

But the Cambridge critics have another string to their bow. In *simpliste* marginal productivity theory, the capital intensity of an economy is uniquely related to relative factor prices; in particular, a decline in the rate of interest or a rise in the rate of wages necessarily raises the average capital–labor ratio of the economy. But whatever version of marginal productivity theory we adopt, argue the Cambridge critics, it is not possible to demonstrate that a fall in the rate of interest will always alter the rankings of the most profitable of all currently available techniques in a unidirectional manner so as to increase the overall capital intensity of the economy. This is because of the phenomenon of *double switching* or *reswitching,* which may occur even under strictly neoclassical conditions of perfect competition, perfect information, instantaneous adjustments, smoothly differentiable microproduction functions, and profit-maximizing behavior. The phenomenon of reswitching is said to destroy the logical coherence of the neoclassical theory of distribution: if there is no strict monotonic relationship between a change in the rate of interest and the capital–labor ratio, we must give up the idea of explaining the rate of interest in terms of the relative scarcity of capital in an economy, which is after all the essence of the marginal productivity theory of interest, and indeed, we must abandon all notions of drawing up the demand for capital as an inverse function of the interest rate.

The 1960s witnessed a great debate on the validity of the concept of reswitching. There is no need to review the history of the "great reswitching debate," which culminated in the unconditional surrender of Samuelson who had earlier denied the possibility of reswitching except in unusual circumstances, because Geoffrey Harcourt (1972, chap. 4) has already provided a blow-by-blow description of this extraordinarily instructive episode in modern economic thought. What exactly is reswitching? The simplest illustration of it is the one given by Samuelson in his 1966 declaration of unconditional surrender involving two processes that require the same length of time to manufacture a given product with the aid of unequal amounts of labor, but without any machines (see Blaug, 1980, p. 523). It is easy to show that the process with less labor will not necessarily be the more profitable one at all rates of interest: if its labor is applied at an earlier date in the production cycle, it will become the more expensive of the two processes at high rates of interest because its wage bill accumulates faster at compound interest. It is also easy to show that there exist patterns in the application of labor to the two processes at which the one with less labor is the more profitable of the two at low rates of interest, the less profitable of the two at somewhat higher rates of interest, and then, at still higher rates of interest, once again the more profitable of the two processes. This is the phenomenon of reswitching. It arises in this simple example from the compound-interest effect of changes in the interest rate on the comparative costs of labor inputs applied at different dates in various technical processes of identical length producing the same good; in more complex examples, it arises both from the staggered application of inputs to identical productive processes, from the different gestation periods of alternative technical processes, and from the fact that the output of such processes sometimes enter as inputs into other processes.

The empirical significance of reswitching

Everyone has now agreed that reswitching is perfectly possible, and everyone has also agreed that its possible occurrence destroys the concept of a necessarily monotonic relationship between capital intensity and relative factor prices. But how likely is it for reswitching to occur? Samuelson, in conceding the validity of the switching theorem, has expressed some doubt about its empirical importance, and Hicks (1973, p. 44) has conjectured that "reswitching looks like being on the edge of the things that could happen." Cambridge economists, on the other hand, have insisted that reswitching and the associated phenomenon of capital reversing (lower instead of higher capital–labor ratios as the rate of interest rises) are extremely likely and indeed the general rule, but they have neither attempted to measure the empirical significance of switching in actual economies nor discussed the problem of how we might go about measuring it. It is clear that it would not be an easy task. Strictly speaking, changes in capital–labor ratios as a consequence of changes in relative factor prices involve instantaneous movements among alternative equilibrium stationary states, which is a far cry from the process of substituting capital for labor in historical time, which we all think of when confronted with the proposition that a capital-abundant economy like America will have a lower rate of interest than a labor-abundant one like India.

Faced with the familiar problem of testing comparative static propositions, and loath to investigate the scope for reswitching by tedious microstudies of the length of production processes and the associated time patterns of inputs, the Cambridge economists have instead taken refuge in analytical theorems about the conditions that are required to rule out switching. The most famous of these shows that to preclude switching in an *n*-sector model of fixed coefficients techniques, we need at least one capital good in our model that is exceptional in the sense that (1) all inputs in the economy enter into the production of that capital good, and (2) it is itself produced by a smooth neoclassical production function with variable coefficients. Cambridge economists appear to find these conditions so strict as to be unlikely to occur in the real world, on which grounds they conclude that reswitching is the rule and not the exception (Harcourt, 1972, p. 171n), but others have followed the same route only to emerge in the end with exactly the opposite conclusion (Eltis, 1973, pp. 115–16, 123–5). Similarly, it has been shown that the empirical significance of switching depends on (1) whether the rate of interest falls below a critical level and (2) whether product prices decline as firms readopt some previously used techniques (Ferguson and Allen, 1970). The upshot of the controversy in the literature so far seems to be that measurement of the likelihood of switching rests on measurement of the degree of input substitutability in an economy and this is an issue that is unlikely to be decisively resolved in the near future.

The favorite models of the Cambridge school always involve linear Leontief technologies – each product in each sector is produced with only one fixed coefficients technique – and this naturally throws the entire burden of factor substitutability on consumers choosing one mix of output rather than another, the different mixes implying different techniques and hence input substitution through the backdoor. In other words, even in the worst case, where input substitution is excluded by assumption, some degree of input substitution in the large is reintroduced by the pattern of final demand, including the demand of overseas buyers. This result is even more likely if we adopt activity analysis as a mode of describing the technical possibilities open to business firms representing a halfway house between completely fixed and completely variable production coefficients (see Blaug, 1980, pp. 431–5). It is not obvious, therefore, that switching among techniques does in fact occur. If reswitching does not occur, it is still possible to have capital reversing (Harcourt, 1972, pp. 128–9, 145–6) but it takes even more tortuous assumptions about technology – such as wide gaps in the input coefficients of different techniques – to obtain that result. If we cannot get ourselves to believe that switching is a common occurrence, it is even more difficult to persuade ourselves that capital reversing is ever likely to happen.

There is, therefore, nothing absurd in Ferguson's (1969, pp. xvii, 266) famous declaration of "faith" in the neoclassical parables until such a time that "the econometricians have the answers for us." Samuelson (1976, p. 618), in the tenth edition of his elementary textbook, voices similar sentiments: "the science of political economy has not yet the empirical knowledge to decide whether the real world is nearer to the idealized polar case represented by (a) the neoclassical parable or (b) the simple reswitching paradigm." Both Joan Robinson (1975, p. 82) and Harcourt (1972, pp. 25, 29, 122; 1976, pp. 37, 58), however, deny that the question can ever be settled by empirical evidence: reswitching and capital reversing, they say, are propositions about alternative equilibrium states and such counterfactual possibilities never can be observed in the real world even in principle.

If this fantastic claim were to be taken seriously, it would succeed in rendering the whole of the neoclassical research program as impervious to empirical refutation. Take the simplest possible example of a standard neoclassical prediction: a tax on butter producers will raise the price of butter because it shifts the butter supply curve to the left; let us take a look at butter prices to verify this prediction, making sure by all means at our disposal that the demand curve for butter has not shifted during the time period of observation. Oh no, we are told by Robinson and Harcourt, you are comparing two alternative equilibrium positions involving the passage of logical and not actual time, and hence your prediction is not capable, strictly speaking, of being empirically falsified. This dodge would certainly make neoclassical economics easier to defend, but only at the cost of exchanging the methodology of falsificationism for the methodology of essentialism (see Chapter 4 above). As a matter of fact, despite Joan Robinson's lip service paid to Popperian ideas (1977, pp. 1318–20, 1323), the writings of the Cambridge school continually lapse into essentialist arguments.

To declare one's faith that the econometricians will one day deliver the goods is quite another matter. The history of both the physical and the social sciences is replete with such examples of "faith," that is, a determination to ignore logical anomalies in a theory until they are shown to be empirically important, rather than to leave whole areas of intellectual endeavor devoid of any theoretical framework. There is nothing irrational, as Popper and Lakatos have shown, about the tendency of scientists to hang on to a research program despite anomalies if no better rival program is available. To continue our earlier example, it is as if one economist, arguing that a specific tax on butter producers is very likely to raise the price of butter, were to be told by another that his reasoning is based on the orthodox idea that all demand curves are negatively inclined and all supply curves positively inclined, equilibrium being found at the intersection of the two curves; the modern theory of consumer behavior shows that demand curves may be positively as well as negatively inclined; therefore, the initial proposition about the specific tax on butter producers is just as likely to be false as true. Most economists when confronted with this argument would reply that positively inclined demand curves, while perfectly possible, are few and far between and that empirical work on statistical demand curves has never in fact produced a single convincing example of one (see Chapter 6 above). Similarly, it may be conceded that reswitching and capital reversing are perfectly possible phenomena, but until they are shown to actually occur, economists are ill-advised to throw away their textbooks on price theory, labor economics, growth theory, and development economics just because the models in them contain some indigestible anomalies.[13]

Hausman (1981b, pp. 81–2) denies that there is an analogy between the existence of Giffen goods and upward-sloping demand curves in the theory of demand, on the one hand, and reswitching and capital reversing in the theory of capital and interest, on the other: " Demand theorists know there are few Giffen goods. They know why there are Giffen goods. They can successfully predict that certain goods in certain economies . . . are likely to be Giffen goods. Capital theorists, on the other hand do not know whether capital reversing is common or rare. Until recently they possessed no theory which made sense of the phenomenon. . . . Capital theorists are also unable to predict when capital reversing will occur. . . . There is no justification for the claim that capital reversing depends only on minor qualifications in simplified capital theories.'' No doubt, but the fact remains that the issue is essentially one of *quantifying* the significance of reswitching and capital reversing; we now know that they may happen but not that they do happen. Members of the Cambridge school agree but deny that the burden of proof rests with them: "the logical possibility of reswitching and capital reversing having been established, it is for those who ignore such possibilities to justify themselves empirically" (Steedman, 1991, p. 441).[13] That is to say, if I demonstrate that green swans may well exist and you deny that they actually exist, the burden of proof is on *you* to travel the world to investigate every siting of swans. What a convenient stance to adopt and what a license to reject every rule that has any exception whatsoever!

Do the Cambridge critics truly believe their avowed agnosticism about capital theory? Would they go as far to deny that, in general, India and China are well-advised to favor labor-intensive techniques? (Sen, 1974). No doubt, in particular cases, we would still have to carry out detailed project appraisals but, surely?, we would be surprised to find a labor-surplus economy adopting the same capital intensive technology as America or Britain. If so, are we not conceding the real-world insignificance of reswitching and capital reversing, at least in gross economic comparisons? In short, we are perfectly justified in retaining the neoclassical theory of distribution, *so far as it goes,* provided we add that it does not go very far.

Burmeister (1991, pp. 470–1), a neoclassical economist if there ever was one, notes the failure of the economics profession in recent years to take much

---

[13] However, some Cambridge critics believe the matter is already settled. Thus, Nell (1972b, p. 511) observes: "Giffen goods and backward-bending labour-supply curves are obviously *special* cases. By contrast, in a multi-sector economy, reswitching and capital-reversing appear to be the general rule, not the exception." No empirical evidence is supplied to justify either assertion.

notice of the phenomenon of reswitching. Heterogeneous capital models are treated as if they were single-capital models, which is strictly speaking incorrect, on the grounds that one-capital goods models give approximately good answers to certain kinds of questions. However, it is not at all clear what these questions are other than purely logical puzzles about one economic model or another. Hausman (1981b, p. 191), in yet another survey of the great reswitching debate, concludes: "Economists do not understand the phenomena of capital and interest. They do not understand why the rate of interest is generally positive (and thus how it is that capitalism can work)." If so, it is a damning indictment of one of the most acrimonious controversies of modern economics. But in point of fact, it is not so. Rather, the reason the rate of interest is positive has little if anything to do with static equilibrium theory, which is the domain of the great reswitching debate; it rests on the presence of uncertainty in a dynamic model of price determination à la Knight and Schumpeter. But that is another story.

11

The Heckscher–Ohlin theory of international trade

The Heckscher–Ohlin theorem

Ricardo found the cause of foreign trade in the relative immobility of capital across national frontiers and he explained the commodity composition of world trade by persistent differences in the productivity of labor between nations; by assuming that relative commodity prices vary proportionately with relative labor costs, he showed that free trade will cause each country to export those goods in which it possessed a comparative price advantage and that such trade will result in mutual gain as compared to a state of self-sufficiency.

Ricardian theory made no attempt to explain the underlying productivity differences that give rise to intercountry variations in comparative costs, which in turn give rise to international trade. In the modern Heckscher-Ohlin theory, these productivity differences themselves are traced to intercountry differences in initial factor endowments, which indeed are made to carry the entire burden of the explanation: the more obvious causes of the commodity composition of foreign trade, such as international differences in the quality of factors, as well as differences in production functions for given products, are deliberately excluded by assumption. The Heckscher–Ohlin theory culminates in what is now generally known as the *Heckscher–Ohlin theorem* (HOT) of the pattern of international trade: a country exports those goods whose production is intensive in the country's relatively abundant factor and imports other goods that use intensively the country's relatively scarce factor. This theorem is plausible but it is also very daring: it explains the commodity composition of foreign trade entirely in terms of supply conditions; if, for example, a country's demand is biased towards those goods that use the abundant factor more intensively, the HOT may fail.

Samuelson's factor-price-equalization theorem

In its present form, the Heckscher–Ohlin model owes more to a number of articles published by Samuelson in the late 1940s and early 1950s than to Heckscher's seminal 1919 article, refurbished and expanded in Ohlin's *Interregional and International Trade* (1933): many of the variables that Heckscher and Ohlin regarded as significant, such as demand conditions and economies of scale, were dropped from the discussion and further developments of the theory departed considerably from the task that the two pioneers set for themselves of explaining the actual observed commodity composition of foreign trade. Inasmuch as international trade is a substitute for international factor movements, both Heckscher and Ohlin conjectured that free trade would work to equalize factor scarcities and hence factor prices around the world but Ohlin, at any rate, also found good reasons why this process would nevertheless fall short of perfect equalization. Samuelson, however, devoted much of his effort to spelling out a corollary of the HOT, namely, the *factor-price-equalization theorem* (FPET): under a number of special conditions (perfect competition, zero transport costs, incomplete specialization, identical linearly homogeneous production functions, identical homothetic preferences, absence of external economies, constant relative factor intensities at all relative factor prices, factors homogeneous in quality, and the number of factors no greater than the number of commodities), free trade will bring about complete and not just partial equalization of factor prices. This elegant formulation was eventually generalized to *n* countries, *n* factors, and *n* goods. The same thing is not true of the HOT, which remains to this day a theorem about the case of two countries, two factors, and two goods (Bhagwati, 1965, pp. 175–6).

The Leontief paradox

Although empirical tests of the "monetary" theory of international trade (or classical theory of the transfer mechanism) go back to the 1920s, the pure or "real" theory of international trade in either its Ricardian or Ohlinian version remained virtually untested until 1951.[14] In that year, Donald MacDougall carried out the first test of Ricardian trade theory and a few years later Wassily Leontief, applying his 1947 input-output table to United States trade patterns, discovered that the country's exports were relatively labor intensive, while its imports were relatively capital intensive, the very opposite of what the HOT would lead us to expect. Neil de Marchi (1976, pp. 114–23) has shown that the reactions to Leontief's apparent refutation of the HOT

[14] There are, of course, older descriptive studies of trade patterns and Ohlin himself repeatedly drew attention to trade patterns and land-labor ratios in nineteenth-century Europe that confirmed the predictions of his factor-proportions theory.

can be divided into four categories. (1) There were those who criticized Leontief's methods, the quality of his data, the exclusion of both natural resources
and human capital embodied in skilled labor, all of which taken together are
capable of reversing his results. (2) There were some who explained away the
findings by a variety of ad hoc arguments: factors and techniques are not
everywhere the same, demand conditions differ between countries just enough
to offset the factor biases in production, factor-intensity reversal is likely within
the relevant range of factor prices, and so on. (3) Others, including Samuelson himself, more or less ignored the Leontief paradox because they pursued
what might be called "the Ohlin-Samuelson research program," whose aim
was to reduce the pure theory of international trade to a special case of general
equilibrium (GE) theory. From their point of view, the factual accuracy of the
HOT was a minor question because it was regarded anyway as only a first
approximation to the real-world conditions of different taxes, tariffs, transport
costs, economies of scale, demand conditions, factor mobilities, and imperfections of competition. Finally, (4) there was a group of mainly business
economists who rejected both the HOT and the Ohlin–Samuelson program;
they seized on the Leontief paradox to support their own loosely constructed
"product cycle" and "technological gap" models, accounting for the pattern
of trade in manufactured goods in terms of the dynamics of product innovations and the information and marketing advantages of producers in high-
income countries.

Very few economists reacted as did Charles Kindleberger: "what he [Leon-
tief] proves is not that the USA is capital-scarce and labour-abundant, but that
the Heckscher–Ohlin theorem is wrong" (cited by de Marchi, 1976, p. 124).
Most trade theorists continued to refine the apparently refuted factor-proportions theory, becoming increasingly preoccupied with the stream of technical
puzzles generated by the Leontief paradox, for example: What is a factor and
how many separate factors enter into production processes? Can factor-intensity reversal be excluded in a multifactor world? What conditions are necessary to ensure the FPET as the number of factors increases?

Earlier in 1941, Samuelson and Stolper had endeavored to establish the
theorem that protective tariffs may benefit the relatively scarcer factor in both
absolute and relative terms. This theorem proved to be a milestone in the
history of the Ohlin–Samuelson research program. Subsequent work on FPET
was intended to demonstrate the uniqueness of a one-to-one relation between
commodity prices and corresponding factor prices in a world of many factors
and many goods, traded in separate but related markets, thus completing the
articulation of a GE framework in which the Ricardian and the Ohlinian models
are viewed simply as special cases, the former arguing forward from given
factor prices to commodity prices, while the latter instead argues from given
commodity prices back to factor prices.

The Ohlin–Samuelson research program

How much would have been lost if the Leontief paradox had been allowed to put a stop to the Ohlin–Samuelson research program? Obviously, the answer to that question is a matter of judgment. Suffice it to say that most trade theorists did not behave as if they were "naive falsificationists": they clung to the "hard core" of the Ohlin–Samuelson program, proscribing all attempts to explain the pattern of world trade without appeal to the GE factor-proportions theory of pricing. Whether the Ohlin–Samuelson program was and continues to be a fruitful, "progressive" research program in the Lakatosian sense of generating a harvest of novel facts is again a difficult matter of judgment; most of the novel insights turned up by the Ohlin–Samuelson approach were less matters of facts than analytical connections between the phenomena of international and domestic trade (de Marchi, 1976, p. 123). What is certain is that the program did much to popularize the *simpliste* marginal productivity theory that has dogged all postwar discussions of distribution problems: the factor-proportions model of international trade encouraged the teaching of parables invoking two countries, two goods, and two factors in the context of aggregate production functions obeying constant returns to scale, thus unifying the treatment of both domestic and international trade by means of a highly simplified, aggregate GE theory that promised more than it was capable of delivering. The assessment of the Ohlin-Samuelson research program thus cannot be separated from the assessment of the wider Hicks–Samuelson–Arrow–Debreu GE research program of which it forms an integral part.

It is ironic that so much of this work was fostered and promoted by the efforts of Samuelson, the supreme advocate of *operationalism* in economic theory, at least in his early days (see Chapter 4 above). "The whole discussion [of factor-price equalization]," one commentator observed, "is, for better or worse, a supreme example of nonoperational theorizing" (Caves, 1960, p. 92). Samuelson frankly conceded that the factor-price differentials actually observed in the real world must be expected to diverge considerably from the idealized equalization of factor prices under static, competitive conditions. Nevertheless, he pressed his investigation of the FPET in the fond belief that it somehow *"does convey insights* into the forces shaping world trade" (cited by de Marchi, 1976, p. 118), a contention reminiscent of the methodology of apriorism that he professed to despise (see Chapter 4 above).

In retrospect, it is difficult to resist the conclusion that:

The factor-price equalisation discussion has been an intellectual game. While it has yielded some incidentally useful results by clarifying the structure of pure theory . . . bringing out the interesting conclusion that in some circumstances trade may not even *tend* to equalise factor prices, the fact remains that no policy-maker has ever expressed a desire to know whether free trade would find the answers of any value in explaining any facts, statistical or otherwise, observable in the real world [Corden, 1965, p. 31].

Further tests

The FPET is clearly violated by the sizable differences in factor prices that are actually observed among countries. But if factor prices around the world are in fact not equalized, it must imply that one or more of the assumptions underlying the Heckscher–Ohlin factor-proportions model of trade is not applicable. We return in the final analysis, therefore, to the empirical validity of the HOT, which rests essentially on the question of whether the commodity composition of trade is more decisively influenced by factor endowments, on the one hand, or by differences in techniques, differences in demand patterns, economies of scale and marketing imperfections, on the other. This issue has been intensively studied in a large number of empirical studies since Leontief, the bulk of which tend in fact to refute the HOT. In the words of the latest survey of these attempts to test trade theories,[15] "the simple Heckscher–Ohlin model does not rest on strong empirical foundations. When natural resources and human capital are taken explicitly into account, the model affords greater insight. . . . [Nevertheless,] intercountry differences in efficiency seem sufficiently well-established to make it most unlikely that the factor-endowments hypothesis is empirically valid universally" (Stern, 1965, pp. 20–1).

Product-cycle, technological-gap, and scale-economies explanations of trade have a somewhat better record but the familiar problems of comparing the looser predictions of quasi-dynamic models with the rigorous predictions of static models, particularly when the latter are accompanied by various ad hoc elaborations, prevents us from awarding a decisive victory to either side. The problem of making the comparison, as Robert Stern (p. 30) says:

. . . is in part a question of theory and also one of empirical methodology. As far as theory is concerned, the issue is that the factor-endowments model has yet to be integrated systematically with an endogenous mechanism of technological change and diffusion. Until more progress is made along these lines, it will be difficult to sort out the various determinants of trade. The methodological issue is to devise ways of discriminating among the various theories and choosing the "best" explanation in the face of highly collinear data sets.

International trade is among the oldest topics studied by economists, and the pure theory of international trade has long been one of the most rigorous branches of economics. Nevertheless, it has also been one of the last areas of

[15] The pure theory of international trade has been repeatedly surveyed in recent years with varying emphases on testing: see the annotated listing in Bhagwati (1969, p. 8) and the fuller listing in Caves and Johnson (1968, p. xii).

economic research to come under the influence of falsificationism and even now it remains a field of economic specialization that seems peculiarly prone to the disease of formalism. Peter Kenen (1975, p. xii), an eminent trade theorist in his own right, summed up the situation circa 1970 in these words:

A full decade after other specialties had been transformed by the application of econometric methods, international trade and finance displayed a stubborn immunity to quantification. They became the last refuge of the speculative theorist. . . . One can cite several significant exceptions. . . . But little was done to verify the fundamental propositions of trade theory or to measure the effects of trade restrictions. The theory was deemed to be immutably true. The task of the trade theorist, then, was merely to spell out its implications for welfare and policy.

The Heckscher–Ohlin–Vanek theorem

Such was the state of play in the late 1970s. Since then, however, Leamer (1984) has contributed a powerful reexamination of the HOT, resolved the Leontief paradox, reinterpreted the HOT for purposes of econometric testing, and provided new support for the factor-proportions theory of international trade. Leamer begins by noting that Leontief himself did not actually measure the factor endowments of trading countries but instead inferred factor proportions in one country, the United States, from measures of trade and the factor intensities of imports and exports. He showed that the United States was a net exporter of both capital and labor services (hence the ''paradox'') but he did so by assuming that the U.S. balance of trade was in balance; that is, he compared the factor contents of imports with those of an equal value of exports.

However, the U.S. balance of trade in 1947 was in surplus and, Leamer argues, in those circumstances what must be estimated are the factors embodied in *net* exports or, what amounts to the same thing, the difference between domestic production and domestic consumption. The HOT states that a country will export those goods produced intensively by its relatively abundant factor and import those produced by its relatively scarcer factor. But when the balance of trade is unbalanced, what must be tested is what Leamer calls the Heckscher–Ohlin–Vanek theorem (HOVT), which states that a country will export the services of abundant factors and import the services of scarce factors. Since Leontief showed that U.S. production in 1947 was more capital-intensive than its consumption and also that the capital-intensity of net American exports exceeded the capital-intensity of domestically consumed goods, his data revealed the United States to be capital-abundant, exactly as we would expect. In other words, the Leontief paradox rests on a conceptual misunderstanding and hence on an inappropriate empirical test.

Leamer's monograph is accompanied by econometric evidence that net export commodity trade across a large sample of countries can be accurately represented as a linear function of national resource endowments, vindicating the HOVT and hence the factor-proportions theory of international trade. However, more comprehensive tests by others have produced negative results and have indeed reinstated Leontief 's paradox.[16] Moreover, it does appear that the replacement of the HOT by the HOVT has subtly altered the question being asked: instead of explaining the trade flows in actual commodities, we end up explaining the factor-content of trade patterns, a harmless procedure if the factor-proportions theory is true but not otherwise.

It would in fact be very surprising if one really could explain all or most of the commodity composition of trade by means only of differences in factor endowments. Consider, for example, the influence of the directly ascertainable noncompetitive market structures in most tradable goods (product differentiation, advertising, maintenance guaranties, price collusion, etcetera), the national differences in patterns of demand at identical income levels, the national differences in domestic taxation, and finally, the more controversial phenomena of static and dynamic scale economies in different countries. The debate surrounding the Leontief paradox provides one of the best examples in economics of the importance of the Duhem–Quine thesis (see Chapter 1 above), repudiating the notion that one can ever decisively and compellingly reject something like the HOT or HOVT by even the most sophisticated statistical test: every test will involve, besides the factor-proportions theory, a whole host of auxiliary hypotheses. That is not a counsel of despair. Here, as elsewhere, we must perforce pass a qualitative judgment on the evidence for and against the theory in question.

---

[16] See Gomes (1990, pp. 127–31) for a succinct review of the recent literature and further references.

12

Keynesians versus monetarists

Fruitless debate?

In taking up this topic, we go to the heart of the furious controversies that have surrounded questions of macroeconomic policy in recent years. The great debate between Keynesian and monetarists over the respective potency of fiscal and monetary policy has divided the economic profession, accumulating what is by now a simply enormous literature. I have no intention of surveying this literature in order to define the differences between the two parties so as to pose the question whether these differences are or are not reconcilable.[17] I shall not even attempt to appraise the degree to which either the Keynesian or the monetarist research program is showing signs of "degeneracy," although it must be said that a steady weakening of the earlier formulations of the monetarist position and an increasing willingness of monetarists to adopt Keynesian modes of analysis provide signs of breakdown in the monetarist counterrevolution. My aim in this section is a more limited one: it is to draw two fundamental, methodological lessons from the Keynesian–monetarist debate. The first is that the methodology of instrumentalism espoused by Friedman (see Chapter 4 above) tends all too easily to turn into naive empiricism, or theory *after* measurement instead of measurement after theory. The second is that the attempt to establish a theoretical position by falsifying a competing theory always produces a sharpening of the issues, as it did in this controversy, that gradually does resolve the outstanding differences.

The last twenty years have seen an unending series of efforts to produce a decisive empirical test of the Keynesian and the monetarist view of the causes of economic fluctuations. A detached observer might be forgiven for thinking

[17] Among numerous surveys at various stages in the debate, I have personally found Chick (1973), Selden (1977), Mayer (1978; 1990, chap. 4), Wood (1981), and Desai (1981) most useful: all contain substantial bibliographies.

that this discussion has proved nothing but that empirical evidence is apparently incapable of making any economist change his mind. But a closer look at the literature reveals a steady tendency towards a narrowing of the gap between different points of view and, in particular, a growing appreciation of the limitations of all the current statistical tests of the relative effectiveness of fiscal and monetary policies. The debate is not simply an endless carousel resulting in stalemate but an ongoing discussion with a definite momentum in which the successive positions taken up steadily improve on earlier ones abandoned. At the same time, it must be admitted that the persistence of this controversy, despite all the moves and countermoves in both camps, can only be explained in terms of certain deep-seated "hard core" disagreements about the self-adjusting capacity of the private sector in mixed economies and, hence, the extent to which fiscal and monetary policy is in fact stabilizing or destabilizing (Leijonhufvud, 1976, pp. 70–1). Once again, the debate between Keynesians and monetarists shows that economists (like all other scientists) will characteristically defend their core of central beliefs from the threat of observed anomalies by first adjusting the auxiliary hypotheses surrounding that central core; they will continue to do so as long as it is possible and only on rare occasions, when they have been repeatedly refuted on every battle ground that they have occupied, will they rethink their basic "hard core" and start afresh.

Friedman's successive versions of monetarism

Let us consider first Friedman's own position in the controversy. His essay on "the methodology of positive economics" preceded his first restatement of the quantity theory of money by several years (Friedman, 1956). A year after launching monetarism, he published *The Theory of the Consumption Function* (1957). That book may be said to exemplify his methodology at its best: after framing a new theory of the consumption function in terms of permanent rather than annual income, implying a number of specific, refutable predictions about aggregate consumption expenditures, Friedman reexamined all the available cross-section and time series data on consumption behavior to show that his theory accounted neatly for evidence that defeated the standard Keynesian doctrine. Whatever may be the ultimate verdict of *The Theory of the Consumption Function*,[18] it must rank as one of the most masterful treatments of the relationship between theory and data in the whole of

---

[18] Mayer (1972) provides a comprehensive summary and evaluation of all the numerous tests of the permanent income hypothesis, concluding that Friedman is at least partially right: the income elasticity of consumption is greater for permanent than for transitory income but, on the other hand, the propensity to consume transitory income is not zero as implied by Friedman's theory.

the economic literature. The story of Friedman's advocacy of monetarism, however, is by way of contrast a caricature of his own methodology.

First came the restatement of the old quantity theory of money as a theory, not of the long-run relationship between the aggregate volume of spending and the total output of an economy – a type of primitive macroeconomics – but of the demand for money on the part of business firms and households. Next came an empirical investigation of the demand for money in the United States over the period 1869–1957, followed by a massive *Monetary History of the United States 1867–1960* (1963) with Anna Schwartz, as well as a number of studies of the lags in the economic effects of monetary policy. At this point in the argument, much was made of the empirical demonstration that the money demand function was relatively stable and that, furthermore, it was insensitive to variations in interest rates (Laidler, 1985, pp. 125–26). In the same year, 1963, there also appeared the famous paper by Friedman and David Meiselman, which produced the first of a number of single-equation or "reduced form" estimates of a simple Keynesian and a simple monetarist model, purporting to show that the income velocity of money was a more stable variable than the Keynesian investment multiplier. This result was reversed by Albert Ando and Franco Modigliani among others, and an entire issue of the 1965 *American Economic Review* was devoted to various comparisons between single-equation Keynesian and monetarist formulations, demonstrating to everyone's satisfaction that reduced-form models, lacking a specification of the underlying set of structural equations, were incapable of discriminating between the two competing models (Brainard and Cooper, 1975, pp. 169–70).

Friedman's theory

We have now arrived at the high point of the debate some seven years after the birth of monetarism, by which time, however, Friedman had still not supplied an explicit theory capable of generating the empirical regularities that were said to support the monetarist position. The publication in 1970 of Friedman's "Theoretical Framework for Monetary Analysis" ushered in what might be called Phase II of monetarism.[19] Alas, some monetarists, such as Brunner and Meltzer (1972, pp. 838–9, 848–9), repudiated Friedman's framework, expressed surprise that Friedman chose to present his argument in terms of the Hicksian IS-LM model, an example of comparative static equilibrium analysis, while arguing at the same time that questions of timing and the relative speed of adjustment of prices and quantities provided the key to the difference in approach of Keynesians and monetarists, in which case the IS-LM model was inadequate to the discussion. And, indeed, apart

[19] Phase I is summed up in Friedman (1968).

from repeatedly insisting that monetarists approach economic problems in the spirit of Marshallian partial equilibrium analysis, while Keynesians do so in a Walrasian GE framework, Friedman denied that there were any theoretical or even ideological differences between the two camps.

The point of adopting the IS-LM model, Friedman argued, is to demonstrate the common ground between them, all differences having to do with different dynamic assumptions about the path of adjustment to discrepancies between the quantity of money the public wants to hold and the amount it actually holds: "the relative speed of adjustment of prices and quantity is still the key to the difference in approach and analysis between those economists who regard themselves as Keynesians and those who do not" (Friedman, 1970, pp. 210–11; also pp. 234–5). Nevertheless, Friedman failed to explain how price and quantity decisions are actually reached in an economy such as that of the United States and in that sense he failed to provide any theory of how the effects of monetary changes are divided between prices and real output (Chick, 1973, pp. 111–13). In consequence, the suggestion that the dynamics of "the transmission mechanism" between money and economic activity holds the key to the dispute between Keynesians and monetarists is untestable, or rather, Friedman himself provided no method of testing it. Monetarists have been accused of holding a "black-box theory" of the transmission mechanism, whereas in fact they view the transmission mechanism as being a matter of adjusting portfolio holdings but they define portfolios so comprehensively that no single variable stands out as dominating the rest. In short, they model the transmission mechanism but they do not provide a theory of it.

The qualitative calculus is, as we know, a powerful method for establishing the directional nature of a postulated causal relationship. But it is a blunt instrument for measuring the actual magnitudes involved in that relationship. If the Keynesian-monetarist debate is fundamentally a matter of the speed of adjustment to changes in various parameters, as Friedman has argued, what is needed is a quantitative calculus. Economic policy seeks to control the economy and not merely to predict its behavior. Controlling an economy usually implies knowledge, not just of the sign of economic effects, but of the precise magnitudes of these effects; some control is possible on the basis of a qualitative calculus but certainly "fine tuning" demands more than a knowledge of the sign of economic changes. The failure to provide anything like a quantitative calculus of monetary changes in effect heralded the demise of the monetarist standpoint.

Phase III of monetarism

In Phases I and II of monetarism, the framework of the discussion is largely that of the Keynesian short run, but the long run enters the argument in Phase II and comes to dominate the scene in Phase III, dating roughly from 1972. Now the argument is that, whatever are the short-run effects of monetary changes on both prices and quantities, economic expectations will automatically adjust themselves to changes in the money supply as a result of which monetary policy has little or no effect on output in the long run – this is Friedman's theory of the "natural" rate of unemployment.

Meanwhile, large econometric models were built that spelled out the various channels by which money influences nominal GNP, real GNP, and the price level. Both "Neanderthal Keynesianism," denying that the monetary authorities have any control over the money supply, and "Neanderthal monetarism," denying any efficacy of fiscal policy even in the short run, have been left far behind. In one sense, to be sure, the monetarists have won: governments now pay far more attention to the money supply than they did a decade ago and a more sophisticated Keynesianism, taking account of the impact effects of monetary policy through several different channels and not just through the effects of interest rate changes on investment, has taken the place of the Mickey Mouse versions of Keynes in the 1950s. In a more profound sense, the monetarists have lost: monetarism never succeeded in clarifying the causal mechanism that produced its empirical results, sometimes even denying that these results required interpretation in the light of a supporting causal theory, and it failed to refute any but a crude travesty of the Keynesian theory it opposed (Johnson, 1971, pp. 10, 13). Keynesianism, on the other hand, proved to be capable of absorbing monetarist ideas in a more sophisticated brand of macroeconomics that appears to be emerging from the fifteen-year-old melee. It is perfectly true that controversy persisted, and still persists, despite mountains of evidence: clearly, economists are not easily swayed by empirical refutations. On the other hand, the debate has shown definite signs of progress, gradually surmounting both simple-minded Keynesianism and simple-minded monetarism, so that by now it is much more difficult to classify macroeconomists neatly into either Keynesians or monetarists.

Recovering the message of Keynes

In retrospect, the Keynesian–monetarist debate of the last two decades must rank as one of the most frustrating and irritating controversies in the entire history of economic thought, frequently resembling medieval disputations at their worst. Again and again, violent polemical claims are made, which are subsequently withdrawn – the quantity theory of money is a theory of the demand for money that is embedded in a neglected Chicago oral tradition; the demand for money is interest-inelastic and the supply of money is an exogenously determined variable; substantial changes in prices and nominal incomes are always the result of changes in the money supply; turning points in the growth of the money supply invariably precede the upper and lower turning points of the business cycle; etcetera – and criticisms are reserved for strawman versions of the opposition. Much of the debate consists of talking at cross-purposes and at times it is difficult to remember what it is that is actually in dispute, a difficulty that is even felt by the main protagonists themselves.[20] Running right through the debate is a continuing quarrel about what Keynes really meant, as if it were impossible to settle substantive issues of economic policy without first deciding how Keynes differed from "the classics." Since *The General Theory* contains at least three, and perhaps more, versions of Keynesian theory,[21] there are endless ways in which its elements can be combined into something called "Keynesianism." Arguments about Keynes's central message thus constitute a doctrinal fog that must be pierced before considering the respective merits of Keynesian and monetarist arguments. Reading this debate, one sometimes gets the feeling that macroeconomists are more concerned with exegesis of *The General Theory* than with advancing knowledge of how the economy actually works.

We come back at the close of this discussion to the first of the two fundamental lessons that can be drawn from the Keynesian–monetarist debate. Friedman indeed followed the methodology of "instrumentalism" in Phase I of the debate, that is, he produced predictions without producing any theoretical explanations of these predictions; in Phase II of the debate, however, even he finally capitulated to the demand for a theory to support his predictions. The theory he supplied proved inadequate to the task and so, in Phase III, he adopted a wholly new theory, resting on the distinction between anticipated and unanticipated inflation. Thus, in the final analysis, Friedman's monetarism abandons the methodology of instrumentalism, apparently not because it is inherently defective but because it is unpersuasive.

[20] Consider, for example, Friedman's (1970, p. 217) summing up: "I regard the description of our position as 'money is all that matters for changes in *nominal* income and for *short-run* changes in real income' as an exaggeration that gives the right flavour of our conclusions. I regard the statement that 'money is all that matters', period, as a basic misrepresentation of our conclusions."

[21] Coddington (1976b) discerns at least three strands in the interpretation of Keynes: (1) *hydraulic Keynesianism* – the 45° diagram type of income-expenditure theory and the IS-LM interpretation, which treats the Keynesian model as a special case rather than a general theory – also known as the "neoclassical synthesis" or "bastard Keynesianism," depending on your point of view; (2) *fundamentalist Keynesianism* – an emphasis on shifting expectations and pervasive uncertainty, as found in chap. 12 of *The General Theory* and Keynes's 1937 article on "The General Theory of Employment," implying that Keynes's approach cannot be reconciled with the neoclassical tradition; and (3) *disequilibrium Keynesianism* – a GE reformulation of Keynes without a Walrasian auctioneer, incomplete and imperfect information, false price signals, and income-constrained quantity as well as price adjustments. See also Blaug (1985, pp. 668–71, 693).

The rise and fall of monetarism

This is what I said in 1980. It is not quite what I would say in 1991 were I to start afresh: still, on balance I would add to, rather than detract from, my earlier remarks. Nevertheless, so much has happened in macroeconomics in the 1980s as to make anything written on monetarism at the beginning of the decade obsolete at the end of it. First of all, monetarism in its Friedmanian version – let us call it Mark I monetarism – came and went in the 1980s. Furthermore, the new classical macroeconomics – let us call it Mark II monetarism – likewise faded in appeal during the 1980s and may well have entered a terminal decline. Finally, there has been a simply amazing resurgence of a new Keynesian economics in the spirit rather than the letter of Keynes: the Keynesian revolution of the 1930s has turned out, in the fullness of time, to have been something of a "permanent revolution" (see Shaw, 1988).

Earlier I characterized Friedman's work on monetarism as standing the methodology of instrumentalism on its head, that is, predicting first and explaining afterwards. Hirsch and de Marchi (1990, p. 204), in their new study of Friedman's methodology, take exception to my claim: "Friedman's pragmatic approach in fact so integrates observation and theorizing that it is somewhat misleading to identify an order in the ongoing process of inquiry." Certainly, they remind us that what divides Friedman from much of the economic mainstream is not just an insistence on policy relevance rather than analytical rigor but also a market antipathy to multiple regression as the premier method of validating theoretical propositions. Friedman prefers instead to rely on a wide array of evidence, some historical and some econometric, frequently testing results from one data set on other data sets; not for him the painstaking derivation of hypotheses from the rational, maximizing behavior of economic agents, followed by an elaborate statistical confirmation of results based upon a single sample.[22] One can only welcome the release from the econometric incubus which this approach offers, emphasizing that historical analysis is a perfectly legitimate method of testing theories, but nevertheless the very diversity of the evidence that Friedman provides makes appraisal of his argument more difficult (see, for example, Hirsch and de Marchi, 1986; 1990, chap. 10).

If that were not bad enough, there is the very complexity of the many strands of argument that go to make up monetarism (see Mayer, 1978). There

---

[22] This is strikingly illustrated by the savage review of Friedman and Schwartz's *Monetary Trends in the United States and the United Kingdom* (1982) by Hendry and Ericsson (1991), exemplifying their own "encompassing" approach to regression analysis, followed by an effective rejoinder by Friedman and Schwartz (1991, especially pp. 48–9).

is (1) the quantity theory of money, in the sense of the causative influence of changes in high-powered money on the level of prices, implying a stable demand function for money, a level of output largely or entirely determined by real forces, and an exogenous money supply under effective control by the government; in consequence, the appropriate target for monetary policy is the growth rate of money and not the rate of interest. Next is (2) the assertion that a monetary growth rule, such that the money supply will grow at the same rate as the long-run trend rate of real output, would be more stabilizing than any discretionary monetary or fiscal policy, which is part and parcel of Friedman's hostility towards all forms of government intervention and a belief in the inherent stability of the private sector. Finally, there is (3) the rejection of an unemployment–inflation trade-off (except for brief transitional periods) in favor of a real, vertical Phillips curve, which can only be altered by supply-side policies.

To assess the track record of all these multiple claims would be no small task and it is perhaps significant that no one has yet attempted to provide such a comprehensive evaluation of monetarism (but see Cross, 1982). On the other hand, it is to Friedman's credit that, unlike so many of his contempories, he has never hedged his predictions with endless ifs and buts, thus facilitating an appraisal of his ideas. In a recent comprehensive essay on the quantity theory of money, which is in effect a retrospective survey of monetarism, Friedman (1987, pp. 16–17) declares: "For most Western countries, a change in the rate of monetary growth produces a change in the rate of growth of nominal income about six to nine months later. . . . The change in the rate of growth in nominal income typically shows up first in output and hardly at all in prices. . . . The effect on prices, like that on income and output, is distributed over time, but comes some 12 to 18 months later, so that the total delay between a change in monetary growth and a change in the rate of inflation averages something like two years. . . . In the short run, which may be as long as three to ten years, monetary changes affect primarily output"; and so forth. One would have thought that such statements are sufficiently precise to permit a more or less definite assessment of the validity of monetarism.

Be that as it may, there is a good deal of evidence that monetarism of the Mark I Friedmanite variety has had its day. In the opinion of Mayer (1990, p. 61), a writer who not so long ago would have been considered a monetarist, "casual observation suggests that, at least in the United States, the number of economists who consider themselves monetarists, or who are sympathetic to monetarism, has shrunk. And what is just as (if not more) serious is that monetarism does not seem to attract as many able recruits as it once did." Mayer advances as many as four different explanations of what he calls the "twilight" of monetarism, of which the most important is the failure of monetarists to corroborate their crucial hypotheses. There is, first of all, the fact that the U.S. demand for money began to grow much more slowly in the 1970s than could have been expected on the basis of past trends, followed by a surprising upward shift in 1981–2 (Laidler, 1985, pp. 146–51; Judd and Scadding, 1982; Roley, 1985). No matter how money is defined, the income-velocity of money exhibited greater instability in the 1980s in both the United States and the United Kingdom than it had ever done before (Mayer, 1990, pp. 70–6) and, of course, a stable money demand function, or what is almost the same thing, a stable velocity of money, is the linchpin of the entire monetarist program. The inability to predict velocity since 1982 was undoubtedly the reason for the abandonment of money supply targets by the Thatcher government in 1985–6, which marked the high point of Friedman's political influence in Whitehall (Goodhart, 1991, pp. 94–100). Similarly, the ability of the Federal Reserve system to control either M-1, M-2, or M-3 came increasingly to be doubted after the so-called "monetarist experiment" of 1979–82 (Mayer, 1990, pp. 81–4).

Secondly, there is the acknowledged shortcoming of the 1963 Friedman–Meiselman single-equation assault on Keynesianism mentioned above, followed thereafter by the battering received by the equally simple 1968 St. Louis Equation of Andersen and Jordan (Mayer, 1990, pp. 76–7). Thirdly, there is the inconclusive historical evidence for the exogeneity of the money supply at the turning points of the business cycle, summed up by the much-contested Friedman–Schwartz claim that the Fed caused the Great Depression of the 1930s (see Temin, 1976, especially pp. 174–8; Fearon, 1979, pp. 36–9). Lastly, there is the checkered career of Friedman's natural-rate hypothesis, which began as a Phillips curve augmented by adaptive expectations permitting a temporary trade-off between inflation and unemployment, but soon graduated into a Phillips curve augmented by rational expectations, which closed the door to any trade-off between inflation and unemployment even in the short run.

I have elsewhere told the story of the Phillips curve and the natural rate of unemployment (NRU) (Blaug, 1985, pp. 678–88, 695–6) and will therefore note only that the existence of a well-defined vertical Phillips curve – *the* NRU – and particularly the stability of such a relationship is as much in doubt today as it ever was. No one denies that there is some rate of unemployment below which demand pressures will cause prices to rise, so that there is something to the idea of an NRU, whatever terminology we employ. What is in question is whether this is not a very thin band rather than a line and whether it does not in fact move about with every change in the institutions affecting labor market as well as the patterns of price-setting by firms. The central implication of Friedman's natural-rate hypothesis was that any attempt by governments to force the unemployment rate below the NRU would simply produce inflation at an ever-increasing rate; indeed, this was his explanation of why the 1970s had seen "stagflation," the simultaneous occurrence of unemployment and inflation. Furthermore, since the NRU was the only level of unemployment at which people's expected rate of inflation was equal to the actual rate of inflation, the way to cure inflation was to keep capacity low and unemployment high for as long as it took to induce people to revise their inflationary expectations downward to the continuously falling inflation rate. Such a period of high unemployment, Friedman promised, need not last very long: at most two years, as we have seen, or in some cases three years, was all that was required to get back completely to the NRU. The Thatcher government of the 1980s came as close to testing this bold prediction as any policy ever can: the fact that despite ten years of deflation, the UK unemployment rate never fell below 8 percent and in five out of the ten years stood above 10 percent had much to do with the collapse of the monetarist cause in Britain. The U.S. government never performed a similar "crucial experiment" but, nevertheless, news travels fast even across oceans.

Yet another nail in the coffin of monetarism was the discovery on both sides of the Atlantic that statistical estimates of the NRU trail behind past rates of unemployment, rising and falling as they do; in the now fashionable language of physics, the NRU shows "hysteresis": its level depends on the path taken to reach it (Cross, 1991). Whether this is a real phenomenon – the larger the proportion of unemployment that is long-term unemployment, the larger is the proportion of the labor force that has become unemployable by virtue of the loss of skills and work habits – or simply a statistical artifact is still an open question but it does undermine the notion that the NRU is a stable bedrock capable of serving as a guide to antiinflationary policies.

New classical macroeconomics

This brings us to the next round in the monetarist saga, the new classical macroeconomics or the theory of rational expectations (RE). The persistence of inflation in the 1970s made it difficult to sustain the notion of an adaptive-expectations mechanism, according to which people persistently underestimate the actual rate of inflation. Surely a rational economic agent would form price expectations on the basis of all available information, whether past or present data, including declared policy intentions? In short, all systematic and predictable elements influencing the rate of inflation will quickly become known and incorporated into price expectations, implying paradoxically that people's price expectations are on average identical to the movement of actual prices. Of course, the economy is subject to random and unforeseen "shocks" – sudden changes in tastes, new technological discoveries, natural disasters, etcetera – and these lead to forecasting errors that take time to be corrected. It is these shocks which alone account for the momentary appearance of short-run Phillips curves. But for them the economy would always stick to its vertical long-run Phillips curve, that is, Friedman's NRU. No wonder then that the theory of RE has been labeled as the new *classical* macroeconomics because the principal implication of RE is that Keynesian stabilization policies can influence nominal variables like the inflation rate but are impotent with respect to real variables, like output and employment.

It is tempting to dismiss the RE revolution as invoking unrealistic assumptions. Are we really to believe that private agents have the same access to economic information as government agencies or that they face identical information processing costs? Can we seriously contend that consumers facing a bewildering variety of conflicting information in, say, the housing market form expectations of future house prices in the same way as professional traders in the financial market form expectations of future interest rates? But systematic forecasting errors in any market, RE theorists point out, create profit opportunities to supply information that will improve private forecasting to the point where all forecasting errors are purely random. Whether this is a convincing reply is besides the point. It would be a serious methodological error to judge the new classical macroeconomics solely on the basis of the realism or plausibility of its assumptions. The history of science (and the history of economics) is littered with powerful, influential and long-lived theories based on assumptions that only came to be regarded as plausible by dint of age and repetition. After all, we hardly ever question the utter implausibility of the heliocentric theory of the solar system: why don't we fall off the earth as it travels around the sun rotating at 1,000 miles an hour? Galileo spent many pages in his *Dialogue on The Two Chief Systems of the World* (1632) explaining away all the common-sense objections of his day to the idea of a rotating, revolving earth but we simply take all that for granted now. The realism or plausibility of assumptions is a highly subjective and historically conditioned reason for rejecting any theory.

This is not to say that the descriptive accuracy of a theory's assumptions is of no consequence whatsoever, for that would be to fall back on the methodology of instrumentalism. Expectations cannot be directly observed but they can be investigated via survey techniques. Studies of this kind have been carried out in a number of markets (Sheffrin, 1983, chap. 4) and their results, while not conclusive, sharpen our notion of how expectations are actually formed. More telling, however, are tests of the implications of RE. One of the central implications of RE – its "novel fact" so to speak – is that the growth path of real output or unemployment should not be correlated with systematic changes in the money supply, the volume of government expenditures, the size of budgetary deficits, the rate of interest, the exchange rate, or policy pronouncements about any of these variables – if they were so correlated, private agents would have incorporated these correlations in their pricing forecasts, in which case they would have appeared as purely nominal adjustments to wages and prices. This is the so-called "policy-neutral" hypothesis, the ultimate radical anti-Keynesian conclusion of the new classical macroeconomics research program. A great many tests of this central implication have been carried out by RE theorists, largely with negative results (Maddock, 1984).

It is true, however, that even these refutations are inconclusive – the Duhem–Quine thesis once again. All the tests involve the joint implication of (1) RE; (2) the notion that all markets clear instantly, so that all variables, both real and nominal, are equilibrium variables; and (3) the proposition that all information is available at the same cost to all economic agents. It may be that (3) is reducible to (2) because there is an "information industry," which is also assumed to clear at every moment of time. In any case, the failure to corroborate the policy-neutral implication of the new classical macroeconomics may mean that expectations are not rational or that some or all markets do not clear during the period of observation. In short, it may be that the insistence on market clearance, or equilibrium everywhere even in labor markets, is more essential to the conclusions of the new classical macroeconomics than is the concept of RE.

Macroeconomics seen through Lakatosian spectacles

Let me now paint with a broad brush to depict the whole history of macroeconomics since the publication of *The General Theory* in 1936 with the aid of the apparatus created by Lakatos. The Keynesian revolution was a sea change unparalleled in the history of economic thought: never before had a new research program conquered the economics profession so quickly and so completely. It's child's play to spell out the "hard core" and the "positive" and "negative" heuristic of Keynesian economics (Blaug, 1986, pp. 243–4) and there is not much doubt that it was not just a theory but a research program for working with a distinct point of view in a large number of different areas in economics. Moreover, as I have argued at length (Blaug, 1990, chap. 4), it was throughout the 1930s, 1940s, and 1950s a "progressive" research program in the strict sense defined by Lakatos: it predicted a whole series of novel facts, which were corroborated by his followers almost as soon as they were announced. The principal novel prediction of Keynesian economics was that the value of the instantaneous expenditure multiplier is greater than unity independent of the public or private character of that expenditure and independent of whether the expenditure is for extra investment or extra consumption. This was a novel prediction, not in the sense that it was totally unknown before Keynes's *General Theory,* but that it was an unsuspected implication of the concept of the consumption function combined with the peculiar Keynesian definition of saving and investment; and not just any consumption function but one in which the marginal propensity to consume lies between zero and one, is smaller than the average propensity to consume, and declines as income rises. Other novel facts predicted by *The General Theory* were that (1) there are significant differences in the marginal propensities to consume of different households defined by their income levels (so that a redistribution of income is capable of raising aggregate demand); (2) the interest-elasticity of investment is very low; (3) the interest-elasticity of the demand for money is very high; and (4) the community's average propensity to consume tends to decline as national income rises (indicating that the threat of secular stagnation in mature economies will get worse as they grow richer). Even this list does not exhaust the novel facts that Keynes's followers predicted as Keynesian economics was further refined in the 1940s. It was this series of successfully corroborated predictions which accounted for the extraordinary ascendancy of Keynesian economics in the years before and during World War II.

The Keynesian research program, however, began to degenerate in the 1950s. It was work on the saving rate and hence the consumption function where the trouble first showed up. The contradiction between cross-section and time-series evidence of the savings–income ratio, the former yielding a declining and the latter a constant average propensity to save, spawned a series of revisions in Keynesian economics from Duesenberry's relative income hypothesis to Friedman's permanent income hypothesis to Modigliani's life-cycle theory of saving. Simultaneously, Harrod and Dormar converted static Keynesian analysis into a primitive theory of growth, while Tobin, Baumol, and Friedman reinterpreted Keynes's liquidity-preference function to bring it into line with a more elegant portfolio theory. Then came the Phillips curve, which at first complemented Keynesian economics with a theory of inflation. The early 1960s saw the profession hopelessly enamored with the Phillips curve. But within a few years doubts about its stability began to accumulate. Empirical studies of inflation-unemployment data increasingly revealed a large degree of variance of actual inflation-unemployment observations about the fitted Phillips curve and the number of variables that had to be introduced to improve the statistical fit soon exhausted the available degrees of freedom in the data. In addition, the last year of the decade of the 1960s produced rising inflation in many countries without any reduction in unemployment, giving way in the early 1970s to "slumpflation," the simultaneous occurrence of rising unemployment and rising inflation rates. Clearly, there was not one stable Phillips curve but rather a whole family of short-run Phillips curves, which shifted over time as a result of influences yet to be determined. One answer to what these influences were was offered by Milton Friedman in his 1968 paper, "The Role of Monetary Policy," which announced the natural-rate hypothesis and thus completed the last strand in his then ten-year-old monetarist counterrevolution.

I have said enough to suggest that monetarism was a progressive research program in the 1960s which produced its own "novel facts," such that demand management affects real output only in the short run; that this short run is typically two years long; that in the longer run only supply-side policies can lower the unemployment rate; and that the firm adoption of money growth targets will cure inflation within two to three years. As Mark I monetarism degenerated in the 1970s, Mark II monetarism took over in the 1980s with the prediction of even more dramatic novel facts bringing with it a new hard core and a new set of positive and negative heuristics.

To sum up 56 years of macroeconomics in one bold generalization is no doubt presumptuous but I remain convinced that the driving force in this long saga was the pursuit of empirical validation. I do not for a moment deny that macroeconomists would like to adopt ideas that suit their ideological and political preconceptions – they are human, after all. There is little doubt that many economists in the 1930s were immediately attracted to Keynesian economics because they wanted to believe in a kind of economics that held out prospects for combating the depression. However, if Keynes's empirical predictions had been refuted, not once but again and again, they would soon have ceased to subscribe to Keynesianism despite all its attractive trappings. In the same way, Friedman's strong defense of free markets, as well as his general political stance, biased right-wing economists in favor of his work on money, just as it biased left-wing economists against his monetarist views. But despite the strong resurgence of right-wing politics in the era of Reagan and Thatcher, monetarism lost support in the 1980s because of its poor empirical track record. Similarly, I would contend that if the new classical macroeconomics had been able to exhibit a series of striking confirmations of its principal predictions, it would by now have earned the allegiance of many economists who might have preferred otherwise.

I cannot claim that this is how everyone views the story of macroeconomics since Keynes. For example, Backhouse (1991) and Maddock (1991) see it roughly as I do but Hoover (1988, 1991) prefers Kuhn to Lakatos and gives greater prominence than I would to the purely technical puzzles generated by successive macroeconomic models. It is no wonder that there should be such disagreements. We are only now beginning to get the Keynesian revolution into perspective. We are only two decades away from the heyday of monetarism and hence will almost certainly revise our view of its rise and fall in the years to come.

13

Human capital theory

Hard core versus protective belt

We turn next to a theory that requires the sort of full-scale treatment that it has rarely received. The birth of human capital theory was announced in 1960 by Theodore Schultz. The birth itself may be said to have taken place two years later when the *Journal of Political Economy* published its October 1962 supplement volume on "Investment in Human Beings." This volume included, among several other path-breaking papers, the preliminary chapters of Gary Becker's 1964 monograph, *Human Capital,* which has ever since served as the *locus classicus* of the subject. Thus, the theory of human capital has been with us for more than twenty-five years, during which time the flood of literature in the field has never abated, at least not until the 1980s. The first textbook exclusively devoted to the subject appeared in 1963 (Schultz, 1963). After a lull in the mid-sixties, the textbook industry started in earnest: between 1970 and 1973 as many as eight authors tried their hand at the task, accompanied by the publication in rapid succession of seven anthologies of classic articles on human-capital-and-all-that; more recent years have seen three more textbooks (Psacharopoulos and Woodhall, 1985; Psacharopoulos, 1985; and Cohn and Geske, 1990). It may be time, therefore, to ask what all this adds up to. Has the theory lived up to the high expectations of its founders? Has it progressed, in the sense of grappling ever more deeply and profoundly with the problems to which it was addressed, or are there signs of stagnation and malaise?

Here is a golden opportunity to apply the MSRP of Lakatos to see what, if anything, it has to teach us about the evaluation of the body of ideas known as human capital theory. Armed with Lakatosian concepts, we may begin by asking: what is the "hard core" of the human capital research program, that set of purely metaphysical beliefs whose abandonment is tantamount to abandoning the program itself? Next, we can ask: what refutations have been
206

encountered in the "protective belt" of the program, and how have the advocates of the program responded to these refutations? Lastly, we may pose the question: is the human capital research program a "progressive" or a "degenerating" research program, which is virtually like asking, has the empirical content of the program increased or decreased over time?

It is easy to show that the so-called theory of human capital is in fact a perfect example of a research program: it cannot be reduced to one single theory, being simply an application of standard capital theory to certain economic phenomena; at the same time, it is itself a subprogram within the more comprehensive neoclassical research program, inasmuch as it is simply an application of standard neoclassical concepts to phenomena not previously taken into account by neoclassical economists. The concept of human capital, or the "hard core" of the human capital research program, is the idea that people spend on themselves in diverse ways, not only for the sake of present enjoyments but also for the sake of future pecuniary and nonpecuniary returns. They may purchase health care; they may voluntarily acquire additional education; they may spend time searching for a job with the highest possible rate of pay instead of accepting the first offer that comes along; they may purchase information about job opportunities; they may migrate to take advantage of better employment opportunities; and they may choose jobs with low pay but high learning potential in preference to dead-end jobs with high pay. All these phenomena – health, education, job search, information retrieval, migration, and in-service training – may be viewed as investment rather than as consumption, whether undertaken by individuals on their own behalf or undertaken by society on behalf of its members. What knits these phenomena together is not the question of who undertakes what, but rather the fact that the decision maker, whoever he or she is, looks forward to the future for the justification of present actions.

It takes only an additional assumption, namely, that the decision maker is a household rather than an individual, to extend the analogy to family planning and even to decisions to marry and to divorce.[23] We are not surprised to see life cycle considerations applied to the theory of saving but prior to what Mary Jean Bowman aptly called "the human investment revolution in economic thought" of the 1960s, it was not common to treat expenditures on such social services as health and education as analogous to investment in physical capital; certainly no one dreamed in those days of finding common analytical grounds between labor economics and the economics of the social services.

There is hardly any doubt, therefore, about the genuine novelty of the "hard

---

[23] The human capital research program has indeed been extended by Becker and others to "the economics of the family"; see Chapter 14 below.

core'' of the human capital research program. Nor is there any doubt of the rich research possibilities created by a commitment to this "hard core." The "protective belt" of the human capital research program is replete with human capital "theories," properly so labeled, and indeed the list is so large that we can hardly hope to give an exhaustive account of them. But few human capital theorists would, I think, quarrel with those we have selected for emphasis.

In the field of education, the principal theoretical implication of the human capital research program is that the demand for postcompulsory education is responsive both to variations in the direct and indirect private costs of schooling and to variations in the earnings differentials associated with additional years of schooling. The traditional pre-1960 view among economists was that the demand for postcompulsory schooling is a demand for a type of consumption good and as such depends on given tastes, family incomes, and the "price" of schooling in the form of tuition costs. There was the complication that this consumption demand also involved an "ability" to consume the good in question but most economists were satisfied to leave it to sociologists and social psychologists to show that this "ability" depended in turn on the social class background of students and particularly on the levels of education achieved by their parents. Since this pre-1960 theory of the consumption demand for education was never used to explain real-world attendance rates in high schools and colleges, it makes little difference what particular formulation of it we adopt.

The point is that the notion that earnings forgone constitute an important element in the private costs of schooling and that students take a systematic, forward-looking view of earnings prospects in the labor market would have been dismissed in the pre-1960 days as implausible, on the grounds that students lack the necessary information to make that prediction and that the available information is in any case known to be unreliable. The human capital research program, on the other hand, while also taking the "tastes" and "abilities" referred to above as given, emphasizes the role of present and future earnings and argues in addition that these earnings are much more likely to exhibit variations in the short term than is the distribution of family background characteristics between successive cohorts of students.

The difference between the old and the new view is, therefore, fundamental and the auxiliary assumptions that convert the "hard core" of the human capital research program into a testable theory of the demand for postcompulsory schooling are almost too obvious to require elaboration: because of imperfections in the capital market, students cannot easily finance the present costs of additional schooling out of future earnings; they are perfectly aware of the earnings they forgo while studying and hence demand more schooling when there is a rise in youth unemployment rates; current salary differentials by years of schooling provide them with fairly accurate estimates of the salary differentials that will prevail when they enter the labor market several years later; etcetera. Furthermore, the theory comes in two versions: it claims modestly to predict total enrollments in postcompulsory schooling and, more ambitiously, to predict enrollments in specific fields of study in higher education and even enrollments in different types of institutions at the tertiary level.

Methodological individualism

As originally formulated by Schultz, Becker, and Mincer, the human capital research program was characterized by *methodological individualism,* that is, the view that all social phenomena should be traced back to their foundation in individual behavior (see Chapter 2 above). For Schultz, Becker, and Mincer, human capital formation is typically conceived as being carried out by individuals acting in their own interests.[24] This is the natural view to take in respect of job search and migration, but health care, education, information retrieval, and labor training are either wholly or in part carried out by governments in many countries.

Familiarity with private medicine and private education, and the almost total absence of government-sponsored training schemes in the American context (at least before 1968), gave support to an emphasis on the private calculus. Whenever health and education are largely in the public sector, however, as is the case in most of Europe and in the Third World, it is tempting to ask the question of whether the human capital research program is also capable of providing new normative criteria for public action. In education, at any rate, the human capital research program did indeed furnish a new social investment criterion: resources are to be allocated to years of schooling and to levels of education so as to equalize the marginal ''social'' rate of return on educational investment and, going one step further, this equalized yield on educational investment should not fall below the yield on alternative private investments. However, this normative criterion was not advocated with the same degree of conviction by all adherents of the human capital research program. Furthermore, the so-called social rate of return on educational investment is necessarily calculated exclusively on the basis of observable pe-

---

[24] Note that the emphasis on individual choice is the quintessence of the human capital research program. It has been argued that education improves allocative efficiency in both production and consumption, accelerates technical progress, raises the saving rate, reduces the birthrate, and affects the level as well as the nature of crime (see Juster, 1975, chaps. 9–14). But unless these effects motivate individuals to demand additional education, they have nothing whatever to do with the human capital research program.

cuniary values; the nonpecuniary returns to education, as well as the externalities associated with schooling, are invariably accommodated by qualitative judgments and these differ from author to author (Blaug, 1972, pp. 202–5). Thus, the same observed social rates of return to investment in education frequently produced quite different conclusions about the optimal educational strategy.

Being normative, the cry to equalize the social rate of return to education raises no questions of empirical testing. In the mood of positive economics, it may be interesting to ask whether governments do indeed allocate resources to the educational system so as to equalize the social yield to all levels and types of education, but few human capital theorists would commit themselves to a definite prediction about the outcome of such a calculation.[25] In the absence of any generally accepted theory of government behavior, the advocates of the human capital research program may be forgiven for slighting the normative implications of their doctrines. Unfortunately, it seems difficult to test any positive prediction about the demand for postcompulsory schooling without taking a view of the norms that underlie government action in the field of education. The world provides few examples of countries in which the demand for postcompulsory education is not constrained by the supply of places that governments decide to make available. In testing predictions about private demand, therefore, we end up testing predictions about the supply function as well as the demand function. To give the human capital research program a run for its money, we must go to such open-door systems of higher education as those of the United States, Japan, India, and the Philippines.

These comments no doubt help to explain why almost all empirical work about the demand for education has been confined to the United States. Nevertheless, even with respect to that country, it is surprising how little attention has actually been devoted to an explanation of the private demand for schooling. Almost nothing with any cutting edge was accomplished before 1970 or thereabouts and even now the demand for education remains a curiously neglected subject in the vast empirical literature exemplifying the human capital approach.

We turn now from formal schooling to labor training. Almost from the

---

[25] Similarly, it is interesting to ask what impact education has on economic growth, irrespective of the motives that lie behind the provision of formal schooling. The attempt to answer this question was at the center of the burgeoning literature on growth accounting in the early 1960s, but recent doubts about the concept of aggregate production functions have virtually dried up all further interest in the question: see Nelson (1973) but also Denison (1974). In retrospect, it seems doubtful in any case whether growth accounting of the Denison type had much to do with the crucial issues in human capital theory (Blaug, 1972, pp. 99–100).

outset, the human capital research program was as much preoccupied with the phenomenon of training as with that of education. Becker's fundamental distinction between general and specific training produced the startling prediction that workers themselves pay for general training via reduced earnings during the training period (see Chapter 9 above), thus contradicting the older Marshallian view that a competitive market mechanism fails to provide employers with adequate incentives to offer optimum levels of in-service training. Predictions about the demand for training fitted neatly with predictions about the demand for education, because formal schooling is an almost perfect example of general training; indeed, Becker's model has the virtue of correctly predicting that employers will rarely pay directly for the schooling acquired by their employees, a generally observed real-world phenomenon unexplained by any alternative research program (except perhaps the Marxist one).

The distinction between two kinds of postschool learning soon led to fruitful discussion about the extent to which training is or is not fully vested in individual workers but it largely failed to inspire new empirical work on labor training in industry (Blaug, 1972, pp. 191–9). In part, this was accounted for by the inherent difficulty of distinguishing costless on-the-job learning from both informal on-the-job and formal off-the-job-but-in-plant training (formal off-the-job-out-of-plant training, or a manpower retraining program, is yet another category of "training"). For the rest, Becker's emphasis on training as the outcome of an occupational choice by workers seemed to ignore complex questions about the supply of training by firms with well-developed "internal labor markets." All in all, it can hardly be said that the human capital approach to labor training has yet been put to a decisive empirical test.

The subject of migration gives rise to similar difficulties in assessing degrees of success or failure. There is a rich economic and sociological literature on geographical migration going back to the nineteenth and even to the eighteenth century, to which the human capital approach adds little except a pronounced emphasis on the role of geographical disparities in real incomes. There is little doubt that recent empirical work on migration has been deeply influenced by human capital considerations but an appraisal of the empirical status of the human capital research program in the field of migration is by no means straightforward (but see Greenwood, 1975).

This leaves us with health care, job search, and labor market information networks. The virtual explosion of health economics in recent years and developments in labor market search theory, or "the microeconomic foundations of employment theory," both have their roots in the human capital research program. Nevertheless, they have quickly grown into independent areas of activity that are now only tenuously related to "the human investment revolution in economic thought.'' We will, therefore, pass them by (but see Culyer, Wiseman, and Walker, 1977; Santomero and Seater, 1978, pp. 518–25; and Kim, 1990).

The scope of the program

If we take all these topics together, the program adds up to an almost total explanation of the determinants of earnings from employment; it predicts declining investments in human capital formation with increasing age and hence lifetime age-earnings profiles that are concave from below. No wonder the bulk of empirical work inspired by the human capital framework has taken the form of regressing the earnings of individuals on such variables as native ability, family background, place of residence, years of schooling, years of work experience, occupational status, and the like – the so-called earnings function.

It is sometimes difficult in all this research to see precisely what hypothesis is being tested, other than that schooling and work experience are more important factors than native ability and family background. Work experience has in turn been reduced to human capital formation by arguing that individuals tend to invest in themselves after completing schooling by choosing occupations that promise general training; in so doing, they lower their starting salaries below alternative opportunities in exchange for higher future salaries as the training begins to pay off. In short, the rate at which earnings rise with additional years of work experience is itself a matter of individual choice. Unfortunately, it is impossible in practice to disentangle the effects of such postschool investments from investment in formal schooling unless it is assumed that all private rates of return to postschool and in-school investments are equalized at the margin. There is simply overwhelming evidence, however, that rates of return to different types of human capital are not in fact equalized, or, alternatively expressed, that equilibrium is never actually attained in human capital markets. All in all, it remains true to say that to this day we have had to make do with rates of return to human capital formation that are actually averages of rates of return to formal schooling and rates of return to different forms of labor training.

In summary, it may be said that the human capital research program has displayed a simply amazing fecundity, spawning new research projects in almost every branch of economics. Nevertheless, a survey of its accomplishments to date shows that the program is actually not very well corroborated in the Popperian sense (Blaug, 1976; Rosen, 1977). That is of course no reason for abandoning the human capital research program. To believe that scientific research programs are given up the moment a refutation is encountered is to fall victim to ''naive falsificationism.'' What is required to eliminate a scientific research program is, first of all, repeated refutations, second, an embarrassing proliferation of ad hoc adjustments designed to avoid these refutations, and third, a rival program that purports to account for the same evidence by a different but equally powerful theoretical framework. Such a rival to the human capital research program may now have made its appearance: it travels under the name of the *screening hypothesis* or *credentialism* and it is linked up in some of its versions to the new theory of dual labor markets, or labor market segmentation. Its origins lie in the theory of decision making under uncertainty and its impact derives from the discovery that the process of hiring workers is merely a species of a larger genus, namely, the problem of selecting buyers or sellers in the presence of inadequate information about their characteristics.

The screening hypothesis

According to human capital theory, the labor market is capable of continually absorbing workers with ever higher levels of education, provided that education specific earnings are flexible downwards. Since the educational hiring standards for occupations are not technical constants but rather decision variables, it matters little whether better educated workers are absorbed into lower-paying occupations, while average earnings per occupation remain constant, or into the same occupations as before at reduced earnings; the mechanism works equally well for the case where wages are determined by the characteristics of jobs as for the case where they are determined by the characteristics of workers. In any case, there is sufficient variance of earnings within occupations to suggest that both of these effects occur simultaneously; in addition, occupations can be redesigned so as to destroy any basis of comparison between old and new occupations. In short, nothing is more alien to the human capital research program than the manpower forecaster's notion of technically determined educational requirements for jobs.

These self-regulating labor markets may or may not work smoothly, in the sense of keeping the demand for educated manpower continuously in line with its supply, but they will not work at all unless employers prefer more educated to less educated workers, everything else being the same. The human capital research program is silent on why there should be such a persistent bias in the preferences of employers: it may be because educated workers possess scarce cognitive skills, it may be because they possess desirable personality traits such as self-reliance and achievement drive, and it may be because they display compliance with organizational rules. But whatever the reason for the preference the fact remains that all of these desirable attributes cannot be known with certainty at the time of hiring. The employer is, therefore, faced with a selection problem: given the difficulties of accurately predicting the future performance of job applicants, he is tempted to treat educational qualifications as a screening device to distinguish new workers in terms of ability, achievement motivation, and possibly family origins, that is, in terms of personality traits rather than cognitive skills; cognitive skills are largely acquired by on-the-job training and employers are, therefore, fundamentally concerned with selecting job applicants in terms of their trainability. This may not be the whole story but it is, surely, a good deal of the story. If so, the observed correlation between earnings and length of schooling, which figures so prominently in the writings of human capital theorists, may disguise a more fundamental correlation between schooling and the attributes that characterize trainability. The contribution of education to economic growth, therefore, is simply that of providing a selection device for employers and the way is now open to consider the question of whether formal schooling is indeed the most efficient selection mechanism that we could design for the purpose. This is the so-called *screening hypothesis* or *theory of credentialism,* which in one form or another, has now been expounded by a large number of writers (see Blaug, 1976, p. 846).

This thesis runs into the objection that it accounts with ease for starting salaries but with difficulty for the earnings of long-time employees. Earnings are not only highly correlated with length of schooling but also with years of work experience. An employer has ample opportunity with long-time employees to acquire independent evidence of job performance without continuing to rely on educational qualifications. Besides, the evidence suggests that the correlation between earnings and length of schooling actually increases in the first ten to fifteen years of work experience, a fact difficult to explain by this weak version of the screening hypothesis (see Blaug 1976, p. 846).

A stronger version of credentialism, however, surmounts these difficulties by adding the consideration that job performance is typically judged within firms on a departmental basis. Each hierarchically organized department operates its own "internal labor market," whose principal function is to maintain output in the face of unpredictable variations in demand, while minimizing the costs of labor turnover to the firm as a whole. In consequence, departments operate with enough manpower slack to ensure every new recruit a well-defined sequence of promotions throughout his working life. In this way, the kind of statistical discrimination based on paper qualifications that operates to determine starting salaries in the weak version of credentialism is hereby extended to lifetime earnings. The argument is strengthened by the introduction of various "institutional" factors such as the tendency of monopsonistic employers to share the costs of specific training with workers, the lagged response of firms to cyclical contractions, the effects of collective bargaining in promoting substitution of more educated for less educated workers and the phenomenon of seller's credentialism, whereby professional associations press for increased educational requirements under state licensing laws.

The theory of credentialism, especially in its stronger version, appears to have radical implications for educational policy. It suggests, for example, that educational expansion is unlikely to have much impact on earnings differentials because an increased flow of college graduates will simply promote upgrading of hiring standards: college graduates will be worse off in absolute terms but so will high school graduates, and hence earnings differentials by education will remain more or less the same. However, there is nothing about this argument that is incompatible with human capital theory. The question at issue is whether upgrading can be carried on indefinitely, implying that college graduates are perfect substitutes for high school graduates and high school graduates for elementary school leavers and, therefore, that the educational system is merely an arbitrary sorting mechanism. Even in this extreme version of credentialism, we are still left with an explanation of the demand for schooling that is the same as that of human capital theory: screening by employers in terms of educational credentials creates an incentive on the part of employees to produce the "signal" that maximizes the probability of being selected, namely, the possession of an educational qualification, and this signaling incentive is in fact conveyed by the private rate of return to educational investment.

If college graduates are not perfect substitutes for high school graduates and so on down the line, there is a genuine social return to educational investment and not just a private return. In that case, what the theory of credentialism amounts to is the charge that human capital theorists have been measuring the wrong thing: the social rate of return to educational investment is a rate of return to a particular occupational selection mechanism and not the yield on resources invested in improving the quality of the labor force. However, no advocate of credentialism has so far succeeded in quantifying the social rate of return understood in this sense.

The screening hypothesis is clearly much less ambitious than the human capital research program: it is silent on questions of health care and geographical migration. It is also obvious that the screening hypothesis concentrates its fire on the demand side in the labor market, whereas the human capital research program is strong, where it is strong, on the supply side. Thus, it may well be true that the two research programs are complements, not substitutes. Indeed, Finis Welch (1975, p. 65) has observed that "the fundamental notion of human capital, of forgoing current income for the prospect of increased future earnings, assumes only that the schooling-income association is not spurious. As such, it is fully consistent with the screening view that schools primarily identify preexistent skills and with the view that market skills are produced in school." If the difference between the two explanations is indeed that of discovering whether schools produce or merely identify those attributes that employers value, the empirical evidence that would be capable of distinguishing between them is presumably evidence about what actually happens in classrooms. However, both sides have instead looked to labor market data with which to assail their opponents. But no market test is likely to discriminate between human capital and screening explanations, because the question is not *whether* schooling explains earnings but rather *why* it does.

It would be difficult to find a better example of the difference between merely predicting a result and explaining it by a convincing causal mechanism. For some purposes, this difference does not matter but for others it is vital. Moreover, the widespread belief that it is not the business of economists to examine the internal workings of economic institutions, such as firms and school systems, combined with scruples about not exceeding the proper scope of economics, may effectively bar the way to the development of a genuine explanation for an observable correlation like the one between education and earnings considered here.

Meanwhile, we are left with the uneasy feeling that the advocates of credentialism are largely content to verify their theory by pointing to "educational inflation" without committing themselves to a decisive prediction that might falsify it. The point of a testable theory is to define states of the world that cannot occur if the theory is true. It is sometimes difficult to see what states of the world are excluded by credentialism, particularly as credentialists have so far studiously avoided any investigation of "educational production functions." But this is not to say that the debate is merely a tempest in a teapot. What is at issue is whether the labor market generates private signals to individuals that are totally at variance with social signals. The debate is about the meaning of the social rather than the private rate of return on investment in human capital. In this sense, the argument is about normative values: do we want to select individuals for the world of work by means of educational credentials? If not, surely, it is not beyond the wit of man to concoct other devices for sorting workers for purposes of assigning them to particular occupations. But as is so often the case with normative problems, there is an underlying positive issue to be settled first: how efficient *is* the educational system in assigning people to jobs? Before joining Ivan Illitch in *Deschooling Society* (1971), we ought to try to answer that question.

I do not doubt that the following social experiment would settle the validity of the screening hypothesis once and for all. Let us pass a law prohibiting employers from demanding any evidence of educational qualifications at the point of hiring. If the screening hypothesis is to be believed, this would immediately cause employers to finance the creation of a National Aptitude Testing Center; they would then ask every new recruit to submit themselves to the center for a graded certificate of competence and this would then serve as the hiring screen. If such a center were cheaper to operate than the present educational system (or rather the difference between that system and the schooling system that would survive to satisfy education-as-consumption) and if the productivity of labor were no less under the new arrangement than under credentialism as it now exists, it would follow that we have all been overestimating the social rate of return to formal education. What a pity that the experiment will never be performed!

A final appraisal

The aim of our discussion was to ask: is the human capital research program "progressing" or "degenerating"? Now that we have rapidly reviewed the development of the program over the last decade, are we any nearer to an answer?

The evaluation of a scientific research program can never be absolute: research programs can only be judged in relation to their rivals purporting to explain a similar range of phenomena. The human capital research program, however, has no genuine rivals of roughly equal scope. The standard, timeless theories of consumer behavior and profit-maximizing firms provide some explanation of such phenomena as school enrollments and on-the-job training but they are powerless to account for the sharing of training costs between employers and workers. Classical sociology certainly furnishes alternative explanations of the correlation between education and earnings; and quasi-sociological theories of dual or segmented labor markets undoubtedly poach in the territory staked out by human capital theorists. The difficulty here is one of lack of precision in formulating hypotheses and, in particular, of commitment to new, falsifiable hypotheses outside the range of the human capital research program. The screening hypothesis presents similar difficulties because its advocates seem largely satisfied with providing different causal explanations for facts discovered by the human capital research program. The Marxist research program, on the other hand, has hardly begun to attack the question of earnings differentials and thus in effect fails to compete in the same terrain with human capital theory (see Blaug, 1986, chap. 10).

We are thus condemned to judge the human capital research program largely in its own terms, which is strictly speaking impossible – even the flat-earth research program, judged in its own terms, is not faring too badly! There are certainly grounds for thinking that the human capital research program is now in something of a "crisis": its explanation of the private demand for education has yet to be convincingly corroborated; it offers advice on the supply of education but it does not begin to explain either the pattern of educational finance or the public ownership of schools and colleges that we actually observe; its account of postschool training continues to underemphasize the role of costless learning-by-doing as a simple function of time, not to mention the organizational imperatives of "internal labor markets"; its rate-of-return calculations repeatedly turn up significant differences in the yields of investment in different types of human capital but its explanation of the distribution of earnings nevertheless goes on blithely assuming that all rates of return to human capital formation are equalized at the margin. Worse still is the persistent resort to ad hoc auxiliary assumptions to account for every perverse result, culminating in a certain tendency to mindlessly grind out the same calculation with new sets of data, which are typical signs of degeneration in a scientific research program.

At the same time, we must give credit where credit is due. The human capital research program has moved steadily away from some of its early naive formulations, and it has boldly attacked certain traditionally neglected topics in economics such as the size distribution of personal income. Moreover, it has never entirely lost sight of its original goal of demonstrating that a wide range of apparently disconnected phenomena in the real world are the outcome of a definite pattern of individual decisions, having in common the features of forgoing present gains for the prospect of future ones. In so doing, it discovered novel facts, such as the correlation between education and age specific earnings, which have opened up entirely new areas of research in economics. Whether this momentum can be maintained in the future is of course anybody's guess but it is noteworthy that the screening hypothesis first emerged in the writings of adherents to the human capital research program, and to this day the most fruitful empirical work in the testing of credentialist hypotheses continues to emerge from the friends rather than the enemies of human capital theory.

Nothing is easier than predicting the future course of scientific development – and nothing is more likely to be wrong. Nevertheless, let me rush in where angels fear to tread. In all likelihood, the human capital research program will never die but it will gradually fade away to be swallowed up by the new theory of signaling, the theory of how teachers and students, employers and employees, and indeed all buyers and sellers select each other when their personal attributes matter for the purpose of completing a transaction, but when information about these attributes is subject to uncertainty. In time, the screening hypothesis will be seen to have marked a turning point in the "human investment revolution in economic thought," a turning point to a richer, still more comprehensive view of the sequential life cycle choices of individuals.

Afterthoughts

The human capital research program has continued to degenerate in the 1980s, endlessly regurgitating the same material without shedding new light on issues of education and training; in a word, nothing new has happened and the subject is stale (Blaug, 1987, chap. 5). Even the screening hypothesis stands today just about where it was in 1975. Further tests on its implications using data on the self-employed or on public-versus-private-sector employ-ment have proved utterly inconclusive (Whitehead, 1981).

Needless to say, this negative verdict is not shared by everyone. Jacob Mincer (1989) displays continued faith in the vitality of the human capital research program and he was of course one of its founding fathers, if not *the* original founder.

14

The new economics of the family

Household production functions

The Chicago theory of the maximizing family, sometimes referred to as the *new home economics,* furnishes us with our last specific illustration of methodological principles. From Gary Becker's 1965 article on the allocation of time and earlier work by Jacob Mincer and Becker on fertility rates, human capital formation, and the labor force participation rates of married women, a wide-ranging research program has been developed that gives a unified interpretation to all the diverse market and nonmarket activities of families: the initial decision to marry, the decision to have children, the division of household tasks between husband and wife, the extent of participation in the labor market and even the final decision to dissolve the family by divorce.

Traditional theory views the family as a one-person household, maximizing a utility function that is defined on goods and services bought in the marketplace. The new economics of the family instead views the family as a multiperson production unit, maximizing a production function whose inputs are market goods and the time, skills, and knowledge of different members of the family. The result is not only to extend the standard tools of microeconomics to problems usually assigned to the domain of sociology, social psychology, and social anthropology but to transform the traditional explanation of consumer behavior.[26] As in Lancaster's theory of characteristics (see Chapter 6

---

[26] In Becker's (1976, p. 169) words: "The traditional theory of the household is essentially a theory of a one-person household, and it is almost, but not quite, sterile (the important theorem [sic] of negatively sloped demand curves saves it from complete sterility). In contrast, the new theory of the household is a theory of the multiperson family with interdependent utility functions, and focuses on the coordination and interaction among members with regard to decisions about children, marriage, the division of labor concerning hours worked and investments in market-augmenting and

above) consumers are said to maximize the utility attributable to goods, and this utility depends on much more than the quantities of goods that are consumed; thus, they do not minimize, say, the quantity of traveling they will do but rather they trade off various attributes of traveling (speed, comfort, costs, etcetera) so that different travel modes become inputs into the family's production of the desirable commodity "traveling." Indeed, household size, age structure, education, race, occupation, and other measures of socioeconomic status are now introduced as explanatory variables of family consumption, in addition to such traditional variables as price and income, via their effects on the shadow prices of home-produced services.

The new research program comes equipped with a new "hard core." There is nothing new about the program's adherence to methodological individualism, or the rationalistic notion that all family decisions, including the very decision to constitute a family unit, are the result of a conscious weighing of alternatives. But what is new is the studious avoidance of any reliance on the twin hypotheses that tastes change over time and that they differ between people. Unspecified changes in tastes over time and unspecified differences in tastes between people are, as we know, capable of accounting for just about any behavior we might observe. Hence, the new research program in the economics of the family takes its stand on a definite "negative heuristic": *de gustibus non est disputandum!* (There's no disputing about tastes.) To express it positively, "widespread and/or persistent human behavior can be explained by a generalized calculus of utility-maximizing behavior, without introducing the qualification 'tastes remaining the same' " (Stigler and Becker, 1977, p. 76; also Becker, 1976, pp. 5, 7, 11–12, 133, 144).

The reason for postulating the assumption of stable and uniform preference functions is thus avowedly methodological: it is to produce unambiguously falsifiable predictions about behavior and to avoid, whenever possible, ad hoc explanations based on changes in tastes, differences in tastes, ignorance, and impulsive or neurotic behavior. It would appear, therefore, that the Chicago research program is firmly committed, as are few other research programs in modern economics, to the methodological norms laid down by Karl Popper. For that reason, if for no other, the program deserves our attention.

However, this is not the place or the time to attempt a full-scale appraisal of the Chicago household production model. Its main outlines are clear but

nonmarket-augmenting skills, the protection of members against hazards, intergenerational transfers among members, and so on. Economists are, therefore, only beginning to attribute to the family the same dominant role in society traditionally attributed to it by sociologists, anthropologists, and psychologists. Whereas the theory of the firm is basically no different than it was thirty years ago, the household has been transformed from a sterile field in economics into one of the most exciting and promising areas."

many of its details remain to be worked out; it has hardly begun to be criticized[27] and without a critical discussion, the strength and weaknesses of any budding research program cannot be fairly judged; besides, an adequate appraisal would involve consideration of alternative sociological and anthropological explanations of family behavior, taking us far afield into ill-charted territories. I will confine myself, therefore, to some provocative comments on Becker's work that may stimulate readers to study the new home economics and to form their own assessment.

Adhockery

As we have said, Becker is determined to minimize immunizing stratagems, as Popper calls them, and in particular to avoid appealing to ad hoc explanations whenever the theory is contradicted by observations. Nevertheless, one is struck by the frequency with which he does resort to ad hoc assumptions to produce testable implications. For example, human capital formation appears in the household production model in the guise of investment in the ''quality'' of children, whereas the decision to have children at all is viewed as investment in their ''quantity''; children are treated as if they were consumer durable goods whose services parents wish to consume. The model predicts that family income is positively related, not to the number of children in the family, but to the utility derived from child services – quality and quantity of children are viewed as substitutes in the family's production function. Moreover, because of the opportunity costs of the mother's time in bringing up children, rising family income causes a time-saving substitution of children's quality for children's quantity: in a word, the rich have fewer, better educated children, while the poor have more, worse educated children. But this central conclusion of the model in respect of fertility behavior – a negative relationship between income and fertility between households at any moment in time and among all households over time – is accounted for, not by the model itself, but by a plausible auxiliary assumption (namely, that the income elasticity of demand for the quality of children is substantially larger than that for the quantity of children) that is introduced to help solve the original maximization problem (Becker, 1976, pp. 197, 199; also pp. 105–6).

[27] But see Leibenstein (1974, 1975), Keeley (1975), and Fulop (1977), all of whom deal only with the economic theory of fertility behavior as one strand in the new research program. Leibenstein (1974, pp. 463, 466, 468–9) makes some interesting remarks on the various methodological attitudes of different members of the Chicago school but he spoils his own case by denying that predictive capacity is the acid test of the validity of a theory (1975, p. 471). See also Ferber and Birnbaum (1977), the only critique to date which attempts to look at the whole of the new economics of the family.

Similarly, in Becker's theory of the economics of altruism, he concludes that an increase in a donor's income will increase his charitable gifts disproportionately, while an increase in the income of the recipients of charity will have exactly the obverse effect (p. 275) and he pours scorn on the ''considerable ad hocery'' that is required in the conventional approach to the economics of charity to produce this well-attested result. Again this conclusion depends critically on what is assumed both about the form of the donor's utility function and the form in which the recipient's welfare enters as an argument in that function.

Or, to mention one more point, Becker cannot produce the central results of his theory of crime, for example, that offenders are more deterred by the probability of conviction than by the severity of punishment when convicted, without resorting to arbitrary assumptions about the preference for risk among offenders (pp. 48–9). In other words, Becker's own method of analysis is almost as ad hoc as the conventional one; the qualitative calculus of the one-period, static household production model is simply incapable of producing definite quantitative conclusions about various aspects of human behavior without the arbitrary addition of extra information.[28]

Some results

Becker's writings lend themselves all too easily to caricature because they employ a cumbersome apparatus to produce implications that are sometimes obvious, if not banal.[29] His theory of marriage begins with the observation that ''since men and women compete as they seek mates, a *market* in marriages can be presumed to exist'' (p. 206). A person decides to marry ''when the utility expected from marriage exceeds that from remaining single or from additional search for a more suitable mate'' (p. 10). The gains from marriage derive from the complementarities between men and women in respect of the productivity of time invested in nonmarket activities and the power to acquire market goods (p. 211). To explain the pattern of marriages actually contracted, Becker applies Edgeworth's theory of the ''core'' of a voluntary exchange economy[30] to show that men and women will sort themselves into

[28] Simon (1987, pp. 29–31) makes the same point, drawing on Becker's *Treatise on the Family* (1981).

[29] See the heavy-handed humor of Blinder (1974) on the economics of brushing teeth and Bergstrom (1976) on the economics of sleeping.

[30] Edgeworth's theory of the ''core'' deals with the case of a set of agents with certain initial holdings of commodities in the absence of anything like a price system; these agents are free to form any blocks and coalitions for the purposes of improving their situation by trade and no redistribution of commodities via trade is allowed unless each and every agent agrees voluntarily to the final outcome. As the number of agents increases, it can be shown, surprisingly enough, that (1) the ''core'' containing all agents that agree to the final distribution of commodities contains the equilibrium

families in such a way that the output of marketable and nonmarketable "commodities" produced by families is maximized over all marriages: "A sorting of persons into different marriages is said to be an equilibrium sorting if persons not married to each other in this sorting could not marry and make each other better off" (p. 10). Having analyzed the gains from "marriages of convenience" in terms of the comparative advantages of men and women in different tasks, he adds the comment:

The gain from marriage also depends on traits, such as beauty, intelligence, and education, that affect nonmarket productivity as well, perhaps, as market opportunities. The analysis of sorting . . . implies that an increase in the value of traits that have a positive effect on nonmarket productivity, market productivity held constant, would generally increase the gain from marriage. Presumably this helps to explain why, for example, less attractive or less intelligent persons are less likely to marry than are more attractive or more intelligent persons [p. 214].[31]

It would be difficult to find a better example in economic literature of the use of a sledgehammer to crack a nut.

A more serious difficulty with Becker's research program is that the household production model is so generally formulated as to be compatible with almost any finding. A central question that arises in the anthropological literature on marital patterns throughout human history is why monogamy has gradually emerged as the dominant pattern around the world and why polygamy, which used to be fairly common, has drastically declined over time. Becker accounts for the predominance of monogamy as "the most efficient marital form" over various forms of polygamy by the assumption that the productivity gains from joining men and women together in households are subject to diminishing returns (p. 211). But reasonable as is this assumption, it is easy to see that if the facts suggested the predominance of communal households, made up of multiple, interacting families, this could be easily accommodated in the model by simply assuming a different form of the gains-from-marriage function.

Indeed, Becker himself admits that there are assumptions about the produc-

allocations of commodities that would result from a price system under perfect competition, and (2) in the limit, the set of competitive equilibria allocations are the only outcomes which satisfy the stability requirements of the "core." For a simplified exposition of this very difficult topic, see Johansen (1978).

[31] This statement ignores the question of "love," which however makes little difference to anything: "At an abstract level, love, and other emotional attachments, such as sexual activity or frequent close contact with a particular person can be considered particular nonmarketable household commodities, and nothing much need be added to the analysis" (Becker, 1976, p. 233). The book is in fact full of such complacent, not to say humorless, sentences.

tivity differences between men that can account for polygyny, a particular version of polygamy (p. 239). In other words, the theory cannot actually predict the predominance of monogamy without adding various cultural constraints on gender-role behavior. As a matter of fact, the new home economics may show that families rationally adapt themselves to the traditional division of household tasks within the family, but, surely, not that the division itself is rational? Husbands and wives are said to allocate household tasks according to the principles of comparative advantage, given the constraints of the labor market that largely condemn wives to be marginal wage earners. Now that we have invoked custom and tradition in respect of the constraints on market opportunities, how can we then rule them out as arguments in the preference functions themselves? (Ferber and Birnbaum, 1977, pp. 20–1).

Apart from accounting for the prevalence of monogamy, Becker's theory of marriage is also directed at explaining the well-corroborated phenomenon of "positive associative mating," in other words, that like tend to marry like, where "like" is defined in terms of such traits as age, height, education, intelligence, race, religion, ethnic origin, value of financial assets, and place of residence. Becker's theory predicts, however, that there will be negative associative mating in respect of the earning power commanded by husbands and wives because they are close substitutes in household production. This prediction turns out to be contradicted by the available evidence. He argues, however, that his theory refers to all mates, whereas the available evidence is biased because it counts only those families in which the wife is working (pp. 224–5). We are left at the end of the argument, therefore, with almost empty conclusions that are presented as being more dramatic than they really are:

. . . the economic approach has numerous implications about behavior that could be falsified. For example, it implies that "likes" tend to marry each other, when measured by intelligence, education, race, family background, height, and many other variables, and that "unlikes" marry when measured by wage rates and some other variables. The implication that men with relatively high wage rates marry women with relatively low wage rates (other variables being held constant) surprises many, but appears consistent with the available data when they are adjusted for the large fraction of married women who do not work. The economic approach also implies that higher-income persons marry younger and divorce less frequently than others, implications consistent with the available evidence but not with common beliefs. Still another implication is that an increase in the relative earnings of wives increases the likelihood of marital dissolution, which partly explains the greater dissolution rate among black than white families [pp. 10–11].

Again and again, the theory is shown to be compatible with all the known evidence on the incidence of marriage and divorce (pp. 214, 220, 221, 224), which is hardly surprising given the flexibility of the model. For example, in order to combine the market goods and services purchased with the own time and skills of different household members into a single aggregate of "full income," it is assumed that the household's "technology" exhibits constant returns to scale and no joint production, and that all the "commodities" produced by households are similarly affected by productivity-augmenting factors such as education (these assumptions guarantee meaningful aggregation of microproduction functions). Dropping the assumption of constant returns to scale and allowing for joint production, as well as the multiplicity of traits by which family members differ, allows almost any observed sorting of mates to be explained (pp. 226, 228).[32]

"Does my analysis justify the popular belief that more beautiful, charming, and talented women tend to marry wealthier and more successful men?" Becker (p. 223) asks. Well, yes and no: positive associative mating is generally optimal and hence will emerge spontaneously, but it is not invariably optimal because differences in earning power dictate negative associative mating. Thus, if beautiful, talented women married poor failures, this would, surely, be hailed as a striking confirmation of the theory? Finally, when we add "caring" anything can happen: "Most people no doubt find the concept of a market allocation to beloved mates strange and unrealistic. And, as I have shown, caring can strikingly modify the market allocation between married persons" (p. 235). Indeed, "caring" is perfectly capable of turning a negative sorting into a positive one (p. 238).

Verificationism again

Despite continued appeal to the methodological norms of falsificationism, the whole of Becker's writings are positively infected by the easier option of verificationism: we begin with the available evidence about human behavior in areas traditionally neglected by economists and then congratulate ourselves that we have accounted for it by nothing more than the application of standard economic logic. But what we never do is to produce really surprising implications directing our attention to hitherto unsuspected "novel facts," that is, facts that the theory was not specifically designed to predict. Moreover, we hail the economic approach as superior to any available alternative, but we restrict the scope of the comparison to our own advantage and we never in fact specify the alternative approaches that we have in mind.[33] Clearly, if these are the rules of the game, we simply cannot lose.

---

[32] Dropping these assumptions also makes it difficult to estimate household protection functions, and yet it is difficult to obtain independent evidence that would exclude decreasing returns to scale and joint production (see Pollak and Wachter, 1975, particularly pp. 256, 270; 1977).

[33] "I do not pretend," Becker (1976, p. 206) disclaims, "to have developed the analysis sufficiently to explain all the similarities and differences in marital patterns across cultures or over time. But the 'economic' approach does quite well, certainly far

In itself, there is nothing particularly commendable about economic imperialism of the intellectual variety, particularly once it is granted, as in Becker (pp. 8, 9, 14), that the economic approach is not applicable with equal insight to all aspects of human behavior. Presumably, the invasion of other areas of knowledge by economists is justified either by the fresh light that they cast on old problems in sociology, anthropology, and political science, or by the feedback effects of such invasions on the traditional concerns of economics. Whatever our view of the Chicago research program on the former score, it is difficult to deny its contributions on the latter. There is little doubt of the explanatory value of the nonpecuniary costs of consumption, notably the cost of time forgone, for purposes of analyzing behavior related to travel, recreation, education, migration, health, and indeed, the search for knowledge of the properties of consumable goods and services.[34]

It is also true that there is something very uncomfortable about the traditional picture of households interacting with firms in factor and product markets in which the household remains essentially a single-person decision maker. Whether the problem of family behavior is best tackled by viewing households as producers rather than consumers remains an open question, but at any rate, the household production model gives us something against which to pit Lancaster's demand approach. Finally, we can have nothing but praise for a research program that dares to prescribe a strong ''positive heuristic,'' and what could be stronger or bolder than the premise that all human behavior reflects a single-minded attempt to maximize a constrained utility function subject to completely stable and totally uniform preferences? Such a theory literally invites severe testing, and if Popper is to be believed, severe testing is the hallmark of scientific progress. I doubt that Becker and company always practice what they preach, but at least they clearly commit themselves to methodological standards by which they can be judged.

Nothing is easier than to kill off new research programs by piling up ideological objections against the ''hard core'' of the program, accompanied by nit-picking of the theories in the ''protective belt.'' The study of economic methodology should teach us how difficult it is to appraise even mature research programs, much less infant ones. The Chicago research program in the economics of the family is a going enterprise that has already attracted a large following.[35] My personal view is that the program works well on crime, less

better than any available alternative.'' Later in the book there are several brief references to studies by sociologists and anthropologists, and that is all we ever hear of competing, noneconomic analyses of marital patterns.

[34] For example, the Chicago program can account for the phenomenon of advertising even under conditions of perfect competition (Stigler and Becker, 1977, pp. 83–7).

[35] Becker (1976) lists most of the contributions up to about 1975. Since then there have been many more: see, for example, Becker, Landes, and Michael (1977); and Fair (1978). See also McKenzie and Tullock (1975), a textbook vulgarization of the new economics of the family.

well on marriage and fertility, and least well on social interactions, not because it fails to deduce "theorems" on these latter subjects, but because the content of those theorems is so empty. No doubt, five years from now I shall think quite differently – and that is exactly as it should be. Only a philistine judges a scientific research program decisively once and for all.

In retrospect

I was wrong to think that the so-called new home economics would flourish and attract ever more followers and that I would come to view it more favorably in 1985 or 1990 than I did in 1980. Becker himself has reworked his earlier *Economic Approach to Human Behavior* (1976) into a more finished *Treatise on the Family* (1981), while applying the economic approach to yet other apparently noneconomic subjects, such as drug addiction. However, very few economists have plowed his furrow while most sociologists have scornfully dismissed the "economic imperialism" implied by the Chicago approach to social behavior (Swedberg, 1990, pp. 28, 46, 325–7). The Chicago research program in what Becker now calls "economic sociology" looked so promising ten or fifteen years ago but strikes one today as virtually a one-man band.

15

The rationality postulate

The meaning of rationality

I have left to the last what some regard as the most characteristic feature of neoclassical economics, namely, its insistence on methodological individualism: the attempt to derive all economic behavior from the action of individuals seeking to maximize their utility, subject to the constraints of technology and endowments. This is the so-called *rationality postulate,* which figures as a minor premise in every neoclassical argument. The economist's measure of "rationality" does not correspond to the layman's understanding of the term. In common parlance, rationality means acting with good reasons and with as much information as possible or, in somewhat more formal terms, consistently applying adequate means to achieve well-specified ends. For the economist, however, rationality means choosing in accordance with a preference ordering that is complete and transitive, subject to perfect and costlessly acquired information; where there is uncertainty about future outcomes, rationality means maximizing expected utility, that is, the utility of an outcome multiplied by the probability of its occurrence.

The economist's meaning of rationality is a relatively recent invention dating from the 1930s but descending from the marginal revolution of the 1870s. To the classical economists, rationality (a term they never used) meant preferring more to less, choosing the highest rate of return, minimizing unit costs and, above all, pursuing one's self-interest without explicit regard to the welfare of others. With the use of marginal utility theory, and particularly with the Hicks–Allen ordinalist interpretation of utility theory, the pursuit of self-interest quietly gave way to the maximization of a consistent preference-ordering under certainty and complete information (Broome, 1991). Neumann and Morgenstorm added the expected-utility interpretation where there is uncertainty and, more recently, the new classical macroeconomics has reinterpreted the concept of perfect information under uncertainty to mean perfect infor-

229

mation about the probability distribution of future prices. But the common thread in all these developments of the rationality postulate over the last 60 years is that of a stable, well-behaved set of preferences and perfect costless information about future outcomes, stochastically interpreted.

So strong and pervasive has been the hold of the rationality postulate on modern economics that some have seriously denied that it is possible to construct any economic theory not based on utility maximization. Obviously, this assertion is false because Keynesian economics with its fixed-price assumptions was not derived from utility maximization and is not easily made compatible with it: an entire generation of macroeconomists has sought to derive microeconomic foundations for Keynesian macroeconomics, that is, to square the Keynesian multiplier with the rationality postulate, and not everyone would agree that the effort has been wholly successful. Similarly, the demand for money is difficult to derive from rational utility maximization in the usual sense of the term and Arrow (1987, p. 70) has gone so far as to assert: "I know of no serious derivation of the demand for money from a rational optimization." Finally, there are Marxian economics, radical economics, and American institutionalism, which have all eschewed the rationality postulate – and to deny that these are a type of economics is, surely?, absurd.

Rationality as sacrosanct

Granted that the rationality postulate is dispensable, the fact remains that its intuitive appeal is so strong that neo-Austrian economists like Lionel Robbins and Ludwig von Mises regarded it as an *a priori* proposition, so obviously true that it only needed to be stated to win immediate assent. That is not to say that they held it as an analytical tautology – everyone maximizes utility because whatever they choose exhibits the utility they maximize – but rather as a Kantian synthetic *a priori,* that is, a proposition about empirical reality which nevertheless cannot ever be false by virtue of language or the meaning of terms, in this case, the term *purposive choice.* The rationality postulate continues to this day to be regarded by some as empirically irrefutable, not in and of itself but as a matter of convention; in short, neoclassical economists have decided as it were to regard the rationality postulate as part of the Lakatosian "hard core" of their research program. It is for this reason that Lawrence Boland (1981) has argued that it would be futile to criticize the rationality postulate and that, in any case, all criticisms of it are misguided. It is certainly true that the treatment of rationality as a metaphysical proposition has gradually become the standard orthodox defense of any criticism of the rationality postulate. New classical macroeconomists, like Sargent and Lucas for example, regard any attempt to introduce parameters in an economic model that are not motivated by individual optimization as an "ad hoc adjustment," that is, one introduced for a particular purpose without having any wider justification for them. "The sin of ad hocness," as Wade Hands (1988, p. 132) put it, "seems to be infidelity to the metaphysical presuppositions of the neoclassical program."

Caldwell (1983) agrees with Boland but for different reasons. He reviews five tests of rational choice by experimental economists and argues that their results are necessarily inconclusive. Because of the Duhem–Quine thesis, any such test is a test not only of rationality but also of the stability of preferences and the completeness of knowledge about alternative opportunities. He therefore concludes that the rationality postulate as such is untestable and, in any case, he denounces such tests as "ultraempiricism" (Caldwell, 1982, p. 158), that is, the unwillingness to entertain any theoretical concept that is not capable of being directly observed.[36]

The idea that rationality is obviously true and is so sacrosanct that it must be protected from criticism by the "negative heuristic" of the ad hoc accusation is very curious in view of the fact that rationality in the strict modern sense of the term cannot be universally true of all economic actions by all economic agents. In general, it is impossible to rule out impulsive and habitual behavior or exploratory choice behavior – learning to want what it is we want – or even forgetfulness, destroying the very notion of consistent preference orderings. Besides, the rationality postulate implies an ability at information processing and calculation that invites ridicule – John Maurice Clark's "irrational passion for rational calculations." It is because of "bounded rationality" that Herbert Simon (1957, chaps. 14, 15) contends that we simply cannot maximize utility; the best we can do is to "satisfice," and satisficing leads to very different predictions of economic behavior from maximizing (see Loasby, 1989, chap. 9).

Still more curious is the fact that the treatment of rationality as a "hard core" proposition was recommended long ago for the whole of the social sciences by Karl Popper himself. He called it "situational logic" or the "zero method" and advocated it initially in *The Poverty of Historicism* (1957) without direct reference to economics. Nevertheless, it is unmistakably the same thing as the rationality assumption of neoclassical economics. And curiouser and curiouser, he later declared that it was false as a substantive proposition but that he advocated it nevertheless because it had proved so fruitful in the past in the investigation of economic behavior (see Hands, 1985; Blaug, 1985; Redman, 1991, pp. 111–16; and Caldwell, 1991, pp. 13–22).

Popper was perfectly correct on both scores and yet it is clear that he misunderstood the role of rationality in economics. The rationality postulate refers to individual motivation but the behavior in which economists are inter-

---

[36] Hargreaves-Heap (1989) in a recent book-length study of rationality takes the same point of view.

ested is the behavior of aggregates of consumers and producers in different markets. Typically, this problem of aggregation is waived by the tacit assumption that all individuals are alike and hence have the same utility function (and even that all firms are alike and have the same technology). Since individuals are clearly not alike in both preferences and endowments – if they were it would imply the absence of trading – it is evident that the successful explanations of economic behavior by economists have been due to more than the use of the rationality postulate. The rationality hypothesis by itself is rather weak. To make it yield interesting implications, we need to add auxiliary assumptions to the general notion of rationality, such as homogeneity of agents in the standard evasion of the problem of aggregation or, more generally, perfect foreknowledge, equilibrium outcomes, perfect competition, and the like (Arrow, 1987, pp. 70–71). In other words, the allegedly impressive track record of neoclassical economics, which impelled Popper to recommend the rationality postulate as the golden key for unlocking all doors in social science, is based on much more than the assumption of rational action.

Criticisms of rationality

Be that as it may, the rationality postulate is probably false, as Popper conceded. Experimental psychologists have shown that individual behavior systematically violates rationality. Such "anomalies" have long been recognized in the literature on the expected-utility model (Schoemaker, 1982) but, paradoxically, they have not been taken seriously in theorizing about rational action under certainty and complete information (Frey and Eichenberger, 1989, pp. 109–10). For example, a widespread finding in many markets is that individuals systematically undervalue opportunity costs compared to out-of-pocket costs, that is, count a dollar spent as more than a dollar lost in opportunities forgone.

Frey and Eichenberger (1989) show that the reaction by economists to the evidence about such anomalies has taken a variety of forms. Insofar as the anomalies refer to individual behavior, the anomalies are frequently ignored or explained away as a result of the artificial nature of laboratory evidence. When the evidence refers not to laboratory experiments but to real-world aggregate behavior, it is argued that the anomalies are randomly distributed and average out in the large, or, more commonly, that competitive markets tend in time to eliminate such anomalies. The Darwinian survival mechanism invoked by Alchian and Friedman to rationalize profit maximization (see Chapter 4 above) is a case in point of such a defense. However, by now we have accumulated sufficient empirical observations to support the belief that competition even in financial markets does not succeed in eliminating all individual-level anomalies at the aggregate level. Thus, Thaler (1987a; 1987b) has shown that abnormal returns in stock market trading occur around the turn of the year, the turn of the month, the turn of the week, and even the turn of the day, not to mention the day before holidays. But according to the so-called "efficient market hypothesis," stock prices follow a random walk if only because stock market traders hold rational expectations and exploit every profit opportunity the moment it occurs. But if the assumption of rational expectations, which is nothing more than the rationality postulate in stochastic dress, breaks down in financial markets, why should it be regarded as tenable in other markets?

We conclude that the classic defense against criticisms of the rationality postulate carries less conviction today than it did in the past. But so what? Are we to reject the whole of neoclassical economics because it rests on the insecure foundation of the dubious rationality postulate? To do so would be to fall prey to "naive falsificationism." We do not discard a research program simply because it is subject to "anomalies" unless an alternative research program is available. However, such alternatives are in fact available as, for example, the "prospect theory" of Tversky and Kahneman (1986), a non-expected utility theory of decision making under uncertainty, or Simon's satisficing theory, which might be described as a non-fully-rational theory of individual action under both certainty and uncertainty. It is true of course that none of these alternative conceptions offer the same rigorous implications that are obtained by standard models with full rationality – not yet at any rate. But this rigor may be purchased at the expense of relevance: if the rationality postulate is truly false, it may be one of the reasons why microeconomics is so poor at explaining the patterns of consumption of many households and the price-setting patterns of firms in many markets.

Needless to say, the trouble may lie in our understanding of information costs or our grasp of competitive mechanisms and not in the use of the traditional rationality postulate. It would be foolhardy to tell fellow economists how to amend mainstream economics to take account of choice anomalies or even to abandon standard microeconomics in favor of one of the dissenting brands of economics that dispense altogether with methodological individualism. However, what is clear is that the direct investigation of rational action, the attempt to test the urgency of the assumption of rationality, should not be dismissed out of hand as "ultraempiricism." This much we do learn from the methodology of economics. So long as tests of the accuracy of predictions remain ambiguous – that is to say, forever – it will remain important also to test the descriptive accuracy of assumptions and to take the results of these tests seriously.

PART IV

What have we now learned about economics?

16

Conclusions

The crisis of modern economics

The 1960s was a decade in which the public esteem of economics and the professional euphoria of economists rose to an all-time pitch. The 1970s, on the other hand, have been full of talk of "crisis," "revolution," and "counterrevolution," amounting at times to a veritable orgy of self-criticism on the part of some of the leading spokesmen of the economics profession. According to Wassily Leontief (1971, p. 3), "Continued preoccupation with imaginary, hypothetic, rather than with observable reality has gradually led to a distortion of the informal valuation scale used in our academic community to assess and to rank the scientific performance of its members. Empirical analysis, according to this scale, gets a lower rating than formal mathematical reasoning." Furthermore, he charged, economists care too little about the quality of the data with which they work and he blamed this attitude on the baleful influence of the methodology of instrumentalism or as-if theorizing (p. 5). Henry Phelps Brown (1972, p. 3), however, went much further: what is basically wrong with modern economics, he argued, is that its assumptions about human behavior are totally arbitrary, being literally "plucked from the air," and he blamed this habit of building make-believe worlds on the failure to train economists in the study of history. David Worswick (1972, p. 78) voiced similar sentiments, adding that "there now exist whole branches of abstract economic theory which have no links with concrete facts and are almost indistinguishable from pure mathematics."[1]

Benjamin Ward devoted an entire book to the question *What's Wrong With*

---

[1] Two government economists, Macdougall (1974) and Heller (1975), have supplied more cheerful assessments, while nevertheless conceding most of the points made by Leontief, Phelps Brown, and Worswick. For these and other expressions of, and reactions to, the "crisis" in modern economics, see Gordon (1976), Hutchison (1977, chap. 4), O'Brien (1974), and Coats (1977).

Economics? and his answer in brief is that economics is basically a normative policy science adorning itself with the fig leaf of hard-headed positivism. Insofar as economics is a positive science, Ward (1972, p. 173) concluded, "the desire systematically to confront the theory with fact has not been a notable feature of the discipline." For him, however, this failure consistently to pursue the task of empirical testing "is not the central difficulty with modern economics" (p. 173). My own contention, by way of contrast, is that the central weakness of modern economics is, indeed, the reluctance to produce the theories that yield unambiguously refutable implications, followed by a general unwillingness to confront those implications with the facts.

Consider, for example, the preoccupation since 1945 of some of the best brains in modern economics with the esoterica of growth theory, when even practitioners of the art admit that modern growth theory is not as yet capable of casting any light on actual economies growing over time.[2] The essence of modern growth theory is simply old-style stationary state analysis in which an element of compound growth is introduced by adding factor-augmenting technical change and exogenous increases in labor supply to an otherwise static, one-period, general equilibrium model of the economy. In view of the enormous difficulties of handling anything but steady-state growth (equiproportionate increases in all the relevant economic variables), the literature has been almost solely taken up with arid brain-twisters about "golden rules" of capital accumulation. To put it bluntly: no economy has ever been observed in steady-state growth and, besides, there are deep, inherent reasons why actual growth is always unsteady and always unbalanced.

Growth theory is usually defended as an abstract formulation of the conditions required for the economy to reproduce itself unchanged in all essential respects from one period to another, which formulation is then supposed to serve as a reference point against which various patterns of unbalanced growth can be studied. But if there is no correspondence whatever between the steady-state path and the actual historical experience of economic development, it is not easy to see how growth theory can be expected to throw light on the causes of unbalanced growth, or on the policies that may be required to manage the economy.[3] This is not to say, therefore, that growth theory is simply

---

[2] As even Hicks (1965, p. 183), a leading modern growth theorist, admits: modern growth theory "has been fertile in the generation of class-room exercises; but so far as we can yet see, they are exercises, not real problems. They are not even hypothetical real problems, of the type 'what would happen if?' where the 'if' is something that could conceivably happen. They are shadows of real problems, dressed up in such a way that by pure logic we can find solutions for them."

[3] Hollis and Nell, it will be remembered (see Chapter 4 above) regarded the study of the conditions for an economy to reproduce itself to be the "essence" of any proper science of economics. Alas, economic systems never reproduce themselves in an unaltered state: the children, so to speak, never completely resemble the parents.

a waste of time but, given its extremely limited practical implications, we may question the magnitude of the intellectual resources that have been devoted to growth theory in recent years. Certainly, it smacks of a subject more devoted to solving logical puzzles than to furthering positive science.

Having more or less faded away in the 1970s, growth theory has recently made a small comeback in the guise of Walrasian models purporting to explain economic growth as an endogenous process due to external economies generated by technical progress. At least this style of growth theory is addressed to stylized facts about growth (Wulwick, 1991) instead of simply providing brain teasers for mathematical economists. Nevertheless, the fascination with technical problems – such as whether the equilibrium growth path of the model is the outcome of a perfectly competitive process or not – continues to haunt the new growth theory as it did the old and so far its contribution to a truly causal explanation of growth in industrialized economics is nil.

But perhaps the example of growth theory is too easy. Consider instead that part of the neoclassical research program that comes closest in matching the rigor and elegance of quantum physics, the modern theory of consumer behavior based on the axioms of revealed preference, to which a long line of great economists have devoted their most intense efforts. There is little sign, as we have seen, that these prodigious labors have had much impact on the estimation of statistical demand curves. Even if this much is denied, it can hardly be argued that the quantity and quality of intellectual effort devoted to rationalizing the negative slope of the demand curve over the last ninety years has been in due proportion to its practical fruits in empirical work.

Or, to switch topics, consider the endless arguments in textbooks on labor economics about the assumptions that underlie the misnamed "marginal productivity theory of wages" at the expense of space devoted to considering what the theory actually predicts about the workings of the labor market. If this is not misplaced emphasis, what is? Consider next the frequently refuted Heckscher–Ohlin theorem in all its $2 \times 2 \times 2$ box-diagram varieties, taught in all textbooks on international trade, not so much as a parable for purposes of limbering up but, on the contrary, as a simplified but nevertheless valid explanation of the pattern of goods traded between countries. Once again, all the emphasis falls on teaching the analytical subtleties of the Heckscher–Ohlin theorem at the expense of time devoted to considering the considerable evidence against the theorem.

Take, finally, the infinite refinements that have been achieved by Arrow, Debreu, McKenzie, and many others in the formulation of existence proofs of general equilibrium (GE). It cannot be denied that such work has generated some deep insights into the logical characteristics of economic theories – the role of money in perfect-certainty models, the requirement of forward markets in all goods to secure competitive equilibrium, the need for noncompetitive disequilibrium transactions to keep competitive equilibria stable, etcetera – but what may be doubted is that GE theory has contributed much to increasing the predictive powers of modern economics. Even this would not constitute a serious criticism of GE theorizing were it not for the fact that the work in the area of GE theory is generally regarded as ranking high in the intellectual pecking order of the economic profession and deemed to be an absolutely essential part of the training of professional economists. And yet GE *theory* as distinct from GE *models* (see Chapter 8 above) is at best a species of "solving the puzzles that we have ourselves created," and time spent in mastering it is time taken away from learning the empirical methods of economics.

The enormous intellectual prestige of GE theory has in recent years given way to a new fashion: game theory. Now there is simply no doubt that the introduction of a game-theoretic approach to economics has brought with it a new "understanding" of what is meant by rationality and interdependence and equilibrium. But the very notion of rationality in game situations explodes into a host of different possible rationality scenarios, each culminating in a different equilibrium concept, none of which can be excluded as psychologically impossible. We end up conceding that "game theory is not a theory which has as output a set of refutable statements, but merely a syntax articulating the vocabulary of interdependent rationality. Game 'theory' *per se* is no more empirically verifiable than an alleged translation from English into an unspoken language. Yet its application to specific economic political or social situations produces many testable statements" (Bianchi and Moulin, 1991, pp. 187–8).

It would be better to say "may" produce testable statements, for such statements have so far been few and far between. The field of industrial organization, for example, has been transformed in recent years by the introduction of noncooperative game theory. Nevertheless, one may search high and low in such leading textbooks as Jean Tirole's *Theory of Industrial Organization* (1988), exemplifying the game-theoretic revolution in industrial organization, without encountering so much as a definite empirical prediction about market behavior. What we find here and elsewhere in the economic literature inspired by game theory is virtually endless conceptual proliferation of the fundamental notions of rational behavior. There is nothing wrong with that provided one remembers that "it does not naturally fit into the category of theories that generate testable hypotheses. . . . It is perhaps better thought of as showing the poverty (degeneration?) of traditional analysis, in that game theory is what one gets if one admits strategic interaction into the analysis of optimizing behavior, yet game theory is unable – so far, anyway – to generate the testable propositions that most positivist defenders of the traditional analysis have implied were there'' (Bianchi and Moulin, 1991, p. 196; see also Roth, 1991). Is that perhaps why it is so popular these days with younger, mathematically inclined economists?

Measurement without theory

But, surely, economists engage massively in empirical research? Clearly they do but, unfortunately, much of it is like playing tennis with the net down: instead of attempting to refute testable predictions, modern economists all too frequently are satisfied to demonstrate that the real world conforms to their predictions, thus replacing falsification, which is difficult, with verification, which is easy. We have seen some striking examples of this attitude in the sources-of-growth literature and in the new economics of the family. The journals abound with papers that apply regression analysis to every conceivable economic problem, but it is no secret that success in such endeavors frequently relies on ''cookbook econometrics'': express a hypothesis in terms of an equation, estimate a variety of forms for that equation, select the best fit, discard the rest, and then adjust the theoretical argument to rationalize the hypothesis that is being tested (Ward, 1972, pp. 146–52). Marshall used to say that scientific explanation is simply ''prediction written backwards.'' But the reverse proposition is false: prediction is not necessarily explanation written forwards. Empirical work that fails utterly to discriminate between competing explanations quickly degenerates into a sort of mindless instrumentalism and it is not too much to say that the bulk of empirical work in modern economics is guilty on that score.

A wild exaggeration? Perhaps, but there are many others who have said as much. Peter Kenen (1975, p. xvi) expresses the same thought in forceful language:

I detect a dangerous ambiguity in our quantitative work. We do not distinguish carefully enough between the *testing* of hypotheses and the estimation of structural relationships. The ambiguity is rampant in economics. . . . We should be spending more time and thought on the construction of tests that will help us to discriminate between hypotheses having different economic implications. It is not enough to show that our favourite theory does as well as – or better than – some other theory when it comes to accounting retrospectively for the available evidence.

Similarly, when asked in an interview what he thought was wrong with the empirical work of economists, Robert Solow replied:

The problem with it, I think, is rather that it's too late for economists to ask themselves seriously, ''Will the data bear the conclusions that I want to push upon them? Am I asking questions so subtle that the statistical methods will give answers which depend on the trivial characteristics of the data?'' They don't ask, ''Is the period of time from which I have taken the data really homogeneous? Might the relationship I am estimating have changed its form somewhere during this period?'' They don't ask whether the assumption that this function is linear so I may do standard statistical estimation on it is a reasonable estimate. They don't ask themselves – and I think this is the worst sin of them all – whether there doesn't exist a different model that would fit the data equally well, and what does that tell me? So I think that the problem with economists is that they do too much uncritical empirical work, and that they deceive themselves with the refinements of their methods [Swedberg, 1990, p. 273].

Those who explicitly revolt against orthodoxy are often infected by the same disease. So-called Cambridge controversies in the theory of capital, which would be better described as controversies in the theory of functional income distribution, have raged on for twenty years without so much as a reference to anything but ''stylized facts,'' such as the constancy of the capital–output ratio and the constancy of labor's relative share, which turn out on closer examination not to be facts at all (see Blaug, 1990, pp. 194–6). The fundamental issue at stake between Cambridge, United Kingdom, and Cambridge, United States, we are told by no less an authority on the debate than Joan Robinson (1973, p. xii), is not so much the famous problem of measuring capital as the question of whether it is saving that determines investment by means of variations in prices or investment that determines saving via changes in the wage–profit ratio. It is clear that a Keynesian-type growth model, assigning a key role to autonomous investment, makes perfectly good sense when there is a situation of less than full employment. On the other hand, if fiscal and monetary policies succeed in maintaining full employment, it would appear that growth depends critically on saving rather than investment, in which case anti-Keynesian, neoclassical growth models appear to be appropriate. The issue of the respective primacy of investment and saving is, therefore, a matter of deciding whether the world is better described by full-employment or by underemployment equilibrium.

However, inasmuch as the entire debate is carried out in the context of steady-state growth theory, and as both sides agree that steady-state growth is never even approximated in the real world, Cambridge controversies as they are currently formulated are incapable of being resolved by empirical research. But this has not prevented either side from battling over the issues with redoubled fury. Protagonists in both camps have described the controversy as a war of ''paradigms'' but in fact the two paradigms intersect and indeed overlap entirely. Rhetoric apart, there is nothing to choose between the styles of theorizing of the two Cambridges.[4] (See Chapter 10 above).

---

[4] For sympathetic surveys of Cambridge, United Kingdom, theories, sometimes labeled ''post-Keynesian economics,'' see Asimakopulos (1977) and Kregel (1977). For an unsympathetic survey, see Blaug (1975, chap. 6; 1990, chap. 9).

Even radical political economists, a growing breed in the United States, have devoted most of their efforts to "telling a new story": the same old facts are given a different interpretation in terms of the paradigm of power conflict rather than the paradigm of utility maximization, as if social science were reducible to "hard cores" selected according to taste (see Worland, 1972; Applebaum, 1977). What little empirical work has appeared in the *Review of Radical Political Economics* on economic imperialism, race and sex discrimination, the financial returns to education and the patterns of social mobility has lacked discriminating, well-articulated hypotheses that could distinguish between mainstream and radical predictions (Bronfenbrenner, 1970; Lindbeck, 1971). But radical economists do at least have the excuse of explicitly announcing their preference on methodological grounds for social and political relevance over empirical reliability as the acid test of "good" theory.[5] Indeed, if radical economists can be said to share a common methodology, it seems to be that of voluntarism or "thinking makes it so" (see Blaug, 1990, chap. 3, especially pp. 60–3).

Similarly, latter-day Austrians claim to derive their economic insights from a priori reasoning unaided by experience and hence repudiate empirical testing as a method for establishing the validity of their conclusions. Likewise, institutionalists purport to model economic behavior in terms of definite patterns and are satisfied to "understand" the workings of an economy even if this implies little power to predict the actual course of economic events. Lastly, Marxists are too deeply committed to the philosophy of essentialism to be willing to run the gauntlet of empirical testing: they hope of course to prophesy correctly, but they have developed an ample store of immunizing stratagems to protect Marxism against any prophecies that have failed to materialize (see Blaug, 1990, chap. 2). In short, radicals, modern Austrians, institutionalists, and Marxists all have very good excuses for not paying much heed to the methodological imperatives of falsificationism.

Falsificationism once again

Mainstream neoclassical economists do not have the same excuse. They preach the importance of submitting theories to empirical tests but they rarely live up to their declared methodological canons. Analytical elegance, economy of theoretical means, and the widest possible scope obtained by ever more heroic simplification have been too often prized above predictability and

---

[5] Franklin and Resnik (1973, pp. 73–4) provide a typical radical methodological pronouncement: "From a radical perspective, in which analysis is closely linked to advocacy of fundamental changes in the social order, an abstract model or category is not simply an aesthetic device [sic]. It is purposely designed to assist in the changes advocated, or in describing the nature of the barriers that must be broken down if the advocated changes are to occur."

significance for policy questions. The working philosophy of science of modern economics may indeed be characterized as "innocuous falsificationism."

To be sure, there are still some, like Shackle or the modern Austrians, who will argue that prediction is absolutely impossible in a subject like economics because economic behavior, being forward-looking, is inherently unpredictable. But these economists are in a minority. For the most part, the battle for falsificationism has been won in modern economics (would that we could say as much about some of the other social sciences). The problem now is to persuade economists to take falsificationism seriously.

Applied econometrics

It is not difficult to think of many good reasons why economists fail to practice the methodology that they preach: all scientists sometimes cling tenaciously to "degenerating" research programs in the presence of "progressive" rivals but economists are particularly prone to this tendency if only because an economic system, unlike the state of nature, cries out to be evaluated and not just to be studied with Olympian detachment. Furthermore, economics continually touches on questions that are subject to government policy, so that major economic doctrines are not only scientific research programs (SRP) in the sense of Lakatos but also political action programs (PAP). This dual function of economic theories allows for situations in which a particular theory is simultaneously a "degenerating" SRP and a "progressive" PAP, that is, one that offers governments an expanding agenda of policy measures. (Marxian economics may be a case in point and monetarism in its latest phase is perhaps an example of exactly the opposite conjunction.) It is only when a theory defines both a "progressive" SRP and a "progressive" PAP that we talk of a "revolution" in economic thought (the obvious example is Keynesian economics in the 1930s).[6]

Be that as it may, the fact that economics is, among other things, a policy science is at least one major reason why Lakatos's methodology of SRP does not fit the history of economics perfectly, or at any rate fits it much less perfectly than it does the history of physics. It is precisely for that reason that the attempt to separate positive from normative propositions in economics, and clearly to specify the conditions for submitting positive propositions to the text of experience, remains a task which is as important to the progress of economics today as it ever was.

Unfortunately, we lack both reliable data and powerful techniques for distinguishing sharply between valid and invalid propositions in positive economics and professional pressures to "publish or perish" continually encourage a "game playing" approach to econometric work that does nothing to improve the data base or the standard techniques that are regularly employed

---

[6] I owe this point to R. G. Lipsey.

for testing economic hypotheses. These weaknesses, not so much of theoretical econometrics as of the actual procedures followed by applied econometricians, go a long way toward explaining why economists are frequently reluctant to follow their avowed falsificationist precepts. In many areas of economics, different econometric studies reach conflicting conclusions and, given the available data, there are frequently no effective methods for deciding which conclusion is correct. In consequence, contradictory hypotheses continue to coexist sometimes for decades or more. To add to the confusion, there is even disarray on pure econometric theory, the ''Bayesians'' such as Leamer and the atheoretical agnostics such as Sims being pitted against the ''classicals'' such as Hendry and Mizon – labels which I borrow from Johnston (1991) if only to save time.[7] For some, this is a good reason for abandoning econometrics altogether.

But that is not an attractive alternative because it would leave economics with almost no way of selecting from among a plethora of possible explanations the one that best explains economic events. Even if we argue that there are other methods for testing economic hypotheses, such as the looser methods of ''colligation'' practiced by economic historians, or the ethnographic methods favored by some institutionalists, the demands of economic policy makers will nevertheless drive us back to the use of econometrics, which alone can provide a quantitative as well as a qualitative calculus. Our only hope, therefore, is to improve both theoretical and applied econometrics, and indeed it is the latter where improvements could come fairly rapidly if only better workaday practices were adopted.

Thomas Mayer (1980) has a number of concrete suggestions to make that would do much to strengthen the claim of economics as a ''hard science.'' First, he echoes Leontief in urging us to place far more emphasis on the problem of data collection. Second, he deplores the tendency to treat econometric results as evidence from a ''crucial experiment,'' which is never to be repeated; on the contrary, most applied econometrics should seek to replicate previous results using a different data set; as we come to rely increasingly on the weight of many pieces of evidence, rather than a single crucial experiment, periodic surveys should pull the evidence together with a view to resolving contradictions between them. Third, he argues that it would help to raise the standards for assessing econometric work if the journals could encourage work on the basis of the likely validity of the results reported and not on the basis of the technical sophistication of the techniques employed. Fourth, he recommends that we guard against data mining by requiring authors to present all the regressions they ran and not just the particular regression that happened to support their hypothesis. Fifth, he proposes that authors should

[7] For another characterization of the disarray, and an illuminating attempt to restate traditional econometric modeling within a falsificationist methodology, see Darnell and Evans (1990).

not use up all their data in fitting their regressions, but leave some as a reserve sample against which to test the regressions; this harks back to the early distinction we drew between estimating a structural relationship and testing an economic hypothesis. Sixth, he urges journals to publish papers that report insignificant results and to require authors to submit their unpublished data so that their work can be easily verified by others. Finally, he adds that "given all the weaknesses of econometric techniques, we should be open minded enough to accept that truth does not always wear the garb of equations, and is not always born inside a computer. Other ways of testing, such as appeals to economic history, should not be treated as archaic" (Mayer, 1980, p. 18).[8] These recommendations are as cogent today as they were in 1980. The only cure for the shortcomings of econometrics, as Pesaran (1987) puts it, is more and better econometrics.

The best way forward

I have argued throughout this book that the central aim of economics is to predict and not merely to understand and I have implied that of all the contending economic doctrines of the past, it is only orthodox, timeless equilibrium theory – in short, the neoclassical SRP – that has shown itself to be willing to be judged in terms of its predictions. Orthodox economics can indeed boast that it has increased the economist's capacity for making predictions. At the same time, it must be emphasized how limited this capacity is even now. We cannot accurately predict the growth of GNP in an economy more than a year ahead and we cannot even predict the growth of NNP in individual sectors of the economy beyond two or three years.[9] This is an

---

[8] On the woeful neglect of economic history as a testing ground for theory (and in the teaching of economics), see Parker (1986).

[9] Thus, Victor Zarnowitz (1968, pp. 435–6) sums up present-day achievements in GNP forecasting in the United States in these words: "The record of economic forecasters in general leaves a great deal to be desired, although it also includes some significant achievements and may be capable of further improvements. According to the current NBER study, the annual GNP predictions for 1953–63 made by some three hundred to four hundred forecasters (company staffs and groups of economists from various industries, government, and academic institutions) had errors averaging $10 billion. Although this amounts to about 2 per cent of the average level of GNP, the errors were big enough to make the difference between a good and bad business year. . . . Had the forecasters assumed that GNP would advance next year by the average amount it had advanced in the preceding postwar years, the resulting average error would not have been greater than $12 billion." Similarly, Hans Theil (1966, chaps. 6, 7) has shown that the use of an input-output model to forecast value added in twenty-seven sectors of the Dutch economy over a ten-year period, given observed final demand in the economy as a whole, predicted better than a simple extrapolation of past trends for periods up to two or three years but predicted much worse for periods longer than three years.

improvement over what can be obtained by mere mechanical extrapolation of past trends (Bodkin, Klein, and Marwah, 1991, pp. 528–9) but nevertheless it is insufficient to support complacency about the state of modern, orthodox economics. Similarly, for a wide variety of problems – demand functions for consumer goods, investment functions, money demand and supply functions, and large-scale econometric models of the entire economy – it turns out that goodness of fit of a regression equation during the sample period invariably proves to be an unreliable guide to what happens subsequently in the post-sample period (Shupak, 1962; Streissler, 1970; Mayer, 1975, 1980; Armstrong, 1978, chap. 13). Clearly, there are still serious limitations in the capacity of economists to predict the actual course of economic events and hence ample room for skepticism about mainstream economics.

There are now a number of alternative research programs in economics that express this sense of disillusionment with the past accomplishments of received economic doctrines. The radical economists have their own house organ, *The Review of Radical Political Economics,* and so do the institutionalists (*The Journal of Economic Issues,* published by the Association of Evolutionary Economics). *Journal of Post-Keynesian Economics* seeks to unite those who hope to develop Keynesian economics in new directions to attack the problems of inflation and income distribution. Likewise, another group of economists are determined to focus their research program on Herbert Simon's concept of "bounded rationality," denoting a central concern with the underlying motivational assumptions of economic theory, and their *Journal of Economic Behavior and Organization* to give expression to their sense of dissatisfaction with contemporary economic theory. In other words, we have entered an era in which there will be too many, rather than too few, competing economic research programs.

It would be very convenient if all of these alternative research programs were addressed to the same set of questions that preoccupy the neoclassical SRP, because then we could choose among them solely, or at any rate largely, on the basis of the empirical evidence. Alas, it is a characteristic feature of many of the rival SRPs that they ask different questions about the real world from those posed by the neoclassical SRP, so that choice among them involves difficult judgments of fruitfulness, that is, promises of empirical evidence to be delivered in the future. Economic methodology, therefore, is unlikely to tell us which of these competing programs is likely most to contribute in the years ahead to substantive knowledge of the workings of economic systems.

What methodology can do is to provide criteria for the acceptance and rejections of research programs, setting standards that will help us to discriminate between wheat and chaff. These standards, we have seen, are hierarchical, relative, dynamic, and by no means unambiguous in terms of the practical advice they offer to working economists. Nevertheless, the ultimate question we can and indeed must pose about any research program is the one made familiar by Popper: what events, if they materialized, would lead us to reject that program? A program that cannot meet that question has fallen short of the highest standards that scientific knowledge can attain.

GLOSSARY

Adduction Black's term for nondemonstrative inferences, or what in common parlance is called induction.

Aggressive methodology Any methodological standpoint that amounts to rejecting some current or past scientific practices as "bad" science, as opposed to "defensive methodology," which seeks to justify whatever scientific activity has gone before.

Alchian thesis The view that competition represents a Darwinian selection mechanism that produces exactly the same outcome that would ensue from a world in which consumers maximized utility and businessmen maximized profits.

Analytic propositions Statements or propositions that are true by the definition of their own terms.

Apriorism A methodological standpoint that regards economic theories as being grounded in a few intuitively obvious axioms or principles that do not need to be independently established.

Characterizing value judgments Judgments about the choice of subject matter to be investigated, the mode of investigation to be followed, the standards of reliability of the data to be selected, and the criteria adopted for judging the validity of the findings, as opposed to "appraising value judgments" that evaluate states of the world.

Conventionalism A methodological standpoint that regards all scientific theories and hypotheses as merely condensed descriptions of events, neither true nor false in themselves but simply conventions for storing empirical information.

Covering-law model of explanation See *Hypothetico-deductive model*.

Demarcation criterion Any principle that separates intellectual activity into two mutually exclusive classes of science and nonscience.

Demonstrative inference A method of making inferences that relies exclusively on deductive logic in which true premises always entail true conclusions.

Descriptivism A degenerate form of conventionalism and instrumentalism, which regards scientific explanations as merely condensed descriptions contributing to accurate predictions.

Duhem–Quine thesis The argument that no individual scientific hypothesis can ever be conclusively falsified, because we necessarily test the hypothesis in conjunction with auxiliary conditions and, hence, can never locate the source of a refutation.

Essentialism A methodological standpoint that regards the discovery of the essence of things as the central task of science and defines the essence of a thing as that element or set of elements without which the thing would cease to exist.

Falsificationism A methodological standpoint that regards theories and hypotheses as scientific if

249

and only if their predictions are, at least in principle, empirically falsifiable; "naive falsificationism" holds that theories can be refuted by a single test, whereas "sophisticated falsificationism" holds that it requires a large number of tests to refute a theory.

Hard core A technical term in the methodology of Lakatos, denoting the purely metaphysical beliefs that unite the protagonists of a SRP; the hard core is surrounded by the "protective belt" of testable theories.

Hypothetico-deductive model The view that all scientific explanations take the form of deducing a statement about an event from at least one universal law combined with a set of initial or boundary conditions (also known as the covering-law model of explanation).

Immunizing stratagems Certain types of stratagems adopted by scientists to protect their theories against refutation, which are severely condemned in Popper's methodology of falsificationism.

Induction The process of inferring general laws from particular events or individual observations, frequently confused with "adduction"; the "problem of induction" is to justify this process of inference on purely logical grounds.

Instrumentalism A methodological standpoint that regards all scientific theories and hypotheses as being nothing more than instruments for making predictions.

Invisible hand theorem The proposition that every perfectly competitive equilibrium is Pareto-optimal and, conversely, that a Pareto-optimal equilibrium is characterized by a perfectly competitive market structure.

Irrelevance-of-assumptions thesis The view espoused by Friedman that the degree of realism of the assumptions of a theory is irrelevant to its validity.

Methodological individualism The view that social theories must be grounded in the attitudes and behavior of individuals, as opposed to "methodological holism," which asserts that social theories must be grounded in the behavior of irreducible groups of individuals.

Methodological monism The view that there is only one common methodology to both the natural and the social sciences, as opposed to "methodological dualism," which argues that the social sciences cannot employ the methodology of the natural sciences.

MSRP The methodology of scientific research programs in the sense of Lakatos.

Neyman–Pearson theory of statistics A method of statistical inference that instructs us to set the chance of Type I error (the mistaken decision to reject a true hypothesis) at some arbitrary small figure and then to minimize the chance of Type II error (the mistaken decision to accept a false hypothesis) for the given Type I error.

Nondemonstrative inference A method of making inferences that does not rely exclusively on deductive logic, so that true premises do not necessarily entail true conclusions.

Operationalism A methodological standpoint that regards theories and hypotheses as scientific if and only if it is possible to specify a physical operation that assigns quantitative values to their basic terms.

Pattern modeling A methodological standpoint that seeks to "understand' ' events or actions by identifying their place in a pattern of relationships that is supposed to characterize a particular economic system.

PPI Potential-Pareto-improvement, meaning any economic change that is capable of making at least one economic agent better off in his own terms without making anyone else worse off, whether or not the former agent compensates the latter to approve the economic change.

Qualitative calculus A technical term we owe to Samuelson that denotes the use of comparative static reasoning to predict the sign rather than the magnitude of a given economic change.

Progressive SRP A technical term in the methodology of Lakatos for a SRP whose successive formulations account for all the facts predicted by a rival SRP and, in addition, predict extra, novel facts; a "degenerating" SRP fails to meet this criterion.

Received view on theories The dominant pattern of thinking in the philosophy of science between the two world wars that emphasized the formal structure of scientific theories and regarded classical physics as the prototype of all science.

SRP Scientific research programs in the sense of Lakatos, that is, clusters of interconnected theories deriving from a common "hard core."

Storytelling A term we owe to Ward that describes a method of theorizing that binds together facts, low-level generalizations, high-level theories, and value judgments in a coherent narrative.

Symmetry thesis The notion that there is a perfect, logical symmetry between the nature of explanation and the nature of prediction, so that explanation is simply prediction-in-reverse; an essential part of the hypothetico-deductive model of scientific explanation.

Synthetic propositions Definite statements or propositions about the real world that are either true or false.

Tendency laws Generalizations that state the effect of a variation in one or more variables subject to a set of other disturbing variables that are assumed to be held constant.

Ultraempiricism A term of abuse to describe methodologists who believe that the assumptions of theories must be tested against the facts as much as the predictions of theories.

Verifiability A methodological standpoint that regards theories and hypotheses as scientific if and only if their predictions are, at least in principle, empirically verifiable.

Verstehen doctrine The view that social science must be grounded in first-person knowledge that is intelligible to us as fellow human beings, and not third-person knowledge corresponding to the measured outcomes of a laboratory experiment.

SUGGESTIONS FOR FURTHER READING

Part I was designed as a child's guide to recent developments in the philosophy of science. Some readers may question my knowledge of what children are able to absorb and they would undoubtedly benefit from a prior reading of Stewart (1979). The first six chapters of Stewart are hard to beat as a systematic introductory account of the philosophy of economic science, and even I cannot claim to have improved on his presentation. He offers a balanced view of the debates in economic methodology, while taking a "softer" view of what is right and wrong with modern economics than I do. Chalmers (1976) too covers almost the same ground as my first two chapters, arriving however at very different conclusions. Losee (1972) is a most useful historical introduction to the philosophy of science from Aristotle up to and including Popper. Nagel (1961) is a block-buster of a book that perfectly reflects the orthodox, interwar view of the philosophy of science but includes an unusual, fresh extension into the philosophy of the social sciences. A much shorter book with a similar viewpoint is Hempel (1966).

All of Popper's books are eminently readable and profoundly instructive, starting with his intellectual biography (1976) and then more or less in the order in which they were written: (1965), (1962), (1972a), (1972b), and (1983): I leave aside (1957), which Popper himself described as "one of my stodgiest pieces of writing" and which, despite its fame, suffers from a tendency to overkill. Magee (1973) is an excellent if hagiographic introduction to the whole of Popper. A more sophisticated, critical treatment, which shows keen awareness of the subtle evolution of Popper's views over the years, is found in Ackermann (1976).

Kuhn (1970) is also very readable and, in any case, must be read if one is to hold up one's head in intellectual circles. A reading of Kuhn should lead straightaway to a short course in the history of science, where Toulmin and Goodfield (1963, 1965, 1967) can be recommended as a perfect starting-point – but only a starting point. Lakatos and Musgrave (1970) will introduce the reader to the great debate on paradigms, while including some Lakatos at his best. Feyerabend (1975) may perhaps sow confusion but at least he forces the reader to take a stand for or against methodology and even for and against science itself.

Kaplan (1964) is perhaps the best book with which to start a course of reading in the philosophy of *social* science, being a sensible account that steers a middle course between a book on methods and a book on methodology proper. Lesnoff (1974) is a shorter, more or less positivist account which must, however, tie for second place with Ryan (1970), another excellent introduction to the methodological problems of the social sciences. A more sociologically inspired book that can be heartily recommended at a later stage in the reading program is Barnes (1974).

Original sources on the economic methodology of yesterday, such as Neville Keynes (1955)

253

and Robbins (1935), will convey the flavor of verificationism as no commentary ever can; besides, both write superbly and are a pleasure to read almost regardless of what they are saying. Literacy in modern economic methodology begins with the essay by Friedman (1953). Among the numerous comments that Friedman's essay has received, McClelland (1975, chap. 3) may be recommended without qualification. Klappholz and Agassi (1967) cover a canvass almost as extensive as our third chapter from a more or less similar standpoint.

Another substitute for my Chapters 1–4 is Caldwell (1982), a good introduction to economic methodology, which plumps for "methodological pluralism" or sitting on the fence; this stance may make for good reading by some. Pheby (1988) is yet another introduction, shorter than most but otherwise undistinguished.

Hutchison (1964) is indispensable and authoritative on the distinction between positive and normative economics. Latsis (1976) and de Marchi and Blaug (1991) contain applications of Lakatos's methodology to various economic controversies as well as some expressions of doubt of its applicability to a subject like economics. Glass and Johnson (1989) provide their own guide to Lakatos and the implications of adopting MSRP in economics. For a useful annotated bibliography on economic methodology, see Redman (1989). Caldwell (1984) and Hausman (1984) are excellent books of readings on the methodology of economics.

Having come this far, the reader can use my references in the text to guide the pursuit of topics that are of special interest to him or her: one of my motives for peppering the text with citations of secondary sources, apart from that of covering my nakedness with the garment of scholarly acknowledgments, was precisely to facilitate further reading of this kind.

BIBLIOGRAPHY

Achinstein, P. 1968. *Concepts of Science*. Baltimore: Johns Hopkins Press.

   1974. History and philosophy of science: a reply to Cohen. In Suppe, 1974, 350–60.

Ackermann, R. J. 1976. *The Philosophy of Karl Popper*. Amherst: University of Massachusetts Press.

Alchian, A. A., and W. R. Allen, 1964. *University Economics*. Belmont: Wadsworth Publishing Company.

Alexander, P. 1964. The philosophy of science 1850–1910. In *A Critical History of Western Philosophy*. D. J. O'Connor (ed.). London: Collier-Macmillan, 402–25.

Anschutz, R. P. 1953. *The Philosophy of J. S. Mill*. Oxford: Clarendon Press.

Applebaum, E. 1977. Radical economics. In Weintraub 1977, 559–74.

Archibald, G. C. 1959a. The state of economic science. *British Journal for the Philosophy of Science*, 10, reprinted in Marr and Ray, 1983, 185–98.

   1959b. Welfare economics, ethics, and essentialism. *Economica*, 26, 316–27.

   1961. Chamberlin *versus* Chicago, *Review of Economic Studies*, 29, 1–28.

   1963. Reply to Chicago. *Review of Economic Studies*, 30, 68–71.

   1965. The qualitative content of maximizing models. *Journal of Political Economy*, 73, 27–36.

   1967. Refutation or comparison? *British Journal for the Philosophy of Science*, 17, 279–96.

Armstrong, J. S. 1978. *Long Range Economic Forecasting*. New York: John Wiley & Sons.

Arrow, K. J. 1987. Economic theory and the hypothesis of rationality. In Eatwell et al., 2, 69–74.

Arrow, K. J., and F. H. Hahn, 1971. *General Competitive Analysis*. San Francisco: Holden-Day.

Asimakopulos, A. 1977. Post-Keynesian growth theory. In Weintraub, 1977, 369–88.

Ayer, A. J. 1970. Has Harrod answered Hume? In *Induction, Growth and Trade: Essays in Honour of Sir Roy Harrod*. W. A. Eltis, M. F. G. Scott, and J. N. Wolfe (eds.). Oxford: Clarendon Press, 20–37.

   1976. *The Central Questions of Philosophy*, London: Penguin Books.

Backhouse, R. E. 1990. Competition. In *Foundations of Economic Thought*, J. Creedy (ed.). Oxford: Basil Blackwell, 58–86.

   1991. The neo-Walrasian research programme in macroeconomics. In de Marchi and Blaug, 1991, 406–29.

   Forthcoming. The constructivist critique of economic methodology.

Barker, S. F. 1957. *Induction and Hypothesis. A Study of the Logic of Confirmation.* Ithaca: Cornell University Press.

Barnes, B. 1974. *Scientific Knowledge and Sociological Theory.* London: Routledge & Kegan Paul.

Barrett, M., and D. Hausman. 1991. Making interpersonal comparisons coherently. *Economics and Philosophy,* 6(2), 293–300.

Barry, N. P. 1979. *Hayek's Social and Economic Philosophy.* London: Macmillan.

Bartlett, M. S. 1968. Fisher, R. A. In Sills, 1968, vol. 5, 485–91.

Baumol, W. J. 1965. *Economic Theory and Operations Analysis.* Englewood Cliffs: Prentice-Hall, 2d ed.

Baumol, W. J., J. Panzar, and R. Willig. 1986. On the theory of perfectly contestable markets. *In New Developments in the Analysis of Market Structure,* J. Stiglitz and F. Mathewson (eds.). Cambridge, MA: Macmillan, 339–65.

Bear, D. V. T., and D. Orr. 1967. Logic and expediency in economic theorizing. *Journal of Political Economy,* 75, 188–96.

Becker, G. S. 1976. *The Economic Approach to Human Behavior.* Chicago: University of Chicago Press.

Becker, G. S., E. M. Landes, and R. T. Michael. 1977. An economic analysis of marital instability. *Journal of Political Economy,* 85, 1141–88.

Bergmann, G. 1951. Ideology. *Ethics,* April, reprinted in *Readings in the Philosophy of the Social Sciences,* 1968. M. Brodbeck (ed.). New York: Macmillan, 1968, 123–38.

Bergstrom, T. C. 1976. Towards a deeper economics of sleeping. *Journal of Political Economy,* 84, 411–12.

Berkson, W. 1976. Lakatos one and Lakatos two: an appreciation. In *Essays in Memory of Imre Lakatos.* R. S. Cohen, P. K. Feyerabend, and M. W. Wartofsky (eds.). Dordrecht: D. Reidel, 39–54.

Bhagwati, J. 1965. The pure theory of international trade: a survey. In *Surveys of Economic Theory Growth and Development.* London: Macmillan, vol. 2, 156–239.

  1969. *International Trade Theory. Selected Readings.* London: Penguin Books.

Bhaskar, R. 1975. Feyerabend and Bachelard: two philosophies of science. *New Left Review,* 94, 31–55.

Bianchi, M., and H. Moulin. 1991. Strategic interactions in economics: the game theoretic alternative. In de Marchi and Blaug, 1991, 181–98.

Black, M. 1970. *Margins of Precision. Essays in Logic and Language.* Ithaca: Cornell University Press.

Blaug, M. 1972. *An Introduction to the Economics of Education.* London: Penguin Books.

  1973. *Ricardian Economics. A Historical Study.* Westport, CT: Greenwood Press.

  1975. *The Cambridge Revolution. Success or Failure?* London: Institute of Economic Affairs.

  1985a. *Economic Theory in Retrospect.* Cambridge: Cambridge University Press, 4th ed.

  1985b. Comment on D. Wade Hands's "Karl Popper and economic methodology: A new look." *Economics and Philosophy,* 1(2), 286–8.

  1986. *Economic History and the History of Economics.* Aldershot, Hants: Edward Elgar.

  1988. *The Economics of Education and the Education of an Economist.* Aldershot, Hants: Edward Elgar.

  1990. *Economic Theories, True or False?* Aldershot, Hants: Edward Elgar.

Blinder, A. S. 1974. The economics of brushing teeth. *Journal of Political Economy,* 82, 887–91.

Bloor, D. 1971. Two paradigms for scientific knowledge. *Science Studies,* 1, 101–15.

Bodkin, R. G., L. R. Klein, and K. Marwah. 1991. *A History of Macroeconometric Model-Building*. Aldershot, Hants: Edward Elgar.

Boland, L. A. 1970. Conventionalism and economic theory. *Philosophy of Science*, 37, 239–48.

1979. A critique of Friedman's critics. *Journal of Economic Literature*, 17, reprinted in Caldwell, 1984, 205–24.

1981. On the futility of criticizing the neoclassical maximization hypothesis. *American Economic Review*, 71, reprinted in Caldwell, 1984, 246–51.

1982. *The Foundations of Economic Method*. London: Allen & Unwin.

1989. *The Methodology of Model-Building After Samuelson*. London: Routledge.

Bordo, M. D. 1975. John E. Cairnes on the effects of the Australian gold discoveries 1851–73: an early application of the methodology of positive economics. *History of Political Economy*, 7, 337–59.

1978. Reply. *History of Political Economy*, 10, 328–31.

Bowley, M. 1949. *Nassau Senior and Classical Economics*. New York: Augustus M. Kelley.

Brainard, W. C., and R. N. Cooper. 1975. Empirical monetary macroeconomics: what have we learned in the last 25 years? *American Economic Review*, 65, 167–75.

Braithwaite, R. B. 1960. *Scientific Explanation*. New York: Harper Torchbooks.

Braybrooke, D., and C. E. Lindblom. 1963. *A Strategy of Decision*. New York: The Free Press.

Brittan, S. 1973. *Is There an Economic Consensus? An Attitude Survey*. London: Macmillan.

Brodbeck, M. 1958. Methodological individualism: definition and reduction. *Philosophy of Science*, 1973, reprinted in O'Neill, 1973, 287–311.

Bronfenbrenner, M. 1970. Radical economics in America: a 1970 survey. *Journal of Economic Literature*, 8, 747–66.

1971. *Income Distribution Theory*. London: Macmillan.

Broome, J. 1991. Utility. *Economics & Philosophy*, 7(1), 1–12.

Brown, A., and A. Deaton. 1972. Models of consumer behaviour: a survey. *Economic Journal*, 82, 1145–1236.

Brunner, K., and A. H. Meltzer. 1972. Friedman's monetary theory. *Journal of Political Economy*, 80, 837–51.

Burger, T. 1976. *Max Weber's Theory of Concept Formation. History, Laws and Ideal Types*. Durham: Duke University Press.

Burmeister, E. 1991. Comment on Steedman. In de Marchi and Blaug, 1991, 460–73.

Burton, J. F., Jr., L. K. Benham, W. M. Vaughan, III, and R. J. Flanagan. 1971. *Readings in Labor Market Analysis*. New York: Holt, Rinehart & Winston.

Bynum, W. F., E. J. Browne, and R. Porter. 1981. *Macmillan Dictionary of the History of Science*. London: Macmillan.

Cahnman, W. J. 1964. Max Weber and the methodological controversy in the social sciences. In *Sociology and History*. W. J. Cahnman and A. Boskoff (eds.). New York: The Free Press, 103–27.

Cairnes, J. E. 1988, *The Character and Logical Method of Political Economy*. London: Frank Cass, 1965.

Caldwell, B. 1980. A critique of Friedman's methodological instrumentalism. *Southern Economic Journal*, 366–74, reprinted in Caldwell, 1983, 225–33.

1982. *Beyond Positivism: Economic Methodology in the Twentieth Century*. London: Allen and Unwin.

1983. The neoclassical maximization hypothesis: comment. *American Economic Review*, 73, reprinted in Caldwell, 1984, 252–5.

1984. *Appraisal and Criticism in Economics. A Book of Readings*. Boston: Allen and Unwin.

1991. Clarifying Popper. *Journal of Economic Literature,* 29 (1), 1–33.

Forthcoming. Hayek the Falsificationist? A Refutation. In *Research in the History of Economic Thought and Methodology,* 10, W. J. Samuels (ed.). Greenwich, CN: JAI Press.

Caldwell, B. J., and A. W. Coats, 1984. The rhetoric of economics: a comment on McCloskey. *Journal of Economic Literature,* 22(2), 575–8.

Canterberry, E. R., and R. J. Burkhardt. 1983. What do we mean by asking whether economics is a science? In Eichner, 1983, 15–40.

Caplan, A. L. 1985. The nature of Darwinian explanation: is Darwinian evolutionary theory scientific? In *What Darwin Began,* L. K. Godfrey. Boston: Allyn and Bacon, 24–39.

Caves, R. E. 1960. *Trade and Economic Structures. Models and Methods.* Cambridge: Harvard University Press.

Caves, R. E., and H. G. Johnson. 1968. *Readings in International Economics.* London: Allen & Unwin.

Chalmers, A. F. 1976. *What Is This Thing Called Science?* Milton Keynes: The Open University Press.

Chick, V. 1973. *The Theory of Monetary Policy.* Oxford: Basil Blackwell, 2nd ed.

Churchman, C. W. 1968. *A Challenge to Reason.* New York: McGraw-Hill.

Clarkson, G. P. E. 1963. *The Theory of Consumer Demand: A Critical Appraisal.* Englewood Cliffs: Prentice-Hall.

Coase, R. H. 1975. Marshall on method. *Journal of Law and Economics,* 18, April, 25–31.

Coats, A. W. 1954. The historist reaction in English political economy, 1870–90. *Economica,* 21, 143–53.

1976. Economics and psychology: the death and resurrection of a research programme. In Latsis, 1976, 43–64.

1977. The current "crisis" in economics in historical perspective. *Nebraska Journal of Economics and Business,* 16 (3), 3–16.

1983. Half a century of methodological controversy in economics: as reflected in the writings of T. W. Hutchison. In *Methodological Controversy in Economics: Historical Essays in Honor of T. W. Hutchison,* A. W. Coats, (ed.). Greenwich, CN: JAI Press.

Coddington, A. 1972. Positive economics. *Canadian Journal of Economics,* 5, reprinted in Marr and Raj, 1983, 69–88.

1975. The rationale of general equilibrium theory. *Economic Inquiry,* 13, 539–58.

1976a. *The Adequacy and Applicability of Economic Theories: A Perspective on the Methodological Views of Robbins and Friedman.* London: Queen Mary College, University of London Occasional Papers, No. 26.

1983. *Keynesian Economics: The Search for First Principles.* London: Allen and Unwin.

Cohen, I. B. 1980. *The Newtonian Revolution.* Cambridge: Cambridge University Press.

(1985). *Revolution in Science.* Cambridge, MA: Harvard University Press.

Cohen, M. R. 1931. *Reason and Nature: An Essay on the Meaning of Scientific Method.* New York: Harcourt, Brace.

Cohen, M. R., and E. Nagel. 1934. *An Introduction to Logic and Scientific Method.* New York: Harcourt, Brace.

Cohn, E., and T. G. Geske. 1990. *The Economics of Education.* Oxford: Pergamon Press, 3d ed.

Colander, D., and A. Klamer. 1987. The making of an economist. *Journal of Economic Perspectives,* 1(2), 95–111.

Collins, H. M. 1985. *Changing Order. Replication and Induction in Scientific Practice.* London: Sage Publications.

Corden, W. M. 1965. *Recent Developments in the Theory of International Trade.* Princeton: Princeton University, International Finance Section.

Cross, R. 1982. The Duhem–Quine thesis, Lakatos and the appraisal of theories in macroeconomics. *Economic Journal,* 92, reprinted in Caldwell, 1984, 285–304.

1991. Alternative accounts of equilibrium unemployment. In de Marchi and Blaug, 1991, 296–327.

Culyer, A. J., J. Wiseman, and A. Walker. 1977. *An Annotated Bibliography of Health Economics.* London: Martin Robertson.

Cyert, R. M., and E. Grunberg. 1963. Assumption, prediction and explanation in economics. *A Behavioral Theory of the Firm.* R. M. Cyert and J. G. March (eds.). Englewood Cliffs: Prentice-Hall, 298–311.

Cyert, R. M., and C. L. Hendrick. 1972. The theory of the firm: past, present, and future. *Journal of Economic Literature,* 10, 398–412.

Darnell, A. C., and J. L. Evans. 1990. *The Limits of Econometrics.* Aldershot, Hants: Edward Elgar.

Darwin, C. 1859. *The Origin of Species.* J. W. Burrow (ed.). London: Penguin Books, 1968.

David, P. A. 1985. Clio and the economics of QWERTY. *American Economic Review,* 75(2), 332–7.

De Alessi, L. 1965. Economic theory as a language. *Quarterly Journal of Economics,* 79, 472–7.

1971. Reversals of assumptions and implications. *Journal of Political Economy,* 79, 867–77.

Dean, P. 1983. The scope and method of economic science. *Economic Journal,* 93, 1–12.

de Marchi, N. 1970. The empirical content and longevity of Ricardian economics. *Economica,* 37, 257–76.

1976. Anomaly and the development of economics: the case of the Leontief paradox. In Latsis, 1976, 109–27.

1988. Popper and the LSE economists. In *The Popperian Legacy in Economics,* N. de Marchi (ed.). Cambridge: Cambridge University Press, 139–66.

1991. Introduction: rethinking Lakatos. In de Marchi and Blaug, 1991. 1–30.

de Marchi, N., and M. Blaug (eds.). 1991. *Appraising Economic Theories.* Aldershot, Hants: Edward Elgar.

Denison, E. F. 1974. *Accounting for U.S. Growth, 1929–1969.* Washington: The Brookings Institution.

Desai, M. 1981. *Testing Monetarism.* London: Frances Pinter.

De Vroey, M. 1990. The base camp paradox: a reflection on the place of tâtonnement in general equilibrium theory. *Economics and Philosophy,* 6(2), 235–54.

Diesing, P. 1971. *Patterns of Discoveries in the Social Sciences.* Chicago: Aldine Atherton.

1985. Hypothesis testing and data intepretation. the case of Milton Friedman. In *Research in the History of Economic Thought and Methodology,* 3, W. J. Samuels (ed.). Greenwich, CN: JAI Press.

Dolan, E. G. (ed.). 1976. *The Foundation of Modern Austrian Economics.* Kansas City: Sheed & Ward.

Dray, W. 1957. *Laws and Explanations in History.* London: Oxford University Press.

1966. *Philosophical Analysis and History.* New York: Harper & Row.

Dror, Y. 1968. *Public Policymaking Reexamined.* San Francisco: Chandler.

1971. *Ventures in Policy Science.* New York: American Elsevier.

Eatwell, J., M. Milgate, and P. Newman (eds.). 1987. *The New Palgrave: A Dictionary of Economics.* London: Macmillan, 4 vols.

Eichner, A. S. (ed.). 1983. *Why Economics Is Not yet a Science.* Basingstoke: Macmillan.

Elster, J. 1989. *Nuts and Bolts for the Social Sciences.* New York: Cambridge University Press.

Eltis, W. A. 1973. *Growth and Distribution.* London: Macmillan.

Eysenck, H. J. 1979. Astrology. Science – or superstition? *Encounter*, 53, 85–90.

Fair, R. C. 1978. A theory of extramarital affairs. *Journal of Political Economy*, 86, 45–62.

Fearon, P. 1979. *The Origin and Nature of the Great Slump 1929–1932*. London: Macmillan Education.

Feiwel, G. R. (ed.). 1987. *Arrow and the Ascent of Modern Economic Theory*. London: Macmillan.

Ferber, M. A., and B. G. Birnbaum. 1977. The "new home economics": retrospects and prospects. *Journal of Consumer Research*, 4, 19–28.

Ferguson, C. E. 1969. *The Neo-Classical Theory of Production and Distribution*. Cambridge: Cambridge University Press.

Ferguson, C. E., and R. F. Allen. 1970. Factor prices, commodity prices, and switches of technique. *Western Economic Journal*, 8, 95–109.

Feyerabend, P. K. 1975. *Against Method. Outline of an Anarchistic Theory of Knowledge*. London: NLB.

  1976. On the critique of scientific reason. In *Method and Appraisal in the Physical Sciences*. C. Howson (ed.). Cambridge: Cambridge University Press, 309–39.

  1978. *Science in a Free Society*. London: NLB.

  1988. *Farewell to Reason*. New York: Routledge.

Finger, J. M. 1971. Is equilibrium an operational concept? *Economic Journal*, 81, 609–12.

Fischer, F. M. 1987. Adjustment processes and stability. In Eatwell et al., 1987, I, 26–9.

Fisher, S. 1991. Recent developments in macroeconomics. In Oswald, 1991, vol. 1, 1–47.

Flew, A. 1984. *Darwinian Evolution*. London: Paladin Books.

Franklin, R. J., and S. Resnik. 1973. *The Political Economy of Racism*. New York: Holt, Rinehart & Winston.

Fraser, L. M. 1937. *Economic Thought and Language. A Critique of Some Fundamental Concepts*. London: A. & C. Black.

Frey, B. S., and R. Eichenberger. 1989. Should social scientists care about choice anomalies? *Rationality and Society*, 1(1), 101–22.

Frey, B. S., W. W. Pommerehne, F. Schneider, and G. Gilbert. 1984. Consensus and Dissension Among Economists: An Empirical Enquiry. *American Economic Review*, 7(5), 986–94.

Friedman, D. 1988. *Economics in Theory and Practice*. London: Harvester Wheatsheaf.

Friedman, M. 1953. *Essays in Positive Economics*. Chicago: University of Chicago Press.

  1956. The quantity theory of money: a restatement. In *Studies in the Quantity Theory of Money*. M. Friedman (ed.). Chicago: University of Chicago Press, 3–21.

  1962. *Capitalism and Freedom*. Chicago: University of Chicago Press.

  1968. Money: Quantity Theory. In Sills, 1968, vol. 10, 433–47.

  1970. A theoretical framework for monetary analysis. *Journal of Political Economy*, 78, 193–238.

  1987. The quantity theory of money. In Eatwell et al., 4, 3–20.

Friedman, M., and A. J. Schwartz. 1991. Alternative approaches to analyzing economic data. *American Economic Review*, 81(1), 39–49.

Fulop, M. 1977. A survey of the literature on the economic theory of fertility behavior. *American Economist*, 21, 5–13.

Geanakoplos, J. 1987. Arrow–Debreu model of general equilibrium. In Eatwell et al., 1987, I, 116–24.

George, W. 1982. *Darwin*. Fontana Modern Masters. London: Fontana Paperbacks.

Gerrard, B. 1990. On matters methodological in economics. *Journal of Economic Surveys*, 4(2), 197–223.

Ghiselin, M. T. 1969. *The Triumph of the Darwinian Method.* Berkeley: University of California Press.

Gilbert, C. L. 1991. Do economists test theories? – demand analysis and consumption analysis as tests of theories of economic method. In de Marchi and Blaug, 1991, 143–54.

Glass, J. C., and W. Johnson. 1989. *Economics. Progression, Stagnation or Degeneration?* New York: Harvester Wheatsheaf.

Goldsmith, D. (ed.). 1977. *Scientists Confront Velikovsky.* Ithaca: Cornell University Press.

Gomes, L. 1990. *Neoclassical International Economics.* An Historical Survey. London: Macmillan.

Gonce, R. A. 1972. Frank Knight on social control and the scope and method of economics. *Southern Economic Journal,* 38, 547–58.

Goodhart, C. 1991. The conduct of monetary policy. In Oswald, 1991b, vol. 1, 82–135.

Gordon, D. F. 1955. Operational propositions in economic theory. *Journal of Political Economy,* reprinted in *Readings in Microeconomics,* W. Breit and H. M. Hochman (eds.). New York: Holt, Rinehart & Winston, 1968, 48–59.

Gordon, S. 1977. Social science and value judgements. *Canadian Journal of Economics,* 10, 529–46.

Gordon, R. A. 1976. Rigor and relevance in a changing institutional context. *American Economic Review,* 66(1), 1–14.

Gordon, S. 1991. *The History and Philosophy of Social Science.* London: Routledge.

Gouldner, A. W. 1971. *The Coming Crisis of Western Sociology.* London: Heinemann Educational Books.

Green, F. 1977. *Empiricist Methodology and the Development of Economic Thought.* London: Thames Polytechnic.

Green, H. A. J. 1976. *Consumer Theory.* London: Macmillan, 2nd ed.

Greenwood, M. J. 1975. Research on internal migration in the United States: a survey. *Journal of Economic Literature,* 13, 397–433.

Grünbaum, A. 1976. Is falsifiability the touchstone of scientific rationality? Karl Popper versus inductivism. In *Essays in Memory of Imre Lakatos.* R. S. Cohen, P. K. Feyerabend, and M. W. Wartofsky (eds.). Dordrecht: D. Reidel, 569–629.

Hahn, F. H. 1972. *The Share of Wages in National Income: An Enquiry into the Theory of Distribution.* London: Weidenfeld & Nicolson.

1984. *Equilibrium and Macroeconomics.* Oxford: Basil Blackwell.

1985. *Money, Growth and Stability.* Oxford: Basil Blackwell.

1987. Review of D. McCloskey, *The rhetoric of economics. Journal of Economic Literature,* 25(1), 110–11.

Hammond, J. D. 1990. Realism in Friedman's *Essays in Positive Economics.* In *Perspectives on the History of Economic Thought,* 4, *Keynes, Macroeconomics and Method,* D. E. Moggridge (ed.). Aldershot, Hants: Edward Elgar, 194–208.

1991. Alfred Marshall's methodology. *Methodus,* 3(1), 95–101.

Hands, D. W. 1985. Karl Popper and economic methodology: a new look. *Economics and Philosophy,* 1(1), 83–99.

1988. Ad hocness in economics and the Popperian tradition. In de Marchi, 1988, 121–38.

1991. The Problem of Excess Content: Economics, Novelty and a Long Popperian Tale. In de Marchi and Blaug, 1991, 58–75.

Hanson, N. R. 1965. *Patterns of Discovery.* Cambridge: Cambridge University Press.

Harcourt, G. C. 1972. *Some Cambridge Controversies in the Theory of Capital.* Cambridge: Cambridge University Press.

1982. *The Social Science Imperialists.* London: Routledge and Kegan Paul.

Harding, S. G. 1976. *Can Theories Be Refuted? Essays on the Duhem-Quine Thesis.* Dordrecht: D. Reidel.

Hargreaves-Heap, S. 1989. *Rationality in Economics.* Oxford: Basil Blackwell.

Harré, R. 1967. Philosophy of Science, History of. In *Encyclopedia of Philosophy.* P. Edwards (ed.). London: Collier-Macmillan, VII, 289–96.

1970. *The Principles of Scientific Thinking.* London: Macmillan.

1972. *The Philosophies of Science. An Introductory Survey.* Oxford: Oxford University Press.

Harré, R., and P. F. Secord. 1972. *The Explanation of Social Behaviour.* Oxford: Basil Blackwell.

Harrod, R. F. 1938. Scope and method of economics. *Economic Journal,* 1938, reprinted in *Readings in Economic Analysis.* R. V. Clemence (ed.). Cambridge, Mass.: Addison-Wesley, vol. 1, 1950, 1–30.

1956. *Foundations of Inductive Logic.* London: Macmillan.

Hausman, D. M. 1981a. Are general equilibrium theories explanatory? In *Philosophy in Economics,* ed. J. Pitt. Dordrecht: Reidel. Reprinted in Hausman, 1984, 344–59.

1981b. *Capital, Profits and Prices. An Essay in the Philosophy of Economics.* New York: Columbia University Press.

1984. *The Philosophy of Economics. An Anthology* Cambridge: Cambridge University Press.

1985. Is falsificationism unpractised or unpractisable? *Philosophy of Science,* 15, 313–19.

1988. An appraisal of Popperian methodology. In de Marchi, 1988, 65–85.

1989. Economic methodology in a nutshell. *Journal of Economic Perspectives,* 3(2), 115–27.

Hayek, F. A. 1960. *The Constitution of Liberty.* Chicago: University of Chicago Press.

1942, 1943. Scientism and the study of society. *Economica,* reprinted in O'Neil, 1973, 27–67.

Heilbroner, R. L. (ed.). 1969. *Economic Means and Social Ends.* Englewood Cliffs: Prentice-Hall.

1973. Economics as a "value-free" science. *Social Research,* 40, reprinted in Marr and Raj, 1983, 337–74.

Heller, W. W. 1975. What's right with economics? *American Economic Review,* 65, 1–26.

Hempel, C. G. 1942. The function of general laws in history. *Journal of Philosophy,* 39, reprinted in *Readings in Philosophical Analysis.* H. Feigl and W. Sellars (eds.). New York: Appleton-Century-Crofts, 1949, 459–71.

1966. *Philosophy of Natural Science.* Englewood Cliffs: Prentice-Hall.

Hempel, C. G., and P. Oppenheim. 1948. Studies in the logic of explanation. *Philosophy of Science,* 1965, reprinted (with a postscript) in C. G. Hempel, *Aspects of Scientific Explanation.* New York: Free Press, 1965, 245–95.

Hendry, D. F., and N. R. Ericsson. 1991. An econometric analysis of U.K. money demand in *Monetary Trends in the United States and the United Kingdom* by Milton Friedman and Anna J. Schwartz. *American Economic Review,* 81(1), 8–38.

Hennipman, P. 1976. Pareto optimality: value judgement or analytical tool. In *Relevance and Precision. From Quantitative Analysis to Economic Policy.* J. S. Cramer, A. Heertje and P. Venekamp (eds.). Amsterdam: North-Holland, 39–69.

Hesse, M. 1973. Reasons and evaluation in the history of science. In *Changing Perspectives in the History of Science.* M. Teich and R. Young (eds.). Dordrecht: D. Reidel, 127–47.

Hicks, J. R. 1956. *Revisions of Demand Theory.* Oxford: Clarendon Press.

1965. *Capital and Growth.* Oxford: Clarendon Press.

1973. *Capital and Time. A Neo-Austrian Theory.* Oxford: Clarendon Press.

Hindess, B. 1977. *Philosophy and Methodology in the Social Sciences*. London: Harvester Press.

Hirsch, A. 1978. J. E. Cairnes' methodology in theory and practice. *History of Political Economy*, 10, 322–8.

Hirsch, A., and E. Hirsch. 1975. The methodological implications of Marshall's economics. In *International Congress of Economic History and History of Economic Theories in Piraeus*. L. Houmanidis (ed.). Piraeus: Piraeus Graduate School of Industrial Studies, 134–52.

1976. The heterodox methodology of two Chicago economists. In *The Chicago School of Political Economy*. W. J. Samuels (ed.). East Lansing: Association for Evolutionary Economics and Michigan State University, 59–78.

Hirsch, A., and N. de Marchi. 1986. Making a case when theory is unfalsifiable. *Economics and Philosophy*, 2(1), 1–21.

1990. *Milton Friedmen. Economics in Theory and Practice*. London: Harvester Wheatsheaf.

Hogarth, R. M., and M. W. Reder (eds.). 1987. *Rational Choice. The Contrast Between Economics and Psychology*. Chicago: University of Chicago Press.

Hollander, S. 1977. Adam Smith and the self-interest axiom. *Journal of Law and Economics*, 20, 133–52.

1985. *The Economics of John Stuart Mill*. Toronto: University of Toronto Press, 2 vols.

Hollis, M., and E. J. Nell. 1975. *Rational Economic Man. A Philosophical Critique of Neo-Classical Economics*. Cambridge: Cambridge University Press.

Hoover, K. D. 1988. *The New Classical Macroeconomics: A Sceptical Inquiry*. Oxford: Basil Blackwell.

1991. Scientific research program or tribe? A joint appraisal of Lakatos and the new classical macroeconomics. In de Marchi and Blaug, 1991, 367–97.

Houthakker, H. S. 1961. The present state of consumption theory. *Econometrica*, 29, 704–40.

Howson, C. (ed). 1976. *Method and Appraisal in the Physical Sciences*. Cambridge: Cambridge University Press.

Hudson, W. D. 1969. *The Is-Ought Question. A Collection of Papers on the Central Problem in Moral Philosophy*. London: Macmillan.

Hutchison, T. W. 1938. *The Significance and Basic Postulates of Economic Theory*. New York: Augustus M. Kelley. 1965.

1941. The significance and basic postulates of economic theory: a reply to Professor Knight. *Journal of Political Economy*, 49, 732–50.

1953. *A Review of Economic Doctrines 1870–1929*. Oxford: Clarendon Press.

1956. Professor Machlup on verification in economics. *Southern Economic Journal*. 22, reprinted in Caldwell, 1984, 118–25, and Hausman, 1984, 188–97.

1960. Methodological prescriptions in economics: a reply. *Economica*, 27, 158–61.

1964. *'Positive' Economics and Policy Judgements*. London: Allen & Unwin.

1966. Testing economic assumptions: a comment. *Journal of Political Economy*, 74, 81–3.

1973. Some themes from *Investigations into Method*. In *Carl Menger and the Austrian School of Economics*. J. R. Hicks and W. Weber (eds.). Oxford: Clarendon Press.

1977. *Knowledge and Ignorance in Economics*. Oxford: Basil Blackwell.

1978. *On Revolutions and Progress in Economic Knowledge*. Cambridge: Cambridge University Press.

1988. The case for falsification. In de Marchi, 1988, 169–82.

Forthcoming. *Changing Aims in Economics*. Oxford: Basil Blackwell.

Forthcoming. Hayek and 'modern Austrian' methodology. Comment on a non-refuting refutation. *Research in the History of Economic Thought and Methodology*, 10, W. J. Samuels (ed.). Greenwich, CN: JAI Press.

Jenkin, F. 1867. The origin of species. *North British Review*, reprinted in *Darwin and His*

Critics. D. L. Hull (ed.). Cambridge, Mass.: Harvard University Press, 1973, 302–50.

Johannson, J. 1975. *A Critique of Karl Popper's Methodology*. Stockholm: Scandinavian University Books.

Johansen, L. 1978. A calculus approach to the theory of the core of an exchange economy. *American Economic Review*, 68, 813–20.

Johnson, H. G. 1968. The economic approach to social questions. *Economica*, 35, 1–21.

1971. The Keynesian revolution and the monetarist counter-revolution. *American Economic Review*, 61, 1–14.

1973. *The Theory of Income Distribution*. London: Gray-Mills.

Johnston, J. 1991. Econometrics: retrospect and prospect. *Economic Journal*, 101, 51–56.

Judd, J., and J. Scadding. 1982. The search for a stable money demand function: a survey of the post-1973 literature. *Journal of Economic Literature*, 20, 993–1023.

Juster, F. T. 1975. Introduction. In *Education, Income and Human Behavior*. F. T. Juster (ed.). New York: McGraw-Hill, 1–43.

Kamerschen, D. R. (ed.). 1967. *Readings in Microeconomics*. Cleveland, OH: World.

Klant, J. J. 1984. *The Rules of the Game: The Logical Structure of Economic Theories*. Cambridge: Cambridge University Press.

Kaplan, A. 1964. *The Conduct of Inquiry. Methodology for Behavioral Science*. New York: Thomas Y. Crowell.

Kaufmann, F. 1944. *Methodology of the Social Sciences*. London: Oxford University Press.

Kearl, J. R., C. L. Pope, G. T. Whiting, and L. T. Wimmer. 1979. A confusion of economists. *American Economic Review*, 69 (2), 28–37.

Keeley, M. C. 1975. A comment on "An interpretation of the economic theory of fertility." *Journal of Economic Literature*, 13, 461–8.

Kendall, M. G. 1968. The history of statistical methods. In Sills, 1968, vol. 15, 224–32.

Kenen, P. B. (ed.). 1975. *International Trade and Finance. Frontiers for Research*. Cambridge: Cambridge University Press.

Kennedy, C., and A. P. Thirlwall. 1972. Technical progress: a survey. *Economic Journal*, 82, 11–72.

Keynes, J. M. 1973. *The Collected Writings of John Maynard Keynes. Vol. XIV. The General Theory and After*. D. Moggridge (ed.). London: Macmillan.

Keynes, J. N. 1891. *The Scope and Method of Political Economy*. New York: Kelley & Millman, 1955.

Kim, J. 1991. Testing in modern economics: the case of job search theory. In de Marchi and Blaug, 1991, 105–32.

Kirzner, I. M. 1960. *The Economic Point of View*. Kansas City: Sheed & Ward.

1976. On The Method of Austrian Economics. In Dolan, 1976, 40–51.

Klamer, A., and Colander, D. 1990. *The Making of an Economist*. Boulder, CO: Westview Press.

Klappholz, K. 1964. Value judgements and economics. *British Journal for the Philosophy of Science*, 15, reprinted in Hausman, 1984, 267–92.

Klappholz, K., and J. Agassi. 1959. Methodological prescriptions in economics. *Economica*, reprinted in Kamerschen, 1967, 23–39.

1960. Methodological prescriptions in economics: a rejoinder. *Economica*, 27, 160–1.

Klappholz, K., and E. J. Mishan. 1962. Identities in economic models. *Economica*, 29, 117–28.

Knight, F. 1940. "What is Truth" in economics? *Journal of Political Economy*, reprinted in *On the History and Method of Economics. Selected Essays*. Chicago: University of Chicago Press, 1956, 151–78.

1941. The significance and basic postulates of economic theory. A rejoinder. *Journal of Political Economy,* 49, 750–3.

Koopmans, T. C. 1957. *Three Essays on the State of Economic Science.* New York: McGraw-Hill.

Koot, G. M. 1975. T. E. Cliffe Leslie, Irish social reform, and the origins of the English historical school of economics, *History of Political Economy,* 7, 312–36.

1987. *English Historical Economics: 1870–1926.* Cambridge: Cambridge University Press.

Kregel, J. 1977. Some post-Keynesian distribution theory. In Weintraub, 1977, 421–38.

Krimerman, I. (ed.). 1969. *The Nature and Scope of Social Science. A Critical Anthology.* New York: Meredith.

Krupp, S. R. 1966. Types of controversy in economics. In *The Structure of Economic Science. Essays on Methodology.* S. R. Krupp (ed.). Englewood Cliffs: Prentice-Hall, 39–52.

Kuhn, T. S. 1957. *The Copernican Revolution.* Cambridge: Harvard University Press.

1970a. *The Structure of Scientific Revolutions.* Chicago: University of Chicago Press. 2nd ed.

1970b. Logic of discovery or psychology of research? Reflections on my critics. In Lakatos and Musgrave, 1970, 1–23, 231–78.

1971. Notes on Lakatos. In *Boston Studies in the Philosophy of Science,* 8. R. S. Cohen and C. R. Bucks (eds.). Dordrecht: D. Reidel, 137–46.

Laidler, D. E. W. 1985. *The Demand for Money: Theories and Evidence.* New York: Harper & Row, 3d ed.

Lakatos, I. 1976. *Proofs and Refutations. The Logic of Mathematical Discovery.* Cambridge: Cambridge University Press.

1978. *The Methodology of Scientific Research Programmes. Philosophical Papers.* J. Worrall and G. Currie (eds.). Cambridge: Cambridge University Press, vols. 1, 2.

Lakatos, I., and A. Musgrave. (eds.). 1970. *Criticism and the Growth of Knowledge.* Cambridge: Cambridge University Press.

Lancaster, K. J. 1962. The scope of qualitative economics. *Review of Economic Studies,* 29, 99–123.

1966a. The solution of qualitative comparative static problems. *Quarterly Journal of Economics,* 80, 278–95.

1971. *Consumer Demand. A New Approach.* New York: Columbia University Press.

1991. *Modern Consumer Theory.* Aldershot, Hants: Edward Elgar.

Lange, O. 1945. The scope and method of economics. *Review of Economic Studies,* reprinted in Kamerschen, 1967, 3–22.

Latsis, S. J. 1972. Situational determinism in economics. *British Journal for the Philosophy of Science,* 23, 207–45.

1974. Situational determinism in economics. Unpublished Ph.D. dissertation of the University of London.

1976a. A research programme in economics. In Latsis, 1976, 1–42.

(ed.). 1976b. *Method and Appraisal in Economics.* Cambridge: Cambridge University Press.

Laudan, L. 1977. *Progress and Its Problems: Towards a Theory of Scientific Growth.* Berkeley: University of California Press.

Lavoie, D. 1985. *Rivalry and Central Planning. The Socialist Calculation Debate Reconsidered.* Cambridge: Cambridge University Press.

1986. Euclideanism versus hermeneutics: a reinterpretation of Misesian apriorism. In *Subjectivism, Intelligibility and Economics Understanding,* I. M. Kirzner (ed.). London: Macmillan, 192–210.

Leamer, E. E. 1984. *Sources for International Comparative Advantage: Theory and Evidence.* Cambridge, MA: MIT Press.

Leibenstein, H. 1989. *The Collected Essays of Harvey Leibenstein*. Aldershot, Hants: Edward Elgar, 2 vols.

Leijonhufvud, A. 1976. School, 'revolutions', and research programmes in economic theory. In Latsis, 1976, 65–108.

Leontief, W. 1937. Implicit theorizing: a methodological criticism of the neo-Cambridge school. *Quarterly Journal of Economics*, reprinted in *Readings in Economic Analysis*. R. V. Clemence (ed.). Cambridge, Mass.: Addison-Wesley, 1950, vol. 1, 31–45.

1971. Theoretical assumptions and nonobserved facts. *American Economic Review*, 61, 1–7.

1982. Academic economics. *Science*, 217, reprinted in Marr and Raj, 1983, 331–6.

Lesnoff, M. 1974. *The Structure of Social Science. A Philosophical Introduction*. London: Allen & Unwin.

Lindbeck, A. 1971. *The Political Economy of the New Left. An Outsider's View*. New York: Harper & Row.

Lindbeck, A., and D. V. Snower. 1985. Explanations of unemployment. *Oxford Review of Economic Policy*, 1(2), 34–59.

Lindblom, C. E. 1965. *Intelligence of Democracy*. New York: The Free Press.

1968. *The Policy Making Process*. Englewood Cliffs: Prentice-Hall.

Lindgren, J. R. 1969. Adam Smith's theory of inquiry. *Journal of Political Economy*, 77, 897–915.

Lipsey, R. G. 1966. *An Introduction to Positive Economics*. London: Weidenfeld & Nicolson, 2nd ed.

1989. *An Introduction to Positive Economics*. London: Weidenfeld & Nicolson, 7th ed.

Lipsey, R. G., and G. Rosenbluth. 1971. A contribution to the new theory of demand: a rehabilitation of the Giffen good. *Canadian Journal of Economics*, 4, 131–63.

Littlechild, S. C. 1978. *The Fallacy of the Mixed Economy. An 'Austrian' Critique of Economic Thinking and Policy*. London: Institute of Economic Affairs.

Loasby, B. J. 1976. *Choice, Complexity and Ignorance*. Cambridge: Cambridge University Press.

1989. *The Mind and Method of the Economist*. Aldershot, Hants: Edward Elgar.

1990. The Firm. In *Foundations of Economic Thought*, ed. J. Creedy. Oxford: Basil Blackwell, 212–33.

Losee, J. 1972. *A Historical Introduction to the Philosophy of Science*. London: Oxford University Press.

Lowe, A. 1977. *On Economic Knowledge. Toward a Science of Political Economics*. White Plains: M. E. Sharpe, 2nd ed.

Lukes, S. 1968. Methodological individualism reconsidered. *British Journal of Sociology*, reprinted in *The Philosophy of Social Explanation*. A. Ryan (ed.). Oxford: Oxford University Press, 1968, 119–29.

McClelland, P. D. 1975. *Causal Explanation and Model Building in History, Economics and the New Economic History*. Ithaca: Cornell University Press.

McCloskey, D. 1985. The rhetoric of economics. *Journal of Economic Literature*, 21, reprinted in Caldwell, 1984, 320–517.

1987. Rhetoric. In Eatwell et al., 1987, 4, 173–4.

1991. Economic Science: a search through the hyperspace of assumptions. *Methodus*, 3(1), 6–16.

MacCrimmon, K. R., and M. Toda. 1969. The experimental determination of indifference curves. *Review of Economic Studies*, 36, 433–51.

MacDougall, D. 1974. In praise of economics. *Economic Journal*, 84, 773–86.

Macfie, A. L. 1967. *The Individual in Society. Papers on Adam Smith*. London: Allen & Unwin.

Machlup, F. 1963. *Essays on Economic Semantics*. Englewood Cliffs: Prentice-Hall.

1978. *Methodology of Economics and Other Social Sciences.* New York: Academic Press.

McKenzie, R. B., and G. Tullock. 1975. *The New World of Economics: Explorations into the Human Experience.* Homewood: Richard D. Irwin.

MacLennan, B. 1972. Jevons's philosophy of science. *The Manchester School of Economic and Social Studies,* 1, 53–71.

Maddock, R. 1984. Rational expectations macrotheory: A Lakatosian case study in program adjustment. *History of Political Economy,* 16(2), 291–309.

1991. The development of new classical macroeconomics: lessons for Lakatos. In de Marchi and Blaug, 1991, 339–62.

Magee, B. 1973. *Popper.* London: Fontana/Collins.

Marr, W. L., and B. Raj. (eds.) 1983. *How Economists Explain. A Reader in Methodology.* Lanham, MD: University Press of America.

Mason, R. S. 1989. *Robert Giffen and the Giffen Paradox.* Deddington, Oxford: Phillip Allan.

Masterman, M. 1970. The nature of a paradigm. In Lakatos and Musgrave, 1970, 59–89.

Mawatari, S. 1982–3. J. S. Mill's methodology of political economy. *The Kaizai Gaku Annual Report of the Economic Society,* Tohoku University, 44(2), 1982; 45(1), 1983; 45(2), 1983, 1–19, 1–21, 33–54, 21–36.

Maxwell, N. 1972. A critique of Popper's views on scientific methods. *Philosophy of Science,* 30, 131–52.

Mayer, T. 1972. *Permanent Income, Wealth and Consumption.* Berkeley: University of California Press.

1975. Selecting economic hypotheses by goodness of fit. *Economic Journal,* 85, 877–83.

1978. *The Structure of Monetarism.* New York: W. W. Norton.

1980. Economics as a hard science: realistic goal or wishful thinking. *Economic Inquiry,* 18, reprinted in Marr and Raj, 1983, 49–60.

1990. *Monetarism and Macroeconomics Policy.* Aldershot, Hants: Edward Elgar.

1992. *Truth vs. Precision in Economics.* Aldershot, Hants: Edward Elgar.

Mayr, E. 1972. The nature of the Darwinian revolution. *Science,* 176, 981–9.

1982. *The Growth of Biological Thought.* Cambridge, MA: Harvard University Press.

Medawar, P. B. 1967. *The Art of the Soluble. Creativity and Originality in Science.* London: Penguin Books.

Melitz, J. 1965. Friedman and Machlup on the significance of testing economic assumptions. *Journal of Political Economy,* 73, 37–60.

Michie, J. 1991. The search for a 'stylized fact' of cyclical wages. In *The Economics of Restructuring and Intervention,* (ed.) J. Michie. Aldershot, Hants: Edward Elgar, 119–37.

Mill, J. S. 1967. *Collected Works, Essays on Economy and Society.* J. M. Robson (ed.). Toronto: University of Toronto Press, vol. 4.

1973. *Collected Works, A System of Logic Ratiocinative and Inductive.* J. M. Robson (ed.), Introduction by R. F. McRae. London: Routledge & Kegan Paul, vols. 7, 8.

Miller, W. L. 1971. Richard Jones: a case study in methodology. *History of Political Economy,* 3, 198–207.

Mincer, J. 1989. Human capital and the labor market. A review of current research. *Educational Researcher,* 18(5), 27–34.

Mises, L. von. 1949. *Human Action. A Treatise on Economics.* London: William Hodge.

1978. *The Ultimate Foundation of Economic Science: An Essay on Method.* Kansas City: Universal Press Syndicate, 2nd ed.

Mishan, E. J. 1961. Theories of consumers' behaviour: a cynical view. *Economica,* February, reprinted in Kamerschen, 1967, 82–94.

Mitchell, E. D. 1974. *Psychic Explorations. A Challenge for Science.* J. White (ed.). New York: G. P. Putnam's Sons.

Morgan, T. 1988. Theory versus empiricism in academic economics: update and comparison. *Journal of Economic Perspectives,* 2(1), 159–64.

Morgenstern, O. 1972. Thirteen critical points in contemporary economic theory: an interpretation. *Journal of Economic Literature,* 10, 1163–89.

Morishima, M. 1991. General equilibrium theory in the twenty-first century. *Economic Journal,* 101, 69–74.

Musgrave, A. 1981. 'Unreal assumptions' in economic theory: the F-twist untwisted. *Kyklos,* 34, reprinted in Caldwell, 1983, 234–44.

Myrdal, G. 1970. *Objectivity in Social Research.* London: Gerald Duckworth.

Nagel, E. 1950. *John Stuart Mill's Philosophy of Scientific Method.* New York: Hafner.

1961. *The Structure of Science. Problems in the Logic of Scientific Explanation.* London: Routledge & Kegan Paul.

1963. Assumptions in economic theory. *American Economic Review,* 53, reprinted in Caldwell, 1984, 179–88.

Naughton, J. 1978. The logic of scientific economics in economics: a response to Bray. *Journal of Economic Studies,* 5(2), 152–65.

Nell, E. J. 1972a. Economics: the revival of political economy. In *Ideology in Social Science.* R. Blackburn (ed.). London: Fontana, 76–95.

1972b. Property and the means of production. A primer on the Cambridge controversy. *Review of Radical Political Economics,* 4, 1–27.

Nelson, R. R. 1973. Recent exercises in growth accounting: new understanding or dead end? *American Economic Review,* 63, 462–8.

Nelson, R. R., and S. G. Winter. 1982. *An Evolutionary Theory of Economic Change.* Cambridge, MA: Harvard University Press.

Ng, Y. K. 1972. Value judgments and economists' role in policy recommendation. *Economic Journal,* 82, reprinted in Marr and Raj, 1983, 33–47.

Nickell, S. 1991. Unemployment: a survey. In Oswald, 1991, vol. 1, 136–84.

Nordhaus, W. D. 1973. Some skeptical thoughts on the theory of induced innovations. *Quarterly Journal of Economics,* 87, 208–19.

Nordquist, G. L. 1965. The breakup of the maximization principle. *Quarterly Review of Economics and Business,* reprinted in Kamerschen, 1967, 278–95.

O'Brien, D. P. 1970. *J. R. McCulloch. A Study in Classical Economics.* London: Allen & Unwin.

1974. *Whither Economics? An Inaugural Lecture.* Durham: University of Durham.

1975. *The Classical Economists.* Oxford: Clarendon Press.

O'Neill, J. (ed.). 1973. *Modes of Individualism and Collectivism.* London: Heinemann.

O'Sullivan, P. 1987. *Economic Methodology and Freedom to Choose.* London: Allen and Unwin.

Oswald, A. J. 1991a. Progress and microeconomic data. *Economic Journal,* 101, 75–80.

1991b. *Surveys in Economics.* Oxford: Basil Blackwell, 2 vols.

Papandreou, A. G. 1958. *Economics as a Science.* Chicago: Lippincott.

1963. Theory construction and empirical meaning in economics. *American Economic Review, Supplement,* 53, 205–10.

Parker, W. N. (ed.). 1986. *Economic History and the Modern Economist.* Oxford: Basil Blackwell.

Patinkin, D. 1982. *Anticipations of the General Theory? And Other Essays on Keynes.* Oxford: Basil Blackwell.

Pen, J. 1971. *Income Distribution.* London: Allen Lane, The Penguin Press.

Perlman, R. 1969. *Labor Theory.* New York: Wiley.

Pesaran, M. H. 1987. Econometrics. In Eatwell et al., 1987, vol. 2, 8–22.

Pheby, J. 1988. *Methodology and Economics: A Critical Introduction.* London: Macmillan.

Phelps Brown, E. H. 1972. The underdevelopment of economics. *Economic Journal,* 82, 1–10.

Pigou, A. C. (ed.). 1956. *Memorials of Alfred Marshall.* New York: Kelley and Millman.

Polanyi, M. 1958. *Personal Knowledge. Towards a Post-Critical Philosophy.* London: Routledge & Kegan Paul.

Pollak, R. A., and L. M. Wachter. 1975. The relevance of the household production function and its implications for the allocation of time. *Journal of Political Economy.* 83, 255–77.

1977. Reply: "Pollack and Wachter on the Household Production Approach." *Journal of Political Economy,* 85, 1083–6.

Pope, D., and R. Pope. 1972a. Predictionists, assumptions and the relatives of the assumptionists. *Australian Economic Papers,* 11, 224–8.

1972b. In defence of predictionism. *Australian Economic Papers,* 11, reprinted in Marr and Raj, 1983, 89–100.

Popper, K. 1957. *The Poverty of Historicism.* London: Routledge & Kegan Paul.

1962. *The Open Society and Its Enemies.* London: Routledge & Kegan Paul, 4th ed., vols. 1, 2.

1959. Reprinted 1965. *The Logic of Scientific Discovery.* New York: Harper Torchbooks.

1970. Normal science and its dangers. In Lakatos and Musgrave, 1970, 51–8.

1972a. *Objective Knowledge. An Evolutionary Approach.* London: Oxford University Press.

1972b. *Conjectures and Refutations. The Growth of Scientific Knowledge.* London: Routledge & Kegan Paul.

1976. *The Unended Quest. An Intellectual Biography.* London: Fontana.

1983. *Realism and the Aim of Science, The Postscript to the Logic of Scientific Discovery,* W. W. Bartley III (ed). London: Huttchinson.

Popper, K., and C. Eccles. 1977. *The Self and Its Brain.* Berlin: Springer-Verlag.

Psacharopoulos, G. (ed.). 1985. *Economics of Education. Research and Studies.* Oxford: Pergamon Press.

Psacharopoulos, G., and M. Woodhall. 1985. *Education and Development. An Analysis of Investment Choices.* New York: Oxford University Press.

Raup, D. M. 1986. *The Nemesis Affair. A Story of the Death of Dinosaurs and the Ways of Science.* New York: W. W. Norton.

Redman, D. A. 1989. *Economic Methodology. A Bibliography with References to Works in the Philosophy of Science, 1860–1988.* New York: Greenwood Press.

1991. *Economics and the Philosophy of Science.* New York: Oxford University Press.

Ricketts, M., and E. Shoesmith. 1990. *British Economic Opinion. A Survey of A Thousand Economists.* London: Institute of Economic Affairs.

Rivett, K. 1970. "Suggest" or "entail"? The derivation and confirmation of economic hypotheses. *Australian Economic Papers,* 9, 127–48.

Rizzo, M. J. 1978. Praxeology and econometrics: a critique of positivist economics. In *New Directions in Austrian Economics.* L. M. Spadaro (ed.). Kansas City: Sheed Andrews & McMeel, 40–56.

1982. Mises and Lakatos: a reformulation of Austrian methodology. In *Method, Process and Austrian Economics,* I. M. Kirzner (ed.). Lexington, MA: D. C. Heath, 53–72.

Robbins, L. 1935. *An Essay on the Nature and Significance of Economic Science.* London: Macmillan, 2nd ed.

1971. *Autobiography of an Economist.* London: Macmillan.

1979. On Latsis: a review essay. *Journal of Economic Literature,* 17, 996–1004.

Robinson, J. 1962. *Economic Philosophy.* London: C. A. Watts.

1973. Foreword to J. A. Kregel, *The Reconstruction of Political Economy.* London: Macmillan, ix–xiii.

1975. The unimportance of reswitching. *Quarterly Journal of Economics,* 89, 32–9.

1977. What are the questions? *Journal of Economic Literature,* 15, 1318–39.

Roley, V. V. 1985. Money demand predictability. *Journal of Money, Credit and Banking,* 17(4), Pt.2, 615,41.

Rosen, S. 1977. Human capital: a survey of empirical research. In *Research in Labor Economics: An Annual Compilation of Research.* R. G. Ehrenberg (ed.). Greenwich: Jai Press, vol. 1, 3–40.

Rosenberg, A. 1976. *Microeconomic Laws. A Philosophical Analysis.* Pittsburgh: University of Pittsburgh Press.

1985. *The Structure of Biological Science.* Cambridge: Cambridge University Press.

1988. Economics is too important to be left to the rhetoricians. *Economics and Philosophy,* 4(1), 129–49.

Roth, A. E. 1991. Game theory as a part of empirical economics. *Economic Journal,* 101, 107–14.

Rothbart, M. N. 1957. In defense of "extreme apriorism." *Southern Economic Journal,* 23, 314–20.

1976. Praxeology: the methodology of Austrian economics. In Dolan, 1976, 119–39.

Rotwein, E. 1959. On "the methodology of positive economics." *Quarterly Journal of Economics,* 73, 554–75.

1973. Empiricism and economic method: several views considered. *Journal of Economic Issues,* 7, reprinted in Marr and Raj, 1983, 133–54.

Rowley, C. K., and A. T. Peacock. 1975. *Welfare Economics: A Liberal Restatement.* London: Martin Robertson.

Roy, S. 1989. *Philosophy of Economics: On the Scope of Reasoning in Economics.* London: Routledge.

Rudner, R. S. 1953. The scientist *qua* scientist makes value judgements. *Philosophy of Science,* 20, 1–6.

1966. *Philosophy of Social Science.* Englewood Cliffs: Prentice-Hall.

Runciman, W. G. 1968. Sociological evidence and political theory. In *Readings in the Philosophy of the Social Sciences.* M. Brodbeck (ed.). New York: Macmillan, 561–71.

1972. *A Critique of Max Weber's Philosophy of the Social Sciences.* Cambridge: Cambridge University Press.

Ruse, M. 1982. *Darwinism Defended. A Guide to Evolution Controversies.* London: Addison-Wesley.

1986. *Taking Darwin Seriously.* Oxford: Basil Blackwell.

Ryan, A. 1970. *The Philosophy of the Social Sciences.* London: Macmillan.

1974. *J. S. Mill.* London: Routledge & Kegan Paul.

Samuels, W. J. 1977. Ideology in economics. In Weintraub, 1977, 467–84.

Samuelson, P. A. 1948. *Foundations of Economic Analysis.* Cambridge: Harvard University Press.

1966. *The Collected Scientific Papers of Paul A. Samuelson.* J. E. Stiglitz (ed.). Cambridge, Mass.: The M.I.T. Press, vols. 1, 2.

1967. The monopolistic competition revolution. In *Monopolistic Competition Theory: Studies in Impact,* R. E. Kuenne (ed.). New York: Wiley & Sons, 105–38.

1972. *The Collected Scientific Papers of Paul A. Samuelson.* R. C. Merton (ed.). Cambridge, Mass.: The M.I.T. Press, vol. 3.

Samuelson, P. A., and W. D. Nordhaus. 1985. *Economics.* New York: McGraw-Hill, 12th ed.

Santomero, A. M., and J. J. Seater. 1978. The inflation-unemployment trade-off: a critique of the literature. *Journal of Economic Literature,* 16, 499–544.

Sargant Florence, P. 1927. *Economics and Human Behaviour. A Rejoinder to Social Psychologists.* London: Kegan Paul, Trench, Trubner.

Scarf, H. E. 1987. Computation of general equilibria. In Eatwell et al., 1987, I, 556–62.

Schoeffler, S. 1955. *The Failures of Economics: A Diagnostic Study.* Cambridge: Harvard University Press.

Schoemaker, P. J. 1982. The expected utility model: its variants, purposes, evidence and limitations. *Journal of Economic Literature,* 20(2), 529–63.

Schultz, T. W. 1963. *The Economic Value of Education.* New York: Columbia University Press.

Schumpeter, J. A. 1954. *History of Economic Analysis.* New York: Oxford University Press.

Scriven, M. 1959. Explanation and prediction in evolutionary theory. *Science,* 130, 477–82.

    1962. Explanation, predictions and laws. In *Minnesota Studies in the Philosophy of Science, 3. Scientific Explanation, Space, and Time.* H. Feigl and G. Maxwell (eds.). Minneapolis: University of Minnesota Press, 170–230.

Selden, R. T. 1977. Monetarism. In Weintraub, 1977, 253–74.

Seliger, M. 1977. *The Marxist Conception of Ideology.* Cambridge: Cambridge University Press.

Sen, A. K. 1970. *Collective Choices and Social Welfare.* Edinburgh: Oliver & Boyd.

    1974. On some debates in capital theory. *Economica,* 41, 328–35.

Shackle, G. S. L. 1973. *Epistemics and Economics: A Critique of Economic Doctrines.* Cambridge: Cambridge University Press.

Shaw, K. 1988. *Keynesian Economics: The Permanent Revolution.* Aldershot, Hants: Edward Elgar.

Sheffrin, S. M. 1983. *Rational Expectations.* Cambridge: Cambridge University Press.

Shubik, M. 1970. A curmudgeon's guide to microeconomics. *Journal of Economic Literature,* 8, 405–34.

Shupak, M. 1962. The predictive accuracy of empirical demand analyses. *Economic Journal,* 72, 550–75.

Sill, D. (ed). *International Encyclopedia of the Social Sciences.* New York: Macmillan and The Free Press, 17 vols.

Simon, H. 1957. *Models of Man.* New York: Wiley & Sons.

    1979. Rational decision making in business organizations. *American Economic Review,* 69, 493–513.

    1987. Rationality in psychology and economics. In Hogarth and Reder, 1987, 25–40.

Skinner, A. S. 1965. Economics and history: the Scottish enlightenment. *Scottish Journal of Political Economy,* 12, 1–22.

    1974. Adam Smith, science and the role of the imagination. In *Hume and the Enlightenment.* W. B. Todd (ed.). Edinburgh: Edinburgh University Press, 164–88.

Smith, A. 1776. *The Wealth of Nations.* A. S. Skinner (ed.). London: Penguin Books, 1970.

Smyth, R. L. (ed.). 1962. *Essays in Economic Method.* London: Gerald Duckworth.

Sowell, 'ı. 1974. *Classical Economics Reconsidered.* Princeton: Princeton University Press.

Steedman, I. 1991. Negative and Positive Contributions: Appraising Sraffa and Lakatos. In de Marchi and Blaug, 1991, 439–54.

Stern, R. M. 1965. Testing trade theories. In *International Trade and Finance. Frontiers for Research.* P. B. Kenen (ed.). Cambridge: Cambridge University Press, 3–49.

Stewart, I. M. T. 1979. *Reasoning and Method in Economics. An Introduction to Economic Methodology.* London: McGraw-Hill.

Stigler, G. J. 1963. Archibald versus Chicago. *Review of Economic Studies,* 30, 63–4.

    1965. *Essays in the History of Economics.* Chicago: University of Chicago Press.

    1966. *The Theory of Price.* New York: Macmillan, 3rd ed.

Stigler, G. J., and G. S. Becker. 1977. De gustibus non est disputandum. *American Economic Review,* 67, 76–90.

Stone, R. 1980. Keynes, political arithmetic and econometrics. In *Proceedings of the British Academy,* 64, 55–92.

Streissler, E. 1970. *Pitfalls in Econometric Forecasting*. London: Institute of Economic Affairs.

Suppe, F. 1974. The search for philosophical understanding of scientific theories. In Suppe, 1974, 6–241.

(ed.). 1974. *The Structure of Scientific Theories*. Urbana, IL: University of Illinois Press.

Swedberg, R. 1990. *Economics and Sociology. Redefining Their Boundaries: Conversations with Economists and Sociologists*. Princeton: Princeton University Press.

Tarascio, V. J. 1966. *Pareto's Methodological Approach to Economics*. Chapel Hill: University of North Carolina Press.

Temin, P. 1976. *Did Monetary Forces Cause the Great Depression?* New York: W. W. Norton.

Thaler, R. H. 1987a. Anomalies: the January effect. *Journal of Economic Perspectives,* 1(1), 197–201.

1987b. Anomalies: weekend, holiday, turn of the month, and intraday effects. *Journal of Economic Perspectives*, 1(2), 169–78.

Theil, H. 1966. *Applied Economic Forecasting*. Amsterdam: North-Holland.

Thompson, H. F. 1965. Adam Smith's philosophy of science. *Quarterly Journal of Economics,* 79, 212–33.

Thurow, L. C. 1975. *Generating Inequality*. London: Macmillan Press.

Tompkins, P., and C. Bird. 1973. *The Secret Life of Plants*. London: Penguin Books.

Toulmin, S. 1972. *Human Understanding*. Oxford: Clarendon Press.

1976. History, praxis and the "third world." Ambiguities in Lakatos. In *Essays in Memory of Imre Lakatos*. R. S. Cohen, P. K. Feyerabend, and M. W. Wartofsky (eds.). Dordrecht: D. Reidel, 227–54.

1977. From form to function: philosophy and history of science in the 1950s and now. *Daedalus*, 106, 143–62.

Toulmin, S., and J. Goodfield. 1963. *The Fabric of the Heavens*. London: Penguin Books.

1965. *The Architecture of Matter*. London: Penguin Books.

1967. *The Discovery of Time*. London: Penguin Books.

Trevor-Roper, H. R. 1969. *The European Witch-Craze of the 16th and 17th Centuries*. London: Penguin Books.

Tversky, A., and D. Kahneman. 1987. Rational choices and the framing of decisions. In Hogarth and Reder, 1987, 67–94.

Urbach, P. 1974. Progress and degeneration in the "IQ debate." *British Journal for the Philosophy of Science*, 25, 99–135, 235–59.

Viner, J. 1958. *The Long View and the Short*. Glencoe: The Free Press.

Walker, D. A. 1984. Is Walras's theory of general equilibrium a normative scheme? *History of Political Economy*, 16(3), 445–69.

1987. Walras's theories of tatonnement. *Journal of Political Economy*, 95(4), 758–74.

Walters, A. A. 1963. Production and cost functions: an econometric survey. *Econometrica*, 31, 1–66.

Ward, B. 1972. *What's Wrong With Economics?* London: Macmillan.

Watkins, J. W. N. 1970. Against "normal science." In Lakatos and Musgrave, 1970, 25–37.

Weber, M. 1949. *The Methodology of the Social Sciences*. E. A. Shils and H. A. Finch (eds.). Glencoe: The Free Press.

Weintraub, E. R. 1977. General equilibrium theory. In Weintraub, 1977, 107–23.

1985. *General Equilibrium Analysis: Studies in Appraisal*. Cambridge: Cambridge University Press.

1989. Methodology doesn't matter, but the history of thought might. In *The State of Macroeconomics*, S. Honkapohja (ed.). Oxford: Basil Blackwell, 263–79.

Weintraub, S. (ed). 1977. *Modern Economic Thought*. Oxford: Basil Blackwell.

Welch, F. 1975. Human capital theory: education, discrimination, and life cycles. *American Economic Review*, 75, 63–73.

West, J. A., and J. G. Toonder. 1973. *The Case for Astrology*. London: Penguin Books.

Whitaker, J. K. 1975. John Stuart Mill's methodology. *Journal of Political Economy*, 83, 1033–50.

Whitehead, A. K. 1981. Screening and education: a theoretical and empirical survey. *British Review of Economic Issues*, 3(8), 44–62.

Wilber, C. K., and R. S. Harrison. 1978. The methodological basis of institutional economics: pattern model, storytelling and holism. *Journal of Economic Issues*, 12, reprinted in Marr and Raj, 1983, 243–72.

Wildavsky, A. 1964. *The Politics of the Budgetary Process*. Boston: Little Brown.

Williams, K. 1975. Facing reality – a critique of Karl Popper's empiricism. *Economy and Society*, 43, 309–58.

Williams, M. B. 1973. Falsifiable predictions of evolutionary theory. *Philosophy of Science*, 40, 518–37.

Williams, P. L. 1978. *The Emergence of the Theory of the Firm*. London: Macmillan.

Winch, D. 1978. *Adam Smith's Politics*. Cambridge: Cambridge University Press.

Winter, S. G. 1962. Economic "natural selection" and the theory of the firm. *Yale Economic Essay*, 4, 225–72.

Wong, S. 1973. The "F-twist" and the methodology of Paul Samuelson. *American Economic Review*, 63, 312–25.

1978. *The Foundations of Paul Samuelson's Revealed Preference Theory*. London: Routledge & Kegan Paul.

Wood, J. H. 1981. The economics of Professor Friedman. In *Essays in Contemporary Fields in Economics: In Honor of Emanuel T. Weiler (1914–1979)*, G. Horwich and J. P. Quirk (eds.). West Lafayette, IN: Purdue University Press, 191–241.

Worland, S. T. 1972. Radical political economy as a "scientific revolution." *Southern Economic Journal*, 39, 274–84.

Worrall, J. 1976. Thomas Young and the "refutation" of Newtonian optics: a case-study in the interaction of philosophy of science and history of science. In *Method and Appraisal in the Physical Sciences*. C. Howson (ed.). Cambridge: Cambridge University Press, 107–79.

Worswick, G. D. N. 1972. Is progress of economic science possible? *Economic Journal*, 82, 73–86.

Wulwick, N. J. 1991. Comment on Hoover. In de Marchi and Blaug, 1991, 398–403.

Yamey, B. S. 1972. Do monopoly and near-monopoly matter? A survey of empirical studies. In *Essays in Honour of Lord Robbins*. M. Peston and B. Corry (eds.). London: Weidenfeld & Nicolson, 290–323.

Zarnowitz, V. 1968. Prediction and forecasting, economic. In Sills, 1968, vol. 12, 425–39.

Ziman, J. 1967. *Public Knowledge. The Social Dimension of Science*. Cambridge: Cambridge University Press.

1978. *Reliable Knowledge. An Exploration of the Grounds for Belief in Science*. Cambridge: Cambridge University Press.

NAME INDEX

Achinstein, P., 31n, 33
Ackermann, R. J., 23n, 26, 30, 44–5n, 253
Agassi, J., 84, 85, 96n, 105, 106, 254
Alchian, A. A., 146, 232
Alexander, P., 4
Allen, R. F., 181
Allen, R. G. D., 140, 141, 229
Allen, W. R., 146
Ando, A., 194
Anschutz, R. P., 62n
Applebaum, E., 243
Archibald, G. C., 90, 93n, 94, 96n, 99,
    101, 102, 124–5, 126, 127
Aristotle, 108
Armstrong, J. S., 247
Arrow, K. J., 162, 163, 165, 166, 167, 168,
    169, 188, 230, 232, 239
Ashley, W., 72n
Asimakopulos, A., 242n
Aumann, R. J., 169
Ayer, A. J., 12n, 16n, 20n, 26, 87, 108
Ayers, C. E., 109

Bachelard, G., 37n
Backhouse, R., xixn, 158, 163, 205
Bagehot, W., 83
Balzer, W., xi
Barker, S. F., 16
Barnes, B., 119, 253
Barrett, M., 119
Barry, N. P., 45n
Bartlett, M. S., 22
Baumol, W. J., 147, 153, 156, 158, 204
Bear, D. V. T., 95n
Becker, G. S., 141n, 175, 206, 207n, 209,
    211, 220–8
Bergmann, G., 119

Bergson, A., 123
Bergstrom, T. C., 223n
Berkson, W., 37n
Bhagwati, J., 186
Bhaskar, R., 37n, 39, 40
Bianchi, M., 240, 241
Bird, C., 41n
Birnbaum, B. G., 222n, 225
Black, M., 17, 113, 114
Blaug, M., 36, 57, 60, 61n, 63n, 65, 67,
    68n, 72n, 107, 110, 111, 123n, 139,
    140, 152, 162, 171, 172, 173, 175,
    178, 179, 181, 197n, 203, 210, 211,
    212, 214, 217, 218, 231, 242, 243, 254
Blinder, A. S., 223n
Bloor, D., 32n
Bodkin, R. G., 247
Böhm-Bawerk, E. von, 80
Boland, L. A., xi, xvi–xvii, 96n, 99, 230,
    231
Bordo, M., 71n
Bowley, A. L., xv
Bowley, M., 54, 56, 122
Bowman, M. J., 207
Brainard, W. C., 194
Braithwaite, R. B., 16–17n, 22, 23n
Braybrooke, D., 130
Bridgman, P., 12, 87, 88, 89
Brittan, S., 134
Brodbeck, M., 46–7, 60
Bronfenbrenner, M., 173, 243
Broome, J., 229
Brown, A., 144, 145
Brunner, K., 194
Burger, T., 44n
Burkhardt, R. J., xxn
Burmeister, E., 183–4

275

SUBJECT INDEX